RESIDENCE, EMPLOYMENT AND SOCIAL RIGHTS OF MOBILE PERSONS

Social Europe Series, Volume 36

RESIDENCE, EMPLOYMENT AND SOCIAL RIGHTS OF MOBILE PERSONS

On How EU Law Defines Where They Belong

Edited by
Herwig VERSCHUEREN

intersentia
Cambridge – Antwerp – Portland

Intersentia Ltd
Sheraton House | Castle Park
Cambridge | CB3 0AX | United Kingdom
Tel.: +44 1223 370 170 | Fax: +44 1223 370 169
Email: mail@intersentia.co.uk
www.intersentia.com | www.intersentia.co.uk

Distribution for the UK and Ireland:
NBN International
Airport Business Centre, 10 Thornbury Road
Plymouth, PL6 7 PP
United Kingdom
Tel.: +44 1752 202 301 | Fax: +44 1752 202 331
Email: orders@nbninternational.com

Distribution for Europe and all other countries:
Intersentia Publishing nv
Groenstraat 31
2640 Mortsel
Belgium
Tel.: +32 3 680 15 50 | Fax: +32 3 658 71 21
Email: mail@intersentia.be

Distribution for the USA and Canada:
International Specialized Book Services
920 NE 58th Ave. Suite 300
Portland, OR 97213
USA
Tel.: +1 800 944 6190 (toll free) | Fax: +1 503 280 8832
Email: info@isbs.com

Residence, Employment and Social Work of Mobile Persons. On How EU Law Defines Where They Belong

ISBN 978-1-78068-407-9
D/2016/7849/94
NUR 825

British Library Cataloguing in Publication Data. A catalogue record for this book is available from the British Library.

PREFACE

Where do I belong? A question all mobile persons are bound to ask themselves at one time or another. When crossing borders individuals establish links with States, which can be the basis for legal claims against these States. This book discusses the issue of these links and, more specifically, the question of how EU law defines the link needed to obtain the right to reside in a Member State and the right to social and employment protection in that State.

The EU legal framework of internal market rules, citizenship rights and immigration rules has developed very different answers to the question of where a mobile person belongs. Indeed, it uses a number of criteria on the basis of which it is determined with which Member State a person has a sufficient link to create rights.

As regards the right of residence, Directive 2004/38 establishes this right for Union citizens and the members of their family on the basis of criteria such as the exercise of an economic activity, the duration of their residence, the burden on the social assistance system, or the threat to public order. In external EU migration law the link between the migrant and the Member State also plays a role in obtaining and retaining a right of residence, links like being economically active, being a family member, having sufficient resources or fulfilling integration requirements. They can be found in instruments such as the Family Reunification Directive 2003/86 and the Long-Term Residence Directive 2003/109.

As for the social rights of mobile Union citizens, the rules of conflict of the social security coordination in Regulation 883/2004 prescribe criteria like the place of work and the place of residence to determine to which legislation the mobile person is subject. The rules of conflict applying to labour law (Rome I Regulation 593/2008, Posting of Workers Directive 96/71) also contain criteria to determine with which Member State a cross-border worker has a sufficient link to make its employment protection applicable, criteria such as the country where the work is habitually carried out or the place of business through which the employee was engaged.

Furthermore, in cases which do not concern the application of secondary Union law, the Court of Justice also uses criteria to determine whether the link between a person and a Member State is sufficient to justify the claim of a right to reside or to social benefits. These criteria are: having a sufficient link with the labour market of the host Member State, the duration of the residence or stay in the host Member State, payment of taxes, education of children, enrolment in higher education or having fulfilled one on these criteria in the past.

So, EU law gives a multitude of answers to the question which link is necessary and sufficient to create an individual's right *vis-à-vis* a State. The definition of this link, the criteria used and the legal consequences differ according to the legal framework the individual finds himself/herself in and the legal instrument he/she invokes.

These issues were discussed at an expert seminar organised on 7–8 May 2015 at the University of Antwerp. Scholars from different legal disciplines were invited to critically analyse, discuss and compare the multitude of criteria used in EU legislation and case-law to determine whether there is a sufficient link between a person and a Member State with a view to making legal claims. The discussions concentrated on the right to reside in a Member State as well as on the social and employment rights a mobile person could claim in that State.

The papers presented at this seminar as well as the comments by some of the respondents to these papers are compiled in this book. It starts with an introductory chapter which summarises the findings in the various chapters. It ends with a more recent comment on 'the settlement for the United Kingdom within the European Union' agreed by the European Council on 18–19 February 2016 with a view to the referendum on UK membership of the EU.

The seminar as well as the publication of this volume were only possible with the help of a number of persons. First I would like to thank Nele Voorspoels for the perfect organisation of the seminar, including the organisation of travel and lodging arrangements for the participants. I also acknowledge the invaluable language checks of the draft chapters by Erika Peeters and Rebecca Pound as well as the editing work of the staff of Intersentia. And finally I am greatly indebted to the meticulous and time consuming work of streamlining the references in the chapters done by Bartłomiej Bednarowicz, PhD researcher at the Faculty of Law of the University of Antwerp.

Herwig Verschueren
May 2016

CONTENTS

Chapter 13.
Conflicting Rules of Conflict: Social Security and Labour Law. A Response

Chapter 14.
Where Does the UK Belong?

LIST OF ABBREVIATIONS

AG	Advocate General
CJ	Court of Justice of the European Union
CML Rev	Common Market Law Review
ECHR	Convention for the Protection of Human Rights and Fundamental Freedoms (European Convention on Human Rights)
ECtHR	European Court of Human Rights
EJML	European Journal of Migration and Law
EL Rev	European Law Review
ELJ	European Law Journal
EU	European Union
EUCO	European Council
EUConst	European Constitutional Law Review
MJ	Maastricht Journal of European and Comparative Law
OJ	Official Journal of the European Union
TEU	Treaty on the European Union
TFEU	Treaty on the Functioning of the European Union

LIST OF CONTRIBUTORS

Sergio Carrera is Senior Research Fellow and Head of the Justice and Home Affairs Research Programme at the Centre for European Policy Studies (CEPS), Brussels. He is also Associate Professor/Senior Researcher at the Faculty of Law of the University of Maastricht.

Rob Cornelissen is Visiting Professor of European Social Security Law at the University of Brussels (VUB). He is also Guest Professor at the Catholic University of Leuven and at the University of Ghent. From 1983 to 2014 he was a civil servant at the European Commission. During that period he was the head of several departments in fields such as free movement of workers, social protection and inclusion, anti-racism, and coordination of social security. He is the author and co-author of several books and numerous articles in the field of free movement of workers and coordination of social security.

Henri de Waele is Professor of International and European Law at Radboud University Nijmegen, where he also serves as Co-Director of the Research Platform on the Europeanisation of Policy and Law (EUROPAL). Since 2010, he has been Guest Professor of European Institutional Law at the University of Antwerp. He is moreover affiliated as a Senior Fellow with the Centre for European Integration Studies at the University of Bonn.

Maximilian Fuchs is Professor Emeritus and had a chair of Civil Law, German and European Labour and Social Law at the Catholic University of Eichstätt-Ingolstadt, Germany. He is co-editor of ZESAR (Zeitschrift für europäisches Sozial- und Arbeitsrecht). He was an analytical expert of trESS and since 2014 he has been an analytical expert of FreSsco. Since 2006 he has been a member of the Advisory Board of the Institute for Labour Law and Industrial Relations in the European Union at the University of Trier. Since 2014 he has been a lecturer on European labour and social security law at the Vienna University of Economics and Business.

Stefano Giubboni is Professor of Labour Law at the Department of Political Sciences of the University of Perugia. He has published extensively on labour law and social security law, from a national as well as a European and comparative perspective.

Alexander Hoogenboom is a PhD Researcher at the Faculty of Law of the Maastricht University, as well as Junior Researcher for the Institute for Transnational and Euregional cross-border cooperation and Mobility (ITEM). His areas of expertise include EU free movement law, student mobility, Union citizenship, EU migration law, and EU competition and State aid law.

Mijke Houwerzijl is Professor of Labour Law at Tilburg University. She also holds a chair in Comparative and European Labour Law at the University of Groningen. She has written widely on Dutch and EU labour law and social policy, with an emphasis on issues concerning workers mobility, labour migration and enforcement of labour law.

Paul Minderhoud is an Associate Professor at the Centre for Migration Law of the Radboud University Nijmegen, the Netherlands. His main research interests are the legal and socio-legal aspects of immigration and social security. He is managing editor of the *European Journal of Migration and Law.*

Jo Shaw holds the Salvesen Chair of European Institutions at the University of Edinburgh, having previously held Chairs at the Universities of Leeds and Manchester. Her research focuses on citizenship, especially EU citizenship viewed in constitutional perspective.

Eleanor Spaventa is Professor of European Union Law at the Law School, Durham University. She specialises in EU law, and in particular in the internal market, Union citizenship, free movement and fundamental rights.

Daniel Thym holds the Jean Monnet Chair of European, International and Public Law at University of Konstanz and is the co-director of the Research Centre Immigration & Asylum Law. He serves as an editor of the *European Law Journal, Review of European Law in Context* and has published widely on diverse issues of European law, with a special focus on asylum, immigration, constitutional affairs and external relations

Anthony Valcke is Visiting Lecturer at the University of Kent in Brussels where he convenes the module 'Teaching EU Migration Law Through Clinical Legal Education'. He also directs the EU Rights Clinic, which is the first law clinic to specialise in EU law that was set up by Kent in collaboration with the non-governemental organisation ECAS. He also serves as Associate Professor of Law at Vesalius College in Brussels where he teaches EU law. He is qualified as a solicitor in England and is also a member of the Brussels and Palermo bars.

Aukje A.H. van Hoek is Professor of Private International Law and Civil Procedure at the University of Amsterdam and honorary justice in the Court of

Appeals 's Hertogenbosch where she sits on labour cases. She is a former member of the Dutch standing committee on private international law and a former chair holder of a Jean Monnet Chair in Transnational Social Justice and European Integration at the University of Tilburg. One of her key research areas concerns the regulation and governance of cross-border employment.

Herwig Verschueren is Professor of International and European Labour and Social Security law at the University of Antwerp. He is also a Visiting Professor at the University of Brussels (VUB). His research concentrates on European employment and social law and more specifically on the legal position of mobile persons with regard to employment and social security rights.

CHAPTER 1
HOW EU LAW DEFINES WHERE MOBILE PERSONS BELONG
An Introduction

Herwig VERSCHUEREN

More than ever individuals cross borders for work, business, studies, tourism, in search of international protection, for family or other reasons. By doing so they establish links with other countries, which could be the basis for legal claims against these States or for the application of their legal order. This book discusses the issue of these links and, more specifically, the question as to how EU law defines the link needed to obtain the right to reside in a Member State and the right to social and employment protection in that State. When it comes to claiming rights from States, traditionally 'nationality' is the answer to the question where a person belongs. However, in the context of European integration and the development of an EU legal framework of internal market rules, citizenship rights and immigration rules, different answers to these questions have been developed.

It follows from the analyses in this book that EU law gives a multitude of answers to the question which link is necessary and sufficient to create an individual's right *vis-à-vis* a State. The definition of this link, the criteria used and the legal consequences differ according to the legal framework the individual finds himself/herself in and the legal instrument he/she invokes. It also appears that the various applicable instruments of EU law all have their own criteria to determine with which Member State a person has a sufficient link to claim rights.

As regards the right of residence for Union citizens and the members of their family, Directive 2004/38 establishes the right of residence on the basis of, *inter alia*, the following criteria: do the persons concerned exercise an economic activity or not, what is the duration of their residence, do these persons constitute a burden on the social assistance system of the host State and is this burden 'reasonable', which family ties are accepted to create rights for members of the family as well, including third-country nationals? The establishment of the right to reside on the basis of these criteria also triggers the right to equal treatment with the nationals of the host State, for instance with regard to social benefits. On the basis of this Directive a host State could also consider an individual as no longer belonging to its society and consequently expel this person on grounds of not having sufficient resources or for reasons of public policy, public security or public health.

As for the social rights of migrant Union citizens, the rules on conflict of laws of the social security coordination in Regulation 883/2004 prescribe criteria like the place of work, the place of residence or the centre of the professional activities to determine to which legislation a migrant person is subject, and hence from which social security system he/she can claim benefits or to which system he/she must contribute financially. The rules on conflict of laws applicable to labour law (Rome I Regulation 593/2008, Posting of Workers Directive 96/71) also contain criteria to determine with which Member State a cross-border worker has a sufficient link to make its employment protection applicable. The criteria used in these instruments concern the habitual place of work, the temporary nature of the employment or posting, place of business or, in general, other circumstances that connect the employment contract more closely to a State. For each of these rules the Court of Justice (CJ) has developed abundant case-law in which it further specifies and completes these rules.

Furthermore, in cases which do not concern the application of secondary EU law but instead fall directly under the Treaty provisions on citizenship and free movement, the CJ also uses criteria to determine whether the link between a person and a Member State is sufficient to justify the claim of a right to reside or to social benefits. These criteria are, amongst others: having a sufficient link with the labour market of the host Member State, the duration of the residence or stay in the host Member State, payment of taxes, education of children, the degree of integration into the host society, enrolment in higher education or having fulfilled one of these criteria in the past.

In external EU migration law too the link between the third-country migrant and the Member State plays a role in obtaining and retaining rights *vis-à-vis* the host State, such as the right of residence or the right to equal treatment regarding employment and social protection. These criteria concern, *inter alia*, being economically active, having family ties, having sufficient resources, fulfilling integration requirements or having legally resided in the host State for a certain period. They can be found in instruments, such as Family Reunification Directive 2003/86 and the Long-Term Residence Directive 2003/109.

From the outset, it should be obvious that EU law gives a lot of answers to the question where a mobile person belongs. Moreover, these answers do not only vary but sometimes also overlap or even conflict, which leads to situations in which a person may claim comparable rights in more than one Member State or, conversely, in which a person falls between two stools since he/she does not fulfil the criteria to claim a certain right in any Member State at all. In addition, the various criteria used in secondary EU law as well as in the case-law of the CJ are subject to discussions on their exact meaning as well as on the way to implement them in specific situations, which may increase and reinforce those conflicting situations.

In this book, scholars from different legal disciplines critically analyse and discuss the multitude of criteria used in EU legislation and case-law to determine whether there is a sufficient link between a person and a Member State with a view to making legal claims. The various chapters concentrate on the right to reside in a Member State as well as on the social and employment rights a mobile person could claim in that State.

It starts with an analysis on how family ties may constitute a sufficient link to create rights to reside or to equal treatment in a Member State, both for Union citizens and for third-country nationals (Chapter 2). In this chapter, Daniel Thym reconstructs the evolution and rationale of the rules in question, which he calls 'a legal jungle'. As far as members of the family of Union citizens are concerned, he points at the generous family reunion regime in the first decades of European integration until the early 2000s, both in legislation and in the case-law of the CJ. The protection of family life was seen as an instrument to foster 'integration' of the migrant worker into the host society and therefore as serving the free movement objectives of the internal market. In some cases, it was even regarded as an end in itself. It also applied when a migrant Union citizen returned to the home State. Recent case-law, however, shows a more restrictive approach, especially for spouses from third countries. Their status lies 'at the crossroads of rules on free movement and migration law', and illustrates 'the cleavage between citizens' rights and migration law', between free movement within the internal market and policy in the area of freedom, security and justice. Daniel Thym also highlights the importance of taking into account fundamental rights issues as well as the broader social and political context, a context that changes over time. This is clearly the case with the Member States' growing concern about immigration policy. In his view, all this explains why the CJ has difficulty in developing a coherent position on this issue.

In his response, Henri de Waele takes the view that the CJ's rulings on family reunion failed to keep up with the times (Chapter 3). But he adds that 'when the desired judicial application to a decisively changed political and societal context finally arrived, it unfortunately took the shape of an *over*reaction, alongside some dubious prevarication'.

The right to reside in a host Member State for economically inactive Union citizens is subject to them having sufficient resources for themselves and their family and a comprehensive sickness insurance (Article 7(1)(b) Directive 2004/38). In Chapter 4, Paul Minderhoud investigates the meaning of these concepts as conditions for being entitled to the right to reside, but also to the right to equal treatment with the nationals of the host State. He analyses the recent case-law of the CJ on this issue, as well as the implementation of these conditions by national administrations and judiciary. He found that the approaches regarding the definition of sufficient resources vary between the Member States. This is also the case with the condition of having comprehensive sickness insurance, in particular in Member States with a residence based national health service. He also refers to the most recent judgments of the CJ in *Dano* and *Alimanovic*, in which the CJ indicated that asking for social assistance automatically means that the economically inactive Union citizen is not fulfilling the sufficient resources condition and hence has no right to reside on the basis of Directive 2004/38 and is not even entitled to equal treatment in the host Member State. For him this case-law raises some fundamental questions about the scope of European citizenship rights which normally should emphasise proportionality and the need for individual assessment.

In his response to this analysis, Stefano Giubboni confirms the retreat in the CJ's discourse on EU citizenship as a source of transnational social solidarity, which, in his view, appears to be very fragile or even illusory (Chapter 5). For him, this recent case-law is a return to obeying a strict mercantile logic and re-introduces the pre-Maastricht cleavage within the status of Union citizenship between economically inactive and economically active migrating Union citizens. He fears a creeping return to the grim logic of the Poor Laws with a 'post-modern rediscovery of the classical remedy of expulsion of the undeserving poor, by sending them back to the parish (or, in our case, to the country) of origin'.

Indeed, these analyses show that for economically inactive Union citizens, the condition of having sufficient resources is applied very strictly when it comes to answering the question whether or not such a person belongs to the circle of solidarity of the host State. This would mean that solidarity is only open to those who do not really need it.

Since residence in a State is a crucial factor when it comes to belonging to that State's legal and social order, it goes without saying that the termination of a person's residence by expulsion measures breaches this physical link between the individual and that State. After having analysed the conditions which have to be satisfied by EU citizens in order to gain residency rights under Directive 2004/38, including the self-sufficiency condition for economically inactive citizens, Eleanor Spaventa examines in Chapter 6 the possibility to expel a citizen who does not fulfil (any longer) these conditions. She argues that 'denial of residency rights cannot be the automatic consequence of recourse to social assistance but has to be justified by also having regard for the particular situation of the claimants'. Next, she considers the circumstances in which lawfully resident Union citizens might be expelled from the host State, i.e. because their conduct amounts to a threat to the host State's public policy or security. It appears that recently the CJ introduced qualitative criteria of integration in addition to the traditional territorial and time factors, and this despite the fact that Directive 2004/38 does not mention any qualitative criteria. No integration test is mentioned in this Directive, which for her is the biggest difference between Union citizens and third-country nationals. For Union citizens, time and place alone should suffice. In her view the reasoning of the Court is 'wholly irrational because it risks depriving the enhanced protection of any effect' and it denies that '"bad" individuals also have a life, families and relationships'. In her view this demonstrates the 'implosion of Union citizenship' since it indicates that Union nationals finally remain the responsibility of the State of which they hold the nationality, even in cases where they do no longer have any personal, social or other ties with that State'. She concludes that, despite the introduction of Union citizenship, the bottom line still is: 'once a foreigner always a foreigner'.

In addition to Spaventa's legal analysis, Anthony Valcke offers us a statistical snapshot of Member States' practices in restricting the free movement rights of EU citizens and their family members (Chapter 7). He found significant divergences between the various Member States in terms of the availability and level of detail of statistical information in this respect. As for the rejection of the application for residence, there seems to be a high refusal rate for applications made by non-EU family members. Based on the information available, it also appears that three out of twenty residence applications are suspected of involving a marriage or relationship of convenience, but that only 2% of the applications were actually rejected for this reason. Regarding expulsion measures, the publicly available statistics are scarce and suggest that for the period 2011–2013 Belgium and France expelled proportionally more Union citizens than other Member States of which we have data.

Sergio Carrera analyses in Chapter 8 the role 'integration' plays in the EU's legal framework on immigration of third-country nationals. He identifies a 'paradigm shift' from integration policies 'used to focus mainly on the facilitation of mobility through non-discrimination, respect for family life and security of residence' to 'integration as a new ground for exclusion of foreigners in EU management of human mobility and identity'. His contribution examines the lawfulness under EU law, more specifically Family Reunification Directive 2003/86, the Long-Term Residence Directive 2003/109, as well as the EU Charter of Fundamental Rights of mandatory civic integration exams as introduced by some Member States. In his view the most recent case-law of the CJ (*P. and S.* and *K. and A.*) on this issue did not produce further legal clarity and consistency on the application of Member States' civic integration programmes. Neither did it sufficiently take account of the role of fundamental rights, meaning that the CJ missed the opportunity to function as a 'fundamental rights adjudicator'. Still, it did draw some 'red lines' on what is not permissible within the scope of EU immigration law as regards the use of mandatory civic integration exams. Finally, he points at the high level of discretion characterising the concept of 'integration'.

Student mobility within the EU is promoted intensively by EU institutions as well as by the Member States, and is frequently attributed a wide range of economic and civic benefits. This is the starting point of Alexander Hoogenboom's analysis in Chapter 9 of the question where these students belong when it comes to claiming rights regarding access to education and study facilitating benefits. As for access to education, students are not required 'to show a degree of connection or genuine link with the host Member State to benefit from equal treatment'. Conversely, regarding access to study facilitating benefits the question of 'belonging' requires a much more intricate answer. Indeed, the analysis of the relevant case-law of the CJ suggests that there are different ways in which an individual can demonstrate his or her integration, such as resident family members, past employment, past schooling and the ability to speak the language of the Member State in question. Even 'nationality' seems, surprisingly, to play a role. As regards access to study grants and/or loans, it is accepted that Member States have more freedom when it comes to restricting the circle of beneficiaries, but in Hoogenboom's view the CJ's case-law should ensure a more coherent legal framework as a result of which the commitment to promote student mobility would be taken more seriously. Member States should be forced to carry out a 'more sophisticated analysis as to who can be considered sufficiently connected', 'while at the same time substantiate more extensively the threat to the financial equilibrium that underlies' their systems.

Subsequently the book turns to the discussion on the social and labour rights of persons migrating within the EU.

Chapter 10 offers an analysis by myself of the role the exercise of an economic activity in a host Member State plays in obtaining rights from that State. The classic way for migrating Union citizens to claim rights in the host Member State is, indeed, being economically active as a worker (see the original Article 48 EEC and now Article 45 TFEU). It appears that, despite the introduction of EU citizenship, including for economically inactive citizens, those who are economically active continue to enjoy a stronger legal position under EU law compared to inactive persons. However, the borderline between the categories of active and inactive EU citizens is still rather muddled and subject to discussion and doubts, resulting in unpredictable qualifications and creating inconsistencies in the implementation by the Member States, their judiciary and even the CJ. The latter's case-law sticks to the traditional binary divide between employment and self-employment and therefore overlooks the economic and social reality of work today. Moreover, even the status of economically active EU migrants does not guarantee full rights in the host State. Recent case-law seems to depart from the previous, almost mechanical, application of the right to equal treatment and to submit the economically active EU migrants to a 'genuine link' test as well, a test which is not always considered to be fulfilled, not even by those who qualify as 'workers'.

In labour law matters, rules established in private international law (PIL) play a central role in determining the legal order which governs the contractual relationship between the employee and the employer. In Chapter 11, Aukje van Hoek and Mijke Houwerzijl critically analyse criteria and concepts used by the PIL rules in the Rome I Regulation 593/2008 as well as in the Posting of Workers Directive 96/71 (and the relevant CJ's case-law) to establish the place(s) where mobile EU workers 'belong' with regard to their rights under labour law. These instruments may be seen as tools to find a balance between the types of 'belonging' involved which, in their view, is not a static fact 'but rather an ongoing game where different weight may be given to the distinct lines of ordering'. These lines concern the protection of the worker as the weaker party in the employment contract as well as the restriction of regulatory competition between workers and between employers (prevention of social dumping), the organisational framework of the undertaking (collective aspects of the employment relationship) and the embeddedness in the social and tax systems applicable to the employment contract. These authors discuss the meaning of and the interference between the different connecting factors used, such as the habitual place of work, the country of engagement, the country with which there is a closer link (to be determined by a number of other connecting factors) and the country in which the posted workers temporarily work in the context of the cross-border provision of services by the employer. It appears that in law as well as in practice it is sometimes difficult to define these factors clearly. Moreover, the authors underline that 'blurring regulatory concepts and criteria also generate opportunities for non-compliance, resulting in violation of labour law and other (fundamental) rights of migrant workers', such as 'underpayment, excessive deduction of costs for lodging and travel, violations of health and safety and working time regulations', the use of letter-box companies, rotational postings or other abuses of internal market law. In addition, such abuses are sometimes difficult to trace and combat, or not even seen as negative by the workers involved when 'they seem to be happy with the job opportunity and do not want to put that in danger by claiming rights' in the host State. Therefore, efficient enforcement by host State authorities or interested third parties seems crucial.

Regarding social security legislation, which remains a matter for the Member States to develop, as early as 1958 the EU started developing conflict of laws rules to be applicable when moving persons are confronted with more than one national system (now Regulation 883/2004). This system is analogous to the PIL conflict of laws rules applicable to employment relationships.

Rob Cornelissen explores in Chapter 12 how the co-existence of these two systems of conflict of laws rules could result in situations in which a worker is subject to the social security legislation of one Member State and to the labour law of another Member State. He starts by explaining in detail which criteria the EU coordination system has developed for the determination of the legislation applicable with a view to preventing negative or positive conflicts of laws. It concerns criteria, such as the place of work (*lex loci laboris*), the place of residence (*lex loci domicilii*), the seat of the company or the centre of a person's economic activity. These rules are binding and exclusive. However, he makes it clear that the exclusive effect is undermined by recent CJ case-law (*Bosmann, Hudzinski/Wawrzyniak, Franzen*) which allows other criteria to be invoked in order to claim benefits from a Member State, such as the fact of being subject to unlimited income tax liability when it comes to social security benefits financed through taxes. The CJ even seems to indicate that it is up to the national courts to decide whether or not there is a sufficiently 'close connection' between the person and the non-competent State. According to Cornelissen this might be a 'tedious exercise' which may lead to legal uncertainty. The question arises whether the Member State with which the person has a 'close connection' may exclude such persons from its social security coverage for the sole reason that they are subject to the legislation of another Member State by virtue of EU law. He notes that for mobile workers and their employers the situation might become rather complicated when the EU rules in the field of labour law and social security law lead to the applicability of different national laws concerning the same subject. This is, for instance, the case with the income protection for sick workers, which may be subject to rules of conflict in social security law as well as in labour law. He analyses in detail some examples of situations of this kind and argues that 'it would go beyond the coordination of social security if the application of the EU rules determining the applicable social security legislation would result in intervention in the rights between employer and worker'.

In his contribution Maximilian Fuchs responds to Cornelissen's analysis of the recent CJ case-law in relation to the exclusive and mandatory character of the EU rules on the determination of the applicable legislation in social security (Chapter 13). On the one hand, he explains how this case-law is in line with, for instance, the case-law of German courts stating that it is not the purpose of the EU conflict of laws rules to keep Member States from achieving aims with are inherent to their legislation. But on the other hand, he is also critical, for instance, of the second part of the CJ's judgment in *Hudzinski/Wawrzyniak* in which, in his view, the CJ gave unjustified significance to tax liability as a connecting factor, denying other essential characteristics of the family benefit at stake. He opines that the CJ, by looking at this issue from the point of view of the prohibition of obstacles to the free movement of workers as guaranteed by the Treaty, 'introduced by the back door a duty to grant' a benefit where the rules of conflict of the EU do not contain such a duty. By doing so the Court introduced a rule requiring application of the most favourable legislation, in fact a 'better law' principle. For the author this gives rise 'to the risk that the aim of legal certainty and predictability of the application of the rules will not be achieved' or undermines the principle that the rules of conflict of laws in social security are neutral as regards the benefits the migrant person is entitled to in the 'competent State'. He also takes the view that the *raison d'être* of the *lex loci laboris* principle is to guarantee the migrant worker's affiliation to the social security scheme of the Member State where he/she works, but that in the case where such an affiliation is not guaranteed, other connecting factors, such as residence should be applied.

In the final Chapter 14, Jo Shaw comments on 'the settlement for the United Kingdom within the European Union' agreed by the European Council on 18–19 February 2016 with a view to the referendum on UK membership of the EU. The measures envisaged would discriminate against citizens of other Member States with regard to their social rights (non-contributory in-work benefits as well as family benefits) and would in some cases restrict their right to reside (and those of the members of their family). She fears 'that UK exceptionalism could end up resulting in a general watering down of the framework for the free movement of persons'. In her view these measures are not based on empirical evidence about the motivation of mobile EU workers or about the exceptional burden they would lay on the national welfare budgets. They must be seen in the context of the 'politicisation and contested application of EU free movement law in the UK over many years' which seems now to be taken over by other Member States. It appears that States increasingly 'seek to exploit any uncertainties and wiggle room that the framework of EU law itself offers' and that 'in relation to social assistance for EU citizens [...] it is clear the protestations of Member States about welfare tourism have not fallen on deaf ears in the Court of Justice'.

After lecture of these chapters it will be clear that EU law takes a whole set of criteria into account to determine with which Member State an individual has a sufficient link to claim rights, more specifically the right to reside and the rights regarding employment and social protection. As a result, the definition of where a mobile person belongs differs from legislation to legislation and from case to case. Furthermore, this could lead to situations in which the answer is that the individual belongs to the legal order of more than one Member State or that he/she does not meet one of these criteria sufficiently to belong to any legal order at all, and therefore finds himself/herself in a kind of no man's land. Moreover, the criteria used in legislation continue to be the subject of problems of interpretation and application, which in turn leads to legal uncertainty or even confusion. No wonder that some of the discussions in this respect have turned political, such as the discussion on 'benefit tourism' of economically inactive EU citizens.

A key question in this matter seems to be whether or not integration into a Member State is the result of granting rights to newcomers or that granting rights to migrants can be made dependent on the pre-requirement of sufficient integration into the society or economy of the host Member State. Recent case-law of the CJ shows that there is a clear shift towards the second approach:

integration no longer as the ultimate goal of granting rights to persons who do not hold the nationality of the Member State concerned, but as a pre-condition to obtain rights. As a result, in spite of the fundamental prohibition of discrimination on grounds of nationality in the TFEU (Article 18) and in the EU Charter of Fundamental Rights (Article 21(2)), nationality could again play a bigger role in the formulation of the definition of where a mobile person belongs.

CHAPTER 2

FAMILY AS LINK

Explaining the Judicial Change of Direction on Residence Rights of Family Members from Third States

Daniel THYM

1. RECONSTRUCTING FREE MOVEMENT AND UNION CITIZENSHIP

Rules on free movement and Union citizenship have always had a predilection towards progressive change. This inherent dynamism reflects the general tendency of the EU to rely on an ongoing process of transformative integration through law and corresponds to the historic weight of invocations of 'citizenship' during earlier struggles for political reform and social inclusion.[1] Within the confines of EU law, rules on citizenship and free movement have evolved considerably over the past decades. This process was driven by Treaty changes or legislative amendments at some points, while Court judgments took the helm at other moments. The first section of this contribution presents the methodological foundations upon which our enquiry rests (see below 1.1) and shows the significance of our object of study: residence rights of family members, in particular those from third states (see below 1.2).

1.1. EVOLUTION OF LEGAL RULES

There was and remains nothing inevitable in the evolution of Union citizenship and free movement. It will be demonstrated later that the original Treaty regime established a framework the legislature had to fill with substance in the

1 See P. MAGNETTE, *Citizenship. The History of an Idea* (Oxford: ECPR Press, 2005), chs. 4 and 5; and D. KOCHENOV, 'The Citizenship Paradigm' (2012/13) 15 *Cambridge Yearbook of European Legal Studies*, 197–226.

1960s.[2] On this basis, the Court of Justice embarked upon the construction of doctrinal figures for free movement, which it applied to family reunion later.[3] Luxembourg's case-law embraced a variety of different scenarios reflecting the complexity of free movement rules whose interpretation was inspired by the subsequent introduction of Union citizenship which the Court famously considered being 'destined to be [a] fundamental status.'[4]

Union citizenship can be understood as an overarching idea supporting the search for coherent solutions for family reunion in the diverse scenarios discussed below. This would establish the citizenship paradigm as the fixed star guiding the resolution of legal questions,[5] reflecting the desire of the legislature to remedy the 'sector-by-sector, piecemeal approach to the right of free movement.'[6] Even where such status convergence happens, change cannot be expected to be linear. Instead, it will often present a process of stratification when different layers supplement and influence each other. Such evolution may result in gradual approximation, but it can also cause frictions or contradictions when later events have a transformative impact upon earlier developments – and vice versa.[7] Arguably, residence rights of family members from third states exemplify such stratification of free movement law. Many of the interpretative cleavages discussed in this chapter can be explained as a result of countervailing forces within the Union's legal order pushing the evolution of the law in different directions, thereby causing doctrinal disparities and conceptual tensions in relation to our object of study.

There are at least three interrelated reasons why the case-law on third-country national family members is bound to remain instable. Firstly, the doctrinal foundations of CJ judgments may be robust, but their application to individual cases at the fringes of citizenship and free movement law remains precarious as the analysis below will establish.[8] Secondly, the very concept of 'citizenship' remains contested with academics promoting different trajectories of how to construe the meaning of a status fluctuating between aspirational accounts that emphasise its dynamic character, a legal perspective highlighting doctrinal rigour

2 See below section 2.1.

3 See below section 3.

4 Case C-184/99, *Grzelczyk*, EU:C:2001:458, para. 31.

5 For a pronounced statement see D. Kochenov, 'The Citizenship Paradigm' (2012–13) 15 *Cambridge Yearbook of European Legal Studies*, 197–226.

6 Recital 4 Directive 2004/38/EC on the right of citizens of the Union and their family members to move and reside freely within the territory of the Member States, OJ 2004, L 158/77 (hereinafter referred to as 'Directive 2004/38').

7 Cf. J.H.H. Weiler, 'The Geology of International Law' (2004) 64 *Heidelberg Journal of International Law*, 549; and D. Thym, 'The Elusive Limits of Solidarity' (2015) 52 *CML Rev*, 18–19.

8 See below 3; and N. Nic Shuibhne, *The Coherence of EU Free Movement Law* (Oxford: OUP, 2013), ch. 2.

and a sociological approach concentrating on the empirical substratum.[9] Thirdly, the broader constitutional context seems to have had a noticeable impact on the case-law when migration law towards third-country nationals within the area of freedom security and justice and related human rights guarantees appeared as a competing frame of reference for rules on family reunion.[10]

Methodologically, this chapter follows an approach one may call contextually embedded doctrinal constructivism, since it assumes, in contrast to US-style legal realism, that legal concepts can have a semi-autonomous significance and that academia may contribute to their rationalisation.[11] Corresponding analyses are based on a reconstruction of the case-law and its doctrinal foundations, thereby ideally supporting a better understanding of the systemic coherence of the law and its internal inconsistencies.[12] Doing so assumes that doctrinal arguments should be taken seriously in a discursive community involving academics in the constant reconstruction of the legal infrastructure.[13] Meanwhile, abstract legal concepts, such as free movement, citizenship or human rights, require a broader constitutional analysis in a process Armin von Bogdandy has aptly described as a doctrinal argument about constitutional principles.[14] This chapter follows this approach by extrapolating the constitutional infrastructure guiding the interaction of the diverse sets of rules on free movement, Union citizenship, human rights and migration.

Although the analysis of this contribution focuses on legal questions of doctrinal interpretation and constitutional reconstruction, it recognises that constitutional principles are not confined to legal debates, since they convey a set of normative values and express basic choices, which change over time.[15] Citizenship, migration and human rights are fields of the law resonating with broader social and political developments. Their conceptual openness was one factor facilitating progressive interpretation by the CJ described by academic observers as a process of judicial transformation transcending the original rationale of market integration.[16] However, such an outcome was and is no foregone conclusion. The

---

9 On these trajectories, see D. Thym, 'Frontiers of EU Citizenship', in D. Kochenov (ed.), *EU Citizenship and Federalism. The Role of Rights* (Cambridge: CUP, 2016), forthcoming.

10 See below section 4.

11 See G. Beck, *The Legal Reasoning of the Court of Justice of the EU* (Oxford: Hart Publishing, 2012); and T. Horsley, 'Reflections on the Role of the Court of Justice as the "Motor" of European Integration' (2013) 50 *CML Rev*, 934–954.

12 See R. van Gestel and H.-W. Micklitz, 'Why Methods Matter in European Legal Scholarship' (2014) 20 *ELJ*, 292–316.

13 See M. Kumm, 'On the Past and Future of European Constitutional Scholarship' (2009) 7 *International Journal of Constitutional Law*, 406–411.

14 See A. von Bogdandy, 'Founding Principles of EU Law: A Theoretical and Doctrinal Sketch' (2010) 16 *ELJ*, 98–100.

15 See R.M. Cover, 'Foreword: *Nomos* and Narrative' (1983) 97 *Harvard Law Review*, 11–44.

16 See E. Spaventa, 'From *Gebhard* to *Carpenter*' (2004) 41 *CML Rev*, 764–768; and S. Kadelbach, 'Union Citizenship', in A. von Bogdandy and J. Bast (eds.), *Principles of European Constitutional Law, 2nd edition* (Oxford: Hart Publishing, 2009), 461–466.

broader social and political context may similarly support restrictive tendencies, thematic shifts or judicial changes of direction.[17] Our analysis will show that rules on family reunion disclose such interpretative reorientation.

This outcome arguably reflects both the current state of Union citizenship and the emergence of migration law within the area of freedom security and justice as a competing frame of reference. While migration and human rights are discussed in greater detail below, the state of Union citizenship has been described elsewhere. Residence rights of family members are not the only area where the CJ has recently become more cautious. In its case-law on access to social benefits, the CJ arguably retreated from the vision expressed in some of its most renowned judgments by emphasising the limits of free movement and the conditions for equal treatment in cases such as *Dano*.[18] Arguably, such an outcome reflects a weakness of the conceptual groundwork for free movement and citizenship at a time when the limits of legal imagination become apparent.[19] This chapter will touch upon the broader social and political context influencing rules on family reunion even if its focus of analysis will be the doctrinal infrastructure and constitutional setting guiding interpretation.

1.2. THE CHALLENGE OF FAMILY REUNION

Rules on family reunion have been at the forefront of academic and political debates about Union citizenship and free movement in recent years. If one considers controversial citizenship cases over the past fifteen years, another common thread besides access to social benefits stands out: residence rights of family members, in particular those from third-states. *Ruiz Zambrano* and *Dereci* are prime examples, but the line of judgments upon which I will build my argument is much longer. Most experts of free movement law are familiar with cases such as *Baumbast*, *Carpenter*, *Akrich*, *Metock*, *Iida*, *O. and S.*, *Teixeira*, *McCarthy* – and, more recently, *Ogieriakhi*, *Singh*, *S. and B.* or *Alimanovic*. Despite the fact that all these cases relate to different aspects of primary and secondary law, they have one thing in common: they concern the interface of migration law and Union citizenship or, to be more precise, residence rights of family members from third states.

17 See D. Kostakopoulou, 'Co-creating European Union Citizenship' (2012/13) 15 *Cambridge Yearbook of European Legal Studies*, 259–266; and J. Shaw and N. Miller, 'When Legal Worlds Collide' (2013) 38 *EL Rev*, 137–166.

18 See D. Thym, 'The Elusive Limits of Solidarity' (2015) 52 *CML Rev*, 21–49; and N. Nic Shuibhne, 'Limits Rising, Duties Ascending: The Changing Legal Shape of Union Citizenship' (2015) 52 *CML Rev*, 889–937.

19 See S. Barbou des Places, 'La cohérence du droit de la libre circulation des personnes à l'épreuve de la mobilité des indigents' (2015) *Revue trimestrielle de droit européen*, 135–137; and D. Thym, 'When Union Citizens turn into Illegal Migrants: the *Dano* case' (2015) 40 *EL Rev*, 259–260.

It seems to me that this focal point is no coincidence, but reflects a deeper ambivalence of Union citizenship and its interaction with broader rules on immigration and asylum. By focusing on the grey zone between citizens' rights and the immigration status of foreigners, we may ideally learn more about the doctrinal interaction and constitutional rationale of both sets of rules. In doing so, this analysis will contribute to the resolution of the overarching research question addressed in the various chapters to this volume which are meant to scrutinise the link connecting 'individuals' and Member States in diverse areas of the supranational legal order. My central argument will be the following: the widespread confusion over the diversity of family reunion rules and the apparent change of direction in CJ case-law can be resolved, at an abstract level of analysis at least, by distinguishing two distinct constitutional frames of reference: one for the free movement of citizens, the other for immigration purposes.

I will structure my argument along the following lines. Firstly, a reminder of the role of family members in the early hours of the integration process will show that the initial impetus for a liberal regime came from the EU legislature subscribing to a generous interpretation of the Treaty articles. Secondly, it will be demonstrated that the Court of Justice built its position on diverse doctrinal scenarios which explain the complexity of the case-law but do not necessarily coalesce to form a coherent approach to family reunion, since they moreover exhibit a change of direction in the application of the European rules to specific scenarios taking place in recent years. Finally, the broader constitutional setting will reveal an alternative frame of reference based upon migration law and human rights, which may rationalise thematic shifts in recent case-law in light of a different constitutional rationale.

2. STARTING POINT: FAMILY AS AN END IN ITSELF

Many experts on EU law may not have realised that Treaty provisions on workers do not mention family members. There was and is nothing on the rights of spouses, children or parents in the wording of the EU Treaties. This suggested that the position of family members had to be determined by the EU institutions: while the legislature took the helm in the 1960s, the CJ entered the scene thereafter. Debates on family members reinforce the impression that social policy objectives accompanied economic considerations from the beginning. The 'market citizen', a term coined by Hans-Peter Ipsen to describe a status in between alienage and nationality,[20] was never supposed to be a factor of production for only whose mobility supports the functioning of the common

[20] See H.-P. Ipsen, *Europäisches Gemeinschaftsrecht* (Tübingen: Mohr Siebeck, 1972), 250–254.

market. Rules on the free movement of persons adopted early on contained elements one could describe as an incipient form of European citizenship.[21] Generous rules on family reunion are an integral element of these original policy debates dominated by economic and social policy objectives, which shaped the definition of family reunion.

2.1. TREATY NEGOTIATIONS AND EARLY LEGISLATION

How did the family reunion regime as we know it today come about? The silence of the EU Treaties on family members meant that the legislature had to define the contours of residence rights. In contrast to the heated political and legal disputes questions of family reunion have been generating these days,[22] the issue did not cause much controversy at the time. In several steps, Member States in the Council agreed on a generous family reunion regime for migrant workers, which concerned the nuclear family first[23] and was later extended to other relatives.[24] Disagreement among Member States on the issue during negotiations was limited with the Commission and Italy pressing for a generous regime accepted by other Member States after initial reticence about the extended family.[25] To this date, the extended family benefits from a quasi-automatic right to accompany or join workers.

One condition had originally been laid down in secondary legislation: appropriate accommodation was a requirement without which family reunion could be rejected.[26] This criterion reflected an important policy challenge at the time: the housing shortage after the Second World War.[27] It was abandoned

---

21 For the early debate on workers and service recipients, see A. Evans, 'European Citizenship' (1982) 45 *Modern Law Review*, 502–510.

22 See the chapter by S. Carrera in this volume.

23 Articles 11–15 Regulation No. 15 on first steps measures towards the realisation of the free movement of workers, OJ 1961, No. 57, 1073, for which no English translation is available, concerned spouses and children (hereinafter referred to as 'Regulation No. 15').

24 See Article 17(1) Regulation 38/64/EEC, OJ 1964, No. 62, 965 (hereinafter referred to as 'Regulation 38/64'), which is not available in English, corresponded to Articles 10–12 Regulation (EEC) 1612/68, OJ English Special Edn. Ser. I Ch. 1968(II), p. 475 (hereinafter referred to as 'Regulation 1612/68') and today's Article 10 Regulation (EU) 492/2011, OJ 2011, L 141/1 on the free movement of workers (hereinafter referred to as 'Regulation 492/2011), as well as Articles 2(2) and 7(1)(d) Directive 2004/38.

25 S. Goedings, *Labor Migration in an Integrating Europe* (The Hague: SDU Uitgevers, 2005), 163–166, 220–221 shows that the Benelux countries and Germany retreated from their earlier opposition during which some members of their delegations had allegedly warned against Mediterranean 'clans' moving North.

26 See Article 11(3) Regulation No. 15, Article 17(3) Regulation 38/64 and Article 10(3) Regulation 1612/68; on unsuccessful attempts by the Commission to delete it, see S. Goedings, *Labor Migration in an Integrating Europe* (The Hague: SDU Uitgevers, 2005), 164–165, 220–222, 245–248.

27 See T. Judt, *Postwar: A History of Europe Since 1945* (London: Penguin, 2005), ch. 3.

without much debate in the early 2000s when the question was no longer deemed as problematic.[28] Moreover, EU Treaties have always provided for an exception on public policy, security and health grounds, which early legislation and later CJ case-law interpreted restrictively.[29] In the absence of a permission to the contrary at Treaty level or in secondary legislation, Member States are prevented from establishing additional hurdles. They cannot, for instance, require economic self-sufficiency as a precondition for the free movement of workers and related family reunion.[30] It seems that the question was not considered pertinent in the early 1960s when it was deemed self-evident that a worker would be able to sustain his family.[31]

Similarly, Member States cannot require Union citizens and family members living abroad to comply with integration conditions, such as learning the local language. The latter cannot be applied differently to workers than from those who are economically inactive.[32] A Portuguese couple may spend their whole life in Marseille without speaking a single word of French and a German national moving across the border to Austria has the right to be joined by his wife from Turkey even if she cannot communicate in either German or any other official language of the European Union.[33] One may speculate whether a hypothetical amendment of the Citizenship Directive 2004/38 requiring Union citizens and/or family members to learn the local language in specific scenarios would be compatible with the EU Treaties.[34] Politically, such an amendment appears

---

28 Directive 2004/38/EC discontinued the criterion along similar lines as previous rules for Union citizens who are economically inactive (students, pensioners and others) in Directive 90/364/EEC, OJ 1990, L 180/26, Directive 90/365/EEC, OJ 1990, L 180/28 and Directive 93/96/EEC, OJ 1993, L 317/59.

29 See Directive 64/221/EEC on the co-ordination of special measures concerning the movement and residence of foreign nationals which are justified on grounds of public policy, public security or public health, OJ English Special Edn. Ser. I Vol. 1963/64, p. 117 (hereinafter referred to as 'Directive 64/221') and today's Articles 27–31 Directive 2004/38.

30 Sufficient resources are required only for those who are economically inactive by Article 7(1)(b) Directive 2004/38, while workers and family members benefit from an unconditional right to reside irrespective of whether they have recourse to social assistance; see for workers Case 139/85, *Kempf*, EU:C:1986:223; for family members Case 157/84, *Frascogna*, EU:C:1985:243; and, for further comment, A.P. van der Mei, *Free Movement of Persons within the European Community. Cross-Border Access to Public Benefits* (Oxford: Hart Publishing, 2003), 133–139.

31 During negotiations, the question of unemployment was not discussed at length, similarly since it was assumed, at a time of full employment, that unemployed workers would always be able to find a new job offer; see S. Goedings, *Labor Migration in an Integrating Europe* (The Hague: SDU Uitgevers, 2005), 259–264.

32 The reason is simple: the Citizenship Directive 2004/38 does not permit such requirement; see also C. Costello, '*Metock*: Free Movement and "Normal Family Life" in the Union' (2009) 46 *CML Rev*, 602–603.

33 Article 2(2) Directive 2004/38 and CJ case-law interpret free movement rules to cover reunion with family members from third states; see below section 3.2.

34 To make residence rights of certain categories of persons conditional upon compliance with language requirements by amending Directive 2004/38, would constitute a restriction of free movement guarantees in Articles 21 and 45 TFEU; it would be up to the CJ to decide whether

unrealistic,[35] since it would be almost impossible to convince the Commission, the European Parliament and the majority of Member States in the Council to support to it.[36]

2.2. UNDERLYING RATIONALE

It has been mentioned above that questions of family unity did not play a prominent role during negotiations. Reading documents about early debates, one realises that family reunion was simply not approached from a migration law perspective as it is the case today. Instead, debates during Treaty negotiations and early legislation were dominated by economic concerns, reflecting the primary focus of the European Economic Community on establishing a common market. Rules on family reunion followed this dominant rationale, which is taken up in Recital 6 of today's Regulation 492/2011 on the free movement of workers:

> 'The right of freedom of movement, in order that it may be exercised […] in freedom and dignity, requires that *equality of treatment* be ensured in fact and in law in respect of all matters relating to the actual pursuit of activities as employed persons and to eligibility for housing, and also that *obstacles to the mobility of workers be eliminated*, in particular as regards the conditions for the *integration of the worker's family* into the host country.'[37]

This official statement about the objectives pursued by the legislature encapsulates three core ideas that have shaped the legal position of third-country national family members ever since. Firstly, family reunion benefited from the central relevance of equal treatment during negotiations on the common market which embraced the pursuit of social policy objectives from the beginning. Member States wanted to ensure that free movement does not undermine legislation protecting workers at domestic level.[38] Against this background, equal

this solution presented a proportionate justification, for instance after years of protracted long-term unemployment.

35 Cf. the rejection of the Commission to table a proposal to amend the Citizenship Directive 2004/38 in response to the *Metock* judgment, although a couple of Member States supported such a step originally.

36 The CJ gains influence if secondary legislation and the EU Treaties are difficult to amend; see A. Stone Sweet, 'The European Court of Justice', in P. Craig and G. de Búrca (eds.), *The Evolution of EU Law, 2nd edition* (Oxford: OUP, 2011), 126–130; moreover, it interprets new and ambiguous legislative provisions not to depart from earlier case-law in cases of doubt; see D. Thym, 'Towards "Real' Citizenship?"', in M. Adams *et al.* (eds.), *Judging Europe's Judges* (Oxford: Hart Publishing, 2013), 159.

37 See Recital 6 of Regulation 492/2011, which replaced the original Recital 5 of Regulation 1612/68; emphasis added.

38 See S. O'Leary, 'Free Movement of Persons and Services', in P. Craig and G. de Búrca (eds.), *The Evolution of EU Law, 2nd edition* (Oxford: OUP, 2011), 499, 382–386; and S. Giubboni, 'Free Movement of Persons and European Solidarity' (2007) 13 *ELJ*, 363–368.

treatment of incoming workers served the double objective of protecting migrant workers and preventing a downward pressure on wages to the detriment of the domestic workforce of the host state.[39] Rules on migrant workers reflect the central relevance of equal treatment in economic and social policy debates.

Secondly, the above-mentioned recital maintains that 'obstacles to the mobility of workers [should] be eliminated.' This resonates with later CJ case-law that free movement should be interpreted generously, since it is essential for attaining the internal market and the concept of Union citizenship introduced later. In other words, the protection of family life was not necessarily perceived as an end in itself but contributed, in part at least, to the realisation of the other, more important Treaty objectives. To this date, it is a recurrent argument in the reasoning of the CJ in judgments on family reunion that the rejection of far-reaching family reunion rights 'might dissuade that citizen from exercising the rights to freedom of movement [...] and would therefore create an obstacle to the effective exercise of the freedom thus guaranteed by the EC Treaty.'[40] This argument, which is central to the case-law discussed below, mirrors the general aversion of economic market integration to allegedly protectionist restrictions by Member States constraining cross-border movements.

Thirdly, the recital employs the term 'integration' which is to be promoted by equality-based family reunion rights. This statement seems to reflect the primary orientation of policy debates at transnational market integration and the protection of social policy standards. Broader social or cultural integration were not discussed, arguably reflecting the expertise of the civil servants involved in the discussion and a general focus on economic issues at the time.[41] By contrast, it will be shown later that it is precisely these arguments that dominate today's debates about family reunion.[42] When the free movement *acquis* was designed, these novel debates were irrelevant – even if empirical evidence demonstrates that social integration of Union citizens may face similar challenges as for third-country nationals.[43] Equality-based rules on mobility enshrined at Treaty level

39 Belgian and France pressed for widespread equal treatment for that reason – both for working conditions generally and for equal pay for men and women in today's Article 157 TFEU; see S. Goedings, *Labor Migration in an Integrating Europe* (The Hague: SDU Uitgevers, 2005), 122–126; and M. Dani, in L. Azoulai, S. Barbou des Places and E. Pataut (eds.), *Ideas of the Person and Personhood in European Union Law* (Oxford: Hart Publishing, 2016, forthcoming).

40 Case C-413/99, *Baumbast and R.*, EU:C:2002:493, para. 52.

41 In the relation to citizens from other Member States, broader cultural or social imperatives would probably have been treated with suspicion as an expression of nationalism the EU was founded to overcome.

42 See below section 3.6.

43 Data from Germany show that Italian migrant workers and their children, in particular, have significant problems on the labour market and in the education system that is not better and sometimes worse than the performance of many third-country nationals; see the 8. Bericht der Beauftragten über die Lage der Ausländerinnen und Ausländer in Deutschland, Juni 2010, 93–94.

were reinforced by the legislature, thereby preventing Member States from applying most facets of their domestic immigration laws to Union citizens.[44]

3. EUROPEAN COURT OF JUSTICE: TOWARDS A NEW ACCENTUATION OF DERIVED RIGHTS

This section presents core judgments on family reunion in the context of EU free movement. It will be shown that judges in Luxembourg construe family as a potential 'link' to a country on the basis of the established principles for transnational activities in the single market.[45] Experts on EU law will be aware that the doctrinal foundations of the case-law were developed for goods first and extended to persons later. Notwithstanding the solidity of the doctrinal groundwork, the interpretation of secondary legislation and the application of the fundamental freedoms require judicial choices about how to reconstruct the contours of the family reunion regime in specific scenarios. It will be demonstrated that there has been a noteworthy shift in direction in recent years with the CJ abandoning its previous emphasis on the self-sufficient maintenance of family life when applying established doctrinal principles.

As starting point, it is worth emphasising that each of the three scenarios discussed below arises within a distinct legal context in the broader framework of Treaty rules governing the free movement of Union citizens. This common point of reference is important, since the Treaty guarantees on transnational mobility apply to Union citizens and cannot be invoked by third-country nationals. The latter can benefit from citizens' rights only indirectly by means of a legal reflex in the form of 'derived rights acquired through their status as members of the beneficiary's family.'[46] It is this derivative character that has been reinforced by the CJ in recent years, thereby recognising the potential overlap with the new constitutional frame of reference on migration discussed below.

3.1. AUTONOMOUS RIGHTS OF CHILDREN AND SPOUSES

The standard scenario of family reunion concerns situations where Union citizens move to or reside in other Member States. It is for these cases that the Citizenship Directive establishes a right for family members to 'accompany or

---

44 See J. Bast, *Aufenthaltsrecht und Migrationssteuerung* (Tübingen: Mohr Siebeck, 2011), 52 *et seq.*; and D. Thym, 'Freizügigkeit in Europa als Modell?' (2011) 56 *Europarecht*, 488–490.

45 For an overview of the doctrinal foundations, see D. Chalmers, G. Davies and G. Monti, *European Union Law. Text and Materials, 3rd edition* (Cambridge: OUP, 2014), 466–516.

46 Case C-256/11, *Dereci et al.*, EU:C:2011:734, para. 55; the formula was used first in Case 40/76, *Kermaschek*, EU:C:1976:157, para. 7.

join'[47] Union citizens. Moreover, legislation provides for an autonomous right of children to stay in the host country to pursue their education.[48] This provision is an excellent example to illustrate the family-friendly tendency in many Court cases. The CJ confirmed early on that it was not necessary for children to live with their parents.[49] In the early 2000s, it went further by applying the provision to children with the nationality of a third state irrespective of whether the family still lived together.[50] Moreover, the CJ assumed that the residence right of a child from a third state may serve as the basis for a derived residence right of parents from third states who are primary carers.[51] It later confirmed this position, although the new rules in the Citizenship Directive could have been read as justifying a different outcome.[52] This line of cases retains an indirect connection at best with economic activities by migrant workers.[53] Autonomous residence rights for children and the maintenance of family relations appeared as the primary motive of the generous CJ case-law.

It later applied the same rationale to the generic right of free movement under Article 21 TFEU in relation to EU citizens who are economically inactive. On this basis, a minor child depending on personal care and financial support by parents from third states may sponsor a residence right for the latter.[54] The Court's emphasis on autonomous residence rights for family members was reinforced by the assumption that motives which prompted the factual situation for claiming residence rights were irrelevant; regardless of whether a domestic court had established that the family deliberately moved to another EU Member State with the intention to benefit from generous free movement case-law upon return to the first state.[55] Thus, family unity thrived on the basis of free movement rights.

---

47 Article 3(1) Citizenship Directive 2004/38; similarly, see the previous Articles 10–11 Regulation 1612/68 and, for those who are self-employed, Article 1(1)(c)–(d) and (2) Directive 73/148/EEC on the abolition of restrictions on movement and residence within the Community for nationals of Member States with regard to establishment and the provision of services, OJ 1973, L 172/14.

48 See Article 10 Regulation 492/2011 reiterating the previous Article 12 Regulation 1612/68 for children of workers, while rules on the self-employed did not embrace a similar guarantee; see also Article 12(3) Citizenship Directive 2004/38.

49 See Joined Cases 389/87 and 390/87, *Echternach and Moritz*, EU:C:1989:130, paras. 16–22.

50 Case C-413/99, *Baumbast and R.*, EU:C:2002:493, paras. 56–62.

51 Case C-413/99, *Baumbast and R.*, EU:C:2002:493, paras. 68–75.

52 See Case C-310/08, *Ibrahim*, EU:C:2010:80, paras. 29–31, 54; Case C-480/08, *Teixeira*, EU:C:2010:83, paras. 36–39, 54–61; and P. Starup and M. Elsmore, 'Taking a Logical or Giant Step Forward? Comment on *Ibrahim* and *Teixeira*' (2010) 35 *EL Rev*, 571–588.

53 For a similar conclusion regarding job-seeking parents who may benefit from more generous derived rights under Article 10 Regulation 492/2011 see the Opinion of Advocate General Wathelet in Case C-67/14, *Alimanovic*, EU:C:2015:210, paras. 117–122.

54 See Case C-200/02, *Zhu and Chen*, EU:C:2004:639, paras. 42–47.

55 See Case C-200/02, *Zhu and Chen*, EU:C:2004:639, paras. 34–41 concerning temporary residence for childbirth in Northern Ireland to acquire Irish citizenship for the newly born on the basis of which the family would claim free movement rights upon their return to

None of the generous positions presented above have been overturned by the CJ. Nonetheless, it accentuated the limits of the approach in a number of more recent judgments. The Court stressed, for instance, that derived residence rights of parents from third states who are primary carers remain derivative in nature and therefore come to an end as a matter of principle, when the (former) child no longer depends on the parent.[56] Moreover, autonomous residence rights of children are attached to a specific Member State and do not bring about an autonomous right to free movement within the EU for the child or family members.[57] In addition, the statutory provision on autonomous residence rights for children concern workers only and cannot be extended to cover the children of service providers.[58] These more restrictive tendencies in follow-up cases may be complemented by more generous positions in other judgments, for instance on the question whether parents support minor children financially if the money comes from grandparents.[59] In short, the Court retains the positions of its more generous earlier case-law, while adapting its line of arguments to avoid extending it to even further domains.

In a number of more recent rulings, the restrictive line embraced the autonomous residence right of spouses after the death of the Union citizen provided that they had lived there for at least one year and have sufficient resources required by secondary legislation.[60] Similar rules apply to divorce after three years of marriage.[61] In recent decisions, the CJ focused on a strict interpretation of the rules in question instead of reactivating the more generous line of argumentation described above. For instance, it found that a derived residence right after a divorce does not come about if the partner left the Member State after the separation of the couple and initiated the divorce proceedings after his departure.[62] The same situation does not prevent the acquisition of permanent residence status by the family member if the Union citizen stays in the country after separation and until divorce.[63] In addition, third-country

England; the basic principle that motives are irrelevant was established by Case C-109/01, *Akrich*, EU:C:2003:491, paras. 55–57; see also C. Costello, 'Citizenship of the Union: Above Abuse?', in R. de la Feria and S. Vogenauer (eds.), *Prohibition of Abuse of Law* (Oxford: Hart Publishing, 2011), 321–354.

56 See Case C-480/08, *Teixeira*, EU:C:2010:83, paras. 76–87; in practice, most Member States will provide channels for continued legal residence by third-country national parents after a couple of years of legal stay in accordance with national immigration laws.

57 See Case C-10/05, *Mattern and Cikotic*, EU:C:2006:220; of course, free movement may be permitted in direct application of free movement rules irrespective of Article 10 Regulation 492/2011 if the conditions of the relevant provisions are met.

58 See Joined Cases C-147/11 and C-148/11, *Czop and Punakova*, EU:C:2012:538, paras. 30–33.

59 See Case C-423/12, *Reyes*, EU:C:2014:16; and J.-Y. Carlier, 'La libre circulation des personnes dans l'Union européenne' (2015) *Journal de droit européen*, 177.

60 See Article 12(2) Citizenship Directive 2004/38; previously, see Article 3(2) Regulation (EEC) No. 1612/68 which erected different conditions.

61 See Article 13(2)(a) Directive 2004/38; this provision was a novelty introduced in 2004.

62 See Case C-218/14, *Singh et al.*, EU:C:2015:476.

63 See Case C-244/13, *Ogieriakhi*, EU:C:2014:2068.

national parents living across the border in another EU Member State cannot invoke derived rights.[64]

Doctrinally, this reorientation of the case-law signals a shift from an interpretation based on the *telos* (purpose) and constitutional principles (human rights, significance of free movement) to an examination based upon the wording, general scheme and drafting history.[65] In doing so, judges accentuate the 'derived character'[66] of residence rights for spouses from third states, thereby rendering less visible the linkage between free movement and family unity which had defined earlier judgments.

3.2. RETURN AND CROSS-BORDER ECONOMIC ACTIVITIES

The family-friendly orientation of the case-law in the early 2000s is most visible in return scenarios when a Union citizen moves to another EU Member State before returning to his home state. In such scenarios, the following question may arise: whether and if so under what circumstances spouses from third states have a residence right, first in the other EU Member State and second in the home state upon return. Since the Citizenship Directive 2004/38/EC does not apply to residence in the home state, these scenarios are assessed directly on the basis of the fundamental freedoms by the CJ, which has to decide whether the denial of residence rights for third-country national spouses by the home state amounts to a restriction of free movement that cannot be justified. While the doctrinal foundations of the notion of restriction are well established, it is less clear what the consequences for return scenarios should be.

In *Singh*, the CJ found for the first time that a denial of residence rights for spouses upon return can amount to an unjustified restriction.[67] On this basis, the Court concluded in *Akrich* that the underlying idea does not justify an extension of this position to cover spouses without residence rights, since Union citizens could expect neither the home state nor the second Member State to regularise illegal stay in the absence of an obligation to the contrary in secondary law.[68] It later qualified this position by highlighting that the *Singh* judgment applied to situations where Union citizens met their spouse while residing in another Member State.[69] Most importantly, however, the CJ overturned the *Akrich* ruling

64 See Case C-40/11, *Iida*, EU:C:2012:2405, paras. 46–65.

65 See D. Thym, 'EU Free Movement as a Legal Construction – not as Social Imagination', Verfassungsblog.de on 12 November 2014.

66 See Case C-40/11, *Iida*, EU:C:2012:2405, paras. 63, 67; and Case C-218/14, *Singh et al.*, EU:C:2015:476, para. 50.

67 See Case C-502/10, *Singh*, EU:C:2012:3076, paras. 19–21.

68 See Case C-109/01, *Akrich*, EU:C:2003:491, paras. 47–54.

69 See Case C-1/05, *Jia*, EU:C:2007:1; Case C-291/05, *Eind*, EU:C:2007:771; and, for more detail, G. Barrett, 'Family Matters: European Community Law and Third-Country Family

in *Metock*, thereby effectively turning free movement law into an instrument for the regularisation of illegal stay on the part of the family member.[70] In these scenarios, the application of the concept of restriction retains only corollary connections with classic notions of transnational free movement, since it is difficult to argue that Union citizens might be deterred from moving if neither the home state nor the host country would have authorised regularisation.[71] Family unity appeared as an end in itself.

Along similar lines, the Court applied the fundamental freedoms to Union citizens living in their home state whenever they are engaged in transnational economic activities from within that state. This was first decided for active service-providers with a customer base abroad, since the separation of the couple 'would be detrimental to their family life and, therefore, to the conditions under which [a Union citizen] exercises a fundamental freedom.'[72] It is noteworthy that in this citation, the Court seems to acquire without caveat the detrimental effects to family life with economic activities. Again, the connection with transnational free movement appeared as a formal criterion for the betterment of family life by the CJ as an end in itself.[73]

For a couple of years, German companies tried to benefit from this situation by offering weekend trips to Denmark for German nationals who wanted to marry a partner from a third state but did not qualify for family reunion under German immigration law.[74] It was argued that, after having married in Denmark, the German national would benefit from the case-law on returning EU nationals. The Federal Administrative Court closed this route without a reference to the CJ arguing that free movement rights had not been exercised effectively[75] – a position that was reaffirmed by the CJ a few years later in the *O. and B.* judgment. Judges in Luxembourg held that short stays abroad below a three-month threshold did not indicate an intention to settle in the

---

Members' (2003) 40 *CML Rev*, 377 *et seq.*

70 See Case C-127/08, *Metock*, EU:C:2008:449, in particular paras. 58–59; and S. Currie, 'Accelerated Justice or a Step too Far?' (2009) 34 *EL Rev*, 310–326.

71 See A. Epiney, 'Von Akrich bis Metock' (2008) 43 *Europarecht*, 847–848; and N. Nic Shuibhne, 'The Outer Limits of EU Citizenship: Displacing Economic Free Movement Rights?', in C. Barnard and O. Odudu (eds.), *The Outer Limits of European Union Law* (Oxford: Hart Publishing, 2009), 179–180.

72 See Case C-60/00, *Carpenter*, EU:C:2002:434, para. 39; and the critical comment by U. Mager, 'Dienstleistungsfreiheit und Schutz des Familienlebens' (2003) *Juristenzeitung*, 204–207.

73 See E. Spaventa, 'From *Gebhard* to *Carpenter*: Towards a (Non-)Economic European Constitution' (2004) 41 *CML Rev*, 764–768; and A. Tryfonidou, 'Family Reunification Rights of (Migrant) Union Citizens' (2009) 15 *ELJ*, 634–653.

74 There is still a website offering the service at www.xn--hochzeit-dnemark-4nb.de (last accessed on 12 August 2015) promising 'a modern, absolutely legal and inexpensive opportunity to register your personal status and to secure residence status in the European Union' (translation by the author).

75 See Federal Administrative Court (Bundesverwaltungsgericht), judgment of 16 November 2010, 1 C 17.09; and judgment of 11 January 2011, 1 C 23.09.

host state 'in a way which would be such as to create or strengthen family life in that Member State.'[76] Accordingly, denial of residence rights for spouses upon return cannot be considered a restriction in need of justification. It is noticeable that this conclusion puts less emphasis on family unity as an end in itself, reinforcing instead the classic concept of transnational mobility as the hallmark of free movement.[77] Along similar lines, the EU legislator may soon force the CJ to revisit its position, since the new settlement for the UK, to which the European Council agreed upon in the run-up to the UK referendum on the EU membership in June 2016, would embrace an amendment of the Directive 2004/28/EC to effectively overturn the effects of the *Metock* judgment.[78] The outcome of the referendum was uncertain at the time of writing.[79]

3.3. SUBSTANCE OF RIGHTS (*RUIZ ZAMBRANO*)

By protecting family members of Union citizens, the Court left the impression that it transcended step by step the functional underpinning of free movement based on transnational mobility even if the judgments discussed above were decided on the basis of the established principles of the internal market.[80] Against this background, it seemed that a crucial threshold had been surpassed in the *Ruiz Zambrano* ruling of March 2011, which commentators applauded as a Rubicon towards 'real' citizenship.[81] It concerned the economically inactive Ruiz Zambrano family whose children had acquired Belgian nationality that was now relied upon as a foundation for residence rights of the parents in the children's home state of Belgium.[82] I have explained elsewhere that doctrinal and methodological considerations justify the theoretical conclusion that the judgment was in essence about citizenship as a vehicle for the promotion of social justice, protecting human wellbeing in a way that is usually assumed by human rights.[83]

---

76 See Case C-456/12, *O. and B.*, EU:C:2014:135, para. 52, while also extending the earlier *Carpenter* conclusion to workers in Case C-457/12, *S. and G.*, EU:C:2014:189, paras. 40–42.

77 See E. Spaventa, 'Family Rights for Circular Migrants and Frontier Workers: *O. and B.*, and *S. and G.*' (2015) 52 *CML Rev*, 764–778; and E. Pataut, 'Citoyenneté de l'Union européenne' (2014) *Revue trimestrielle de droit européen*, 791.

78 Case C-127/08, *Metock*, EU:C:2008:449.

79 See further on this settlement the chapter by J. Shaw in this volume.

80 See N. Nic Shuibhne, 'The Resilience of EU Market Citizenship' (2010) 47 *CML Rev*, 1611–1618; and F. Wollenschläger, 'A New Fundamental Freedom beyond Market Integration' (2011) 17 *ELJ*, 14–29.

81 See M. Nettesheim, 'Der "Kernbereich" der Unionsbürgerschaft' (2011) *Juristenzeitung*, 1030, 1032–1033; and D. Kochenov, 'A Real European Citizenship' (2011) 18 *Colombia Journal of European Law*, 95 *et seq.*

82 See Case C-34/09, *Ruiz Zambrano*, EU:C:2011:124; and K. Hailbronner and D. Thym, 'Case Note *Ruiz Zambrano*' (2011) 48 *CML Rev*, 1253–1270.

83 See D. Thym, 'Towards "Real" Citizenship?"', in M. Adams *et al.* (eds.), *Judging Europe's Judges* (Oxford: Hart Publishing, 2013), 166–167, 171–172.

It is quite revealing that the Court explained its brief reasoning in *Ruiz Zambrano* essentially by way of a teleological argument: the 'fundamental status' the Court had Union citizenship previously identified as being 'destined to be.'[84] Invoking the *telos* can be perceived as an attempt on the side of the Court to focus on the citizenship concept instead of the doctrinal foundations of transnational free movement.[85] This move precipitated creative proposals by EU experts suggesting that the Court ought to deploy citizens' rights as an instrument to overhaul national immigration laws[86] or to enhance the reach of EU fundamental rights via Union citizenship.[87] However, judicial developments did not follow this advice. The Court was quick to minimise the impact of the newly established 'substance of rights' test in follow-up cases. Space precludes an extensive analysis,[88] but three conclusions deserve our attention, since they illustrate the inherent change of direction from an aspirational trajectory to a more modest approach which effectively reigned in the revolutionary potential of the judicial innovation:

Firstly, it is worth quoting a passage from the *Dereci* judgment: 'the mere fact that it might appear desirable [...] for economic reasons or in order to keep his family together [...] to be able to reside with [third-country national spouses] in the territory of the Union, is not sufficient in itself to support' the activation of the substance of rights test.[89] This relegation of a crucial family link – the cohabitation of spouses – to a mere desire that can be legally irrelevant stands in striking contrast to earlier assumptions in judgments such as *Metock* which had provided almost unconditional protection to family reunion. To be sure, the different positions can be distinguished doctrinally, since *Metock* concerned a restriction to the fundamental freedoms, while *Dereci* was about the stricter 'deprivation' test in line with the Court's reconstruction of the *Ruiz Zambrano* ruling.[90] Moreover, the Court had second thoughts on its strict position in *O. and S.* in relation to persons taking care, within the context of patchwork families, of

84 Case C-34/09, *Ruiz Zambrano*, EU:C:2011:124, para. 31; the French formulation '*a vocation à être*' emphasises the inspirational and forward-looking intention even stronger, which tends to be lost in other language versions, such as German.

85 See D. Thym, 'Frontiers of EU Citizenship', in D. Kochenov (ed.), *EU Citizenship and Federalism. The Role of Rights* (Cambridge: CUP, 2016), forthcoming, section 4.

86 See B. Huber, 'Die ausländerrechtlichen Folgen des EuGH-Urteils *Zambrano*' (2011) *Neue Zeitschrift für Verwaltungsrecht*, 856–858.

87 Cf. A. von Bogdandy *et al.*, 'Reverse *Solange* – Protecting the Essence of Fundamental Rights against EU Member States' (2012) 49 *CML Rev*, 489–512.

88 See M. Wendel, '§18: Unionsbürgerrechte, Freizügigkeit', in C. Grabenwarter (ed.), *Enzyklopädie Europarecht, Volume 2* (Baden-Baden: Nomos, 2014), paras. 107–115; A. Tryfonidou, 'Redefining the Outer Boundaries of EU Law' (2012) 18 *European Public Law*, 493–526; and N. Nic Shuibhne, 'Recasting EU Citizenship as Federal Citizenship', in D. Kochenov (ed.), *EU Citizenship and Federalism. The Role of Rights* (Cambridge: CUP, 2016), forthcoming.

89 Case C-256/11, *Dereci et al.*, EU:C:2011:734, para. 68; similarly, see Case C-87/12, *Ymeraga et al.*, EU:C:2013:291, paras. 38–39.

90 See S. Reynolds, 'Exploring the "Intrinsic Connection" between Free Movement and the Genuine Enjoyment Test' (2013) 38 *EL Rev*, 385–386; and K. Lenaerts, 'The Court's Outer

minor EU context citizens living in their home state.[91] Notwithstanding these caveats, the different subtext of the judicial positions is palpable.

Secondly, the Court emphasised in the following cases the derivative nature of residence rights of family members who are not covered by citizens' rights to free movement but benefit from the fundamental freedoms by means of a legal reflex in the form of 'derived rights' mentioned at the outset.[92] This re-activation of a classic formula featured prominently in judgments on family reunion in recent years, thereby emphasising at a semantic level that the rulings are not about abstract visions of social justice, as indicated in *Ruiz Zambrano*, but about transnational free movement.[93] This emphasis on the derivative character in recent decisions replaced earlier invocations of the human right to family life in Article 8 ECHR in generous judgments on family reunion in the context of free movement. These had signalled that the CJ was primarily concerned with maintaining family unity.[94]

Thirdly, it is no coincidence that the newly found prominence of the 'derived rights' formula replaced earlier invocations of human rights, since the latter are usually activated to articulate considerations of social justice in legal terms.[95] Notwithstanding the limited impetus provided by international human rights law for supplanting national immigration laws on matters of family unity,[96] the CJ's turn away from human rights emphasised that its analysis is shaped by a different concern: free movement of Union citizens. It reinforced this impression

---

and Inner Selves', in M. Adams *et al.* (eds.), *Judging Europe's Judges* (Oxford: Hart Publishing, 2013), 50–51.

91 See Case C-356/11 and C-357/11, *O. and S.*, EU:C:2012:776, paras. 52–56 requiring domestic courts to embark upon an assessment of legal, financial and emotional dependence, although it had discarded these factors as being irrelevant in *Dereci*; for comments, see D. Thym, 'Grenzen der Unionsbürgerschaft. Zur Rechtsstellung von Familienmitgliedern aus Drittstaaten im Lichte der Kernbereichs-Rechtsprechung des EuGH' (2015) *Europarecht Beiheft 1*, 146–148; and M. Almhofer, 'Zum Aufenthaltsrecht Drittstaatsangehöriger zwei Jahre post Ruiz Zambrano' (2013) *Neue Zeitschrift für Verwaltungsrecht*, 1134 (1135).

92 See Case C-256/11, *Dereci et al.*, EU:C:2011:734, para. 55; the formula was used first in Case 40/76, *Kermaschek*, EU:C:1976:157, para. 7.

93 The formula was taken up after *Dereci et al.* and the previous chamber judgment in Case C-434/09, *McCarthy*, EU:C:2011:277, para. 42; Case C-40/11, *Iida*, EU:C:2012:2405, para. 58; Case C-356/11 and C-357/11, *O. and S.*, EU:C:2012:776, para. 55; Case C-87/12, *Ymeraga et al.*, EU:C:2013:291, paras. 31, 35; Case C-86/12, *Alokpa and Moudoulou*, EU:C:2013:645, para. 34; Case C-456/12, *O. and B.*, EU:C:2014:135, paras. 36 *et seq.*; Case C-457/12, *S. and G.*, EU:C:2014:189, paras. 33–35; Case C-244/13, *Ogieriakhi*, EU:C:2014:2068, para. 37; and Case C-218/14, *Singh et al.*, EU:C:2015:476, paras. 50–51.

94 See, in particular, Case C-60/00, *Carpenter*, EU:C:2002:434, paras. 41–44 integrating the human rights analysis into the application of the fundamental freedoms (in a conclusion which is much more generous than the position of the ECtHR) and Case C-109/01, *Akrich*, EU:C:2003:491, paras. 58–60 under reference to the more restrictive ECtHR case-law; see also N. Nic Shuibhne, *The Coherence of EU Free Movement Law* (Oxford: OUP, 2013), 50–54.

95 See A. Sen, *The Idea of Justice* (Harvard: HUP, 2009), ch. 17; and H. Lindahl, 'Breaking Promises to Keep Them', in H. Lindahl (ed.), *A Right to Inclusion and Exclusion?* (Oxford: Hart Publishing, 2009), 154–155.

96 See below section 4.1.

when it stated, in *Dereci*, that the non-applicability of free movement rules did not imply that family members from third states could not invoke human rights. It crucially continued with the idea that human rights are not inherently connected to Union citizenship: domestic courts should apply domestic constitutional guarantees and/or the European Convention on Human Rights.[97] This guides the resolution of the cases towards an alternative frame of reference: the right of Union citizens to transnational free movement is replaced by universal human rights.

3.4. HOW TO EXPLAIN THE JUDICIAL CHANGE OF DIRECTION?

It has been mentioned at the outset that the doctrinal foundations of the case-law on transnational free movement first applied to goods and was extended to cover persons. From a historic institutionalism perspective, this judicial transfer may be read as an expression of path dependency with the CJ employing doctrinal concepts which had proven their utility in one domain to related questions.[98] However, the initial success of this undertaking does not imply that the parallelism is persuasive from a broader normative perspective.[99] How can we explain the change of direction in applying the case-law to family members from third states? It seems to reflect an introspection on the side of the Court how to operationalise the interaction of citizens' rights to free movement and immigration statuses of third-country nationals. In line with the introductory comments, this reconsideration of the legal regime can be analysed on doctrinal

97 See Case C-256/11, *Dereci et al.*, EU:C:2011:734, paras. 70–74; this conclusion prevents an indirect transfer of powers from Member States to the EU, see D. Thym, 'Towards "Real' Citizenship?"', in M. Adams *et al.* (eds.), *Judging Europe's Judges* (Oxford: Hart Publishing, 2013), 168–169; the EU Charter will be applicable only when the facts of the case concern the implementation of Union law, if not the ECHR will be applicable and the CJ won't have jurisdiction, see the Opinion of Advocate General Mengozzi in Case C-256/11, *Dereci et al.*, EU:C:2011:626, paras. 37–38; K. Lenaerts, 'The Court's Outer and Inner Selves', in M. Adams *et al.* (eds.), *Judging Europe's Judges* (Oxford: Hart Publishing, 2013), 51–52; S. Reynolds, 'Exploring the "Intrinsic Connection" between Free Movement and the Genuine Enjoyment Test' (2013) 38 *EL Rev*, 382–384; and M. Wendel, 'Aufenthalt als Mittel zum Zweck: zu Grund und Grenzen derivativer Aufenthaltsrechte Drittstaatsangehöriger' (2014) *Die Öffentliche Verwaltung*, 141–142.

98 See S. Schmidt, 'Who Cares About Nationality? The Path-Dependent Case-Law of the ECJ from Goods to Citizens' (2012) 19 *Journal of European Public Policy*, 8–24 explaining how the transfer can be explained from the perspective of historic institutionalism.

99 See E. Spaventa, 'From *Gebhard* to *Carpenter*: Towards a (Non-)Economic European Constitution' (2004) 41 *CML Rev*, 743–773; J. Snell, 'And Then There Were Two: Products and Citizens in Community Law', in T. Tridimas and P. Nebbia (eds.), *European Union Law for the Twenty-First Century, Volume 2* (Oxford: Hart Publishing, 2005), 52–55; and F. de Cecco, 'Fundamental Freedoms, Fundamental Rights, and the Scope of Free Movement Law' (2014) 15 *Georgetown Law Journal*, 385–401.

grounds, in relation to the constitutional context and regarding the socio-economic underpinning of the law in political discourses.[100] This leads to three remarks seeking to rationalise the change of direction.

Firstly, the doctrinal foundations of the case-law may be robust, but its continued interpretation and application to specific scenarios is not. This is illustrated by the novel emphasis on 'derived rights' formula, which builds directly on the concept of restrictions but supports different conclusions than earlier rulings on similar topics. Moreover, the implications of the notion of Union citizenship for the resolution of specific cases are less stable than the term may suggest. Recent judgments on social benefits for Union citizens[101] can be conceptualised as signalling a shift away from a residence-based understanding of citizenship based on equal treatment towards an integration-based approach emphasising a qualitative assessment of the behaviour of the individual citizen concerned.[102] Against this background, the emphasis on the wording and general scheme instead of the *telos* (purpose) and constitutional context in recent judgments on family reunion seems to follow a general trend in the doctrinal construction of judgments on free movement and Union citizenship.

Secondly, experts on free movement law tend to analyse the case-law primarily from an internal perspective. The debate is often framed as an evolution from (old) transnational market integration towards (new) social or political citizenship with more rights.[103] Although such accounts have many merits, we should recognise that they remain based upon a citizenship-centred analysis designing free movement as the central axis for the resolution of individual cases. This, however, is not the full picture. As a constitutional court of a supranational polity, the CJ will consider implications for the constitutional order at large, including the federal balance of power and the horizontal interaction between judges and the EU legislature. Arguably, it is these constitutional considerations which motivated the Court to move towards a more restrictive reasoning in the follow-up to *Ruiz Zambrano*, since doing otherwise would have seriously

---

100 See above section 1.1.

101 See D. Thym, 'The Elusive Limits of Solidarity' (2015) 52 *CML Rev*, 21–49; and N. Nic Shuibhne, 'Limits Rising, Duties Ascending: The Changing Legal Shape of Union Citizenship' (2015) 52 *CML Rev*, 889–937; and S. Barbou des Places, 'La cohérence du droit de la libre circulation des personnes à l'épreuve de la mobilité des indigents' (2015) *Revue trimestrielle de droit européen*, 135–137; and D. Thym, 'When Union Citizens turn into Illegal Migrants: the *Dano* case' (2015) 40 *EL Rev*, 259–260.

102 See D. Thym, 'The Elusive Limits of Solidarity' (2015) 52 *CML Rev*, 35–39; and L. Azoulai, 'La Citoyenneté européenne, un statut d'intégration sociale', in *Chemins d'Europe. Mélanges en l'honneur de Jean Paul Jacqué* (Paris: Dalloz, 2010), 1–28.

103 For example, see the varied accounts by D. Kochenov, 'The Citizenship Paradigm' (2012–13) 15 *Cambridge Yearbook of European Legal Studies*, 205–211; E. Spaventa, 'Seeing the Wood despite the Trees?' (2008) 45 *CML Rev*, 14–30; A. Tryfonidou, *Reverse Discrimination in EC Law* (The Hague: Kluwer, 2009), ch. 4; and J. Shaw, 'Citizenship: Contrasting Dynamics at the Interface of Integration and Constitutionalism', in P. Craig and G. de Búrca (eds.), *The Evolution of EU Law, 2nd edition* (Oxford: OUP, 2011), 598–600.

undermined the federal balance of power between the EU and its Member States by restricting the purely internal rule and/or applying the Charter of Fundamental Rights outside the scope of EU legislation.[104]

Along similar lines, the status of family members from third states touches upon new legislative instruments adopted within the framework of the area of freedom, security and justice, such as the Family Reunion Directive 2003/86/EC and the Long-Term Residents Directive 2003/109/EC.[105] On closer inspection, a number of important judgments on family members mentioned above discuss these instruments alongside the Citizenship Directive 2004/38.[106] They thereby recognise the potential significance, in terms of the status of family members, of migration law which the Court had brushed aside in earlier cases.[107] With regard to the Turkish association agreement, the Court explicitly recognised that it pursued different objectives than EU citizenship and that, therefore, 'the two legal schemes in question cannot be considered equivalent.'[108] Arguably, the change of direction regarding family reunion can be explained, in part at least, by a recognition, on the part of judges, that the EU Treaties have more to say on family reunion than free movement and citizens' rights.[109] In contrast to classic notions of path dependency, this change of direction can be conceptualised as a process of adaptation to a modified legal and constitutional context brought about by the adoption of new legislation and the entry into force of the Treaty of Lisbon in 2009 in line with the comments in the next section.[110]

---

104 See D. Thym, 'Towards "Real' Citizenship?"', in M. Adams *et al.* (eds.), *Judging Europe's Judges* (Oxford: Hart Publishing, 2013), 168–169; and D. Thym, 'Frontiers of EU Citizenship', in D. Kochenov (ed.), *EU Citizenship and Federalism. The Role of Rights* (Cambridge: CUP, 2016), forthcoming, section V.B.

105 Cf. Directive 2003/86/EC on the right to family reunification, OJ 2003, L 251/12 (hereinafter referred to as 'Directive 2003/86/EC'); and Directive 2003/109/EC concerning the status of third-country nationals who are long-term residents, OJ 2004, L 16/44.

106 See Case C-256/11, *Dereci et al.*, EU:C:2011:734, paras. 71–72; Case C-40/11, *Iida*, EU:C:2012:2405, paras. 78–81; Case C-356/11 and C-357/11, *O. and S.*, EU:C:2012:776, para. 59; and Case C-87/12, *Ymeraga et al.*, EU:C:2013:291, para. 42; see also A. Lansbergen and N. Miller, 'European Citizenship Rights in Internal Situations: An Ambiguous Revolution?' (2011) 7 *EUConst*, 300–301.

107 Despite calls to the contrary by Opinion of Advocate General Geelhoed in Case C-127/08, *Metock*, EU:C:2008:335, paras. 59–62; Case C-1/05, *Jia*, EU:C:2006:258, paras. 26–35; the CJ neglected the immigration dimension in Case C-127/08, *Metock*, EU:C:2008:449, para. 66; cf. C. Costello, '*Metock*: Free Movement and "Normal Family Life" in the Union' (2009) 46 *CML Rev*, 602–603.

108 Case C-371/08, *Ziebell*, EU:C:2011:809, para. 74 concerning expulsion; for more comments, see D. Thym, 'Constitutional Foundations of the Judgments on the EEC-Turkey Association Agreement', in D. Thym and Z. Zoeteweij-Turhan (eds.), *Rights of Third-Country Nationals under EU Association Agreements* (Leiden: Brill Nijhoff, 2015), 14–24.

109 See the case study by T. Horsley, 'Reflections on the Role of the Court of Justice as the "Motor" of European Integration' (2013) 50 *CML Rev*, 956–963; and, in more abstract terms, K. Lenaerts, 'The Court's Outer and Inner Selves', in M. Adams *et al.* (eds.), *Judging Europe's Judges* (Oxford: Hart Publishing, 2013), 28–39.

110 The literature on judicial institutions and path dependency is often written on the basis of experiences in common law jurisdictions, like the US and the UK, see A. Stone Sweet, 'Path

Thirdly, the broader socio-economic outlook may have changed in comparison to the 1950s and 1960s when the Treaty of Rome and implementing legislation were drafted against the background of an equality-based rationale reflecting economic and social policy imperatives at the time.[111] By contrast, today's debates about family reunion are less concerned with social policy and transnational market integration: they revolve around broader social and cultural issues in many Member States. Family reunion emerged as a hot political topic in the 1980s as a result of an increase of inward migration despite an official freeze on labour migration in Western European countries.[112] A few years later, immigration policy started focusing on questions of social integration from the 1990s onwards when it became clear that the former guest workers and their children would remain in their new home countries indefinitely.[113] At EU level, this debate came to the fore in the mid-2000s when the EU legislature was engulfed into heavy debates on the contents of the Family Reunion Directive and the Long-Term Residents Directive.[114]

The intense political reactions to both the *Metock* judgment and the *Ruiz Zambrano* ruling signalled to the CJ that this novel frame of reference reflected deep-seated concerns on the side of Member States,[115] which need not necessarily be presented as a xenophobic trend overturning the more migrant-friendly approach of free movement rules[116] even if the new policy design coincided with the emergence of right-wing populist parties in some Member States.[117] The socio-economic context of family reunion will vary between Member States and along the timeline, but it signals that the original convergence of economic and social policy rationales which lay beneath the

Dependence, Precedent, and Judicial Power', in M. Shapiro and A. Stone Sweet (eds.), *On Law, Politics, and Judicialization* (Oxford: OUP, 2002), 117–133; by contrast, civil law jurisdictions and the CJ will pay more attention to written rules in the Treaties or secondary legislation which, arguably, played a prominent role in the change of direction on residence rights of third-country national family members, see G. Beck, *The Legal Reasoning of the Court of Justice of the EU* (Oxford: Hart Publishing, 2012).

111 See above section 2.2.

112 See S. Castles, H. de Haas and M. Miller, *The Age of Migration, 5th edition* (Basingstoke: Palgrave, 2013), 111–113; and J. Hollifield, *Immigrants, Markets and States* (Harvard: HUP, 1992), ch. 4.

113 See C. Joppke, *Citizenship and Immigration* (Cambridge: Polity Press, 2010), ch. 4; and S. Sassen, *Guests and Aliens* (New York: New Press, 1999), 116–124.

114 See S. Carrera, *In Search of the Perfect Citizen?* (Leiden: Martinus Nijhoff, 2009), chs. 3–4; and D. Thym, 'Legal Framework for EU Immigration Policy', in K. Hailbronner and D. Thym (eds.), *EU Immigration and Asylum Law. Commentary, 2nd edition* (C.H. Beck and Oxford: Hart Publishing, 2016), forthcoming, paras. 43–47.

115 See N. Nic Shuibhne and J. Shaw, 'General Report', in Neergaard *et al.* (eds.), *Union Citizenship: Development, Impact and Challenges. The XXVI FIDE Congress in Copenhagen* (Copenhagen: DJØF, 2014), 139–150.

116 See C. Joppke, *Citizenship and Immigration* (Cambridge: Polity Press, 2010), ch. 4.

117 See D. Kostakopoulou, S. Carrera and M. Jesse, 'Doing and Deserving', in E. Guild *et al.* (eds.), *Illiberal Liberal States* (Farnham: Ashgate, 2009), 180–184.

original family reunion regime has given way to a more nuanced outlook on immigrant integration.[118] Arguably, it is this change in the socio-economic context that buttresses doctrinal adaptation and constitutional change in relation to family reunion, thereby reinforcing the judicial change of direction in relation to residence rights for family members.

4. CONSTITUTIONAL CONTEXT: MIGRATION AND HUMAN RIGHTS

From today's perspective, the EU Treaties have more to say on family reunion than free movement and Union citizenship, which both do not embrace family members *expressis verbis* to this date. The picture looks different if we broaden our analysis to rules on migration as amended by the Treaty of Lisbon, which entered into force in December 2009. Various legislative instruments have been adopted on their basis, including on family reunion. These rules on migration can be construed as an alternative frame of reference for residence rights of third-country national family members explaining, as one factor among many, the change of direction in CJ case-law. This section will present the novel constitutional frame for migration. In doing so, it transcends an analytical recount of the case-law and embarks instead on an exercise of doctrinal constructivism exploring the constitutional infrastructure for migration law towards third-country nationals on the basis of the amendments brought about by the Treaty of Lisbon.[119]

Distinguishing free movement and migration law does not suggest that it will be possible to separate citizens' rights and migration law ingeniously. There will always be grey areas of overlap between both regimes, in particular for family members of Union citizens from third states. Moreover, the Court's approach to free movement may guide the interpretation of secondary legislation on migration, in particular when similar terminology or a comparable doctrinal structure are used (like in the case of the association agreement with Turkey).[120] However, such overlap does not invalidate the identification of constitutional principles for citizens and third-country nationals, which may guide the reconstruction of the legal regime when addressing more specific questions of statutory interpretation.

118 See S. Bonjour, 'The Power and Morals of Policy Makers' (2011) 45 *International Migration Review*, 106–113; and A. Staver, 'Free Movement and the Fragmentation of Family Reunification Rights' (2013) 15 EJML, 82–85.

119 On methodology, see above section 1.1.

120 See K. Groenendijk, 'Recent Developments in EU Law on Migration: The Legislative Patchwork and the Court's Approach' (2014) 16 EJML, 324–334; and K. Hailbronner and D. Thym, 'Constitutional Framework', in K. Hailbronner and D. Thym (eds.), *EU Immigration and Asylum Law. Commentary, 2nd edition* (C.H. Beck and Oxford: Hart Publishing, 2016), forthcoming, paras. 10–20.

This chapter builds upon earlier contributions which have developed the underlying theoretical argument in greater detail.[121] It presents the human rights perspective first and focuses on Treaty objectives thereafter.

4.1. HUMAN RIGHTS (ARTICLE 8 ECHR)

It is mentioned above that the CJ explained in the *Dereci* judgment that the non-applicability of free movement rules did not imply that family members from third states had no constitutional guarantees on their side. To the contrary, they may invoke human rights enshrined in either national constitutions, the European Convention on Human Rights or the EU Charter whose disentanglement depends on the circumstances of the individual case.[122] Indeed, human rights are the classic point of reference for scrutinising the compatibility of statutory rules on family reunion with higher-ranking constitutional guarantees. In this respect, the case-law of the ECtHR takes centre stage, since judges in Strasbourg activated human rights to limit the traditional sovereign authority of states to decide on the admission and expulsion of foreigners. Having said this, it is settled ECtHR case-law that different rules apply to first admission and expulsion. Whereas the Court grants Member States principled discretion in first admission cases, it has considerably limited the freedom of states regarding expulsion.

More specifically, the ECtHR dismissed most claims for first admission, since the Convention 'cannot be considered as extending to a general obligation [...] to respect the choice by married couples of the country of their matrimonial residence.'[123] To date, no more than three applications claiming admission for

---

121 See D. Thym, 'EU Migration Policy and its Constitutional Rationale. A Cosmopolitan Outlook' (2013) 50 *CML Rev*, 709–736.

122 See Case C-256/11, *Dereci et al.*, EU:C:2011:734, paras. 70–74; this conclusion prevents an indirect transfer of powers from Member States to the EU, see D. Thym, 'Towards "Real Citizenship?"', in M. Adams *et al.* (eds.), *Judging Europe's Judges* (Oxford: Hart Publishing, 2013), 168–169; the EU Charter will be applicable only when the facts of the case concern the implementation of Union law, if not the ECHR will be applicable and the CJ won't have jurisdiction, see the Opinion of Advocate General Mengozzi in Case C-256/11, *Dereci et al.*, EU:C:2011:626, paras. 37–38; K. Lenaerts, 'The Court's Outer and Inner Selves', in M. Adams *et al.* (eds.), *Judging Europe's Judges* (Oxford: Hart Publishing, 2013), 51–52; S. Reynolds, 'Exploring the "Intrinsic Connection" between Free Movement and the Genuine Enjoyment Test' (2013) 38 *EL Rev*, 382–384; and M. Wendel, 'Aufenthalt als Mittel zum Zweck: zu Grund und Grenzen derivativer Aufenthaltsrechte Drittstaatsangehöriger' (2014) *Die Öffentliche Verwaltung*, 141–142; the decisive factor delineating the scope of the EU Charter is the applicability of Union law in accordance with Article 51(1) EU Charter and relevant case-law, see F. Fontanelli, 'Implementation of EU Law through Domestic Measures after *Fransson*' (2014) 39 *EL Rev*, 682–701.

123 ECtHR, 28 May 1985, *Abdulaziz, Cabakes and Balkandali v the United Kingdom*, nos. 9214/80, 9473/81 and 9474/81, para. 68 and, more recently, ECtHR, 31 January 2006, *Rodrigues da Silva and Hoogkamer v the Netherlands*, no. 50435/99, para. 39.

purposes of family reunion, which had not been resolved domestically,[124] have been successful, thereby emphasising that family reunion can be requested under Article 8 ECHR only in exceptional circumstances.[125] By contrast, the case-law on expulsion of family members from the country in which they are living is much stricter.[126] This conclusion extends to the EU Charter of Fundamental Rights, since its Article 7 must be interpreted in accordance with Article 8 ECHR.[127] When the CJ assesses the compatibility of EU legislation on migration with the EU Treaties, it concentrates on these human rights guarantees instead of free movement.[128]

All of the above may sound rather abstract, but it can have tangible consequences for our topic. The ECtHR case-law entails that the High Contracting Parties may pursue public policy objectives in relation to third-country nationals which are taboo for Union citizens under the auspices of the fundamental freedoms. Three examples illustrate the pertinence of the distinction between human rights and free movement.

Firstly, free movement law prohibits any expulsion of Union citizens not based exclusively on the personal conduct of the individual concerned; previous criminal convictions as such shall not constitute grounds for taking such measures.[129] This is much stricter than the standard established by the ECtHR even if the latter similarly restrict state discretion on expulsions to a considerable extent.[130] Notwithstanding these limits in the context of free movement, judges in Strasbourg found that a severe criminal conviction, for instance for drug trafficking, may justify an expulsion in the light of human rights

---

124 Most claims for family reunion with reasonable grounds for success will never reach the ECtHR, since national immigration laws and the Family Reunification Directive 2003/86 establish individual statutory rights to family reunion.

125 See ECtHR, 21 December 2000, *Şen v the Netherlands*, no. 31465/96; ECtHR, 1 December 2005, *Tuquabo-Tekle et al. v Netherlands*, no. 60665/00; and, in a specific scenario involving earlier stays in the host country, ECtHR, 14 June 2011, *Osman v Denmark*, no. 38058/09; for an overview of the case-law, see P. Boeles *et al.*, *European Migration Law, 2nd edition* (Antwerp – Oxford: Intersentia, 2014), 223–229.

126 See D. Thym, 'Legal Framework for EU Immigration Policy', in K. Hailbronner and D. Thym (eds.), *EU Immigration and Asylum Law. Commentary, 2nd edition* (C.H. Beck and Oxford: Hart Publishing, 2016), forthcoming, paras. 53–55.

127 On parallel interpretation, see Article 52(3) EU Charter; and Case C-400/10 PPU, *McB.*, EU:C:2010:582, para. 53.

128 See, by way of example, Case C-540/03, *Parliament v Council*, EU:C:2006:429, para. 59 on an action for annulment brought by the European Parliament against the Family Reunification Directive 2003/86.

129 See Article 27(1) Citizenship Directive 2004/38 in accordance with Article 3 Directive 64/221; as well as Case 67/74, *Bonsignore*, EU:C:1975:34, paras. 4–5; and Case C-482/01 and C-493/01, *Orfanopoulos and Olivieri*, EU:C:2004:262, paras. 62–71.

130 See, again, D. Thym, 'Legal Framework for EU Immigration Policy', in K. Hailbronner and D. Thym (eds.), *EU Immigration and Asylum Law. Commentary, 2nd edition* (C.H. Beck and Oxford: Hart Publishing, 2016), forthcoming, paras. 53–55.

requirements.[131] Recent judgment highlighted that parents and children can be indefinitely separated without Article 8 ECHR stipulating a different solution on human rights grounds.[132]

Secondly, the Family Reunion Directive requires Member States to reject family reunion in the absence of stable and regular financial resources.[133] Notwithstanding limitations developed by the CJ on the basis of statutory interpretation, it did not call into question the compatibility of this condition with human rights.[134] Indeed, the ECtHR held that states may regularly reject family reunion in the absence of sufficient resources.[135] This confirms that Union citizens benefit from privileges under free movement law that are not available to foreigners under human rights.

Thirdly, free movement law precludes Member States from requiring Union citizens to learn the local language. A German national moving across the border to Austria has the right to be joined by his wife from Turkey irrespective of whether she speaks German,[136] although family reunion can regularly be rejected in the same scenario if the German national stays at home. The compatibility of this rule with the Family Reunion Directive has recently been confirmed by the CJ with the proviso that a hardship clause is available.[137] There is similar case-law of the ECtHR emphasising the relevance of social and cultural ties with the host society.[138]

None of the above is meant to claim that states can do as they please. To the contrary, there are considerable human rights constraints on the basis of ECtHR case-law. The main purpose of the examples above was to highlight, by means of stark contrast, the constitutional variation between free movement rules and migration law. In the field of migration law, it is for the prerogative of the legislature to lay down the conditions for family reunion within the limits stipulated by human rights. The EU Treaty does not prescribe a specific policy design: the choice whether migration policy towards third-country nationals shall be 'open' or 'closed' rests with the political process and the CJ will regularly accept its outcome.

---

131 See ECtHR, 23 June 2008, *Maslov v Austria*, no. 1638/03, paras. 71, 75, 80; and ECtHR, 6 December 2007, *Chair v Germany*, no. 69735/01, para. 24.

132 See ECtHR, 14 February 2012, *Antwi and others v Norway*, no. 26940/10; and ECtHR, 30 July 2013, *Berisha v Switzerland*, no. 948/12.

133 See Article 7(1)(c) Directive 2003/86.

134 See Case C-578/08, *Chakroun*, EU:C:2010:117.

135 See ECtHR, 26 April 2013, *Konstatinov v the Netherlands*, no. 16351/03, para. 50.

136 See Article 2(2) Directive 2004/38/EC and CJ case-law interpret free movement rules to cover reunion with family members from third states.

137 See Case C-153/14, *K. and A.*, EU:C:2015:453 and the chapter by S. Carrera in this volume.

138 See D. Thym, 'Residence as *de facto* Citizenship?', in R. Rubio-Marin (ed.), *Human Rights and Immigration* (Oxford: OUP, 2014), 138–143.

4.2. MIGRATION GOVERNANCE

It is incorrect, as it is sometimes claimed,[139] that the Treaty regime was subject to revisionist interpretation when the CJ found that the free movement of workers concerned Union citizens only: there was clear understanding that third-country nationals should not be covered.[140] Instead, the Treaty of Rome left immigration and asylum largely to Member States. This changed gradually when a sequence of Treaty amendments established the area of freedom, security and justice as a distinct Treaty regime for those without an EU passport. Its realisation became a freestanding objective with the Treaty of Lisbon,[141] which also set out separate objectives for migration policy.[142] Article 79(2)(a) TFEU lays down an express competence for the EU legislature to harmonise immigration rules – and Article 7 of the Charter of Fundamental Rights protects family life.

Reading the Treaty objectives for immigration and asylum, which entered into force in 2009, the contrast with the rules on Union citizenship stands out. They are typified by a collection of diverse – and contradictory – intentions, including 'enhanced measures to combat illegal immigration', 'fair[ness] towards third-country nationals,' 'compliance with the principle of *non-refoulement*,' and, generally, 'the efficient management of migration flows.'[143] It is important to note that the discrepancy between migration and free movement extends to the EU's Charter of Fundamental Rights, which generally takes pride in presenting itself as an avant-garde catalogue.[144] In terms of migration, the Charter principally reaffirms existing rules under EU law and the ECHR.[145] Put differently, it reiterates citizens' rights and sanctions a lesser degree of protection for third-country nationals. Article 15 illustrates the point: whereas paragraph 2 reaffirms the citizens' right to free movement,[146] the third paragraph deals with

---

139 See E. Guild and S. Peers, 'Out of the Ghetto?', in E. Guild, S. Peers. and N. Rogers (eds.), *EU Immigration and Asylum Law. Text and Commentary* (Leiden: Martinus Nijhoff, 2006), 114.

140 Although Article 48 EEC Treaty (1957) and today's Article 45 TFEU are not limited to nationals of the Member States explicitly, there was agreement during negotiations that third-country nationals should not be covered and an explicit nationality clause was discarded in reaction to Franco-Italian disputes about the status of workers from Algeria and German concerns about compatriots from communist East Germany; cf. S. Goedings, *Labor Migration in an Integrating Europe* (The Hague: SDU Uitgevers, 2005), 128–135.

141 See Article 3(2) TEU (before the single market in Article 3(3) TEU); for detail see J. Monar, 'The Area of Freedom, Security and Justice', in A. von Bogdandy and J. Bast (eds.), *Principles of European Constitutional Law, 2nd edition* (Oxford: Hart Publishing, 2009), 564-569.

142 See Articles 77–80 TFEU, which are identical with Articles III-265–268 Treaty establishing a Constitution for Europe, OJ 2004, C 310/1, which never entered into force.

143 Articles 79(1), 67(2), 78(1) and TFEU.

144 See recital 4 of the Charter, OJ 2007, C 303/1, and, by way of illustration, the prohibition of reproductive cloning (Article 3(2)(d)) or equal treatment of gays and lesbians (Article 21(1)).

145 The argument in this section builds upon D. Thym, 'EU Migration Policy and its Constitutional Rationale. A Cosmopolitan Outlook' (2013) 50 *CML Rev*, 718–723.

146 Article 52(2)(7) EU Charter and the official Explanations, OJ 2007, C 303/17 at 23 confirm that this provision is to be interpreted in line with Articles 45, 49 and 56 TFEU.

non-citizens: 'Nationals of third countries *who are authorised to work* [...] are entitled to working conditions equivalent to those of citizens of the Union.'[147]

This sounds progressive, but the substance is meagre: whereas EU citizens possess an individual right with constitutional status to seek employment abroad, third-country nationals benefit from equal working conditions only. This is undoubtedly well intentioned, but undisputed politically (at least in today's Europe). In particular, it does not change the absence of a prior right to take up employment without state authorisation: admission of workers remains a public prerogative with few human rights limitations.[148] Acknowledging this disparity between human rights and the fundamental freedoms sets the stage for the recognition of migrants' constitutional status. Human rights may, conceptually and in substance, stay short of citizenship, but they reject traditional notions of alienage without the protection of the law nevertheless.[149] If that is correct, we should be careful not to be trapped in false dichotomies. Our debate is not 'open borders' versus 'fortress Europe.' There is room for intermediate solutions, which I have proposed elsewhere to construe as the 'cosmopolitan outlook' of EU migration law.[150] It is in this alternative framework in which the CJ defers in more recent citizenship cases such as the *Dereci* judgment.

5. CONCLUSION

Rules on family reunion rest on unstable grounds, since they are situated in a grey zone of overlap between free movement guarantees for Union citizens and new rules governing migration law. This structural instability arguably explains why CJ case-law on residence rights of family members of Union citizens from third states has been subject to protracted legal and political disputes over the past years. This article set out to explore the evolution of the legal regime, thereby disclosing a change of direction in CJ case-law on the matter. As starting point, it examined the rationale underlying rules on family reunion in the EU Treaties and secondary legislation adopted in the 1960s at a time when debates on free movement followed an essentially economic reasoning with the objective of securing unhindered market access and widespread equal treatment in host states in pursuit of economic and social policy objectives. This rationale

147 Article 15(3) EU Charter; emphasis added.

148 In a similar vein, the Charter distinguishes between citizens and foreigners in relation to intra-European movements in Article 45(1) and (2).

149 It should be noted that the EU Charter supplements the ECHR with novel guarantees; see A. Wiesbrock, *Legal Migration to the European Union* (Leiden: Martinus Nijhoff, 2010), 169–207; and T. Gross, 'Migrationsrelevante Freiheitsrechte der EU-Grundrechtecharta' (2013) *Zeitschrift für Ausländerrecht*, 106–110.

150 See D. Thym, 'EU Migration Policy and its Constitutional Rationale. A Cosmopolitan Outlook' (2013) 50 *CML Rev*, 725–735.

permeates the generous family reunion regime for Union citizens. At the time, social and cultural questions defining today's debates about family reunion in many Member States were not discussed.

Closer inspection of the CJ case-law concerns a variety of distinct legal settings ranging from statutory provisions to the abstract notion of Union citizenship. Notwithstanding these different contexts, a common thread characterises the evolution of the case-law. When deciding individual cases, judges in Luxembourg supported the maintenance of family life in a number of generous judgments throughout the 1990s and early 2000s before moving towards a more restrictive approach in recent years. This evolution can be traced in judgments on autonomous residence rights for children and spouses under secondary legislation, in relation to Union citizens returning to their home state after residence abroad and for the novel 'substance of rights' test established by the *Ruiz Zambrano* judgment. From a methodological perspective, the change of direction in the case-law exposes a shift from interpretation based on the purpose and constitutional principles to an examination focusing on the wording and general scheme. In doing so, judges accentuate the 'derived character' of residence rights for spouses from third states, thereby severing the linkage between free movement and family unity in earlier judgments.

This change of direction can be explained by a collection of different factors. Firstly, the concept of Union citizenship is less stable than the term suggests: family reunion is not the only field where the Court altered its standpoint on citizens' rights. Secondly, the constitutional setting now embraces migration as a self-sufficient policy field with distinct policy objectives and legal bases introduced by the Treaty of Lisbon. Thirdly, the socio-economic context of debates on family reunion transcended the equality-based reasoning of social policy and internal market integration which had defined the design of the original Treaty regime. On this basis, the contribution concluded with an exploration of the new constitutional rules on migration revolving around the area of freedom, security and justice together with the Charter of Fundamental Rights. They illustrate the cleavage between citizens' rights and migration law, while ensuring that third-country nationals have constitutional guarantees on their side: they can invoke human rights even if their level of protection differs from rules on free movement.

The status of family members of Union citizens from third states lies at the crossroads of rules on free movement and migration law and it can be difficult to disentangle them neatly when deciding individual cases. This confusion arguably presents the deeper reason why the CJ struggles to develop a coherent position on the basis of clear standards on how to resolve cases involving family members of Union citizens from third states. The aim of this contribution is to support readers in orientating themselves when entering the legal jungle of rules on family reunion.

CHAPTER 3
THE DIRECTION OF THE COURT'S FAMILY REUNIFICATION CASE-LAW
A Plea for (Timely) Moderation

Henri DE WAELE

1. AIM

This succinct contribution does not aim to engage with what one might call the 'micro-electronics' of the family reunification rules. The marvellous exposé of Daniel Thym, also contained in this volume, does a more than adequate job in that respect.[1] Moreover, the present author wholeheartedly agrees with the gist – or perhaps one should say 'essence' or '*Kernbereich*' – of his chapter. In a way, this short chapter serves to further buttress his conclusions. On the other hand, it posits an argument that travels along a distinctly different path. The focus lies on the underlying dynamics of the Court's family reunification case-law, and consequently, the present chapter deals more with process than with substance. Said dynamics can be analysed (section 2) and critiqued (section 3). In equally traditional fashion, though often regarded symptomatic of the typical complacency of legal scholars, suggestions for improvement may be advanced, which here take the form of a plea for moderation (section 4).

2. ANALYSIS

Since the early 1960s, both the Community legislature and the Court have been almost relentlessly pushing the family reunification agenda. While at the time, the Parliament remained largely side-lined, the first batch of secondary instruments offers ample testimony of the Commission's and (to a lesser

1 See moreover his 'Zur Rechtsstellung von Familienmitgliedern aus Drittstaaten im Lichte der Kernbereichs-Rechtsprechung des EuGH' (2015) *EuR-Beiheft* 1, 135–155.

extent) the Council's great zeal.[2] In supporting and occasionally leading the charge, however, the Court seems to have gotten caught up in its own systemic algorithm.[3] In part, that entanglement appears to have spilled back into the legislative apparatus, particularly from the moment the Parliament became seriously involved. Thereby, the algorithm managed to acquire an apodictic credibility, without the original programming that fostered its development coming across as sufficiently sound.

Obviously, the preceding sentences beg for clarification. Let us first recall that at the inception of the Communities, family reunification rights were no component of the European integration franchise. Over time, beyond the economically active, the desire to include other persons entered into the main stream, leading to an expansion of the reach of EU law without proper premeditation. This main stream gradually turned into a maelstrom, as expressed by the surge of secondary law and Court judgments alluded to above. At pains to explain the amplified momentum, the pundits have traced the forces at play here. As magisterially exposed by Davies, one could regard the EU as a tragic captive of its primordial DNA – the *telos* that was unmistakably engrained in the Treaties. This *telos* suggests that 'the only way is up', or to race further ahead, on the road to ever closer Union.[4] The relatively generous rules enacted by the legislator and pronouncements from the Court come across then as a logical corollary of that DNA; for if indeed European citizenship is 'destined to be the fundamental status of nationals of the Member States',[5] that ought to benefit their family members, of whatever provenance, too. Yet, for the longest time, the Treaties themselves continued to make no mention of the rights of the latter.[6]

That fact notwithstanding, the Court took a crucial step in the *Surinder Singh* case, extending protection to the spouse of the returning EU worker.[7] It thus strengthened the cause of those engaged in, what has been dubbed, 'circular migration' – and quite precipitously so. As known, this threw the door

---

2 See e.g. Article 11 of Regulation (EC) 15/61 on initial measures to realise free movement of workers within the Community, OJ 1961, 57/1073; Article 17(3) of Regulation (EEC) 38/64 on freedom of movement for workers within the Community, OJ 1964, L 62/965; Article 10(3) of Regulation (EC) 1612/68 on freedom of movement for workers within the Community, OJ 1968, L 257/2 (hereinafter referred to as 'Regulation 1612/68').

3 Alongside the judgments referenced below, see e.g. Case 40/76, *Kermaschek*, EU:C:1976:157; Case 157/84, *Frascogna*, EU:C:1985:243. Instead of 'the Court', one should perhaps say 'the case-law', since the institution was never the monolith some commentators make it out to be. The appointment of subsequent generations of judges also means that they are confronted with an overriding narrative, to which the individual members merely add titbits of their own (not unlike the vision of written philosophy as a chain letter, outlined in: P. Sloterdijk, *Regeln für den Menschenpark* (Berlin: Suhrkamp, 1999)).

4 See G. Davies, 'Democracy and Legitimacy in the Shadow of Purposive Competence' (2015) 21 *ELJ*, 2–22.

5 Case C-184/99, *Grzelczyk*, EU:C:2001:458, para. 31.

6 Today, albeit in a slightly different key, such references are to be found in Title V TFEU.

7 Case C-370/90, *Singh*, EU:C:1992:296.

wide open for the infamous 'Europe route', exploited with gusto by *inter alia* Dutch nationals through Belgium, and German nationals through Denmark. Once *Singh* was laid down, the transposition of the employed reasoning to the non-economically active, recently showcased in *O. and B.*, obtained the character of something inevitable.[8] The sceptical observer may wonder whether there is truly so much inevitability in EU law; but in considering the design of the Treaties and the 'spirit' that permeates it, the Court has long been convinced that the free movement regime invites the placing of little puzzles on its docket, whereby there are incontestable 'right answers' flowing from the objectives of the *pères-fondateurs* that may be squarely premised on an *effet utile* argument.[9] This, then, is the pernicious systemic algorithm alluded to above.[10]

3. CRITIQUE

With the course locked in, the Court compounded matters by clinging to its familiar formulaic and self-referential style, which has already oft before been subjected to criticism.[11] Without attempting to reinforce its earlier holding, *O. and B.* was to the mind of the judiciary a logical corollary of *Singh* – as much as *Köbler*, for instance, was a logical corollary of *Francovich*: just the next piece of the jigsaw that had to slide into place.[12] With the systemic algorithm dictating the outcome, there simply was no viable alternative. We should take notice though of the more rare moments when the same *telos* and spirit of the Treaties apparently do allow for a tougher conservative position. Judgments like those in *Plaumann*, *Unibet* and *Inuit*, for example, demonstrate that effective protection of EU rights is not always such a strong command.[13] In addition, we may note that the Court's approach in its most generous pronouncements is both dubious

8 Case C-465/12, *O. and B.*, EU:C:2014:135. See also, earlier, Case C-291/05, *Eind*, EU:C:2007:771.

9 Emblematic of which technique is of course Case 26/62, *van Gend & Loos*, EU:C:1963:1.

10 Put differently, the dynamics could also be tagged as an autocatalytical process: in chemistry, this term is used when the products of a reaction provoke its own catalysis.

11 See e.g. J.H.H. Weiler, 'Epilogue: The Judicial *Après Nice*', in G. De Búrca and J.H.H. Weiler (eds.), *The European Court of Justice* (Oxford: OUP, 2001), 225; S. Weatherill, 'The Court's Case Law on the Internal Market: "A Circumloquacious Statement of the Result, Rather than a Reason for Arriving at It?"', in M. Adams, H. De Waele, J. Meeusen and G. Straetmans (eds.), *Judging Europe's Judges – The Legitimacy of the Case Law of the European Court of Justice* (Oxford: Hart Publishing, 2013), 87–108; G. De Búrca, 'After the EU Charter of Fundamental Rights: The Court of Justice as a Human Rights Adjudicator?' (2013) 20 *MJ*, 176–177.

12 Case C-224/01, *Köbler*, EU:C:2003:513; Joined Cases C-6/90 and C-9/90, *Francovich and Bonifaci*, EU:C:1991:428.

13 Case 25/62, *Plaumann*, EU:C:1963:17; Case C-432/05, *Unibet*, EU:C:2007:163; and Case C-583/11, *P Inuit Tapiriit Kanatami*, EU:C:2013:625.

and deceptive, since with regard to the Union citizenship regime, one can hardly indicate a fixed end-goal or *finalité* that must absolutely be attained.[14]

The legislator has dutifully followed in the wake of many of the Court's rulings nonetheless.[15] Moreover, it did not shy away from bold statements, such as that 'the right of freedom of movement, in order that it may be exercised, by objective standards, in freedom and dignity, requires that obstacles to the mobility of workers be eliminated, in particular as regards the worker's right to be joined by his family and the conditions for the integration of the worker's family into the host country'.[16] Empirical data to support the finding that deviant national rules inhibiting free movement ought to be *ipso facto* classified as obstacles, and that family reunification rights facilitate integration in the host society, is however found wanting.[17] For sure, the analogies and extrapolations practised by the EU institutions are, at least in hindsight, entirely predictable. Yet to contend that this is 'the European way' offers an explanation instead of a justification.[18]

The foregoing definitely does not mean to overlook that limitations have been imposed as well. In *O. and B.*, for example, the Court has reiterated the requirement that circular migrants have been genuinely resident abroad before returning to their Member State, meaning that only a protracted stay can unlock the craved entitlement to be joined by family members.[19] Nevertheless, the general vector or macro-trajectory remains undisputed. In the past two decades, it thus seems that the Court has acted as a frontrunner when there was no lack of support for an expansion of the relevant rights; we could draw a tentative line through the case-law from the past two decades that stretches from *Martínez Sala* all the way to *Ruiz Zambrano*.[20]

All the same, it was only when the consequences of quasi-unfettered free movement were most felt, and the political tide had already irreversibly turned, that the case-law belatedly caught on with the prevailing societal sentiments – with the *Dereci* and now *Dano* rulings as notable samples.[21] This reversing of

---

14 In the same vein D. Thym, 'Towards "Real" Citizenship? The Judicial Construction of Union Citizenship and Its Limits', in M. Adams, H. De Waele, J. Meeusen and G. Straetmans (eds.), *Judging Europe's Judges – The Legitimacy of the Case Law of the European Court of Justice* (Oxford: Hart Publishing, 2013), 174.

15 As illustrated e.g. by the copy-pasting of several of the CJ's *dicta* in the Citizens' Free Movement Directive 2004/38/EC.

16 Regulation 1612/68, preamble, recital 5; cf. Regulation 492/2011 on freedom of movement of workers within the Union, OJ 2011, L 141/1, preamble, recital 6.

17 D. Thym, 'Zur Rechtsstellung von Familienmitgliedern aus Drittstaaten im Lichte der Kernbereichs-Rechtsprechung des EuGH' (2015) *EuR-Beiheft* 1, 138.

18 Cf. F.G. Jacobs, *The Sovereignty of Law – The European Way* (Cambridge: CUP, 2007).

19 Moreover, the Court's interpretation only applies to those family members listed in Article 2(2) of Directive 2004/38, not those mentioned in Article 3(2), thereby excluding *inter alia* same sex registered partners.

20 Case C-85/96, *Martínez Sala*, EU:C:1998:217; Case C-34/09, *Ruiz Zambrano*, EU:C:2011:124.

21 Case C-256/11, *Dereci*, EU:C:2011:734; and Case C-333/13, *Dano*, EU:C:2014:817. For a harsh contrast with *Ruiz Zambrano*, see also Case C-86/12, *Alokpa*, EU:C:2013:645.

tracks can be criticised for its tardiness. In mundane terms, one might say that the Court neglected to 'go with the flow' when it was well-advised to do so. After all, it could not possibly have escaped the Court that the *Singh* doctrine as such was never benevolently received by the Member States, and that they were unlikely to look kindly upon further incursions in their migration policies.[22]

4. PLEA

The heart of the matter therefore appears to lie in an adjudication that failed to keep up with the times, and which has been insufficiently procyclical when that was exactly what was desired. Whilst not perfectly countercyclical either, in some periods the case-law displayed a visibly more progressive course than the political and societal environment was willing to condone.[23] Worse, when attempting to realign itself, it 'applied the brakes' much too vehemently. *Dano* seems to have relegated the sweeping dictum of *Sala* that a Union citizen lawfully resident in the territory of the host Member State can rely on Article 18 TFEU in all situations that fall within the scope *ratione materiae* of EU law.[24] In *Brey*, the precept that migrating citizens may not impose an 'unreasonable burden' was interpreted with palpable emphasis on the 'burden' aspect, where previously (e.g. in *Grzelczyk*), the 'unreasonable' aspect was stretched to the max.[25] By the looks of *Caves Krier* and *Giersch*, even (frontier) workers have been sucked up in the mêlée, as suggested by the startling introduction of a genuine link requirement for the economically active.[26] Cases such as *Onuekwere* raise the suspicion that the Court is currently (re)viewing Union citizenship through a prism of integration, with the latter increasingly denoting a *prerequisite* for acquiring rights, no longer the *goal* of long-term residence.[27] If so, it echoes a

---

22 E. Spaventa, 'Family Rights for Circular Migrants and Frontier Workers: *O and B*, and *S and G*' (2015) 52 *CML Rev*, 754.

23 The procyclical and countercyclical terminology is commonly derived from the economic theory popularised by J.M. Keynes (*The General Theory of Employment, Interest and Money* (MacMillan, 1936)), whereby governments are thought to best increase their expenditure in times of downturn, so as to be able to limit their spending again once consumption picks up, and market investments can happily take over. In a pro-cyclical approach, that strategy ought only to be applied during a boom. Both ideas never lost traction, despite scholarly scepticism.

24 Cf. H. Verschueren, 'Preventing "Benefit Tourism" in the EU: A Narrow or Broad Interpretation of the Possibilities Offered by the ECJ in *Dano*?' (2015) 52 *CML Rev*, 378; *contra* D. Thym, 'The Elusive Limits of Solidarity: Residence Rights of and Social Benefits for Economically Inactive Union Citizens' (2015) 52 *CML Rev*, 40.

25 Case C-140/12, *Brey*, EU:C:2013:565. See on this H. Verschueren, 'Free Movement or Benefit Tourism: The Unreasonable Burden of *Brey*' (2014) 16 EJML, 147–179.

26 Case C-379/11, *Sàrl*, EU:C:2012:798; Case C-20/12, *Giersch*, EU:C:2013:411. On this see further the contribution of H. Verschueren to this volume.

27 Case C-378/12, *Onuekwere*, EU:C:2014:13; see S. Coutts, 'Union Citizenship as Probationary Citizenship: *Onuekwere*' (2015) 52 *CML Rev*, 437.

discourse that reached its apogee in most Member States in the late 1990s.[28] A decade after its adoption, Directive 2004/38, originally meant as a consolidating tool that attaches importance to quantitative factors, is presently deployed as a limitation device, and combined with qualitative criteria for which there is no explicit conformation in the text.[29] In reference to the EU–Turkey association agreement, though not a massive retreat, *Demirkan* forms a crucial (restrictive) signal that one would also have expected somewhat earlier.[30] An unhelpful product of the Court's new-found reticence is the cleavage that has emerged between the citizenship regime on the one hand, and the 'pure' migration rules on the other.[31]

In sum, when the desired judicial adaptation to a decisively changed political and societal context finally arrived, it unfortunately took the shape of an *over*reaction, alongside some dubious prevarication. This goes to show that procyclism does not solely depend on proper timing; it equally presumes *moderation*, i.e. the delivery of precisely the right doses. In contrast, inept, let alone random successions of rights-extending and rights-curtailing decisions convey the impression of a badly thought-out hit and miss strategy. The upshot is an awkward string of cases in which paradigm shifts founder halfway through and become arrested developments. We consequently have to contend with Copernican revolutions that fail to revolve completely, as underscored e.g. by the *Rottmann–Ruiz Zambrano–Dereci* saga.[32]

To be sure, the proposal here is not that the European Court adopt the posture of, say, the International Court of Justice. Whereas the latter is often regarded a shining beacon of procyclical adjudication, emulating that example risks to result in a tribunal deciding in a perilously retrospective manner; an overly timid demeanour, which obviously does not befit the EU system.[33] Besides, a certain measure of countercyclical adjudication remains warranted – for no court should shy away from occasionally rowing against the stream, instead of constantly succumbing to external constraints.[34] Yet, without foregoing its independence, we should wish that the Court exhibits a more immediate sensibility to what, at any given time, is considered the appropriate response

---

28 But cf. T. Sarrazin, *Deutschland schafft sich ab* (Berlin: Suhrkamp, 2010).

29 S. Coutts, 'Union Citizenship as Probationary Citizenship: *Onuekwere*' (2015) 52 *CML Rev*, 544; see further the contributions of H. Verschueren and E. Spaventa to this volume.

30 Case C-221/11, *Demirkan*, EU:C:2013:583.

31 On which, see further the contribution of D. Thym to this volume.

32 Cf. M. Dougan, 'The Bubble that Burst: Exploring the Legitimacy of the Case Law on the Free Movement of Union Citizens', in M. Adams, H. De Waele, J. Meeusen and G. Straetmans (eds.), *Judging Europe's Judges – The Legitimacy of the Case Law of the European Court of Justice* (Oxford: Hart Publishing, 2013), 127–154.

33 Cf. G.I. Hernández, *The International Court of Justice and the Judicial Function* (Oxford: OUP, 2014).

34 Cf. A. Bickel, *The Least Dangerous Branch. The Supreme Court at the Bar of Politics* (Indianapolis: Bobbs-Merill, 1963); J.H. Ely, *Democracy and Distrust* (Cambridge (US): HUP, 1981).

from the side of the judiciary. This especially holds true where it concerns the delicate theme of family reunification – an area of law situated in a political minefield, at the borderline of national and European law.[35] Such sensibility may, nonetheless, be advocated not just in light of the patchy and erratic family reunification jurisprudence, but also when reflecting on adjacent domains.

The requested moderation, and the concomitant sensibility, would for now militate in favour of a prudent approach towards the EU Charter of Fundamental Rights. Of course, that document actually seems to offer an incentive to shift the existing boundaries. Yet, lest we forget, in the interpretation of its Article 9, the vested limitations on Article 8 ECHR ought to be embraced as well. Pursuant to its Article 52(3), the European Court of Justice is moreover bound to toe the lines drawn by the European Court of Human Rights, in a string of generally more procyclical pronouncements.[36] In so doing, it would arguably preserve the modicum of legitimacy needed to occasionally forge ahead – a legitimacy that it can earn, but is not automatically due.

---

35 E. Spaventa, 'Family Rights for Circular Migrants and Frontier Workers: *O and B*, and *S and G*' (2015) 52 *CML Rev*, 753.

36 Evidenced *inter alia* by the restrictive interpretation of Article 8 ECHR it opted to adhere to in the mid-2000s – ostensibly coinciding with the changing dynamics in the free movement of persons after the accession to the Union of the EU-10 and EU-2. Further on this, see the contribution of D. Thym to this volume.

CHAPTER 4
SUFFICIENT RESOURCES AND RESIDENCE RIGHTS UNDER DIRECTIVE 2004/38

Paul MINDERHOUD

According to Article 7(1)(b) of Directive 2004/38/EC Union citizens, who are not workers or self-employed, only have the right of residence on the territory of another Member State for a period of longer than three months if they have sufficient resources for themselves and their family members not to become a burden on the social assistance system of the host Member State during their period of residence and have comprehensive sickness insurance cover in the host Member State.

This chapter seeks to investigate the meaning of the concept of sufficient resources under Directive 2004/38.[1, 2] In section one the question when an inactive citizen has sufficient resources is dealt with by looking at the history of the concept, the national approaches and the Dutch case-law on this issue. The second section gives an overview of the relevant case-law of the CJ, distinguishing two important topics: the level of resources in relation to social assistance benefits and the origin of the resources. This section addresses the most challenging problems of this moment. The third section pays attention to the other condition laid down in Article 7(1)(b) Directive 2004/38, to have comprehensive sickness insurance.

1. SUFFICIENT RESOURCES

Directive 2004/38/EC makes a distinction between residence up to three months, residence from three months to five years and residence for longer than five years. Different preconditions for residence apply in each of these three categories. Furthermore, the treatment of economically inactive persons differs from the treatment of economically active persons.

1 Directive 2004/38/EC of the European Parliament and of the Council of 29 April 2004 on the right of citizens of the Union and their family members to move and reside freely within the territory of the Member States, OJ 2004, L 158/77 (hereinafter referred to as 'Directive 2004/38).

2 It does not deal with the concept of sufficient resources as it is developed in other Directives, like the Family Reunification Directive 2003/86.

The Directive gives in Article 6 all EU citizens a right to entry to any EU Member State without any conditions or formalities, other than the requirement to hold a valid identity card or passport, for three months. It is, however, explicitly stated in Article 24(2) that the host Member State shall not be obliged to confer any entitlement to social assistance during these first three months of residence.

According to Article 7(1) of Directive 2004/38/EC Union citizens only have the right of residence on the territory of another Member State for a period of longer than three months if they:

(a) are workers or self-employed persons in the host Member State; or
(b) have sufficient resources for themselves and their family members not to become a burden on the social assistance system of the host Member State during their period of residence and have comprehensive sickness insurance cover in the host Member State; or
(c) are enrolled at a private or public establishment, accredited or financed by the host Member State on the basis of its legislation or administrative practice, for the principal purpose of following a course of study, including vocational training; and have comprehensive sickness insurance cover in the host Member State and assure the relevant national authority, by means of a declaration or by such equivalent means as they may choose, that they have sufficient resources for themselves and their family members not to become a burden on the social assistance system of the host Member State during their period of residence; or
(d) are family members accompanying or joining a Union citizen who satisfies the conditions referred to in points (a), (b) or (c).

When Union citizens have resided legally for a continuous period of five years in the host Member State they shall have the right of permanent residence there.[3] This right of permanent residence is given to Union citizens (and their family members), without any further conditions, even if these persons do not have sufficient resources or comprehensive sickness insurance cover any more after these five years.

For the purpose of this chapter I will limit myself to the category of inactive EU citizens who fall under Article 7(1)(b) and who need sufficient resources (and comprehensive sickness insurance) to have a right to reside under Directive 2004/38. But it is good to emphasise that these conditions regarding sufficient resources and comprehensive sickness insurance neither apply to workers and self-employed persons, nor to persons who stopped being economically active but who do retain this status pursuant to Article 7(3) Directive 2004/38. Nor do they apply to jobseekers who entered the territory of the host Member State in order to seek employment. Such persons may not be expelled for as long as they

3 Article 16(1) Directive 2004/38.

can provide evidence that they are continuing to seek employment and that they have a genuine chance of being engaged.[4]

Sufficient resources are also of relevance for the persons who fall under the scope of Articles 12 and 13 of Directive 2004/38. According to these articles family members in the event of death or departure of the Union citizen or in the event of divorce, annulment of marriage or termination of registered partnership retain under conditions their right of residence. But it is explicitly provided that (unless they are workers or self-employed persons) before acquiring the right of permanent residence they are required to have sufficient resources for themselves and their family members not to become a burden on the social assistance system of the host Member State during their period of residence and have comprehensive sickness insurance cover in the host Member State.

1.1. WHEN DOES AN INACTIVE UNION CITIZEN HAVE SUFFICIENT RESOURCES?

One of the crucial questions is when do inactive Union citizens have sufficient resources in order to obtain a right of residence under Directive 2004/38. The Commission has tried to provide some guidance in answering this question in its guidelines, published in 2009. According to these guidelines the notion of 'sufficient resources' must be interpreted in the light of the objective of the Directive, which is to facilitate free movement, as long as the beneficiaries of the right of residence do not become an unreasonable burden on the social assistance system of the host Member State.[5]

The first step to assess the existence of sufficient resources should be whether the EU citizen (and family members who derive their right of residence from him or her) would meet the national criteria to be granted the basic social assistance benefit. EU citizens have sufficient resources, according to the Commission's guidelines, where the level of their resources is higher than the threshold under which a minimum subsistence benefit is granted in the host Member State. Where this criterion is not applicable, the minimum social security pension should be taken into account.

At the same time Article 8(4) of Directive 2004/38, which is the important provision in this context, prohibits Member States from laying down a fixed

4 Article 14(4)(b) Directive 2004/38. See F. Van Overmeiren, E. Eichenhofer and H. Verschueren, 'Social Security Coverage of Non-Active Persons Moving to Another Member State', in E. Guild, C. Gortazar Rotaeche and D. Kostakopoulou (eds.), *The Reconceptualization of European Union Citizenship* (Leiden-Boston: Nijhoff, 2014), 231.

5 COM (2009) 313 final, Communication from the Commission to the European Parliament and the Council on guidance for better transposition and application of Directive 2004/38/EC on the right of citizens of the Union and their family members to move and reside freely within the territory of the Member States, Section 2.3.1. Sufficient resources.

amount to be regarded as 'sufficient resources', either directly or indirectly, below which the right of residence can be automatically refused. The authorities of the Member States must take into account the personal situation of the individual concerned. The text of this provision fully reads:

> 'Member States may not lay down a fixed amount which they regard as "sufficient resources", but they must take into account the personal situation of the person concerned. In all cases this amount shall not be higher than the threshold below which nationals of the host Member State become eligible for social assistance, or, where this criterion is not applicable, higher than the minimum social security pension paid by the host Member State'.

Unfortunately, this text has a rather ambivalent character. On the one hand a fixed amount is prohibited, but on the other hand a threshold at the level of a social assistance benefit is indicated. During the negotiations in 2002 and 2003 on the establishment of Directive 2004/38 the wording of this provision regarding the determination of what 'sufficient resources' should mean was highly debated by some Member States and the Commission, which has probably contributed to this ambivalence in the text.

1.2. HISTORY OF THE CONCEPT OF SUFFICIENT RESOURCES UNDER DIRECTIVE 2004/38[6]

Regarding an earlier proposed text of at that time paragraph 5 of Article 8 that Member States may not lay down an amount which they regard as sufficient resources, scrutiny reservations were made during the negotiations in July 2002 by Denmark, Germany and the Netherlands. According to these countries the Member State should be able to decide what were sufficient resources, e.g. by reference to the level of resources below which the host Member State granted social assistance to its nationals.[7] The Commission however could not share that view, arguing that:

- the concept of 'sufficient resources' depended on numerous factors (free accommodation, benefits arising from links with other people, etc.) and could not be assessed by the person alone;
- there were no conditions on the personal possession of resources; they could come from another person;

6 This paragraph is partly based on H. Oosterom-Staples, 'Artikel 8 Richtlijn 2004/38/EG', *SDU Commentaar Europees Migratierecht* (The Hague: SDU, 2013).

7 Students are simply required to assure the relevant national authority, by means of a declaration or by such equivalent means as they may choose, that they have sufficient resources for themselves and their family members not to become a burden on the social assistance system of the host Member State during the period of residence.

- financial situations can change and it would be unrealistic to regard the fact that at a given moment a person possessed a given amount of resources as a guarantee;
- the declaration constituted an undertaking by the person, which, as such, carried legal consequences.

The Commission also said that the system which was proposed to extend to all EU citizens was already being applied in the case of students.[8]

In answer to the question asked during the negotiations in February 2003: 'Should the proposal define a sufficient level of resources? If so, on what basis and at what level?' Germany, Italy and Austria thought that it was not necessary. But Denmark and the Netherlands, now supported by Belgium, Spain and the UK replied that a sufficient level of resources should be defined. Denmark and the Netherlands thought that the condition of resources at, or above, the threshold below which the host Member State may grant social assistance to its nationals should be applied to all categories of people, apart from students. Belgium proposed that it should also be specified that the means of subsistence had to be the person's own resources. Spain and the United Kingdom held the opinion that Member States should be entitled to set the amount of resources they considered sufficient.[9] The German delegation then submitted the following amendment proposal:

> 'Member States may not lay down *schematically* an amount, which they regard as sufficient resources for Union citizens and to *support themselves and their families. The possibility of taking into account the specific circumstances of a given case must not be ruled out*' (emphasis added).[10]

This did not solve the problem at that time. Italy, Portugal and Spain preferred the Commission proposal, Denmark and Austria preferred the German proposal but the Netherlands and the United Kingdom had a scrutiny reservation on the German proposal.

The Commission was opposed to this German proposal, believing that it introduces the concept of a threshold of resources which was contrary to the underlying idea of the initial proposal and that was contrary to the existing *acquis* concerning students.

In the political agreement of 5 September 2003 there is a text which is very similar to the text of what has become Article 8(4) in the end. As far as the definition of a sufficient level of resources is concerned, Belgium, Denmark, Spain, the Netherlands, Sweden and the UK supported this new wording and

8 Council Doc. 10572/02, p. 25, nt. 45.
9 Council Doc. 6147/03, p. 23, nt. 38.
10 Council Doc. 6147/03, p. 23, nt. 39.

entered a positive scrutiny reservation. Germany welcomed the first part but entered a scrutiny reservation on the restrictive second part that 'in all cases this amount shall not be higher than the threshold below which nationals of the host Member State become eligible for social assistance, or, where this criterion is not applicable, higher than the minimum social security pension paid by the host Member State'.

Greece and Portugal had scrutiny reservations as well, preferring the initial Commission proposal based on a declaratory system.[11] But the final text did not change any more.

1.3. NATIONAL APPROACHES REGARDING SUFFICIENT RESOURCES

This ambivalence of prohibiting a fixed amount but indicating a threshold at social assistance benefit level at the same time is reflected in the practice of various Member States as well.

A comparative study of the application of Directive 2004/38 published in 2009 showed that the approaches regarding the definition of sufficient resources differed in the various Member States. Some Member States set out an amount as to what constitutes sufficient resources (France, Greece, Hungary, Ireland, Italy, Latvia, Luxembourg, Romania, Slovenia and the United Kingdom), others apply a threshold together with an examination of the personal circumstances of the citizen (Belgium, the Netherlands and Luxembourg). The study distinguishes four trends in the Member States. Firstly, some Member States have given a liberal and expansive definition to sufficient resources to the point of eliminating any resources requirements for EU migrants. Spain, for instance, does not require EU migrants to provide any information related to resources and in Poland the documentation related to sufficient resources has been kept to a minimum as Union citizens are only requested to provide a declaration to the authorities stating that they have sufficient resources (no supporting evidence is required). Secondly, some Member States have inserted a requirement of sufficient resources in their legislation but have not set out how the sufficient resources threshold may be satisfied. This has, for example, been the case for the implementation of the Directive into Estonian law. Although this does not necessarily mean that a restrictive approach could be taken, the absence of clear published guidelines can result in uncertainty and can itself act as an obstacle to free movement. The lack of transparency and the amount of discretion given to individual officials can result in unequal treatment and can deter Union citizens from taking advantage of their residence rights.

11 Council Doc. 12218/03, p. 22, nt. 22.

Thirdly, the nature of transposing legislation may be ambiguous, causing problems for citizens. An example is the transposition by the United Kingdom. The legislation specifies that resources are regarded as sufficient if they exceed the maximum level for resources which a UK national may possess if he is to become eligible for social assistance under the United Kingdom benefit system, whereas Article 8(4) of the Directive stipulates that sufficient resources 'shall not be higher than the threshold below which nationals of the host Member State become eligible for social assistance'. This transposition creates, at the very least, unnecessary ambiguities, in fact, the terminology prescribed in this case is detrimental to transparency for Union citizens as the figure representing the 'maximum level of resources which a UK national may possess if he is to become eligible for social assistance' remains difficult to quantify.

Fourthly, other Member States have chosen to include additional requirements not provided for in the Directive. Italy, for example, has retained a law which requires Union citizens to prove the legality and authenticity of their sufficient resources.

In sum, the large number of definitions linked to the concept of 'sufficient resources' will undoubtedly give rise to confusion amongst Union citizens exercising their free movement rights. In particular, the evidence required to prove sufficient resources, the lack of transparency and the varying attitudes in different Member States result in a patchwork of uneven legislation.[12]

When we try to look at more recent national practices, there is little information available. Shaw and Nic Shuibhne describe that in most of the national reports, written for the 2014 FIDE conference on Union citizenship, it was clear that national implementing measures expressly incorporate the obligation to evaluate the personal circumstances of the individual concerned, as required by Article 8(4) of the Directive.[13] But it was less clear what this exactly meant for the amount of money involved. In the report for Poland, for example, it is noted that proof of sufficient resources can be demonstrated by means such as the possession of a credit card 'or a certification of having funds at a bank or other financial institution confirmed by a seal and a signature of an authorised officer of the bank or institution, issued one month before submitting an application for registration of stay at the latest'. The report for France alludes to the fact that, as confirmed by EU case-law, financial resources can be provided

12 European Citizen Action Service, Comparative study on the application of Directive 2004/38/EC of 29 April 2004 on the right of citizens of the union and their family members to move and reside freely within the territory of the member states, European Parliament's committee on Legal Affairs, PE 410.650 (Brussels, 2009), 165 *et seq*.

13 J. Shaw and N. Nic Shuibhne, 'General Report: Union Citizenship: Development, Impact and Challenges', in U. Neergaard, C. Jacqueson and N. Holst-Christensen (eds.), *Union Citizenship: Development, Impact and Challenges, The XXVI FIDE Congress in Copenhagen* (Copenhagen: DJØF Publishing, 2014), 91.

on behalf of the Union citizen by a third person;[14] but the relevant national guidance requires, in such situations, that the Union citizen must justify the sufficiency and duration of such resources. However, more problematically, it also appears that some States either have in the past imposed or continue to impose minimum quantitative thresholds for the determination of sufficient resources. There is a reference to the reports for Cyprus, Denmark, and France. In Denmark a person who was in possession of less than €35 (corresponding to the price of a night at a hostel) was regarded as lacking sufficient resources. In Cyprus these conditions are not addressed only to citizens who are not engaged in economic activity; but administrative practice requires also that workers demonstrate certain income for themselves and their families to recognise their right to residence under Article 7(1) Directive 2004/38.

1.4. DUTCH CASE-LAW ON SUFFICIENT RESOURCES

Based on the information of the FIDE 2014 report the impression is justified that there is not much case-law available on the issue of sufficient resources and its consequences in the Member States. In the Netherlands for example, only a few court cases on this issue could be detected. A very noteworthy judgment was given by the Dutch State Council on the issue of the granting of a residence permit.[15] This case concerned a Dutch–Jordanian couple who stayed (involuntarily) in Belgium for a period of five months in the Antwerp University Hospital, due to necessary emergency medical treatment for the Dutch husband. The Jordanian wife who had travelled to the Netherlands on a short term visa just the day before the unexpected hospitalisation of her husband took place, stayed during that entire period in the hospital guesthouse in Belgium. After returning to the Netherlands the couple applied for a residence permit for the Jordanian wife based on European law. The Dutch immigration authorities and the District Court rejected this application on the basis that the couple did not have sufficient resources during their stay in Belgium and therefore need not built up a residence right based on Article 7(1)(b) Directive 2004/38 in Belgium so European law was not applicable. The State Council however granted the application referring to Article 8(4) of the Directive arguing that the personal situation of the individual concerned has to be taken into account. In this case all the hospital costs had been paid by the sickness insurance company and the couple had not applied for any social assistance during their stay in Belgium and therefore were supposed to fulfil the condition of sufficient resources and had

---

14 e.g. Case C-200/02, *Zhu and Chen*, EU:C:2004:639.

15 State Council 12 November 2009, *Rechtspraak Vreemdelingenrecht* 2009, 31, ECLI:N:RVS:2009:BK3910.

residence on the basis of Article 7(1)(b) Directive 2004/38 for the last two months of the five months they stayed in Belgium.

In another court case the Dutch District Court of The Hague (Zutphen) ruled that the Dutch authorities were not allowed to request from two Romanian citizens that they have to fulfil a threshold income equivalent to a Dutch social assistance benefit to have a residence right under Article 7(1)(b) Directive 2004/38. Both Romanians did not have a social assistance benefit but stated to rely on the income of their father and partner and could proof the income of the father and the partner. According to the Court the approach of the Dutch authorities that the norm of the Dutch Social Assistance Act is an absolute minimum norm, is not in line with Article 8(4) Directive 2004/38, and therefore the Dutch authorities had to reconsider their decision.[16]

Another case of the District Court of The Hague concerned a German minor who asked for registration as an EU citizen by the Immigration and Naturalisation Service (IND). This was refused because the IND held the opinion that the mother of the child did not have sufficient resources because she did not meet the threshold of a one parent standard under the Dutch Social Assistance Act. The Dutch Court ruled that this decision was not in line with Article 8(4) Directive 2004/38, because the personal situation of the mother was not taken into account. The fact that the mother received a monthly alimony allowance of €600 (which is substantially lower than the given Social Assistance Act threshold) was seen as sufficient resources. The Court took also in account the fact that the mother already during more than two year lived on this alimony allowance without applying for any social assistance benefit.[17]

The District Court of The Hague (Middelburg) ruled in September 2014 that the decision of the immigration authorities that a bank declaration of €8,000 was not seen as sufficient resources for a Moroccan woman to stay with her Spanish children in the Netherlands could not hold. The financial help of her sisters, as well as the alimony paid by the Spanish former husband for the children, also had to be taken into account. According to the Court, the 2009 guidelines of the European Commission clearly forbid the requirement of a fixed standard as well as the requirement of a sustainable amount of money.[18]

In another case before the Dutch State Council the condition of sufficient resources was discussed in the context of the situation of a German minor who wanted to attend a primary school in the Netherlands. His financial means were supported by his father, who holds the Turkish nationality and who did not have a regular income himself, but received a monthly donation by an Islamic foundation. The Dutch authorities had rejected the application for a residence

---

16 District Court The Hague (Zutphen) 4 November 2009, *Rechtspraak Vreemdelingenrecht* 2009, 33, ECLI:N:RBSGR:2009:BK3936.

17 District Court The Hague 14 November 2011, ECLI:RBSGR:2011:BV1155.

18 District Court The Hague (Middelburg) 18 September 2014, *Jurisprudentie Vreemdelingenrecht* 2014/362, ECLI:N:RBDHA:2014:11638.

permit because the child did not have sufficient resources of his own. According to the State Council the origin of the resources (referring to the judgments of the CJ in *Zhu and Chen*[19] and *Commission v Belgium*)[20] is not of importance for the decision on the right of residence in the Netherlands. The amount of the monthly donation of €800, which is below the threshold of the Dutch social assistance benefit, is seen as sufficient resources by the State Council.[21]

From these Dutch court cases it can be concluded that the Dutch immigration authorities tend to apply a fixed amount at the level of a social assistance benefit as a condition of sufficient resources, not taking into account Article 8(4) Directive 2004/38, while the courts do take into account the personal situation of the EU citizen and tend to accept a lower amount of money to fulfil the condition of sufficient resources. But it has to be stated that in all these court cases it seems that no application for a social assistance benefit has been made.

2. SUFFICIENT RESOURCES IN THE CASE-LAW OF THE CJ

When we have a look at the case-law of the CJ regarding sufficient resources two important issues can be distinguished. The first issue concerns the level of resources and the relation to social assistance benefits, the other issue concerns the origin of the resources.

The *Commission v Netherlands* case made clear that Member States could not require standard norms regarding sufficient resources.[22] In order to obtain a residence permit, the Dutch authorities required that non-active and retired EU citizens had to prove that they had sustainable resources, which meant they had to prove in a systematic way having enough resources to be able to stay for at least a year, based on the threshold of a social assistance benefit. The Court declared that the Netherlands by requiring this condition had failed to fulfil its obligations under the Directives, regulating the right of residence before they were replaced by Directive 2004/38.[23] The personal situation of the person concerned must be taken into account to establish the amount of sufficient resources, according to the Court.

19 Case C-200/02, *Zhu and Chen*, EU:C:2004:639.

20 Case C-408/03, *Commission v Belgium*, EU:C:2006:192.

21 State Council 3 September 2013, *Rechtspraak Vreemdelingenrecht* 2013, 33, ECLI:N:RVS:2013:1068.

22 Case C-398/06, *Commission v Netherlands*, EU:C:2008:214.

23 Council Directive 68/360/EEC of 15 October 1968 on the abolition of restrictions on movement and residence within the Community for workers of Member States and their families, Council Directive 90/364/EEC of 28 June 1990 on the right of residence and Council Directive 90/365/EEC of 28 June 1990 on the right of residence for employees and self-employed persons who have ceased their occupational activity.

The judgment of the Court in the *Ziolkowski and Szeja* case could be seen as a support of the approach that EU citizens having a social assistance benefit will never fulfil the sufficient resources condition of Article 7(1) Directive 2004/38 and therefore do not have a right of residence based on Directive 2004/38.[24] Mr Ziolkowski and Ms Szeja, Polish nationals, arrived in Germany before the accession of Poland to the European Union and were granted a right of residence on humanitarian grounds, which was duly extended in accordance with German law. In 2005, after the accession of Poland to the European Union, they applied for permanent residence in Germany under Article 16 of Directive 2004/38, which was refused on the grounds that they were not in employment and were unable to prove that they had sufficient resources to support themselves. Since entering Germany Mr Ziolkowski had been entitled to social assistance benefits[25] and Ms Szeja and her children were not in a position to support themselves and were informed in 2005 that they would be expelled to Poland.[26]

The Court recalls that for periods of residence of longer than three months, the right of residence is subject to the conditions set out in Article 7(1) of Directive 2004/38 and, under Article 14(2), that right is retained only if the Union citizen and his family members satisfy those conditions.[27] The concept of legal residence implied by the terms 'have resided legally' in Article 16(1) of Directive 2004/38 should be construed as meaning a period of residence which complies with the conditions laid down in the Directive, in particular those set out in Article 7(1).[28] Consequently, a period of residence which complies with the law of a Member State but does not satisfy the conditions laid down in Article 7(1) of Directive 2004/38 cannot be regarded as a 'legal' period of residence within the meaning of Article 16(1).[29] Therefore Article 16(1) of Directive 2004/38 must be interpreted as meaning that a Union citizen who has been resident for more than five years in the territory of the host Member State on the sole basis of the national law of that Member State cannot be regarded as having acquired the right of permanent residence under that provision if, during that period of residence, he did not satisfy the conditions laid down in Article 7(1) of the Directive.[30]

---

24 Case C-424/10 and C-425/10, *Ziolkowski and Szeja*, EU:C:2011:866.

25 The English version of the Conclusion of Advocate General G. Bot where this information can be found speaks by mistake of social security benefits, but the German version speaks of '*Sozialhilfe*', the Dutch version of '*socialebijstandsuitkeringen*' and the French version of '*l'assistance sociale*'. See Opinion of Advocate General Bot in Case C-424/10 and C-425/10, *Ziolkowski and Szeja*, EU:C:2011:575, para. 16.

26 Opinion of the Advocate General Bot in Case C-424/10 and C-425/10, *Ziolkowski and Szeja*, EU:C:2011:575, para. 27.

27 Joined Cases C-424/10 and C-425/10, *Ziolkowski and Szeja*, EU:C:2011:866, para. 40.

28 Joined Cases C-424/10 and C-425/10, *Ziolkowski and Szeja*, EU:C:2011:866, para. 46.

29 Joined Cases C-424/10 and C-425/10, *Ziolkowski and Szeja*, EU:C:2011:866, para. 47.

30 Joined Cases C-424/10 and C-425/10, *Ziolkowski and Szeja*, EU:C:2011:866, para. 51. See also Case C-325/09, *Dias*, EU:C:2011:498, para. 55.

In the *Brey* case this tension between the condition of sufficient resources and applying for a social assistance benefit is also at the heart of the problem.[31] This case concerned a German national, who was in receiving a German invalidity pension of €1,087.74 and who had transferred together with his wife his residence to Austria where he applied for an Austrian compensatory supplement which aimed at guaranteeing the person concerned a minimum subsistence income in Austria.[32] The Austrian authorities refused to grant this benefit because Mr Brey did not meet the conditions required to obtain the right to reside, due to a lack of sufficient resources. The Court held the view that the fact that an economically inactive national from another Member State may be eligible, in the light of a low pension, to receive that compensatory supplement benefit, could be an indication that the national in question does not have sufficient resources to avoid becoming an unreasonable burden on the social assistance system of the host Member State, for the purposes of obtaining or retaining the right to reside under Article 7(1)(b) of Directive 2004/38. However, this is just 'an indication'. The Court recalls that it should be noted that the first sentence of Article 8(4) of Directive 2004/38 expressly states that Member States may not lay down a fixed amount which they will regard as 'sufficient resources', but must take into account the personal situation of the person concerned.[33] Therefore, it follows that, although Member States may indicate a certain sum as a reference amount, they may not impose a minimum income level below which it will be presumed that the person concerned does not have sufficient resources, irrespective of a specific examination of the situation of each person concerned.[34] National authorities first have to carry out an overall assessment of the specific burden which granting that benefit would place on the national social assistance system as a whole, by reference to the personal circumstances characterising the individual situation of the person concerned. The CJ stressed that any limitation upon the freedom of movement as a fundamental principle of EU law, must be construed narrowly and in compliance with the limits imposed by EU law and the principle of proportionality. The Member States' room for manoeuvre may not be used in such a manner as to compromise attainment of the objective of Directive 2004/38, more specifically its objective to facilitate and strengthen the primary right to free movement.[35] On the basis of these elements the Court confirms that EU law recognises a certain degree of solidarity between nationals of a host Member State and nationals of other Member States. The mere fact that a national of a Member State receives social assistance is not sufficient to demonstrate that he constitutes an unreasonable burden on the social assistance system of the host Member State. For that reason the Austrian legislation, by

31 Case C-140/12, *Brey*, EU:C:2013:565.
32 Case C-140/12, *Brey*, EU:C:2013:565, para. 63.
33 Case C-140/12, *Brey*, EU:C:2013:565, para. 67.
34 Case C-140/12, *Brey*, EU:C:2013:565, para. 68.
35 Case C-140/12, *Brey*, EU:C:2013:565, paras. 65–71.

virtue of which the mere fact that an economically inactive migrant EU citizen has applied for the 'compensatory supplement' is sufficient to preclude that citizen from receiving it, is not compatible with EU law.[36] This automatic refusal keeps the national authorities from carrying out an overall assessment of the specific burden.[37]

Although the Court does not explicitly refer to this, in my opinion it can be concluded that Mr Brey has a residence right under Article 7(1)(b) Directive 2004/38, even if he receives this compensatory supplement.

In his case note under the *Brey* judgment Verschueren refers to the final judgment the Austrian Supreme Court delivered after the ruling of the CJ.[38] The Austrian Supreme Court recognised that the host Member State of a migrant not economically active Union citizen may limit this person's right to reside on its territory when he becomes an unreasonable burden on its social assistance system.[39] In order to assess this unreasonability, the national authorities must take into account the various elements to which the CJ refers in *Brey*. A mechanism, as in place in the Austrian legislation, whereby nationals of other Member States who are not economically active are automatically barred from receiving a particular social security benefit, does not enable the competent authorities of the host Member State to carry out such an assessment. Yet the Austrian Supreme Court concluded that as long as Union citizens reside lawfully in Austria, they may rely on EU law, including as regards the principle of equal treatment, to receive social benefits, even if this could subsequently compromise their right of residence. Until the competent Austrian authorities have put an end to the lawful residence of Mr Brey by a formal decision, including in this case the withdrawal of the certificate of residence in accordance with the provisions of Directive 2004/38, he has the right to equal treatment for social benefits, such as in this case the 'compensatory supplement', according to the Austrian Supreme Court.

A year later, however, the CJ delivered its judgment in the *Dano* case and here the approach on the issue of sufficient resources is different from the one in *Brey*.[40] In this case two Romanian nationals, mother and son Dano, who lived in Germany were refused to be granted access to benefits under the German basic provision. Ms Dano had not entered Germany to seek employment and although she applied for benefits reserved to job-seekers the case file showed that she had not been looking for a job. She had no professional qualifications and had not

36 Case C-140/12, *Brey*, EU:C:2013:565, para. 77.

37 See in more detail H. Verschueren, 'Free Movement or Benefit Tourism: The Unreasonable Burden of Brey' (2014) 16 *EJML*, 147–179.

38 H. Verschueren, 'Free Movement or Benefit Tourism: The Unreasonable Burden of Brey' (2014) 16 *EJML*, 147–179.

39 OGH 17 December 2013, ECLI:AT:OGH0002:2013:010OBS00152.13W.1217.000, available at www.ris.bka.gv.at (last accessed on 20 January 2016).

40 Case C-333/13, *Dano*, EU:C:2014:2358.

exercised any profession in Germany nor Romania. The Court held that nationals of other Member States as regards their access to social benefits are only entitled to be treated equally as a national of the host Member State if their residence in the territory of the host Member State meets the requirements of Directive 2004/38. According to the Court, the Directive thus seeks to prevent Union citizens from using the host Member State's social assistance system to fund their means of subsistence. The Court consequently considers in paragraphs 77 and 78 that the possibility that Union citizens who have used their freedom of movement and of residence are being treated differently from the host Member State's own nationals with regard to social benefits is an inevitable consequence of Directive 2004/38. This potentially unequal treatment is in fact based on the link between sufficient resources being a residence requirement on the one hand and, on the other, the desire to prevent the burden on the social assistance system of the Member States, established by the Union legislator in Article 7 of that Directive. A Member State must therefore, in accordance with Article 7 of that Directive, have the possibility of refusing to grant social benefits to economically inactive Union citizens who exercise their right to free movement for the sole purpose of obtaining another Member State's social assistance, although they do not have sufficient resources in order to qualify for a right of residence. According to the Court, Ms Dano and her son lack sufficient resources and, pursuant to Directive 2004/38, are therefore not entitled to a right of residence in Germany, nor are they entitled to benefits under the German basic provision.

A big problem with this approach in the *Dano* case is that it does not clarify what role could still be played by the provision of Article 8(4) Directive 2004/38 to which the Court does not refer at all. The fact that Ms Dano asked for a social assistance benefit is seen by the Court as proof that she had no sufficient resources. It is even stated without any further investigation that she did not have any sufficient resources upon arriving in Germany. It should be recalled that at the moment of application for the German basic provision Ms Dano received child benefits amounting to €184 per month and an advance on public maintenance payments of €133 per month and she had accommodation because she lived in the home of her sister. Given the wording and history of Article 8(4) Directive 2004/38 in my view it could be defended that given her personal situation she would have had sufficient resources (and therefore a right of residence on the basis of Article 7(1)(b) Directive 2004/38) during the time she did not ask for social assistance. The judgment in the *Dano* case seems to imply that the fact that economically inactive EU citizens (residing for less than five years in another Member State) apply for a social assistance benefit would mean automatically that they have no sufficient resources (and no residence right under Directive 2004/38) anymore.[41] This reasoning would also lead to the paradox that such a Union citizen would only be entitled to any

[41] See also D. Thym, 'The elusive limits of solidarity: residence rights of social benefits for economically inactive Union citizens' (2015) 52 *CML Rev*, 42.

social assistance if he has sufficient resources and therefore is not in need of any social assistance.[42] This seems to be a real Catch-22 situation.

The latest development in seeking a balance between the requirement of fulfilling the condition of sufficient resources and the possibility to apply for social assistance is given in the opinion of Advocate General Wathelet, delivered in the *Alimanovic* case on 26 March 2015.[43]

Ms Alimanovic and her three children, are all Swedish nationals. The three children were born in Germany. After living abroad for ten years, the family re-entered Germany in June 2010. Between then and May 2011, Ms Alimanovic and her elder daughter, worked for less than a year in short-term jobs or under employment-promotion measures in Germany. The two women have not worked since. From 1 December 2011 to 31 May 2012, they received subsistence allowances for beneficiaries fit for work ('SGB II benefit'), while the other children received social allowances for beneficiaries unfit for work. Subsequently, the competent German authority stopped paying those allowances, because according to the German legislation, non-nationals (and members of their family), whose right of residence arises solely out of the search for employment, may not claim such benefits.[44] The conclusion of the AG takes as a starting point that following the *Dano* judgment, it is established that the Member States may – but are not obliged to – refuse to grant social assistance to Union citizens who enter their territory without intending to find a job and without being able to support themselves by their own means.[45] The AG notes that the unusual stir that that Court judgment has caused in the European media and all the political interpretations that have accompanied it confirm the importance and sensitivity of the subject.[46] This case however is concerned with the situation in which a Union citizen, after working for less than a year in the territory of a Member State of which he is not a national, applies for subsistence benefits in the host State.[47] But, unlike in the *Vatsouras and Koupatantze* case,[48] the contested SGB II benefit is now primarily seen as a social assistance benefit and not as a benefit facilitating access to the labour market.[49]

---

42 See H. Verschueren, 'Preventing "benefit tourism" in the EU: A narrow or broad interpretation of the possibilities offered by the ECJ in *Dano*?' (2015) 52 *CML Rev*, 381.

43 Opinion of Advocate General Wathelet in Case C-67/14, *Alimanovic*, EU:C:2015:210.

44 This was a consequence of the fact that Germany had excluded this SGB II benefit from the scope of the European Convention on Social and Medical Assistance on 19 December 2011. See P. Minderhoud, 'Directive 2004/38 and Access to Social Assistance', in E. Guild, C. Gortazar Rotaeche and D. Kostakopoulou (eds.), *The Reconceptualization of European Union Citizenship* (Leiden-Boston: Nijhoff, 2014), 216.

45 Opinion of Advocate General Wathelet in Case C-67/14, *Alimanovic*, EU:C:2015:210, para. 5.

46 Opinion of Advocate General Wathelet in Case C-67/14, *Alimanovic*, EU:C:2015:210, para. 4.

47 Opinion of Advocate General Wathelet in Case C-67/14, *Alimanovic*, EU:C:2015:210, para. 7.

48 Joined Cases C-22/08 and C-23/08, *Vatsouras and Koupatantze*, EU:C:2009:344.

49 Opinion of Advocate General Wathelet in Case C-67/14, *Alimanovic*, EU:C:2015:210, paras. 58–72.

According to the AG restrictions of the grant of social assistance to Union citizens who have not, or no longer, a worker status, that are established on the basis of Article 24(2) of Directive 2004/38, must be legitimate.[50] The AG therefore proposes that three situations should be distinguished. Firstly, a national of one Member State who enters the territory of another Member State and stays there (for less than three months or for more than three months) *without* the aim of seeking employment there, may, as the Court held in the judgment in *Dano*, legitimately be excluded from social assistance benefits, in order to maintain the financial equilibrium of the national social security system. Secondly, such exclusion is also legitimate, for the same reasons, in respect of a national of one Member State who moves to the territory of another Member State in order to seek employment there.[51]

On the other hand, as regards, thirdly, a national of one Member State who stays for more than three months in the territory of another Member State and has worked there, the Advocate General considers that such a person (like Ms Alimanovic) may not automatically be refused the benefits in question.

It is true that an EU citizen having worked in national territory for less than one year may, in accordance with EU law, loses the status of worker after six months of unemployment.[52] Nevertheless, it runs counter to the principle of equal treatment to exclude automatically an EU citizen from entitlement to social assistance benefits such as those at issue beyond a period of involuntary unemployment of six months after working for less than one year without allowing that citizen to demonstrate the existence of a genuine link with the host Member State.[53] In that regard, in addition to matters evident from the family circumstances (such as the children's education), the fact that the person concerned has, for a reasonable period, in fact genuinely sought work is a factor capable of demonstrating the existence of such a link with the host Member State. Having worked in the past, or even the fact of having found a new job after applying for the grant of social benefits, should also be taken into account to that end.[54]

The Court avoids any reflections on the importance of a possible demonstration of the existence of such a 'genuine link' on the access to social benefits in its judgment which was delivered on 15 September 2015.[55] It first confirms that the contested SGB II benefit is a social assistance benefit and not a benefit facilitating access to the labour market, revoking its earlier position in the *Vatsouras* and *Koupatantze* judgment definitively. According to the Court

50 Opinion of Advocate General Wathelet in Case C-67/14, *Alimanovic*, EU:C:2015:210, para. 86.
51 This category is also called first time jobseekers.
52 Based on Article 7(3)(c) Directive 2004/38. This happened in the case of Ms Alimanovic and her daughter in December 2011.
53 Opinion of Advocate General Wathelet in Case C-67/14, *Alimanovic*, EU:C:2015:210, para. 110.
54 Opinion of Advocate General Wathelet in Case C-67/14, *Alimanovic*, EU:C:2015:210, para. 111.
55 Case C-67/14, *Alimanovic*, EU:2015:597.

Ms Alimanovic and her daughter were not covered by the Directive as former workers anymore because on the basis of Article 7(3)(c) of the Directive Union citizens who have worked in a host Member State for less than a year retain their right of residence for at least six months after becoming unemployed, after which the Member State (as Germany did) can terminate the worker status. It is only for those six months that they are entitled to equal treatment with nationals of the host State.[56]

This does not mean, however, that Ms Alimanovic and her daughter can be expelled.[57] As long as they are job seekers and they continue to have a genuine chance of being engaged expulsion is not possible. But after six months of job seeking, they no longer retain the status of worker and go back to being first-time job seekers who are not entitled to social assistance.[58] Interestingly, according to the CJ Ms Alimanovic and her daughter can rely in that situation on a right of residence directly on the basis of Article 14(4)(b) Directive 2004/38.[59] The big difference between Ms Alimanovic and Ms Dano is that the first one has a residence right under Directive 2004/38 and the latter does not. The resemblance is that they both have no access to social assistance benefits.

It is interesting that, going beyond the referred questions in this case, the AG emphasised that, if it is demonstrated that the two children are duly continuing their education within an establishment in Germany (which it is for the German court to ascertain), they – like their mother – enjoy a right of residence in German territory under Article 10 Regulation 492/2011. The children of a national of one Member State who works or has worked in the host Member State and the parent who is their primary carer can claim a right of residence in the latter State owing to the sole fact that EU law confers on those children a right of access to education. Referring to the *Ibrahim*[60] and *Teixeira*[61] cases of the CJ, the AG recalls that that right of residence is not dependent on the conditions laid down in Directive 2004/38 and therefore there are no requirements of having sufficient resources and comprehensive sickness insurance.[62] In those circumstances, according to the AG, the exclusion from the SGB II benefit, is not applicable to the situation of Ms Alimanovic or to that of her two younger children, since this applies only to persons 'whose right of residence arises solely out of the search for employment and their family members'.[63] It should,

56 Case C-67/14, *Alimanovic*, EU:2015:597, para. 53.

57 Case C-67/14, *Alimanovic*, EU:2015:597, para. 54.

58 Case C-67/14, *Alimanovic*, EU:2015:597, para. 58.

59 Case C-67/14, *Alimanovic*, EU:2015:597, paras. 52–57.

60 Case C-310/08, *Ibrahim*, EU:C:2010:80.

61 Case C-480/08, *Teixeira*, EU:C:2010:83.

62 Case C-310/08, *Ibrahim*, EU:C:2010:80, paras. 56–59; and Case C-480/08, *Teixeira*, EU:C: 2010:83, para. 70.

63 But I doubt whether it would be as simple as that. In my view Ms Alimanovic would still be excluded in that case but now on the base of point 1 (and not point 2) of the second sentence of paragraph 7(1) SGB II, which excludes: 'foreign nationals who are not workers or self-

however, be noted that Ms Alimanovic derives her right of residence in this situation from Regulation 492/2011 and not from Directive 2004/38 and this right could end if all children reach the age of majority. The Court did not reflect on this alternative possibility in any way.

2.1. ORIGIN OF THE SUFFICIENT RESOURCES

Another important issue the Court of Justice had to deal with was the origin of the sufficient resources. Regarding this issue, the Court of Justice has made clear that these need not to be generated by the EU citizen himself or herself, but could be provided by someone else such as a family member. In the *Zhu and Chen* case a young minor (baby Catherine) got a right of residence in the UK because she had sufficient resources, provided by her parents.[64] According to the Court it was clear from the order for reference that Catherine had both sickness insurance and sufficient resources, provided by her mother, for her not to become a burden on the social assistance system of the host Member State.[65] The objection raised by the Irish and the United Kingdom governments that the condition concerning the availability of sufficient resources means that the person concerned must, in contrast to Catherine's case, possess those resources personally and may not use for that purpose those of an accompanying family member, such as Ms Chen, is unfounded.[66] According to the very terms of Article 1(1) of Directive 90/364[67] it is sufficient for the nationals of Member States to 'have' the necessary resources, and that provision lays down no requirement whatsoever as to their origin.[68] The Court argues that the correctness of that interpretation is reinforced by the fact that provisions laying down a fundamental principle such as that of the free movement of persons must be interpreted broadly.[69] An interpretation of the condition concerning the sufficiency of resources within the meaning of Directive 90/364, in the terms suggested by the Irish and the United Kingdom governments would add to that condition, as formulated in that Directive, a requirement as to the origin of the resources which, not being necessary for the attainment of the objective pursued, namely the protection of the public finances of the Member States, would constitute a disproportionate interference with

employed persons in the Federal Republic of Germany and do not enjoy the right of freedom of movement under Paragraph 2(3) of the Law on freedom of movement of Union citizens [(Freizügigkeitsgesetz/EU, "the FreizügG/EU")], and their family members, for the first three months of their residence'.

64 Case C-200/02, *Zhu and Chen*, EU:C:2004:639.

65 Case C-200/02, *Zhu and Chen*, EU:C:2004:639, para. 28.

66 Case C-200/02, *Zhu and Chen*, EU:C:2004:639, para. 29.

67 Directive 90/364, OJ ENG 1990, L180/26 is one of the predecessors of Directive 2004/38.

68 Case C-200/02, *Zhu and Chen*, EU:C:2004:639, para. 30.

69 Case C-200/02, *Zhu and Chen*, EU:C:2004:639, para. 31.

the exercise of the fundamental right of freedom of movement and of residence upheld by Article 18 EC (now Article 21 TFEU) according to the Court.[70]

Another important case in this respect is *Commission v Belgium* on the right of residence of a Portuguese woman who was living with a Belgian man who financially supported her. The Belgian authorities excluded this income of the Belgian partner in the absence of an agreement concluded before a notary and containing an assistance clause.[71]

The Court repeats its considerations of the *Zhu and Chen* case holding that according to the very terms of the first subparagraph of Article 1(1) of Directive 90/364, it is sufficient for the nationals of Member States to 'have' the necessary resources, and that provision lays down no requirement whatsoever as to their origin.[72] An interpretation of the condition concerning the sufficiency of resources within the meaning of Directive 90/364 to mean that the person concerned must himself have such resources and may not rely on the resources of a member of the family accompanying him would add to that condition, as formulated in that Directive, a requirement as to the origin of the resources which, not being necessary for the attainment of the objective pursued, namely the protection of the public finances of the Member States, would constitute a disproportionate interference with the exercise of the fundamental right of freedom of movement and of residence upheld by Article 18 EC (now Article 21 TFEU).[73] Therefore Belgium had failed to fulfil its obligations under Article 18 EC and Council Directive 90/364/EEC of 28 June 1990 on the right of residence when applying that Directive to nationals of a Member State who wish to rely on their rights under that Directive and on Article 18 EC.

Guild *et al.* raised in this context the question whether an economically inactive Union citizen may always be regarded as possessing sufficient resources if such resources are derived from his or her third-country national spouse.[74] According to them the approach to considering this question will depend upon whether it is claimed that sufficient resources exist prior to the move or whether it is argued that the citizen would possess sufficient resources only if the third-country national spouse were permitted to access the labour market of the host Member as contemplated by Article 23 Directive 2004/38, which authorises family members of Union citizens to engage in economic activity in the host Member State.

If prior to relocating a Union citizen can be shown that the family unit has sufficient resources, it is in their view immaterial whether such resources derive from the Union citizen or from another person, including a third-country

70 Case C-200/02, *Zhu and Chen*, EU:C:2004:639, para. 33.
71 Case C-408/03, *Commission v Belgium*, EU:C:2006:192.
72 Case C-408/03, *Commission v Belgium*, EU:C:2006:192, para. 40.
73 Case C-408/03, *Commission v Belgium*, EU:C:2006:192, para. 41.
74 E. Guild, S. Peers and J. Tomkin, *The EU Citizenship Directive. A Commentary* (Oxford: OUP, 2014), 129.

national family member. The situation is less clear-cut where an economically inactive Union citizen claims that he would have sufficient resources if the spouse were permitted to take up employment in the host Member State. On a strict interpretation, third-country nationals would only be able to derive a right to reside and work after the Union citizen has established his right of residence, which, in turn, is conditional on that citizen having met the conditions laid down in Article 7(1). On the other hand, could a teleological approach lead to an opposite conclusion. As the primary objective of Directive 2004/38 is to facilitate free movement and the sufficient resources requirement is a restriction designed to prevent excessive pressure being placed on the social assistance system of the host Member State, once a family unit is self-sufficient, this system is not burdened and therefore it should be immaterial whether the source derives from the Union citizen or the third-country national family member.

This problem was extensively dealt with by Advocate General Mengozzi in the *Alokpa* case.[75] This case concerned a Togolese national with French children (born in Luxembourg) and a dispute regarding a refusal to grant Ms Alokpa a right of residence and an order for her to leave Luxembourg. Ms Alokpa and her children were reliant on the Luxembourg State although she had been offered a job, which her lack of residence and work permit prevented her from commencing. Unlike in the *Zhu and Chen* case, Ms Alokpa did not possess sufficient resources for herself and her children so she had to rely on Luxembourg's social security system. AG Mengozzi considered that 'sufficient resources' for the purpose of Article 7(1)(b) of the Directive were capable of being satisfied by the definite prospect of future resources which would stem from the offer of a job of unlimited duration.[76] He suggested that the referring court should, in principle, examine the job offer with a view to determining whether the Union citizen children would have sufficient resources under the Directive should Ms Alokpa commence work. According to the AG it was clear from the order for reference that Ms Alokpa never intended to become a burden on the Luxembourg State and that she has been offered a job for an indefinite period in Luxembourg, subject to the sole condition that she obtained a residence permit and a work permit in Luxembourg.[77] Consideration must be given to the relevance of the job offer, and therefore to the possibility of taking into account resources which are not current but rather future or potential, for the purposes of satisfying the condition of 'sufficient resources' laid down in Article 7(1)(b) of Directive 2004/38.[78] Like the German government and the Commission, the AG considered that the condition of 'sufficient resources' is capable of being satisfied by the definite prospect of future resources which would stem from a job offer

---

75 Case C-86/12, *Alokpa*, EU:C:2013:645.

76 Opinion of Advocate General Mengozzi in Case C-86/12, *Alokpa*, EU:C:2013:197.

77 Opinion of Advocate General Mengozzi in Case C-86/12, *Alokpa*, EU:C:2013:197, para. 23.

78 Opinion of Advocate General Mengozzi in Case C-86/12, *Alokpa*, EU:C:2013:197, para. 24.

to which a Union citizen or a member of his family responded successfully in another Member State. A different interpretation would deprive the freedom of movement enjoyed by citizens of the Union of its practical effect, whereas the objective of Directive 2004/38 is precisely to strengthen the right to freedom of movement.[79]

The AG recalls that with regard to the amount of sufficient resources, Article 8(4) of Directive 2004/38 requires Member States to take into account the personal situation of the person concerned. Accordingly, when taking into account the specific situation of a person, the fact that he has been offered a job from which he will be able to derive income enabling him to satisfy the condition laid down in Article 7(1)(b) of Directive 2004/38 cannot be overlooked. Any interpretation to the contrary would lead to the individual situations of Union citizens and their family members being treated unfairly, thus rendering Article 8(4) of that Directive meaningless, according to the AG.[80]

In interpreting Article 7(1)(b) of the Directive, the Court, referring to the *Zhu and Chen* case, found indeed that to 'have' sufficient resources means that these resources are available to the Union citizens, regardless of its origin. But unlike AG Mengozzi, the Court did not consider whether the promise of future earnings meant sufficient resources for the Union citizen children to 'have', and instead left this as a question of fact for the referring court. If the conditions of Article 7(1) of the Directive were not satisfied, Article 21 TFEU would be interpreted as not precluding Luxembourg from refusing a right of residence to Ms Alokpa.[81]

A more explicit and detailed answer could have been given by the Court on this issue regarding preliminary questions asked by the High Court of Ireland in May 2014 in the *Singh and Others* case.[82] This case concerned three third-country nationals who got a right of residence in Ireland as spouse of an EU citizen and who wanted to retain this right after the EU citizen had left Ireland and a divorce had become official. The sufficient resources for the former right of residence of the EU citizen had been partly based on resources of the non-EU citizen spouse. According to the Irish Minister for Justice and Equality this is problematic because this interpretation of the concept of sufficient resources could lead to situations of abuse in which Union citizens could easily start working for a short period of time to create a right to work for their third-country national spouse and stop working themselves immediately afterwards. The most important part of this case is on the question whether the right of residence of the three foreign husbands in Ireland could be retained when the divorce took place after their EU

79 Opinion of Advocate General Mengozzi in Case C-86/12, *Alokpa*, EU:C:2013:197, para. 28.
80 Opinion of Advocate General Mengozzi in Case C-86/12, *Alokpa*, EU:C:2013:197, para. 29.
81 Case C-86/12, *Alokpa*, EU:C:2013:645, paras. 27–30.
82 Case C-218/14, *Singh and Others*, EU:C:2015:476.

wives had left the country, which right was denied by the CJ. But the High Court also asked the following two questions:

> 'Are the requirements of Article 7(1)(b) of Directive 2004/38/EC met where an EU citizen spouse claims to have sufficient resources within the meaning of Article 8(4) of the Directive partly on the basis of the resources of the non-EU citizen spouse? If the answer to the second question is "no", do persons such as the applicants have rights under EU law (apart from the Directive) to work in the host Member State in order to provide or contribute to "sufficient resources" for the purposes of Article 7 of the Directive?'

The Court answered in line with the *Zhu and Chen* judgment that Article 7(1)(b) of Directive 2004/38 must be interpreted as meaning that a Union citizen has sufficient resources for himself and his family members not to become a burden on the social assistance system of the host Member State during his period of residence even where those resources derive in part from those of his spouse who is a third-country national.[83] And therefore did not have to answer the third question.

3. THE CONDITION OF COMPREHENSIVE SICKNESS INSURANCE

Article 7(1)(b) imposes not only a requirement that economically inactive EU migrants have sufficient resources to avoid becoming a burden on social assistance, but also that they have comprehensive sickness insurance. So far, it seems that there has not been paid much attention to this condition, not at the level of the Member States, nor at European level. The first 1979 proposal of which became later Directive 2004/38 did not even require economically non-active EU citizens to have any sort of sickness insurance cover.[84] There is for instance also no mention made on the (lack of) fulfilment of this condition in both the *Brey* judgment and the *Dano* judgment. The only important information in the case-law of the CJ on this issue is provided in the *Baumbast* case,[85] in which the Court said that under the circumstances of that case the refusal to allow Mr Baumbast to exercise the right of residence which is conferred on him by Article 18(1) EC (now Article 21(1) TFEU) by virtue of the application of the

83 Case C-218/14, *Singh and Others*, EU:C:2015:476, para. 77.

84 Proposal for a Council Directive on a Right of Residence for Nationals of Member States in the Territory of another Member State, COM(1979)215 final of 26 July 1979. See M. Meduna *et. al.*, 'Institutional report', in U. Neergaard, C. Jacqueson and N. Holst-Christensen (eds.), *Union Citizenship: Development, Impact and Challenges, The XXVI FIDE Congress in Copenhagen* (Copenhagen: DJØF Publishing, 2014), 236.

85 Case C-413/99, *Baumbast*, EU:C:2002:493.

provisions of Directive 90/364 (one of the predecessors of Directive 2004/38) on the ground that his sickness insurance did not cover the emergency treatment given in the host Member State would amount to a disproportionate interference with the exercise of that right.[86] Important for this decision in my opinion was that Mr Baumbast fulfilled all other conditions, as emphasised by the Court in para 92:

> 'In respect of the application of the principle of proportionality to the facts of the Baumbast case, it must be recalled, first, that it has not been denied that Mr Baumbast has sufficient resources within the meaning of Directive 90/364; second, that he worked and therefore lawfully resided in the host Member State for several years, initially as an employed person and subsequently as a self-employed person; third, that during that period his family also resided in the host Member State and remained there even after his activities as an employed and self-employed person in that State came to an end; fourth, that neither Mr Baumbast nor the members of his family have become burdens on the public finances of the host Member State and, fifth, that both Mr Baumbast and his family have comprehensive sickness insurance in another Member State of the Union.'

In the 2009 guidelines[87] the Commission defined sickness insurance as any insurance cover, private or public, contracted in the host Member State or elsewhere, which would be acceptable in principle, as long as it provides comprehensive coverage and does not create a burden on the public finances of the host Member State. In protecting their public finances while assessing the comprehensiveness of sickness insurance cover, Member States must act in compliance with the limits imposed by Community law and in accordance with the principle of proportionality.[88] Pensioners fulfil the condition of comprehensive sickness insurance cover if they are entitled to health treatment on behalf of the Member State which pays their pension.[89] The European Health Insurance Card offers such comprehensive cover when the EU citizen concerned does not move the residence in the sense of Regulation (EEC) No. 1408/71 (now Regulation 883/2004) to the host Member State and has the intention to return, e.g. in case of studies or posting to another Member State.

Sickness insurance does not necessarily have to derive from the host Member State: it may be contracted in another Member State if cover is granted in the

86 Case C-413/99, *Baumbast*, EU:C:2002:493, para. 93.

87 COM (2009) 313 final, Communication from the Commission to the European Parliament and the Council on guidance for better transposition and application of Directive 2004/38/EC on the right of citizens of the Union and their family members to move and reside freely within the territory of the Member States, section 2.3.2.

88 Here the guidelines make a reference to the *Baumbast* case.

89 A reference is made to Articles 27, 28 and 28a of Regulation (EEC) No. 1408/71 on the application of social security schemes to employed persons, to self-employed persons and to the members of their families moving within the Community. As of 1 March 2010, Regulation (EC) No. 883/04 has replaced it but the same principles apply.

host Member State too. Differences between Member States arise from the fact that whilst some Member States have a national health service (e.g. Denmark, Finland, Ireland, Italy and the UK), others have a health insurance scheme (e.g. Belgium, Germany, Luxembourg, the Netherlands and Romania). If we have a closer look at the level of the Member States problems in the United Kingdom and in Sweden can be detected.

3.1. PROBLEMS IN THE UNITED KINGDOM

Anyone who is 'ordinarily resident' in the United Kingdom is entitled to use the public National Health System (NHS). But according to the UK authorities the NHS cannot be seen as comprehensive sickness insurance for economically inactive EU migrants.[90] For this category the UK authorities require a private health insurance. However, according to the Commission the UK has breached EU law by not considering entitlement to treatment by the NHS as sufficient to allow EU citizens who live but have no job in the UK to stay in the country for more than three months. The Commission has launched an infringement procedure in 2012 against the UK, requesting it to comply with EU rules by considering NHS cover as sufficient sickness insurance when assessing whether or not a non-active EU citizen is entitled to remain in the UK under the free movement rules. The UK is required to amend national rules and to bring UK law in line with EU law.[91] The Commission has not yet taken any decision whether or not to bring the matter before the Court of Justice. They are still analysing the possible impact of the *Brey* and *Dano* judgments on this issue.[92]

The UK Court of Appeal (CA) supports the view of the UK authorities and considered in July 2014 in *Ahmad v Secretary of State for the Home Department (SSHD)* that the requirement on an EEA national who is exercising a treaty right in the UK as a student to have comprehensive sickness insurance, cannot be met by having access to the NHS.[93] The UK Court used the argument that the public healthcare system of the host state could not be included because that would defeat the object of the Directive, namely relieving the state of the cost of providing healthcare in the first five years of the EEA national's presence in that state. According to the UK Court the conditions in Article 7(1) Directive 2004/38 must not be interpreted dynamically. Instead, in line with the CJ decision in *Brey*

90 See S. De Mars, 'Economically inactive EU migrants and the United Kingdom's National Health Service: unreasonable burdens without real links' (2014) 6 *EL Rev*, 770–789.

91 See http://europa.eu/rapid/press-release_IP-12-417_en.htm?locale=en (last accessed on 20 January 2016).

92 Information received from DG Justice on 12 February 2015.

93 *Ahmad v Secretary of State for the Home Department* [2014] EWCA Civ 988 (16 July 2014).

the conditions required strict and literal interpretation but remained subject to the general principles of EU law such as proportionality.[94]

Against this opinion of the UK Court of Appeal one could point out the fact that the part of Article 7 Directive 2004/38 which says 'not to become a burden on the social assistance system of the host Member State' only refers to the sufficient resources requirement and not to the comprehensive sickness insurance requirement. This indicates that even in a strict and literal interpretation the appeal to the NHS can not be regarded as an appeal to the social assistance system of the Member State.[95]

3.2. PROBLEMS IN SWEDEN

Different problems can be identified in Sweden. A 2014 publication by the Swedish National Board of Trade shows that getting the right health insurance is not always an easy task.[96] In Sweden a S1 form grants an EU citizen access to health care if he or she does not live in the country where he or she is insured. The person must request such a S1 form from the home country's social insurance agency (in Sweden, this is the Swedish Social Insurance Agency). According to Union law it is up to each Member State to organise its healthcare system and to decide when to grant a S1 form. But the differences between Member States can mean that one Member State requests a S1 form from the home country when the home country will not grant one. The publication gives the example of a Hungarian pensioner who wanted to move to Sweden, joining her son there. In order to exercise her right of residence and to be entered into the Swedish population registry, she needed a S1 form from Hungary. But in order to obtain a S1 form from Hungary, she had to prove that Swedish authorities considered her a resident of Sweden. And again, Swedish authorities required a S1 from Hungary before they would allow her to reside in Sweden. The problem was not resolved, and the pensioner could not be entered into the Swedish population registry.

The alternative to a S1 form is to purchase a private insurance coverage. But this can lead to problems as well. In evaluating private insurance policies, the Swedish Tax Agency requires that several conditions be met. The policy must be personal, and must not have a monetary ceiling for necessary health care. Private

94 https://asadakhan.wordpress.com/2014/07/21/arden-lj-on-csic-and-permanent-residence/ (last accessed on 20 January 2016).

95 See F. Van Overmeiren, E. Eichenhofer and H. Verschueren, 'Social Security Coverage of Non-Active Persons Moving to Another Member State', in E. Guild, C. Gortazar Rotaeche and D. Kostakopoulou (eds.), *The Reconceptualization of European Union Citizenship* (Leiden-Boston: Nijhoff, 2014), 254.

96 National Board of Trade, *Moving to Sweden; Obstacles to the Free Movement of Citizens* (Stockholm, 2014), 7–8. See: www.kommers.se/Documents/dokumentarkiv/publikationer/2014/Moving-to-Sweden_webb.pdf (last accessed on 20 January 2016).

insurance policies may contain no disclaimers that deny coverage for certain illnesses, and they must cover health care for injuries resulting from sports, risky activities, and so on. The National Board of Trade contacted about twenty insurance companies to learn whether they sell insurance policies that comply with these criteria. None of them did. A person without a S1 form therefore has difficulty acquiring the comprehensive sickness insurance that is required by the Swedish Tax Agency. In sum, EU citizens who plan to work in Sweden for less than one year and those who are non-workers have difficulty gaining access to health care in Sweden because they encounter obstacles involving the population registry. The report gives another example of two German EU citizens, who had difficulty obtaining a S1 form from Germany and therefore bought a private insurance that was equivalent to the German state insurance. However, because the policy included disclaimers that denied coverage of care for self-inflicted injuries and addiction, this insurance was not accepted by the Swedish Tax Agency. These EU citizens were therefore denied inclusion in the population registry.[97]

4. CONCLUSION

This chapter focused on the position of inactive EU citizens who need sufficient resources (and comprehensive sickness insurance) to have a right to reside under Article 7(1)(b) Directive 2004/38. The question when an inactive citizen has sufficient resources is not an easy one to answer. The history of the negotiations regarding the concept of 'sufficient resources' shows that there is an ambivalence in prohibiting a fixed amount of money on one side and the indication of a threshold at social assistance benefit level on the other side. This ambivalence is reflected in the practice of various Member States as well. The approaches regarding the definition of sufficient resources vary between the various Member States. It appears that there is not much case-law available on the issue of sufficient resources and its consequences at the level of the Member States. From the scarce Dutch case-law it can be concluded that the Dutch immigration authorities tend to apply a fixed amount at the level of a social assistance benefit as a condition of sufficient resources, while the courts do take into account the personal situation of the EU citizen and tend to accept a lower amount of money to fulfil the condition of sufficient resources. It should be noted that in all the presented court cases neither the EU citizen nor the family member seem to have made an application for a social assistance benefit.

When we have a look at the case-law of the CJ regarding the notion of sufficient resources two important issues can be distinguished. The first issue

97 National Board of Trade, *Moving to Sweden; Obstacles to the Free Movement of Citizens* (Stockholm, 2014), 8.

concerns the level of resources and the relation to social assistance benefits, the other issue concerns the origin of the resources. Regarding the origin of the resources it is clear from the case-law of the CJ that to 'have' sufficient resources means that these resources are available to the Union citizens, regardless of its origin. They can be derived from another person, including a third national family member. But it is still disputed whether the prospect of future earnings can mean that the condition of sufficient resources is fulfilled as well. Another question to be solved concerns the interpretation of the concept of sufficient resources in situations in which Union citizens start working only for a short period of time to create a right to reside and work for their third-country national spouse and stop working themselves immediately afterwards.

Article 7(1)(b) imposes not only a requirement that economically inactive EU migrants have sufficient resources, but also that they have comprehensive sickness insurance. So far, the impression is given that there has not been paid much attention to this second condition, not at the level of the Member States, nor at European level. Only problems in the UK and in Sweden could be detected. According to the UK authorities the public National Health System cannot be seen as comprehensive sickness insurance for economically inactive EU migrants. For this category the UK authorities require a private health insurance. The European Commission has a different view on this issue and has started in 2012 an infringement procedure against the UK. In Sweden EU citizens who are non-workers have difficulty gaining access to health care because they encounter obstacles involving the population registry. Administrative differences between Member States result in not providing the right forms, which leads to insurance problems. Non recognition of private insurances from other Member States is another problem.

Most interesting at the moment is the challenge for the Court to find a balance between the requirement of fulfilling the condition of sufficient resources and the possibility to apply for social assistance. The shift noted in the case-law – from asking for social assistance being an indication of lack of resources to becoming a certainty that no longer requires an individualised examination of the case and decision – raises some fundamental questions about the scope of EU citizenship and seems to go against the Court's well established way of interpreting EU citizenship rights that emphasis proportionality and the need for individual assessment. The Court's approach in *Dano* and *Alimanovic* will undoubtedly have an impact upon how fundamental EU citizenship is as a status and whom it can actually capture. An interpretation where economically non-active EU citizens must always have resources sufficient not to qualify for any social assistance benefit may lead to an effective exclusion of most economically non-active EU citizens by providing for a social benefit with a very high resource threshold in national laws.

CHAPTER 5
FREE MOVEMENT OF PERSONS AND EUROPEAN SOLIDARITY
A Melancholic Eulogy

Stefano GIUBBONI*

'But people loved darkness instead of light.'
John, III, 19

1. PROLOGUE

For almost fifteen years, the epic of the constitutionalisation of the European citizenship was based on the famous promise of 'a certain degree of financial solidarity'[1] among the nationals of different Member States. The idea that a Union citizen could have access to a new 'status of social integration',[2] directly defined at the supranational level starting from a fundamental freedom of movement, actually seemed to be able to open up a new constitutional dimension to European citizenship, finally able to transcend the nation States' particular allegiances in order to revive and expand the universal and 'omni-inclusive'[3] promise of a society of free and equal individuals based on the jus-naturalistic foundations of modern citizenship.

---

* This article draws its inspiration from the author's participation in different conferences and seminars in 2015, all related to the crisis of European solidarity and respectively held in Antwerp on 7–8 May (*Where do I belong? EU law and the adjudication on the link between individuals and Member States*), Madrid on 11–12 June (*Solidarity in hard times. Solidarity and the European social model in times of economic crisis*) and York on 4–5 September (*The impact of the financial-economic crisis on the guarantee of social welfare rights*). I take the opportunity to publicly express my gratitude to all participants in such events for their comments and suggestions; of course, the usual disclaimer applies.

1 Case C-184/99, *Grzelczyk*, EU:C:2001:458, para. 44.

2 L. AZOULAI, 'La citoyenneté européenne, un statut d'intégration sociale', in *Chemins d'Europe. Mélanges en l'honneur de Jean Paul Jacqué* (Paris: Dalloz, 2010), 1.

3 C. MARGIOTTA, *Cittadinanza europea. Istruzioni per l'uso* (Rome-Bari: Laterza, 2010), 7.

Such a process of constitutionalisation of the weak provisions on citizenship introduced by the Maastricht Treaty[4] has been carried out by the Court of Justice along two convergent trajectories, beginning with the path-breaking case of *Martínez Sala*.[5]

Along the first trajectory a new universal status for transnational access to social rights on an equal footing with the nationals of the host country was progressively attached to the freedom of the (economically inactive) European citizen to move to and establish residence in another Member State. As a result of this, the main feature of this first jurisprudential movement can be identified in the fact that the Court of Justice has progressively extended those same powerful mechanisms of de-nationalisation (and partly of de-territorialisation) of social citizenship rights to every citizen of the Union *qua talis*.

These mechanisms had originally been reserved by the Treaty of Rome to economically active persons, and to workers in particular, as a fundamental means for the functional integration of the common market.[6] The fragility of this first ideational pillar of such a sophisticated endeavour as making European citizenship the fundamental status of the individual in the European Union's constitutional order is probably due to the intrinsic contradiction pervading the conceptual categories used by the Court for such an ambitious purpose. The attempt to overcome the functionalistic logic and the mercantile *ratio* historically underpinning the guarantee of social security rights to migrant workers[7] actually took place through a sort of radicalisation and generalisation of those same conceptual premises under the new universalistic and unifying rhetoric of European citizenship. However, the pseudo-universal allure of transnational social solidarity, which is expected to result from European citizenship, could not (and cannot) for this very same reason sever the original connection with the market citizen coinage,[8] which overwhelmingly re-emerged (and re-surfaced) during the hard times of EU crisis. The 'resilience' of such a model[9] – and the reappearance of its intrinsic limits – is therefore actually due to the contradictions underlying the attempt to build the status of social integration

4 'Little more than a cynical exercise in public relations on the part of the High Contracting Parties', as was famously said by J.H.H. Weiler, *The Selling of Europe: The Discourse of European Citizenship in the IGC 1996*, Harvard Law School, Jean Monnet Working Paper Series, 1996, Issue 3, 1.

5 Case C-85/96, *Martínez Sala,* EU:C:1998:217.

6 S. Giubboni, 'European Citizenship and Social Rights in Times of Crisis' (2014) 15 *German Law Journal, Special Issue – EU Citizenship: Twenty Years On*, 935 *et seq.*

7 G.F. Mancini, 'The Free Movement of Workers in the Case Law of the European Court of Justice', in G.F. Mancini, *Democracy and Constitutionalism in the European Union* (Oxford-Portland, Oregon: Hart Publishing, 2000), 123.

8 *Ex plurimis* M. Everson, 'The Legacy of the Market Citizen', in J. Shaw and G. More (eds.), *New Legal Dynamics of European Union* (Oxford: Clarendon Press, 1995), 73 *et seq.*

9 N. Nic Shuibhne, 'The Resilience of EU Market Citizenship' (2010) 47 *CML Rev*, 1605.

of (economically inactive) European citizens over an individual freedom of movement built in the image and likeness of the transnational economic actor.[10]

The other trajectory for constitutionalisation is even more ambitious. In *Zambrano*,[11] the Court seemed eager even to overcome the transnational perspective, with the aim of 'disconnecting citizenship from mobility'.[12] The integration loop potentially envisioned by such a move would have in fact brought the constitutional trajectory of European citizenship to a sort of federal completion, in so far as the Union would no longer be seen simply as 'the sum of the physical territories of the Member States but as a new common space, a space of distribution of rights and common value'.[13]

But this second trajectory, being based on even more fragile assumptions, was soon interrupted, even before the new territories of the common space of distribution of rights and political values could be explored by their disoriented holders. The great crisis has rather caused the Union to precipitate in a new *terra incognita*, which is exactly the opposite of the land promised by the Maastricht Treaty. Instead of welcoming the 'magnificent and progressive destinies'[14] of an ever-closer union between the peoples of Europe, tightened by the political project of common citizenship and currency, the great crisis has created deep rifts and reciprocal distrust between the Member States, threatening to disintegrate the whole project, beginning above all with the recurring risk of fracture of the Eurozone.

This chapter is meant to give a critical overview of the rapid rise and equally sudden decline of the normative ideal of the European citizenship as a status of transnational social integration. The watershed can be quite easily identified with the great changes in the course of European integration since the mid-2000s. On the one hand the rapid enlargement of the EU in Eastern Europe, and on the other the great political-financial crisis in the Eurozone, have totally altered the political economy of European integration and weakened the optimistic and neo-illuminist assumptions underpinning that normative ideal in a scarcely reversible way. The Court's case-law – especially with the much-discussed *Brey*[15]

10 A. Somek, Solidarity Decomposed: Being and Time in European Citizenship (2007) *EL Rev* 187; A. Somek, 'From Workers to Migrants, from Distributive Justice to Inclusion: Exploring the Changing Social Democratic Imagination' (2012) 18 *ELJ*, 711; A.J. Menéndez, 'European Citizenship after Martínez Sala and Baumbast: Has European Law Become More Human but Less Social?', in M. Poiares Maduro and L. Azoulai (eds.), *The Past and Future of EU Law. The Classics of EU Law Revisited on the 50th Anniversary of the Rome Treaty* (Oxford-Portland, Oregon: Hart Publishing, 2010), 363.

11 Case C-34/09, *Ruiz Zambrano*, EU:C:2011:124.

12 C. Margiotta, *Cittadinanza europea. Istruzioni per l'uso* (Rome-Bari: Laterza, 2010), 150.

13 L. Azoulai, 'Euro-Bonds. The Ruiz Zambrano Judgment or the Real Invention of Union Citizenship' (2011) 3 *Perspectives on Federalism* 2, 34.

14 For the benefit of the non-Italian reader, I would like to recall that this is the verse of one of Giacomo Leopardi's most famous poems, *La ginestra*, composed in 1836. The citation from John's Gospel, appearing in exergue, is also taken from Leopardi's poetry.

15 Case C-140/12, *Brey*, EU:C:2013:565.

and *Dano*[16] judgments – shows a clear retreat, or maybe a retrenchment, in the discourse on EU citizenship as a source of transnational social solidarity, with an indisputable step back to a strict functional interpretation of the Treaty provisions in their relationship with secondary law (Directive 2004/38/EC and Regulation 883/2004).

Nonetheless, it is always hazardous and surely premature at this stage to predict possible future directions. At least in theory – in a hypothetical European reform agenda – alternative paths are still available, and even the effective meaning of *Brey* and *Dano* is sufficiently ambiguous to leave alternative interpretative pathways open. But optimism regarding the democratic and socially-inclusive future of European citizenship is hardly compatible with the political dynamics currently dominant in the Union. It is no coincidence that the same proposals announced by the Commission with the so-called Labour Mobility Package seem broadly consistent with the overall regressive path that the Union has been following since a crisis which called into question, above all, its identity and *finalité*.

2. TRANSNATIONAL SOLIDARITY IN ITS ASCENDING PHASE

'During the golden era of the Welfare State a concrete freedom of movement was inconceivable without the guarantee of the right to social security'.[17] This is the reason why workers' free movement rights and, even before, the social security coordination system, introduced in 1958, could be considered the beginning of European citizenship.[18]

The Court of Justice's case-law played a decisive role in the founding phase of the constitutionalisation of the Community legal order, especially in relation to the freedom of movement and social rights of migrant workers.[19] During the heroic phase of the origins, during which the constitutional foundations for the common market were established, the freedom of movement of workers was intended to be broader than what the mere functional logic of market integration would suggest.[20]

16 Case C-333/13, *Dano*, EU:C:2014:2358.

17 C. Margiotta, *Cittadinanza europea. Istruzioni per l'uso* (Rome-Bari: Laterza, 2010), 55.

18 L. Levi Sandri, 'La sicurezza sociale dei lavoratori migranti nell'ambito della Comunità economica europea', in L. Riva Sanseverino and G. Mazzoni (eds.), *Nuovo trattato di diritto del lavoro*, III (Padova: Cedam, 1971), 941. See S. Giubboni, 'L'azione comunitaria in materia di sicurezza sociale in prospettiva storica. Omaggio a Lionello Levi Sandri', in A. Varsori and L. Mechi (eds.), *Lionello Levi Sandri e la politica sociale europea* (Milan: Franco Angeli, 2008), 175 *et seq.*

19 J.H.H. Weiler, 'The Transformation of Europe' (1991) 100(8) *Yale Law Journal*, 2403 *et seq.*

20 E. Spaventa, *Free Movement of Persons in the European Union. Barriers to Movement in their Constitutional Context* (Alphen aan den Rijn: Kluwer Law International, 2007), 2 *et seq.*

It should not be forgotten that the Court has in fact accepted an extremely broad definition of worker, as far as it encompasses all the activities, having any effectiveness and a minimum of economic consistency, that are performed under the direction of a different person in return for remuneration. The Court has also allowed the holders of such a fundamental freedom of movement, and their family members, to have access to the whole panoply of social rights guaranteed to the nationals of the host Member State under full equal treatment. As for the first aspect, the Court was also able to extend the guarantee of equal treatment in the host Member State – in accordance with the current Article 45 of the TFEU – to workers with employment contracts that are different from the standard model of a permanent full-time job, already undermined during the early 1980s by the gradual spread of atypical work relations. As for the second aspect, the Court assigned an important integrative function to the guarantee of equal treatment, generally extended to social advantages by Article 7 of Regulation 1612/68 even in the domain of social assistance and welfare rights, thus opening up the inner circles of national solidarity systems to migrant workers and their families.[21]

In this case-law, 'social integration into the host society is seen by the ECJ as an instrument for promoting participation within the EU internal market and within its economic objective of free movement of factors of production, even when their productivity may be rather low. The rationale behind this case-law has more to do with the internal market than with combating of social exclusion, even if this actually contributes to the letter'.[22] The model of integration endorsed by the Court is certainly based on the idea that the migrant worker (and his/her family members) should be included, from the beginning and without exceptions, in the social protection system of the host Member State, in its entirety, as they contribute to the well-being of the society that is hosting them through their (although reduced) economic activity.[23]

One outcome of social integration in the country of election – extended to all persons whose contribution to the internal market is actually only potential or at the very best only indirect – has thus been already firmly secured by the Court's historical case-law on the freedom of movement of workers and their families. If read in light of this *acquis*, it can be said that the judgments through which the Court has also extended the principle of equal treatment in the access

21 M. Ferrera, *The Boundaries of Welfare. European Integration and the New Spatial Politics of Social Protection* (Oxford: OUP 2005), 53 *et seq.*

22 H. Verschueren, 'Union Law and the Fight against Poverty: Which Legal Instruments?', in B. Cantillon, H. Verschueren and P. Ploscar (eds.), *Social Inclusion and Social Protection in the EU: Interaction between Law and Policy* (Cambridge-Antwerp-Portland: Intersentia, 2012), 217.

23 M. Dougan and E. Spaventa, 'Wish You Weren't Here ... New Models of Social Solidarity in the European Union', in M. Dougan and E. Spaventa (eds.), *Social Welfare and EU Law* (Oxford-Portland, Oregon: Hart Publishing, 2005), 181.

to social and welfare rights acknowledged by the host country to economically inactive European citizens – from the leading case *Martínez Sala* to *Zambrano* – have done nothing but generalise a status of social integration already widely acquired, although in a more limited way.

This case-law was supposed to have the merit of universalising the logic of social integration originally anchored to the functioning of the internal market, as free movers not carrying out an activity of economic nature were also granted equal protection status based on European citizenship. The innovative feature of this case-law was to be found in the universalistic projection of the model of transnational social solidarity, already foreshadowed by the Treaty of Rome in favour of economic migrants. Therefore, some have recognised a change of the very normative paradigm of European social solidarity: if access to the social protection systems of Member States was previously tied to the internal market's full effectiveness, according to such case-law, widely codified by Directive 2004/38, it has now become an autonomous constitutive element of Union citizenship, seen as a fundamental status of social integration totally unrelated to the mercantile *ratio* and the original idea of *homo oeconomicus*. On this view, a constitutional citizenship status of transnational value was thus created,[24] which – overcoming the old category-based model of market justice and occupational solidarity – underpins a general claim for social integration within the host Member State, not dissimilar to what occurs in federal-type polities.

But the fragility of this conceptual construction has been brutally unmasked by the great EU crisis. Such an idea of compassionate transnational solidarity rested in fact on a huge misunderstanding,[25] the hypocrisy of which has been mercilessly revealed by the drama of the European crisis. The great crisis has quite inevitably dissolved the ability of the core northern European Member States to host nationals of other Member States in need in their (still relatively) generous welfare systems: as social chauvinism resurfaced in the face of the well-cultivated *spectre* of 'benefit tourism', the swift political reaction everywhere has only been to close the porous borders of the so-called transnational solidarity.

Hypocrisy indeed has its shortcomings: in our case, such limits are all included in a post-modern model of abstract solidarity, which – in so far as it relies not on a common welfare and fiscal system but on the ability of some Member States to host migrants in social need – by definition cannot provide economically inactive European citizens with either unconditional freedom of residence or equal access to the host country's system of social protection, at least until they acquire long-term resident status under Article 16 Directive

24 L. Azoulai, La citoyenneté européenne, un statut d'intégration sociale', in *Chemins d'Europe. Mélanges en l'honneur de Jean Paul Jacqué* (Paris: Dalloz, 2010), 8.

25 C. Barnard, 'EU Citizenship and the Principle of Solidarity', in M. Dougan and E. Spaventa (eds.), *Social Welfare and EU Law* (Oxford: Hart Publishing, 2005), 157 *et seq.*

2004/38/EC. In fact, the right to take up residence in another Member State for a period exceeding three months remains conditional on the reverse means test of having comprehensive health insurance coverage as well as sufficient resources to prevent the economically inactive citizen from becoming a burden on that State's social assistance system (Article 7 of Directive 2004/38/EC). The unfortunate accident of becoming such an unreasonable burden on the host country's Welfare State system gives the national authorities the power to expel the unwelcome parasitic EU citizen, even without rude automatism and in compliance with the principle of proportionality (Article 14(3)). Moreover, transnational access to a Member State's social solidarity system under the requirement of equal treatment with that State's nationals follows in any case an incremental criterion, since the inactive Union citizen must show proof of a sufficient degree of integration into the society of the host country.

Such limits have a specific *ratio*, which has gone back to showing all its selective duress and disciplining power with the great crisis.[26] The very roots of the Eurozone crisis lie in the total lack of any real European solidarity, and it is not by accident that the most prominent feature of the new EU crisis management law is that authentic tribute to de-solidarisation unpopularly known as Fiscal Compact.[27] As there is no form of Europeanisation or sharing of national social protection systems, each Member State may legitimately require that access to its welfare system depend on a given degree of social integration already legitimately acquired by the European citizen.

The exclusively transnational dimension of social solidarity connected to European citizenship necessarily deals with this underlying tension,[28] which inevitably re-emerges anytime a freedom of movement not functional to the needs of the market ends up impinges on the finances of the welfare state.[29] If in times of economic growth this tension can easily be disguised by a vaguely cosmopolitan and post-modern rhetoric of transnational solidarity that is more or less equally distributed among the Member States,[30] in times of crisis – and when the new highly asymmetrical Eurozone economic governance rules draw a non-negotiable line between the self-proclaimed financial virtues of the northern countries and the irresponsibility of the southern ones, dismantling

---

26 Almost prophetic were the analysis dedicated to German Ordo-liberalism by M. Foucault, *Nascita della biopolitica. Corso al Collège de France (1978–1979)*, Italian edition under the supervision of F. Ewald (Milan: Feltrinelli, 2005), especially at 113 *et seq.*

27 A. Supiot, 'Introduction', in A. Supiot (ed.), *La Solidarité. Enquête sur un principe juridique* (Paris: Odile Jacob, 2015), 8 *et seq.* and S. Rodotà, *Solidarietà. Un'utopia necessaria* (Rome-Bari: Laterza, 2014), 126 *et seq.*

28 S. Giubboni, 'Free Movement of Persons and European Solidarity' (2007) 13 *ELJ*, 360.

29 See also F. De Witte, 'Transnational Solidarity and the Mediation of Conflicts of Justice in Europe' (2012) 18 *ELJ*, 694.

30 R. Bellamy, *The Liberty of Post-Moderns? Market and Civic Freedom within the EU*, London School of Economics and Political Science, LEQS Paper No. 01/2009.

any resemblance of isonomy within the Union[31] – such a rhetoric reveals its illusory and dangerous fragility.

In essence, this is the lesson learned from *Brey* and *Dano*.

3. *BREY* AND *DANO*

It is worth remembering that thanks to one of the most acrobatic[32] passages already present in the *Martínez Sala* ruling, the Court of Justice had come to infer that economically inactive European citizens fall within the scope *ratione materiae* of Article 18 of the TFEU merely by exercising their freedom of movement, even outside the conditions defined by Article 7(1)(b) Directive 2004/38/EC. That very fact could indeed mean that the mobile EU citizen is covered by the principle of equal treatment even in the case of full access to non-contributory social benefits in the host Member State. In *Martínez Sala*, as well as in other later cases, the residence permit held by an economically inactive European citizen was actually granted not on the basis of EU law but according to national law.[33] Nevertheless, the effective exercise of the freedom of movement and subsequent residency by Mrs Martínez Sala was sufficient to mean that she fell within the scope of the principle of equal treatment, irrespective of her nationality.[34]

However, that certainly daring argumentative passage appeared to be in line with the overall political meaning of the Court's interpretative efforts at that time, where it openly took – with both that ground-breaking judgment and with other paradigmatic rulings of the same period[35] – a bold view of constitutionalisation of the freedom of movement attributed to the European citizen by the Maastricht Treaty.[36] On such a view, the conditions or limits imposed by secondary law on the freedom of movement of the (economically

---

31 On the importance of isonomy in the Aristotle's philosophy of justice classically see C. Perelman, *Justice et Raison* (Brussels: Presses Universitaires de Bruxelles, 1963), 9 *et seq.*, and A. Giuliani, *Giustizia ed ordine economico* (Milan: Giuffrè, 1997), 3 *et seq.*

32 See in particular the sharp criticism by K. Hailbronner, 'Union Citizenship and Access to Social Benefits' (2005) 42 *CML Rev*, 1245 *et seq.*

33 H. Verschueren, 'EU Free Movement and Member States' Solidarity Systems: Searching for a Balance', in E. Guild and P. Minderhoud (eds.), *The First Decade of EU Migration and Asylum Law* (Leiden-Boston: Martinus Nijhoff Publishers, 2012), 62.

34 A.P. Van Der Mei, 'EU Law and Education: Promotion of Student Mobility versus Protection of Education Systems', in M. Dougan and E. Spaventa, *Social Welfare and EU Law* (Oxford: Hart Publishing, 2005), 225–226.

35 See especially the judgment of 17 September 2002 in the Case C-413/99, *Baumbast*, EU:C:2002:493, in which, for the first time, the Court explicitly states the direct effect of the fundamental right to reside in the territory of another Member State granted to the European citizen by Article 21 of the TFEU.

36 K. Lenaerts, 'European Union Citizenship, National Welfare Systems and Social Solidarity' (2011) 18 *Jurisprudencija/Jurisprudence* 2, 397 *et seq.*

inactive) EU citizen must be – coherently – very restrictively considered, while the maximum *effet utile* must be accorded to the rules of the Treaty in guaranteeing equal treatment in all relevant situations in order to effectively exercise that right *magis ut valeat*.[37]

As observed by Michael Dougan, at least since the *Förster*[38] judgment of 2008 the Court of Justice's constitutional narrative has gradually undergone some reshaping with an undeclared 'backtrack from the technique of indirect judicial review previously cultivated by its case law on Union citizenship'.[39] Nonetheless, in its essence this constitutional path was not completely abandoned by the Court, at least until *Brey*. The *Brey* judgment marks in our opinion the first essential separation from the expansive logic of Union citizenship as a fundamental status of Member State nationals, since it marks a paradigmatic retreat to a sort of interpretative legalistic minimalism, according to which secondary law rules strictly determine the applicative limits of the Treaty, and not conversely.

Despite its irresistible ambiguity,[40] *Brey* nonetheless apparently does not yet imply a significant retreat from the old judicial course concerning a certain degree of social solidarity 'among strangers'. In that judgment, in fact, the Court confirms that EU law – requiring a certain degree of transnational solidarity – precludes considering that the mere fact that an economically inactive citizen of a Member State applies for social assistance is sufficient to prove that the s/he has become an unreasonable burden on the welfare system of the host country, therefore depriving her/him of the right to reside in that country. The Court also states that the competent national authorities are entrusted with the task, and the duty, to carry out a careful assessment of the peculiar characteristics of each individual situation according to the principle of proportionality, without there being any automatic consequence attributable to the request of enjoyment of welfare benefits by the citizen of another Member State.

However, at the same time the *Brey* judgment prepares the ground soon after explored by *Dano* for returning to a strict functional interpretation – and a true de-constitutionalisation – of the freedom of movement and residence of the (economically inactive) EU citizen, in two important ways.

On the one hand, the judgment anticipates the focal point of the argumentative line in *Dano* on the relationship between Directive 2004/38/EC and Regulation 883/2004, essentially attributing an improper hierarchical

37 S. Giubboni, *Diritti e solidarietà in Europa* (Bologna: Il Mulino, 2012), 186 *et seq.*

38 Case C-158/07, *Förster*, EU:C:2008:630.

39 M. Dougan, 'The Bubble that Bursts: Exploring the Legitimacy of the Case Law on the Free Movement of Union Citizens', in M. Adams, H. de Waele, J. Meeusen and G. Straetmans (eds.), *Judging Europe's Judges. The Legitimacy of the Case Law of the European Court of Justice* (Oxford-Portland, Oregon, Hart Publishing, 2013), 141.

40 H. Verschueren, 'Free Movement and Benefit Tourism: The Unreasonable Burden of Brey' (2014) 16 *EJML*, 147 *et seq.*

dominance of the former over the latter. As stated in *Brey*, and then repeated in *Dano*, the main issue is whether recourse to social assistance, and a request by an economically inactive citizen who has exercised his/her freedom of movement for a special non-contributory benefit according to Regulation 883/2004, could imply that the same European citizen risks losing the right to reside in the host country, as provided for by Directive 2004/38/EC under the conditions defined by Article 7. The Court's response is exactly that, although through the filter of the proportionality test, such a request for social assistance may actually endanger the status of legal residence under the Directive, due to the loss of the condition of economic self-sufficiency imposed by the latter in order to safeguard the financial stability of the welfare systems of the host Member States.

On the other hand, among the possible configurations of the assessment of the alleged existence of an unreasonable burden on the public finances of a Member State, *Brey* accepts the most rigorous version, effectively defined by Daniel Thym as a 'systemic' type of evaluation as opposed to an 'individual' one.[41] As elusive as it may be, the systemic type of assessment in fact tends to privilege the importance of the overall global implications that may result on national public finances by the effective or potential increasing mobility of economically inactive Union citizens in need, therefore strengthening the protection of Member States' purses against – real or only imaginary – 'benefit tourism'.

Following the pathway opened by *Brey*, in *Dano* the Court of Justice takes the decisive step to overturn the constitutional dynamic which, from *Martínez Sala* on, has essentially promoted economically inactive citizens' access to the welfare systems of the host countries basically under the conditions of equal treatment with the host Member State's nationals. Only the fulfilment of the conditions of economic self-sufficiency (and of comprehensive health insurance coverage) imposed by Article 7(1)(b) Directive 2004/38/EC grants a European economically inactive citizen the right to reside in the host Member State and therefore to benefit from equal treatment in access to benefits in the territory of the latter. Only a prior condition of legal residence under the requirements strictly set out by Article 7 of the Directive allows the economically inactive citizen (who must also prove a sufficient degree of integration in the society of the host country) to access the welfare system of the latter, without putting into jeopardy the right of that citizen to reside in that State. Article 24(1) Directive 2004/38, read in conjunction with Articles 4 and 70 of Regulation 883/2004, therefore does not prohibit Member States from excluding economically inactive European citizens from the enjoyment of a special non-contributory benefit provided to their nationals if those Union citizens do not enjoy the right to legally reside under Article 7 of the Directive.

---

41 D. Thym, 'The Elusive Limits of Solidarity: Residence Rights of and Social Benefits for Economically Inactive Union Citizens' (2015) 52 *CML Rev*, 28–29.

This is in fact a spectacular retreat from the 'magnificent and progressive destinies' of transnational solidarity towards the nationals of other Member States that the Court performs with sublime ease in name of the new European *Realpolitik*, which evidently urges for further reassurances to the hegemonic countries of northern Europe, both continental and insular.[42] This new case-law reintroduces a sharp line of demarcation in the European *status civitatis*, returning to a strict mercantile logic or, rather, to a new census model of citizenship. 'Two citizenships'[43] in fact re-emerge, characterised by totally different levels of protection:[44] first-class citizenship is reserved to persons who are active in the internal market (as workers, providers or merely as individuals receiving services in return for remuneration) and to those who, although not economically active, can nonetheless prove their economic self-sufficiency; second-class citizenship – essentially devoid of any transnational protective status – is for the indigents. The latter are in fact trapped in a typical Catch-22 situation,[45] since claiming social assistance in the host Member State almost automatically implies that they do not satisfy the requirements of Directive 2004/38/EC in order to legally reside for a period exceeding three months.

From a technical point of view, the keystone of what, in hindsight, seems to be the restoration of the system prior to the Maastricht Treaty, needs to be identified once again in the re-construction of the relationship between Directive 2004/38/EC and Regulation 883/2004. In relation to this, *Dano* is firmly in the wake of *Brey*.

As Rob Cornelissen and Herwig Verschueren have shown,[46] the interpretation adopted by the Court in fact overturns the terms of the political compromise behind the contextual adoption of the Regulation and the Directive in 2004. This compromise reaffirmed the political balance already achieved in 1992,[47] with the introduction of a special system of coordination for non-contributory cash benefits, characterised by the express and exceptional

---

42 The influence of the bold political position expressed by the governments of Austria, Germany, the Netherlands and the United Kingdom in the joint letter addressed by the competent ministers of those countries to the presidency of the Union in April of 2013 is evidently perceivable. The main theme put abruptly on the political table was the limitation of the freedom of movement only to economically inactive citizens meeting the legal requirements set by Directive 2004/38/EC.

43 J.-M. Belorgey, 'La protection sociale dans une union de citoyens' (1998) *Droit social*, 160 *et seq*.

44 Cf. H. Verschueren, 'Free Movement of EU Citizens: Including the Poor?' (2015) 12 *MJ*, 1.

45 Cf. the contribution of P. Minderhoud in this volume.

46 R. Cornelissen, 'EU Regulations on the Coordination of Social Security Systems and Special Non-Contributory Benefits: A Source of Never-Ending Controversy', in E. Guild, S. Carrera and K. Eisele (eds.), *Social Benefits and Migration. A Contested Relationship and Policy Challenge in the EU* (Brussels: Centre for European Policy Studies – CEPS, 2013), 82 and H. Verschueren, 'Preventing Benefit Tourism in the EU: A Narrow or a Broad Interpretation of the Possibilities Offered by the ECJ in Dano?' (2015) 52 *CML Rev*, 363.

47 Through Regulation No. 1247/92, that modified Regulation No. 1408/71 by introducing the new sub-system for the coordination of special non-contributory cash benefits. Cf.

provision of a derogation to the general principle of exportability, offset however by the attribution of the responsibility of the payment of such benefits to the Member State of actual residence of the beneficiary according to the *lex loci domicilii*. Yet the notion of residence also used by Regulation 883/2004, for this very reason, is based on parameters that are inherently and essentially factual, as opposed to Directive 2004/38/EC, which gives a much stricter legal definition instead, anchored as it is to requirements of legal-substantial nature. Therefore, the original idea was precisely that, as often as the merely factual situation of habitual residence in the host country recurred,[48] the EU economically inactive citizens covered by the Regulations on social security would certainly be entitled to non-contributory benefits provided for by the legislation of the host Member State in which that citizen placed his/her centre of interests. Thus, at least within the semi-universal scope of application *ratione personae* of Regulation 883/2004, the right to have access to non-contributory benefits in the country of actual/factual habitual residence could certainly allow, or at least legitimately help, the European economically inactive citizen to meet the requirement of economic self-sufficiency set forth by Article 7 Directive 2004/38/EC.

Evidently, that compromise was overwhelmed by the interpretation of the relationship between the social security Regulation and the citizenship Directive endorsed by the Court in *Brey* and even more boldly in *Dano*. Only the status of legal residence – in full compliance with the Directive[49] – will allow access to special non-contributory/social assistance benefits under tendential conditions of equal treatment with the nationals of the host Member State. However, this means reintroducing a decisive division within the status of Union citizenship, with a premature *de profundis* for the normative ideal that, in the name of solidarity 'among strangers', aimed at making EU citizenship the main constitutional vehicle for transnational social integration.

4. EPILOGUE

Even after *Dano*, there are still many uncertain and controversial aspects that require a conclusive answer from the Court. The jurisprudential framework is still developing and the darkest scenarios, although clearly visible on the horizon, hopefully do not necessarily need to take place, as the insuperable Leopardi's pessimism on the unhappiness of the human condition would predict.

S. Giubboni, 'Cittadinanza comunitaria e sicurezza sociale: un profilo critico' (1997) *Argomenti di diritto del lavoro*, 67.

48 See Case C-20/96, *Snares*, EU:C:1997:518; Case C-297/96, *Partridge*, EU:C:1998:280; and Case C-90/97, *Swaddling*, EU:C:1999:96.

49 Further, see the judgment delivered by the Court in the joined Cases C-424/10 and C-425/10, *Ziolkowski and Szeja*, EU:C:2011:866.

Different interpretations of *Dano*, perhaps more in tune with the socially inclusive idea of European citizenship endorsed in the ascending phase of the discourse on transnational solidarity, may still be possible, as Herwig Verschueren has tried to argue with his usual tireless and passionate argumentative accuracy.[50] Indeed, Advocate General Wathelet, in his recent conclusions in *Alimanovic*,[51] suggested that the Court follow a path firmly anchored to the principle of proportionality, which is context sensitive and moderately socially liberal.

However, our fear is that the most likely outcome, in line with the new neurotic and intolerant European *Zeitgeist*, is a creeping return to the grim logic of the Poor Laws, with a post-modern rediscovery of the classic remedy of the expulsion of the undeserving poor, by sending such persons back to the parish (or, in this case, to the country) of origin.[52] It is no coincidence that, among the different possible reforms for providing a solution to the new transnational social question of the movement of inactive Union citizens, there are some that are strikingly similar to the old 'non-resident relief', which under the Law of Settlement from the Elizabethan period exceptionally allowed the expulsion of the stranger poor to be prevented if the parish of origin agreed to take on the burden of supporting them.[53] A scenario in which, at least partially or even temporarily, such a burden is transferred to the State of origin of the migrant European citizen[54] perhaps unwittingly (but no less clearly) harks back to that historic tradition. If this were to be made a reality in the new context of the Union, the deep asymmetries between core and periphery countries created by the great crisis would be exacerbated, again to the detriment of the Member States at the outer (Mediterranean or eastern) edges of the EU and to the benefit of the northern bloc under the German track (as well as the motherland of the Poor Laws, of course).

Moreover, pessimism is justified by the ever more explicit and disturbing signs of an even broader and more general – not to say 'systemic' – questioning of the same assumptions of the freedom of movement of persons, i.e. of workers, within the Union.[55] One such sign is now clearly discernible in the case-law of the

---

50 Cf. H. Verschueren, 'Preventing Benefit Tourism in the EU: A Narrow or a Broad Interpretation of the Possibilities Offered by the ECJ in Dano?' (2015) 52 *CML Rev*, 370 *et seq.*

51 Case C-67/14, *Alimanovic*, EU:C:2015:597.

52 K. Groenendijk, 'Access for Migrants to Social Assistance: Closing the Frontiers or Reducing Citizenship?', in E. Guild, S. Carrera and K. Eisele (eds.), *Social Benefits and Migration. A Contested Relationship and Policy Challenge in the EU* (Brussels: Centre for European Policy Studies – CEPS, 2013), 1 *et seq.*

53 N. Landau, 'The Regulation of Migration, Economic Structures and Definitions of the Poor in Eighteenth-Century England' (1990) 33 *Historical Journal*, 541 *et seq.*

54 For a review of the various hypothesis of reform see H. Verschueren, 'Free Movement of EU Citizens: Including the Poor?' (2015) 12 *MJ*, especially at para. 4.

55 Cf. the Editorial Comments, 'The Free Movement of Persons in the European Union: Salvaging the Dream while Explaining the Nightmare' (2014) 51 *CML Rev*, 729 *et seq.*

Court of Justice, which quite frequently – in a sort of reverse cross-fertilisation – demands that the same economic migrants, especially frontier workers, provide proof of a certain degree of integration in the society of the host country in order to have access to social advantages and benefits on a par with the nationals of that State.[56] If this trend were to continue, such an interpretative reorientation, or detour, would evidently undermine one of the pillars of free movement within the internal market and of the model of social integration it embodied: that is to say, the unconditional right for migrant workers to have access to all the social benefits guaranteed by the host country (Article 7 Regulation 1612/68 and Regulation 492/2011).[57]

Even the Labour Mobility Package recently announced by the European Commission, although not yet fully defined in its operational details, seems to be going in that same wrong direction, as I mentioned in the introduction to this melancholic eulogy on the free movement of persons and European solidarity in the EU. The package would entail a substantial restriction of migrant workers' rights to social protection rights, supinely endorsing once again the requests set of the stronger northern European countries – especially Germany and the United Kingdom – which carry forward – in this regard – substantially convergent political positions.

If these scenarios of the counter-reformation of EU law were to become a reality, we would be witnessing, as lost and disoriented as ever, not only the final and inglorious sinking of any misplaced hope of transnational social solidarity, but the obliteration of an entire history of achievements of civilisation in the long march towards the freedom of movement of workers in the European Union. It would be not only a return to a de-socialised idea of the market citizen, but also a stronger premonition of the forthcoming disintegration of the whole European project.

---

56 Cf. Case C-213/05, *Geven*, EU:C:2007:438; Case C-379/11, *Krier*, EU:C:2012:798; and Case C-20/12, *Giersch*, EU:C:2013:411.

57 Cf. the contribution of H. Verschueren in this volume.

CHAPTER 6

ONCE A FOREIGNER, ALWAYS A FOREIGNER

Who Does Not Belong Here Anymore? Expulsion Measures

Eleanor SPAVENTA

1. INTRODUCTION

The right to enter and reside in any of the Member States, subject to the conditions provided for in Directive 2004/38,[1] is one of the most important rights granted to citizens of the Union. In order to make this right fully effective EU law also restricts the discretion of Member States in refusing entry and terminating residency rights of Union citizens; and it provides for procedural safeguards in order to guarantee the effective enjoyment of Union rights by Union citizens.

In this chapter I am going to focus on two different issues: first of all, I will analyse the conditions which have to be satisfied by the citizen in order to gain residency rights. In particular, for stays of between three months and five years, the Union citizen must be either economically active or economically independent, which is to say have sufficient resources and comprehensive health insurance so as not to become a 'burden' on the host welfare system. The question arises as to when, if the citizen fails, or ceases, to meet those conditions, can a Member State expel a Union citizen.[2] Secondly, I will analyse expulsion

---

1 Directive 2004/38/EC of the European Parliament and of the Council of 29 April 2004 on the right of citizens of the Union and their family members to move and reside freely within the territory of the Member States, OJ 2004, L 158/77 (hereinafter referred to as 'Directive 2004/38').

2 See e.g. Case C-408/03, *Commission v Belgium*, EU:C:2006:192, in relation to the Belgian practice of automatically expelling citizens who could not produce the supporting documents (including proof of personal resources) in order to obtain the residence permit.

measures justified on public policy/public security grounds.[3] My overall conclusion is that the Court has retreated from a purposive interpretation of Union citizenship and Directive 2004/38, so that it is only 'good' citizens that enjoy rights arising from membership of the European Union family. The errant, the poor and the diverse might find that they have limited rights from Member States other than their own: thus Union citizenship, as recently interpreted, reinforces traditional notions of 'belonging' by nationality, so that responsibility for the weaker and less attractive members of society continues to be vested on their state of origin, regardless of the actual link that the citizen has with the latter and the host Member State respectively.

2. THE RIGHT TO RESIDE PURSUANT TO DIRECTIVE 2004/38: SHORT- AND MEDIUM-TERM RESIDENCE

Directive 2004/38 provides for three types of residence: short-term residence, which is unconditional and (broadly speaking)[4] does not entitle the beneficiary access to social assistance; medium-term residence, which is conditional and allows, in various degrees, membership of the host welfare community; and permanent residence, which is conditional upon having spent five years in the host country whilst also satisfying the conditions provided for in Directive 2004/38,[5] and which allows for full membership of the host welfare community. After briefly recalling the regime for short-term residents, we will focus on medium-term residence and the conditions attached therein to assess when Member States can terminate the right to reside provided for by the Treaty and detailed in the Directive. In this section we are only concerned with termination of the right to reside for failing to fulfil the conditions stipulated in the Directive. In the following section we will look at cases in which deportation is justified on public policy/security concerns triggered by the migrant's own behaviour; in this respect it should be recalled that once the Union citizen has acquired the right to permanent residency she can only be deported on public policy or security grounds.

3 I will not look at the limitation to the right to exit; for recent case-law see e.g. Case C-249/11, *Byankov*, EU:C:2012:608; and Case C-434/10, Aladzhov, EU:C:2011:750.

4 See the opinion of Advocate General Wathelet in Case C-299/14, *Garcia-Nieto*, EU:C:2015:366, advocating the possibility for equal treatment (on the basis of Article 45 rather than Directive 2004/38) in relation to benefits aimed at facilitating access to the employment market for workseekers, safe for the possibility to justify indirect discrimination on the grounds that the workseeker has not established a rela link with the employment market.

5 See e.g. Joined Cases C-424/10 and C-425/10, *Ziolkowski and Szeja*, EU:C:2011:866.

2.1. SHORT-TERM RESIDENCE

Article 6 of Directive 2004/38 provides for the right to move to any Member State for up to three months without having to satisfy any conditions or formalities. Article 24(2) of the same instrument provides that short term residents and workseekers do not have the right to 'social assistance', and Article 14(1) provides that the short term residence is maintained 'as long as [the citizens] do not become an unreasonable burden on the social assistance system of the host Member State',[6] whilst paragraph 3 of the same Article provides that expulsion cannot be the automatic consequence of recourse to social assistance. It therefore seems that only a repeated/protracted use of social assistance by short term visitors would justify an expulsion measure; however, given the very limited length of short term residence this is unlikely to happen and in fact there is no EU level case-law on expulsion measures motivated by abuse of welfare resources. It is of course open to the Member State to rely on the public policy/security derogations in relation to those visitors either to deny entry or to expel them.[7] In any event, the fact that Member States cannot impose any formality for stays under three months means also that, even should expulsion take place, it might go unrecorded; furthermore there are concerns about the extent to which procedural rights are effectively guaranteed in those cases.[8]

2.2. MEDIUM-TERM RESIDENCE: THE COMPREHENSIVE HEALTH INSURANCE AND SUFFICIENT RESOURCES CRITERIA

As mentioned above, short term stay is very limited in duration and unconditional so that a discussion on termination of residence is almost redundant; not so for medium term residence. Here the very nature of Union citizenship is increasingly contested, not least by political elites, and the case-law is becoming confused, both because of the experimental 'nature' of Union citizenship and because of the Court's permeability to political discourse. We will proceed in steps in particular to assess whether the failure to meet the conditions in Article 7(1)(b) authorises Member States to expel Union citizens, or whether there is a differential application of Directive 2004/38.

---

6 Emphasis added.

7 That would more likely be the case in particular situations such as fans violence in football tournaments; see C. Barnard, *The Substantive Law of the EU – The Four Freedoms, 4th edition* (Oxford: OUP, 2013), 516; or drug related offences, see e.g. Case C-348/96, *Calfa*, EU:C:1999:6.

8 See e.g. C. Barnard, *The Substantive Law of the EU –The Four Freedoms, 4th edition* (Oxford: OUP, 2013), 516; and A. Valke in the comments to this chapter.

We will consider only the situation of economically inactive citizens, since those are the most vulnerable to the whim of the Member States and the wavering of the Court. That is not to say that economically active individuals might not face difficulties in the host country, in particular in relation to a changing labour market where security of employment is much reduced, employment might be unpaid (in the form of internships, zero-hour contracts), and oscillation between in and out of work periods more common. However, as a matter of EU law (if not of national practice), once a citizen is defined as economically active her rights derive directly by the Treaty, as expansively interpreted by the Court, and she will enjoy significant protection.

2.3. RIGHT TO MEDIUM-TERM RESIDENCE FOR ECONOMICALLY INACTIVE CITIZENS

If one were to visualise the rights of economically inactive citizens over time one could picture it as a circle. The 1990 residence directives are the starting point;[9] there economically inactive individuals derived rights to the extent to which they fell within the personal scope of the Directives by fulfilling the conditions contained therein; to a second (constituent and expansive) phase where the Court gave effect to the Treaty citizenship provisions,[10] and a third phase, where inactive citizens are protected only insofar as they fall within the personal scope of Directive 2004/38 by satisfying the sufficient resources/comprehensive health insurance requirement. I have analysed these developments elsewhere;[11] what interests me here is whether the most recent case-law signals the end of the

9 Council Directive 90/364/EEC of 28 June 1990 on the right of residence, OJ 1990, L 180/26; Council Directive 90/365/EEC of 28 June 1990 on the right of residence for employees and self-employed persons who have ceased their occupational activity, OJ 1990, L 180/28; and Council Directive 93/96/EEC of 29 October 1993 on the right of residence for students, OJ 1993, L 317/59. We could also take as a starting point Joined Cases 286/82 and 26/83, *Luisi and Carbone*, EU:C:1984:35; Case 186/87, *Cowan*, EU:C:1989:47; and *the Museum entry* cases (e.g. Case C-45/93, *Commission v Spain*, EU:C:1994:101), but those are really about short term residence. Given the exclusion of service reception as a ground for residence in Directive 2004/38, it is open to debate whether that case-law would apply beyond the first three months of residence. Rather it is likely that the short term residence was intending to absorb that case-law (so that, for instance, Luisi and Carbone obviously would have a right to move, Cowan would have the right to compensation as that is not social assistance, ditto with museum entry).

10 e.g. Case C-85/96, *Martínez Sala*, EU:C:1998:217; Case C-184/99, *Grzelczyk*, EU:C:2001:458; Case C-413/99, *Baumbast*, EU:C:2002:493; and Case C-209/03, *Bidar*, EU:C:2005:169.

11 See E. Spaventa, 'Economic justifications and Union Citizenship: Reallocating welfare responsibilities to the State of origin', in P. Koutrakos, N. Nic Shuibhne and P. Syrpis (eds.), *Exceptions from EU Free Movement Law – Derogation, Justification and Proportionality* (Oxford: Hart Publishing, 2016), forthcoming and E. Spaventa, 'Earned Citizenship – Understanding Union Citizenship Through its Scope', in D. Kochenov (ed.), *Citizenship and Federalism in the European Union: the Role of Rights* (Cambridge: CUP, 2016), forthcoming.

proportionality assessment in relation to the right to reside of Union citizens. I will recall briefly the most pertinent judicial developments, before focusing more specifically on the conditions to be fulfilled in order to obtain a right to reside. In this respect, it should be remembered that if a Union citizen is found not to have a right of residence (either pursuant to the Treaty or to secondary legislation), then the Member State will be entitled to expel her from its territory without having recourse to the public policy and security derogations. To understand the scope of the residency rights is therefore of paramount importance both for Union citizens and in order to understand the (r)evolving nature of Union citizenship.

It might be recalled that in *Baumbast*[12] the Court found that the fact that Mr Baumbast did not meet all the conditions required by Directive 90/364 to obtain a right to reside in the host country did not mean that he could not derive such a right directly from the Treaty. Rather, since the right to move and reside across the territory of the Union was, following the Maastricht innovations, contained in the Treaty, it was the latter that formed the basis for the right to reside, whilst the residency directives were to be understood as the '*limitations and conditions*' to which Article 21 TFEU refers.[13] Consistently then, the limitations to the Treaty derived right to reside had to be interpreted in the light of the general principles of Union law and in particular the principle of proportionality. In concrete terms, this meant that national authorities could not deny a residence permit to a Union citizen simply because she did not fulfil the conditions in one of the residence directives: rather, the authorities had to conduct an assessment based on the personal circumstances of the claimant, taking into account a number of factors (e.g. length of stay; family ties; extent to which the claimant had relied on welfare assistance in the past, etc.).

In another line of case-law,[14] the Court held that EU citizens lawfully resident in a host State, by virtue of either national or EU law, would be able to rely on the equal treatment right also in relation to welfare provision. In that respect the two conflicting interests, effectiveness of Union citizenship and national welfare societies with limited resources, were balanced at the stage of justification: thus it was open to the Member State to justify the unequal treatment of the non-economically active citizen, for instance on the grounds that the rules were aimed at ensuring a real link between claimant and host welfare society; it was however open to the claimant to demonstrate to have established said real link. For this reason, also in relation to the right of equal treatment, a personal assessment was necessary, so that a rule which in theory might have been

12 Case C-413/99, *Baumbast*, EU:C:2002:493.

13 Case C-413/99, *Baumbast*, EU:C:2002:493.

14 Case C-85/96, *Martínez Sala*, EU:C:1998:217; Case C 184/99, *Grzelczyk*, EU:C:2001:458; Case C-209/03, *Bidar*, EU:C:2005:169.

consistent with Union law, in practice would need to be applied having regard to the circumstances specific to the claimant at issue.[15]

It was quite natural then, for many, to just give for granted that these two lines of case-law could be read together: a citizen would derive a right to reside through the Treaty citizenship provisions, even if she did not meet all the criteria listed in secondary legislation; and as a lawfully resident Union citizen she would also derive a right to equal treatment, safe for the Member State's ability to justify its rules; and to terminate residence should the citizen become an 'unreasonable burden'. This approach seemed also to be supported by Directive 2004/38 which incorporated the principle of proportionality when it clarified that an expulsion measure cannot be the 'automatic' consequence of the citizen's or her family's recourse to social assistance. And yet, Directive 2004/38 is like its predecessors (the residence directives) and the case-law in one important element: in relation to medium-term residence, the Directive specifies that economically inactive citizens must have sufficient resources and comprehensive health insurance so as not to become a 'burden' on the social assistance system of the host State. The notion of 'unreasonable burden' in the Directive's Preamble is then to a certain extent in tension with the broader notion of 'burden' as contained in Article 7(1)(b). The former led the Court to deduce that Union citizens could be 'reasonable' burdens, and could therefore expect at least *some* transnational solidarity; the notion of 'burden' however suggests more limited space for transnational solidarity and, in particular, might suggest that any form of continuing reliance[16] on the social assistance of the host Member State might transform the Union citizen in a burden that might in turn lead to the loss of residence, without there being any possibility of a proportionality assessment.[17]

Furthermore, the Court has recently given a restrictive interpretation of the relationship between primary and secondary legislation: in *Dano* it held that the right to equal treatment can be invoked – at least insofar as economically inactive citizens are concerned – only to the extent to which the claimant meets the conditions of sufficient resources and comprehensive health insurance provided for in Directive 2004/38.[18] Much has been said about *Dano*, and whether the

15 This approach can still be seen in relation to rules relating to the exportability of welfare benefits (and entitlement to said benefits when residing abroad); see e.g. Case C-503/09, *Stewart*, EU:C:2011:500.

16 As said above Article 14(3) Directive 2004/38 provides that recourse to social assistance cannot lead to automatic expulsion, hence envisaging the fact that the Union citizen might draw temporary support, without for that reason becoming a burden and losing her right to reside.

17 Although the principle of proportionality still plays a role in the review of the expulsion measures *per* Article 31(3) Directive 2004/38.

18 Case C-333/13, *Dano*, EU:C:2014:2358.

Court's approach is consistent with previous case-law on Union citizenship;[19] whether it modifies the accepted hierarchy of norms between Treaty and secondary legislation;[20] whether it is compatible with the system of social security co-ordination set up by Regulation 883/2004 and its predecessor.[21] However, there is another question which has remained unexplored, namely whether the *Dano* interpretation affects the *Baumbast* case-law. In other words, does a Union citizen have to satisfy the conditions provided for in Directive 2004/38, without any possibility of recourse to proportionality, only in order to be able to enjoy the right to equal treatment; or also in order to be able to claim a right to reside?

3. *DANO* AND THE RIGHT TO RESIDE

As said above, the Court in *Dano* clarified that those Union citizens who do not satisfy the black letter conditions contained in the Directive are excluded from the right to equal treatment provided for in Article 24 Directive 2004/38, which, according to the Court, is *lex specialis* over Article 18 TFEU, and therefore might exhaust the right not to be discriminated against. There is not much to be said in favour of the *Dano* ruling, but it undeniably relieves pressure from the citizenship project and from the Court itself. Writing about the *Sala* ruling, O'Leary noted how the Court's generous interpretation in that case might backfire: if the Member States were obliged to guarantee a right to equal treatment to anyone who was lawfully present within their territory, they might be tempted to police more closely whether Union citizens actually *had* title to reside in their territory.[22] Therefore, she argued, *Sala* might have a regressive effect: far from freeing Union citizens to live where they please, it might restrict their possibilities: Member States who were pretty *laissez-faire* in relation to residence of non-economically active migrants might become more strict if hospitality came with a price tag attached. Now, it is possible that *Dano* might have the effect of counteracting *Sala*: if it is only residence pursuant to the strict conditions contained in Directive 2004/38 that allows the Union citizen a right to equal treatment, and if compliance with those conditions can be assessed

---

19 D. Thym, 'The elusive limits of solidarity: residence rights of and social benefits for economically inactive Union Citizens' (2015) 52 *CML Rev*, 17; E. Spaventa, 'Economic justifications and Union Citizenship: Reallocating welfare responsibilities to the State of origin', in P. Koutrakos, N. Nic Shuibhne and P. Syrpis (eds.), *Exceptions from EU Free Movement Law – Derogation, Justification and Proportionality* (Oxford: Hart Publishing, 2016), forthcoming.

20 P. Syrpis, 'The relationship between primary and secondary law in the EU' (2015) 52 *CML Rev*, 461.

21 H. Verschueren, 'Preventing "benefit tourism" in the EU: a narrow or broad interpretation of the possibilities offered by the ECJ in *Dano*?' (2015) 52 *CML Rev*, 363.

22 S. O'Leary, 'Putting flesh on the bones of European Union citizenship' (1999) 24 *EL Rev*, 68.

when the citizen applies for a welfare benefit, then there is much less of an incentive for Member States to police the fulfilment of those conditions before the citizen becomes a claimant. It is not surprising then that the *Dano* ruling was welcomed by many politicians as a 'sensible move',[23] and to be fair at a time when benefit tourism is, wrongly, one of the main issues discussed in relation of the costs of the UK membership in the EU, the ruling in *Dano* comes as a helping hand.

Yet the remaining question, and that that is crucial for our investigation, is the extent to which *Dano* affects the *Baumbast* case-law, i.e. whether in order to be able to stay in the host country the migrant must always fulfil the black letter conditions provided in Directive 2004/38, or whether she is still able to derive residual protection from Article 21 TFEU.

4. CONFLICTING CASE-LAW: *ALOKPA v BREY*

I have argued elsewhere that *Dano* cannot be seen in isolation: rather it is part of a broader trend that sees the Court retreating from a generous interpretation of citizenship rights. For instance, the significance of the ruling in *Ruiz Zambrano*[24] has been much reduced in following cases,[25] where the Court made clear that it is only in the most exceptional circumstances that a citizen would be able to rely on the Treaty citizenship provisions against her own Member State lacking any migratory element. In relation to the derived right to reside enjoyed by the parents of Union citizens residing in a State different from that of nationality, the Court also gave a very narrow interpretation in *Alokpa*.[26] Here the Togolese mother of French citizens who had been born and cared for in Luxembourg found that she could not derive a right to reside and work in the latter country from her children's citizenship rights. In the case

23 See e.g. 'EU "benefit tourism" ruling is common sense, says Cameron', reported on bbc.co.uk 11 November 2014, available at www.bbc.com/news/uk-politics-30002138 (last accessed on 20 January 2016); 'UK and Germany press on with welfare curbs after ECJ ruling', FT.com 11 November 2014, available at www.ft.com/cms/s/0/552497e6-6981-11e4-9f65-00144feabdc0.html#axzz3y4ba3nud (last accessed on 20 January 2016).

24 Case C-34/09, *Ruiz Zambrano*, EU:C:2011:124.

25 Case C-434/09, *McCarthy*, EU:C:2011:277; Case C-256/11, Dereci, EU:C:2011:734.

26 Case C-86/12, Alokpa, EU:C:2013:645. The narrow interpretation in *Alokpa* contrasts with the generous interpretation given to the derived right to reside of parents of Union citizens who are in education, when either or both of the migrant parents have been employed (see e.g. Case C-310/08, *Ibrahim*, EU:C:2010:80; Case C-480/08, *Teixeira*, EU:C:2010:83); the difference is due to the fact that Article 10 Regulation 492/2011 on freedom of movement for workers within the Union, OJ 2011, L 141/1 (previously Article 12 Regulation 1612/68) guarantees a right to access and equal treatment in education for the children of those who are or have been employed in the host Member State. In Joined Cases C-147/11 and C-148/11, *Czop and Punakova*, EU:C:2012:538, the Court clarified that Article of 10 Regulation 492/2011 does not apply to the self-employed.

at issue, and unlike the case of the wealthy Chen family,[27] Ms Alokpa did not have 'inherent' resources: rather she had potential resources in the form of a job offer of unlimited duration the taking up of which was, however, conditional upon possessing a work permit, which was in turn conditional upon residency status. Proportionality might have suggested that if Mrs Chen derived a right of residence from her baby's Union citizenship rights, then Ms Alokpa should not be denied the same right on the sole ground that she had to work in order to acquire resources, especially given that she would have been in work as soon as the permit had been granted. Moreover, Ms Alokpa had no ties, family or friends in the state of nationality of her children (France), her children had been born and cared for in Luxembourg and had been there for their entire life (more than three years). Yet the Court found that the children would have a right to reside only to the extent to which they met the conditions set out in Article 7(1)(b) of Directive 2004/38 (sufficient resources and comprehensive health insurance) so that lacking those the mother could not derive a right to reside (and work) from her children's citizenship rights. Furthermore, the Court also found that if the conditions provided for in Directive 2004/38 are not satisfied, then Article 21 TFEU is of no help (and neither are fundamental rights which are not mentioned).[28] It is obvious that this approach constitutes a departure from the *Baumbast* case-law insofar as meeting the conditions specified in secondary legislation becomes a prerequisite to bring oneself within the scope of the Treaty.

The question then arises as to whether *Alokpa,* also read together with *Dano*, signals a definitive change of approach; or rather whether it is justified on policy considerations, and in particular having regard to the fear that the Union citizenship provisions might become a tool to circumvent national rules concerning residence rights of third-country nationals. In other words, would the *Alokpa* approach also apply to a Mr Baumbast, a Union citizen who meets some, but not all, of the conditions provided for in the Directive, and whose right to reside is not derivative? Here it might be useful to recall the case of *Brey*,[29] decided before the *Dano* ruling. In that case, a pensioner moved with his wife, who did not have any income of her own, from Germany to Austria. When Mr Brey applied for a compensatory supplement, he fell within a Catch-22: the very fact that he had applied for the supplement meant that his earnings were low and that therefore he lacked sufficient resources, therefore failing to fulfil

27 Case C-200/02, *Chen*, EU:C:2004:639; it might be recalled that that case related to the reisdency rights of the Chinese mother of a baby who had been born in Northern Ireland (where the mother had traveled in order to give birth) and, under the rules at they stood at the time, had thus gained Irish citizenship. The baby did not obviously have resources but the mother did and the Court (rightly) found that the mother's resources could be taken into consideration to establish the baby's economic independence.

28 Case C-86/12, *Alokpa*, EU:C:2013:645, para. 31.

29 Case C-140/12, *Brey*, EU:C:2013:565.

the conditions provided for in Directive 2004/38 to obtain a right to reside. The Court, rather differently from *Dano*, found that it was true that the fact that a Union citizen applied for the compensatory supplement at issue might be an indication that he lacked sufficient resources pursuant to Article 7(1)(b); however, it remained to be assessed whether that fact alone would transform the citizen in an 'unreasonable' burden. Only in the latter case could the Union citizen be refused residency rights. Furthermore, the Court also restated the centrality of the proportionality principle when performing those assessments: in particular, national authorities should have regard to both the cumulative burden imposed on the welfare resources by all Union citizens applying for that particular benefit; and to the particular conditions of the applicant. Finally, consistently with the *Baumbast* line of case-law, the Court made clear that the conditions of sufficient resources and comprehensive health insurance provided for in Article 7(1)(b) limit a Treaty right and as such must be interpreted restrictively.[30]

As said above, the ruling in *Brey* was delivered before the ruling in *Dano*: the question is therefore whether the latter overruled the former, or whether the conditions for the right to reside differ from the applicability of the right to equal treatment. Thus, if the Union citizen's equal treatment right is conditional upon satisfying the black letter criteria provided for by Article 7(1)(b) Directive 2004/38 then there is little harm in allowing a citizen who does not meet all of those criteria the possibility to reside in the territory of the Member State, especially as doing so would not transform the citizen in a 'burden' (reasonable or unreasonable) on the social assistance system of the host State. In this way the principle of proportionality would once again play a role in the assessment of the citizenship rights. The citizen might of course still be demanded to meet some of the criteria but this interpretation would ensure a more meaningful notion of Union citizenship. Furthermore, this reading would also allow for consistency with the *Alokpa* ruling: in that case the Court assumed that future earnings through employment were not relevant in order to assess whether the claimants would have sufficient resources. That assumption was very questionable: it means that the citizenship rights of Union citizens' children of third-country nationals can only be enjoyed by those whose families are wealthy, in that they have resources without having to work. And yet, once the assumption is made, then it is true that Ms Alokpa was failing to meet, in their entirety, the conditions provided for in Directive 2004/38. Consistently with the ruling in *Trojani* then,[31] the principle of proportionality might be of use when the Union citizen fails to meet *some* of the requirements contained in secondary legislation, not when she has no resources whatsoever.

---

30 Case C-140/12, *Brey*, EU:C:2013:565, para. 70.

31 Case C-456/02, *Trojani*, EU:C:2004:488.

5. EXPULSION MEASURES FOR LACK OF RESOURCES

I have argued so far that the more recent case-law, which undoubtedly constitutes a retreat from the earlier purposive interpretation of the citizenship rights and the ensuing right to equal treatment, should be interpreted only as a partial break with the hermeneutic principles previously established by the Court. Thus, whilst in order to enjoy a full right to equal treatment in relation to social assistance the Union citizen must bring herself within the personal scope of Directive 2004/38 through either economic activity or economic self-sufficiency, matters are different in relation to the residency rights. In this respect, the *Brey* ruling indicates that the Treaty rights of free movement can still supplement the rights of residence detailed in Directive 2004/38, so that denial of residency rights cannot be the 'automatic' consequence of recourse to social assistance but has to be justified also having regard to the particular situation of the claimants, especially since the *Dano* interpretation means that the claimant would not be entitled to social assistance and therefore would be less likely to become a burden on the host State. However, when the citizen fails to meet the conditions provided for in secondary legislation her expulsion would be most likely proportionate. This interpretation is not by any means perfect, and yet it would allow to save, post *Alokpa* and *Dano*, some of the Union citizenship ideas.

It is now time to consider the circumstances in which lawfully resident Union citizens might be expelled from the host State because their conduct amounts to a threat to the public policy or security of the host State.

6. EXPULSION ON GROUNDS OF PUBLIC POLICY AND SECURITY

The original Treaty provided that the free movement rights could be limited only on grounds of public policy, public security and public health (with which we are not concerned).[32] Council Directive 64/221[33] detailed the conditions

32 We are not concerned with the public health derogation since the conditions for it to be invoked are very strict (see Article 29 Directive 2004/38): Member States can rely on the public health derogation only for diseases with epidemic, infectious or parasitic diseases and only in the first three months of stay of the citizen in their territory since, beyond that time, the illness would have either being contracted in the host State or would have had already the chance to spread. The list of diseases that allow for restrictive measures is provided by the WHO; beyond that Member States can invoke the public health derogation only in relation to diseases that are also the subject of protection measures in relation to own nationals. There is no case-law on the public health derogation not least since when there is an outbreak of serious infectious illnesses it is in everybody's interest that potential carriers are quarantined and treated rather than being requested to travel further.

33 Council Directive 64/221/EEC on the co-ordination of special measures concerning the movement and residence of foreign nationals which are justified on grounds of public policy, public security, or public health, OJ 1964, 056.

for the legitimacy of measures adopted pursuant to the Treaty derogations; thus it clarified that the grounds for derogation could not be invoked to serve economic ends (Article 2); that measures taken on grounds of public policy and public security had to be based exclusively on the personal conduct of the individual concerned (Article 3);[34] and for procedural safeguards for the persons affected by the measures taken pursuant to a derogation (Articles 5–9). Broadly speaking the Court interpreted the derogations very narrowly: it held that public policy, although clearly a national concept, was to be subjected to control by the Community institutions,[35] and that only behaviour that constituted a 'genuine and serious threat to the requirements of public policy affecting one of the fundamental interests of society'[36] allowed the State to invoke the public policy derogation. Furthermore, in *Adoui and Cournaille* the Court introduced a principle of equivalence of sanctions: only behaviour that would be sanctioned when engaged in by nationals could be grounds for an expulsion measure.[37]

It should be noted that the interpretation of the Court, pre-Directive 2004/38, was very narrow so much so that it is only in *Van Duyn* (and indirectly in *Calfa*)[38] that the Court accepted the compatibility of an expulsion measure with EU law. Furthermore, the interpretative criteria elaborated by the Court are codified in full in Directive 2004/38. Thus, Article 27 of that Directive provides *inter alia* that measures adopted in pursuance of public policy and security must be proportionate and not serve economic ends; the conduct of the individual must represent a genuine and sufficiently serious threat to one of the fundamental interests of society; and previous criminal convictions are not in themselves sufficient to invoke a public policy/security derogation.

Article 28 of Directive 2004/38 lists (not exhaustively) the elements that must be taken into consideration when deciding upon expulsion: length of stay in the host country, age, family and economic ties, social and cultural integration in the host country and extent of links with the country of origin are all relevant factors when considering the expulsion of a Union citizen on public policy or security grounds. It also, true to the incremental nature that characterises rights in Directive 2004/38, provides for enhanced protection for those who have the right of permanent residence, who cannot be expelled 'except on serious grounds of public policy or public security'; moreover if the citizen has resided in the host State for at least ten years (or is a minor) they cannot be expelled other than on 'imperative grounds of public security'.[39]

---

34 This provision has been held to be directly effective in Case 41/74, *Van Duyn*, EU:C:1974:133.

35 Case 41/74, *Van Duyn*, EU:C:1974:133, para. 18.

36 Case 30/77, *Bouchereau*, EU:C:1977:172.

37 Joined Cases 115/81 and 116/81, *Adoui and Cornuaille*, EU:C:1982:183.

38 Case C-348/96, *Calfa*, EU:C:1999:6.

39 It is interesting to note how these enhanced protection clauses are phrased: thus, whilst Article 27 is phrased in positive terms (Member States *may* restrict the freedom to move and reside on grounds of public policy, public security or public health), the presumption for long

Articles 27 and 28 of the Directive therefore impose strict conditions upon Member States in order to be able to expel Union citizens; in fact, given the very inconsistency between the notion of Union citizenship and that of public policy/security derogation, it could have been thought that the Court would allow expulsions only in the most serious of circumstances. After all, if before Union citizenship the Court was reluctant to allow national authorities the possibility to expel nationals of other Member States, it should be even more so in the changed landscape after Union citizenship – especially if the latter were to really be considered the 'fundamental status' of Union citizens.[40] In this respect, the elimination of the State power to ban a person from the community to which they belong might be seen as one of the key aspect of modern notions of citizenship.[41] The continued existence of the possibility to expel a foreign Union citizen on public policy and security grounds then highlights, in the most tangible way, the limits of the notion of supranational citizenship: after all, the very fact of excluding someone from the community because of their behaviour highlights the transient nature of their membership of the host community. It could have been expected, therefore, that the Court would interpret the public policy/security derogations even more strictly that it had done before the creation of Union citizenship. And yet, as we shall see in more detail below, the case-law post-Directive 2004/38 seems more inclined to condone Member States willingness to expel the foreign Union citizen. This, together with those trends examined above in relation to equal treatment, might therefore tell us something about how Union citizenship is (r)evolving.

6.1. RECENT CASE-LAW ON THE PUBLIC POLICY AND SECURITY DEROGATIONS

Cases on expulsions have never been very plentiful: this might be because of (i) egregious breaches of EU law, so that individuals are not made aware (let aside granted) their rights, even their procedural rights (see e.g. the cases of expulsion of Italian citizens from Belgium;[42] the expulsion of Roma – and Romanian –

term residents is that they *cannot* be expelled *except* on serious grounds of public policy/ security; and on imperative ground of public security. As we shall see further below, this nuance seems to be lost on the Court.

40 Case C-184/99, *Grzelczyk*, EU:C:2001:458.

41 See also Article 9 of the Universal Declaration of Human Rights; in the UK it is possible to revoke citizenship in certain instances; see generally: http://researchbriefings.files.parliament.uk/documents/SN06820/SN06820.pdf (last accessed on 21 May 2016).

42 In 2013, 2712 EU citizens were refused a residence permit or/and asked to leave because they did not meet the sufficient resources and comprehensive health insurance criteria in Belgium see www.linkiesta.it/espulsione-cittadini-europei-belgio (last accessed on 20 January 2016); amongst those the case of Silvia Guerra, who was an Italian citizen, a street artist, who was expelled from Belgium notwithstanding the fact that she had been a

citizens from Italy and France);[43] and/or (ii) because of the fact that individuals who face those measures are very seldom 'empowered' both economically and culturally, and might not be aware/be confident about their rights; and/or (iii) because the national courts resist referring questions, either because they believe the law is clear or because they '*want*' to believe the law is clear.[44] Those cases, by nature, are also less likely to reach the highest courts and trigger the duty to refer pursuant to Article 267 TFEU. In this regard it is useful to look at the 2014 FIDE Report on Union citizenship: a questionnaire was sent to national rapporteurs to understand, *inter alia*, whether the guarantees contained in Directive 2004/38 are *in practice* effective. The general report concluded that 'it can be noted from the outset that, regrettably, the gap between the articulation of citizenship law in principle and the application of citizenship law in practice is perhaps wider here than we found for any other part of the questionnaire'.[45] In particular, a common problem is expulsion as a consequence of a criminal conviction.[46]

Be as it may we have very little case-law both before and after Directive 2004/38. If anything, in comparative terms, references have increased after the Directive, possibly because it clarified the rights of EU citizens by codifying the case-law; possibly as an indirect result of the combination of enlargement with a major economic recession and of the ensuing tensions in relation to free movement of persons.

In *Tsakouridis*,[47] Mr Tsakouridis was a Greek national who had arrived in Germany, where his father was employed, soon after his birth. He had resided in Germany for 30 years, most of his life, and had undergone all of his schooling

---

worker and that her eight-year-old son was at school there and had been for some time (see http://bologna.repubblica.it/cronaca/2013/12/23/news/silvia_l_artista_espulsa_dal_belgio_passer_il_natale_a_bologna-74361409/ (last accessed on 20 January 2016). This case was then seized as an example of the gap between the EU and its citizens; see e.g. www.beppegrillo.it/listeciviche/forum/2013/12/silvia-guerra-espulsa-da-bruxelles-belgio-perche-disoccupata.html (last accessed on 20 January 2016).

43 See generally, the website of the European Roma Rights Centre, www.errc.org/ and in particular the report on forced expulsions perpetrated by France: ERRC, 'Census: Forced evictions of migrant Roma in France', *Website of the European Roma Rights Centre* (2014), available at www.errc.org/article/violent-unfair-unlawful-and-shameful-france-evicted-close-to-3-romani-settlements-per-week-in-2014/4351 (last accessed on 20 January 2016); see European Union Agency for Fundamental Rights, 'Opinion 1/2013 on the situation of equality in the European Union 10 years on from the initial implementation of the Equality directives', *Website of the European Union Agency for Fundamental Rights* (2013), available at http://fra.europa.eu/sites/default/files/fra-2013-opinion-eu-equality-directives_en.pdf (last accessed on 20 January 2016).

44 For a detailed analysis see the comments on this chapter by A. Valcke.

45 U. Neergaard, C. Jacqueson and N. Holst-Christensen (eds.), *Union Citizenship: Development, Impact and Challenges*, the XXVI FIDE Congress in Copenhagen 2014, Congress Pubblications Vol. 2 (Copenhagen: DJØF Publishing, 2014), 125.

46 See e.g. Case C-50/06, *Commission v Netherlands*, EU:C:2007:325.

47 Case C-145/09, *Tsakouridis*, EU:C:2010:708.

there. He was absent from Germany for comparatively short periods when he went to Rhodes to run a pancake stall. Whilst he was in Rhodes the German authorities issued a European Arrest Warrant; upon his return he was convicted of several offences, in particular dealing in narcotics as part of an organised group, and received a custodial sentence of just over six years. The German authorities issued an expulsion order based on '*imperative grounds of public security*': this, in their view, was justified by the fact that the custodial sentence exceeded five years and by the seriousness of the crime, dealing in narcotics, and the harmful effect that it has on society. Furthermore, it was found that Mr Tsakouridis' recent stays in Rhodes indicated that he would have no trouble reintegrating in his Member State of 'origin'. As for fundamental rights, the interference with Mr Tsakouridis' right to family life as protected by Article 8 ECHR was justified in the interest of prevention of crime and disorder.

On appeal from the authorities' order, the national court of first instance annulled the measure. It found that even though Mr Tsakouradis might well pose a threat to public policy, his expulsion could not be justified on the higher threshold of '*imperative grounds of public security*'. In the view of that court, those grounds could be invoked only in relation to a threat to 'the existence of the State and its institutions or the survival of its population'.[48] On appeal, the national court enquired with the Court of Justice as to the interpretation to be given to the 'imperative grounds of public security' and the significance of Mr Tsakouridis' absences from Germany for his ability to benefit from the enhanced protection provided by Article 28(3)(a).

The Court started, quite naturally, by providing the guidelines to determine whether absences from the host territory had affected the ten-year residence requirement, and consequently the enhanced protection provided for in Article 28(3)(a). It found that the assessment would have to be made having regard to the individual case; in particular the national court would need to investigate whether, having regard to frequency, length (also cumulative) and reasons for absences the individual had transferred the 'personal, family or occupational interests' in another Member State. The Court then proceeded to provide guidelines for the interpretation of the concept of imperative grounds of public security; after having found that public security covers both the internal and the external security of the State,[49] it found that the fight against crime in relation to drug dealing as part of an organised group was not 'necessarily' excluded from that concept. This would be the case, in particular, if drug trafficking as part of an organised group reached a 'level of intensity that might directly threaten the calm and physical security of the population as a whole or

48 Case C-145/09, *Tsakouridis*, EU:C:2010:708, para. 20.

49 It held that 'threat to the functioning of the institutions and essential public services and the survival of the population, as well as the risk of a serious disturbance to foreign relations or to peaceful coexistence of nations, or a risk to military interests, may affect public security', Case C-145/09, *Tsakouridis*, EU:C:2010:708, para. 44.

a large part of it'.[50] The Court of Justice then instructed the national court as to the elements to be taken into account in determining whether the conduct of the individual could represent a threat to 'imperative grounds of public security', including family ties, strength of link with the host State, fundamental rights consideration and so on. It then added 'in the case of a Union citizen who has lawfully spent most or even all of his childhood and youth in the host Member State, very good reasons would have to be put forward to justify the expulsion measure'.[51] The interpretation in *Tsakouridis* then, signals a first step towards a broader interpretation of the public security derogation; it however also respects the letter and spirit of the Directive when instructing the national court to take into account the personal circumstances of the claimant, giving particular weight to the fact that he had spent most of his life in Germany.

In *P.I.*,[52] the Court further broadens the interpretation of public security. Here, the claimant was an Italian national who had resided in Germany for 19 years before being arrested, and convicted, for particularly serious and protracted sexual assaults and violence on a child. Again the question referred to the Court was on the interpretation of 'imperative grounds of public security'. After having recalled several paragraphs from the ruling in *Tsakouridis*, the Court linked the notion of 'imperative grounds of public security' to the Union competence to act to combat certain forms of crime with a cross-border dimension. Thus it held:

> 'it is apparent from the above that it is open to the Member States to regard criminal offences such as those referred to in the second subparagraph of Article 83(1) TFEU as constituting a particularly serious threat to one of the fundamental interests of society, which might pose a direct threat to the calm and physical security of the population and thus be covered by the concept of "imperative grounds of public security", capable of justifying an expulsion measure under Article 28(3) of Directive 2004/38'.[53]

The link between Article 83(1) TFEU and the notion of '*imperative grounds of public security*' is questionable for two reasons: first of all, Article 83(1) TFEU does not identify or seek to identify the 'most serious' offences, rather it seeks to identify serious offences with a cross-border dimension that might therefore benefit from some EU co-ordination. However, the Court simply established a nexus between Union competence and public security which does not necessarily hold up to scrutiny. Secondly, the Court has held over and over again that public policy and security are concepts to be defined at national not European level; to link public security with EU competence does not appear to be very persuasive.

50 Case C-145/09, *Tsakouridis*, EU:C:2010:708, para. 47.
51 Case C-145/09, *Tsakouridis*, EU:C:2010:708, para. 53.
52 Case C-348/09, *PI*, EU:C:2012:300.
53 Case C-348/09, *PI*, EU:C:2012:300, para. 28.

More generally, it has been doubted in the scholarship,[54] whether sexual assaults against children can really be defined as a threat to imperative grounds of public security, at least if the latter should be given its ordinary meaning. This is of course not to deny that those are particularly serious and hideous crimes: but rather that the enhanced protection provided for in Directive 2004/38 is based on the idea that the Union citizen might, with time, become a member of the host society in all but nationality so that even should she misbehave, she would remain the responsibility of the host society. The preamble to Directive 2004/38 is in this respect very clear: 'only in *exceptional circumstances*, where there are imperative grounds of public security, should an expulsion measure be taken against Union citizens who have resided for many years in the territory of the host Member State, in particular when they were born and have resided there throughout their life' (emphasis added).[55] The Court however takes a different approach, so that at the end of the day the Union citizen remains the responsibility of the home Member State, even when she might have spent more time in the host State than in the State of nationality. For this reason, a serious crime might be qualified as a public security threat. The reason behind this choice is that the Court has decided that it is not passage of time alone that secures integration in the host State; rather, it is the passage of time coupled with *qualitative* criteria. For instance in *Dias*, in relation to the right to permanent residence, the Court held 'the integration objective which lies behind the acquisition of the right of permanent residence laid down in Article 16(1) of Directive 2004/38 is based not only on territorial and time factors but also on *qualitative elements*, relating to the level of integration in the host Member State' (emphasis added).[56] This despite the fact that Article 16 of Directive 2004/38 does not mention any 'qualitative criteria': indeed the Union legislature decided, for better or worse, not to include any integration test or similar as a condition to benefit from the rights contained in Directive 2004/38. As said above, the presumption (which the wording of Directive suggests to be irrefutable) is that passage of time alone establishes that link of integration that brings with it entitlement to enhanced protection, in terms of permanent residence and protection from expulsion.

In *Onuekwere* and *M.G.*[57] the Court further pushed the 'qualitative element' discourse: in the former case,[58] consistently with *Dias*, it held that the Union legislature made the acquisition of the right of permanent residence subject to the 'integration' of the Union citizen in the host society. This despite the fact that Article 16(1) does not mention, even in passing, integration as a relevant

---

54 See e.g. D. Acosta Arcarazo, 'Trapped in the lobby: Europe's revolving doors and the other as Xenos' (2014) 39 *EL Rev*, 362.

55 Recital 24 of the Preamble of Directive 2004/38.

56 Case C-325/09, *Dias*, EU:C:2011:498, para. 64.

57 Case C-400/12, *M.G.*, EU:C:2014:9.

58 Case C-378/12, *Onuekwere*, EU:C:2014:13.

criterion for entitlement; rather it simply states that 'Union citizens who have resided legally for a continuous period of five years in the host Member State *shall* have the right to permanent residence' (emphasis added). It is continued legal residence[59] for a period of five years that determines *entitlement* to permanent residence. The Court then proceeded in this (very misguided) direction: integration which is a precondition for the enjoyment of the rights of permanent residence is based not only on territorial and temporal factors (as one might have gathered from the text of the Directive) but also on *qualitative* elements, so much so that the undermining of the link of integration justifies the loss of permanent residence even beyond what provided for by the Directive. And, self-evidently in the eyes of the Court, the imposition of a prison sentence affects the integration of the citizen in the host State.

In *M.G.*,[60] decided the same day by the same chamber, this line of reasoning reaches paradoxical results: here, Ms G. was a Portuguese national, married to another Portuguese national, who had resided in the UK since 1998. In 2009 she was condemned to 21 months in prison for cruelty and beating of a person under the age of 16. Both crimes were committed against her children who had been placed into care as a result of the suspected (and then confirmed) violence. Ms G. applied for permanent residence whilst she was in prison; the Secretary of State refused the application and ordered that she should be deported on public policy and public security grounds. She was detained beyond her sentence pending her deportation. The Secretary of State took the view that, despite having lived in the UK for more than twenty years when she was condemned, Ms G. did not qualify for enhanced protection as that protection is dependent upon the 'integration' of the Union citizen in the host society, which cannot take place whilst the Union citizen is in prison. The Secretary of State also found that Ms G. did not have permanent residence and therefore was not entitled to the protection provided for in Article 28 Directive 2004/38, and that in any event there were 'serious' grounds of public policy for expelling her. And, that *a fortiori* she was not entitled to the basic level of protection provided for in Article 27. The immigration tribunal (first tier) found that since Ms G. had resided in the UK for more than ten years, she was entitled to enhanced protection; and that the Secretary of State had failed to show that there were imperative grounds of public security justifying her deportation.

On appeal, the Secretary of State conceded that Ms G. should be treated as a permanent resident, but contested the way the ten years had been calculated; the parties also disagreed on the interpretation of the 'serious grounds' of public policy and security (the protection available to permanent residents), as provided for in Article 28(2) Directive 2004/38. The Upper Tribunal (Immigration and

59 Also interpreted narrowly by the Court, see e.g. Joined Cases C-424/10 and C-425/10, *Ziolkowski and Szeja*, EU:C:2011:866.

60 Case C-400/12, *M.G.*, EU:C:2014:9.

Asylum), the appeal tribunal from the first tier court, then referred the case for a preliminary ruling; in particular the national court enquired whether periods spent in prison would break the continuity of residence in order to benefit from the enhanced protection provided in Article 28(3) Directive 2004/38; whether the ten years of residence needs to be continuous; and whether the ten-year period should be calculated backwards from expulsion or forward from the start of the citizen's residence. The latter question was the crucial one: if the ten years have to be calculated forward from the start of the citizen's residence, then the citizen would benefit from enhanced protection provided she had already lived in the host country for ten years at the time of imprisonment. However, if the period is calculated backwards from the order of deportation; *and* imprisonment had the effect of breaking continuity of residence, it would become very difficult for an errant migrant to ever benefit from the enhanced protection provided for in the Directive.

The Court, delivered a ruling which is both nonsensical and unclear; it is particularly telling that the case was assigned to a chamber, and that it was rendered after hearing the Advocate General so that it was deemed not necessary for an opinion to be delivered, despite this being the first case of its kind to be heard by the Court, and despite the obvious repercussions for Union citizens. The Court held that the ten-year period should be calculated from the date in which the expulsion order was made. It then found that, in principle, the ten-year residence period should be continuous. The Court then restated that the system of protection devised in Article 28 of Directive 2004/38 is based on the degree of integration of the person concerned, so that the greater the degree of integration, the more difficult it is for the Member State to deport them. This is undeniably true; however, much as it was the case in *Onuekwere*, the Court then leaped to a different level of discourse, one wholly unsupported by the aims and text of the Directive. Thus, it decided that the progressive degree of integration which justifies the enhanced protection contained in the Directive is also based on *qualitative* elements so that periods spent in prison would affect continuity of residence: by breaking the law, the Court reasoned, the Union citizen has broken that bond with the host society that indicated her integration therein. For this reason, 'it follows that periods of imprisonment cannot be taken into account for the purposes of granting the enhanced protection provided for in Article 28(3)(a) of Directive 2004/38 and that, in principle, such periods interrupt the continuity of the period of residence for the purposes of that provision'.[61] The Court then indicated that the assessment of whether the straying Union citizen will benefit from enhanced protection will be based on the circumstances of the particular case, and that the fact that the Union citizen has lived in the host State for ten years or more must form part of the assessment of the national court based on individual circumstances. This was the case even though there seems to be no

61 Case C-400/12, *M.G.*, EU:C:2014:9, para. 33.

such discretion in the Directive: the ten-year requirement is an objective not subjective fact.

This ruling is therefore remarkable for three different reasons: first of all, it deviates from previously established hermeneutic principles pursuant to which limitations to Treaty rights must be interpreted narrowly. Thus, the Court departs from the text and aims of Directive 2004/38, and superimposes qualitative criteria which had been left out from its provisions (most probably deliberately). The Directive is based on a mere incremental criterion: the longer the Union citizen resides in the host State, the more rights she will acquire: short stays carry limited rights; medium-term stays carry more rights but are also subject to the economic activity/independence conditions; long stays transform the Union citizen in a full member of the host community, who no longer needs to satisfy any condition to be considered a member of the host welfare and social community. At no point does the Directive allow Member States to impose an integration test: not *before* the right to permanent residency, not *in order* to gain permanent residency. This is possibly the greatest difference between Union citizens and third-country nationals: the former are considered, by the legislature at least, to be many steps above the latter: it is their belonging to the European family that allows for the integration link to be given for granted, so that time and place alone suffice. It is their belonging to the European family that removes executive discretion, and with it the need to 'conform' to whatever requirements drive the political fancy of the moment.

However, the Court, at least in relation to expulsion measures, turns the system of the Directive upside down so that the enhanced protection is nothing more than a proportionality assessment: rather than being available as a matter of right, it will depend on the actual circumstances of the claimant, at least in those cases in which there has been a custodial sentence.

Secondly, the reasoning of the Court is wholly irrational because it risks depriving the enhanced protection of any effect: after all, it is very unlikely, also because of the case-law of the Court and the protection against expulsion provided for in Directive 2004/38, that a Member State would be allowed to rely on the public policy/security derogation in relation to individuals that have carried themselves in exemplary terms. Rather, the protection in the Directive is there for those individuals who, for one reason or the other, deviate from societal norms of behaviour; it is a recognition that also 'bad' individuals have a life, families and relationships which are likelier to become stronger as time goes by. It is exactly to protect those individuals that Directive 2004/38 devised an incremental protection against expulsion: but if anyone who has spent periods in prison, and whose deportation order follows from that detention, is deprived of the enhanced protection, who exactly is going to benefit from Article 28(3)(a) Directive 2004/38? The Catch-22 situation seems not to have escaped national courts: thus, for instance the Upper Tribunal (Immigration and Asylum) when faced with a case involving an expulsion order made against a person detained in prison, held 'if the analysis in the Secretary of State's grounds is accurate [whereby following the ruling in M.G. prison would interrupt residence for the purposes of enhanced protection], then the Secretary of State could defeat all such appeals simply by making a deportation decision whilst an appellant is in prison (and thereby incapable of satisfying the condition of ten years' continuous residence). As the grounds appear to acknowledge, the real issue in this case is the status of the ten years' residence which these appellants have enjoyed before *they* were imprisoned' (emphasis added).[62]

Thirdly, these rulings also demonstrate the implosion of Union citizenship: after all, what the Court is indicating is that Union nationals residing in a host Member State remain the responsibility of their State of origin. It is for the state of origin alone to deal with straying members of society: it matters little in this respect that the citizen might have grown up in the host State which then arguably would carry a greater (moral and possibly factual) responsibility towards the misbehaving citizen. Rather, criminal behaviour is seen in its most simplistic terms – as a sort of original sin (hence responsibility of the State of origin) that is totally severed from environmental factors, which would include a responsibility of the State of residence in cases of long-term residence. As we have seen above, this same trend, that of a traditional allocation of responsibilities so that it is nationality and not choice that determines the relationship between citizen and society, is visible also in other strands of case-law relating to the right to equal treatment of economically inactive individuals.

7. CONCLUSION

Union citizenship is an experiment in progress and whether the case-law analysed above in relation to both residency rights and expulsion measures on grounds of public policy and security is to be welcomed will depend very much on the view one takes of the significance of supranational citizenship. In this respect, a narrow interpretation of Union citizenship might be justified by the fact that the latter does not intend to replace national citizenship, including the fact that is the state of nationality that bears primary responsibility for its citizens. As a result, only acquisition of the nationality of the host State (a matter entirely regulated by national law) will transform the migrant Union citizen in a full member of the host society. And yet, such a narrow interpretation, which is that favoured by the Court at present, seems to betray the transnational roots

62 *Secretary of State for the Home Department v M Essa and others*, Upper Tribunal (Immigration and Asylum) unreported, appeal number DA/02037/2013; and DA/02038/2013, available at https://tribunalsdecisions.service.gov.uk/utiac/da-02037-2013-da-02038-2013 (last accessed on 20 January 2016).

of Union citizenship: after all, the very idea behind it should be to allow Union citizens, at least to a certain extent, to decide where they *want* to belong, so as to replace the belonging-by-birth typical of the national state rhetoric, with a new belonging-by-choice, more in line with the ambitions of a 'special space', the European Union, which is neither national nor international. It is possible that something of this ideal might be saved, especially by restating a role for Article 21 TFEU in relation to the rights to reside of Union citizens. Yet the Court's interpretation of when the Member States are entitled to severe a Union citizen from her polity of choice is a stark reminder that, at least in the eyes of the Court, Union citizenship impacts very little on imbedded notions of self and otherness. Once a foreigner, always a foreigner.

CHAPTER 7

WHO DOES NOT BELONG HERE ANYMORE?

A Statistical Snapshot of Member States' Practices

Anthony VALCKE

In the ten years since the entry into force of Directive 2004/38,[1] there has been a noticeable increase in the number of references for preliminary rulings made by the national courts to the EU Court of Justice concerning the expulsion of EU citizens and their family members. As Eleanor Spaventa rightly points out in her contribution, the codification by Directive 2004/38 of the Court's case-law under previous instruments and EU enlargement in 2004 and 2007 have certainly contributed to this rise in preliminary references. A further contributing factor appears to be the increasing propensity of Member States to have recourse to measures that restrict the free movement rights of EU citizens and their family members for reasons that do not necessarily relate to public order or public security. The purpose of this chapter is to provide a brief empirical review of the practices of the Member States in restricting the free movement rights of EU citizens and their family members, based upon official statistical data that have been made available by the Member States.

1. AVAILABILITY OF DATA ON EU RESIDENCE RIGHTS

Unlike the situation of third-country nationals covered by the EU's common visa and migration policies,[2] Member States are not required to publish detailed

1 Directive 2004/38/EC of the European Parliament and of the Council of 29 April 2004 on the right of citizens of the Union and their family members to move and reside freely within the territory of the Member States, OJ 2004, L 158/77 (hereinafter referred to as 'Directive 2004/38').

2 Regulation (EC) No. 862/2007 of the European Parliament and of the Council of 11 July 2007 on Community statistics on migration and international protection, OJ 2007, L 199/23

statistical information regarding the application of Directive 2004/38. At present, Member States are only required to furnish data on the overall number of EU migrants having their usual residence in their territory, annual migration flows into and out of their territory, as well as the number of EU citizens who have acquired the nationality of the host Member State.[3] It is therefore up to each Member State to determine what – if any – data to collate on the application of Directive 2004/38. They also determine whether to make such data available to the public in accordance with the legal framework governing access to such information.

Nonetheless, Member States do not have an absolute discretion in this regard. The Court of Justice has had an opportunity to examine the limitations that EU law places on the collection of information by Member States in connection with EU citizens who reside on their territory. In *Huber*,[4] the Court found that the storing of personalised (as opposed to anonymised) information relating to EU citizens for statistical purposes on a central register kept by the German immigration office (*Bundesamt für Migration und Flüchtlinge*) could not be considered necessary within the meaning of the EU Data Protection Directive.[5] The Court did not however call into question the power of Member States to store personalised data that is necessary for the practical application of Directive 2004/38 by the competent national authorities,[6] nor the ability of Member States to keep anonymous information on EU citizens for statistical purposes.[7]

In view of the scarcity of harmonising EU legislation on the matter, it is not surprising to find significant divergence between Member States in terms of the availability and the level of detail of statistical information on the entry and residence of EU citizens and their family members. According to a 2013 study on residence formalities undertaken for the European Commission,[8] information on the issue of residence documents is available in most Member

(hereinafter referred to as 'Regulation 862/2007'). This instrument requires the Member States to collate detailed statistical information on persons having applied for international protection including levels of applications and rejections. The Regulation also requires Member States to furnish information on the situation of third-country nationals present on their national territory, including covering the issue of residence permits, measures taken to prevent illegal entry and stay, as well as measures taken to return illegal migrants. Member States are also required to provide statistics on the number of Schengen visas issued under Article 46 of Regulation (EC) No. 810/2009 of the European Parliament and of the Council of 13 July 2009 establishing a Community Code on Visas, OJ 2009, L 243/1.

3 Article 3 Regulation 862/2007.

4 Case C-524/06, *Huber*, EU:C:2008:724.

5 Case C-524/06, *Huber*, EU:C:2008:724, para. 68.

6 Case C-524/06, *Huber*, EU:C:2008:724, paras. 57–62, 66.

7 Case C-524/06, *Huber*, EU:C:2008:724, paras. 63–65.

8 ICF GHK and Milieu, 'Evaluation of EU rules on free movement of EU citizens and their family members and their practical implementation' (20 October 2013), available at http://ec.europa.eu/justice/citizen/document/files/evaluation_of_eu_rules_on_free_movement-final_report.pdf (last accessed on 31 July 2015).

States. However, statistical data on rejection rates of residence applications is only available from sixteen Member States. Furthermore, no data exists on entry bans and the data on expulsions is only publicly available in four Member States, even though these constitute some of the most restrictive measures that Member States can take against EU citizens and their family members. Moreover, the UK is the only Member State that has published data on appeals brought against administrative decisions that restrict the free movement rights of EU citizens and their family members. Several EU officials have unofficially expressed the view that the absence of publicly available statistical data on an EU-wide basis restricts the ability of the Commission to monitor and enforce the EU free movement rules in a way that goes beyond transposition of Directive 2004/38.

Table 1 provides an overview of the availability of data on EU residence rights across the Member States.

Table 1. Availability of statistical information on residence rights of EU citizens and their family members

Member State	Issue of documents	Refusals	Abuse*	Expulsions	Administrative appeals	Judicial appeals	Source of data
Austria	√	√	n/a	n/a	n/a	n/a	Ministry of the Interior
Belgium	√	n/a	√	√	n/a	n/a	Immigration Office
Bulgaria	√	√	√	n/a	n/a	n/a	Ministry of the Interior
Croatia[(1)]	n/a	n/a	n/a	n/a	n/a	n/a	Ministry of the Interior
Cyprus	√	√	√	n/a	n/a	n/a	Ministry of the Interior
Czech Republic	√	√	√	n/a	n/a	n/a	Ministry of the Interior
Denmark	√	√	√	n/a	√	n/a	Immigration Service
Estonia	√	√	√	n/a	n/a	n/a	Ministry of the Interior
Finland	√	√	√	n/a	n/a	n/a	National Police Board
France	√	n/a	n/a	√	n/a	n/a	Ministry of the Interior
Germany	√	n/a	√	n/a	n/a	n/a	Ministry of the Interior
Greece	√	√	n/a	n/a	n/a	n/a	Ministry of the Interior
Ireland	√	√	√	n/a	n/a	n/a	Irish Naturalisation & Immigration Service

Member State	Issue of documents	Refusals	Abuse*	Expulsions	Administrative appeals	Judicial appeals	Source of data
Italy(2)	n/a	n/a	n/a	n/a	n/a	n/a	–
Latvia	√	n/a	√	n/a	n/a	n/a	Office of Citizenship and Migration Affairs
Lithuania	√	√	n/a	n/a	n/a	n/a	Ministry of the Interior
Luxembourg	√	n/a	n/a	n/a	n/a	n/a	Ministry of Foreign Affairs
Malta	n/a	n/a	n/a	n/a	n/a	n/a	–
Netherlands(3)	√	√	√	√	n/a	n/a	Immigration and Naturalisation Service
Poland	√	√	√	n/a	n/a	n/a	Migration Authority
Portugal	√	n/a	√	n/a	n/a	n/a	Immigration & Border Service
Romania	√	n/a	n/a	n/a	n/a	n/a	Ministry of the Interior
Slovakia	√	n/a	n/a	n/a	n/a	n/a	Alien Police Department Office
Slovenia	√	√	n/a	n/a	n/a	n/a	Ministry of the Interior
Spain	√	√	n/a	n/a	n/a	n/a	Ministry of Interior
Sweden	√	√	√	n/a	n/a	n/a	Migration Board
UK	√	√	√	√	√	√	UK Visas & Immigration

Sources: ICF GHK/Milieu 2013 study on residence formalities, with additional research by the author.
Notes:

* Abuse cases include marriages and partnerships of convenience; data on such cases are not systematically published but are in the public domain.

(1) Croatia was not included in 2013 survey; no statistics could be found on Ministry of Interior's website.

(2) Italy ceased the publication of statistics relating to EU citizens in 2008; no response was received from the Ministry of Interior or the Italian Statistical Authority following the author's official request for access to information.

(3) The IND does not publish these statistics, but expulsion figures have been disclosed in parliament.

Further examination of this data reveals some important trends in connection with the practical implementation of the EU free movement rights in the Member States.

2. DATA ON RESIDENCE APPLICATIONS BY EU CITIZENS AND THEIR FAMILY MEMBERS

Most Member States publish data on the issue of residence documentation, with the exception of Croatia, Italy and Malta. However, such data is of limited value when analysing the implementation of Directive 2004/38 because such figures tend only to concern applications by EU citizens and their family members that have been successful.

Data on the rates of rejection of such applications provides a much more useful indication of the existence of problems in the practical implementation of Directive 2004/38. The data reveals a wide range of variation across the Member States as Table 2 shows.

Table 2. Issue and refusal of residence documentation in 2012 (data for 2012 unless otherwise indicated)

Member State	Number of applications received	Refusal rate* (all applications)	Refusal rate** (TCN family members)	Refusal rate*** (Singh cases)
Austria	48,422	3%	3%	n/a
Belgium	64,871	n/a	n/a	n/a
Bulgaria	7,685	0%	0%	n/a
Cyprus	23,058	4%	30%	n/a
Czech Republic	14,676	8%	15%	n/a
Denmark(1)	30,059	1%	1%	64%
Estonia	3,768	0%	0%	n/a
Finland	16,033	3%	3%	n/a
France(2) (3) (4)	13,531	n/a	n/a	n/a
Germany(5)	11,500	n/a	n/a	n/a
Greece	22,400	0.2%	n/a	n/a
Hungary	19,210	0.1%	31%	n/a
Ireland(5) (6)	2,338	n/a	37%	96%
Italy	n/a	n/a	n/a	n/a
Latvia(2) (3)	1,584	n/a	n/a	n/a
Lithuania(3)	1,343	0.4%	4%	n/a
Luxembourg(2)	23,347	n/a	n/a	n/a
Malt	n/a	n/a	n/a	n/a
Netherlands(7)	10,980	n/a	n/a	n/a
Poland	8,446	2%	3%	n/a
Portugal(2)	15,765	n/a	n/a	n/a
Romania(2)	52,501	n/a	n/a	n/a

Member State	Number of applications received	Refusal rate* (all applications)	Refusal rate** (TCN family members)	Refusal rate*** (Singh cases)
Slovakia(2)	4,459	n/a	n/a	n/a
Slovenia(6) (8)	14,365	3%	n/a	n/a
Spain	116,016	13%	34%	n/a
Sweden	34,074	22%	29%	n/a
UK	83,644	43%	65%	n/a
	EU average	**7%**	**20%**	–

Sources: ICF GHK/Milieu 2013 study on residence formalities, with additional research by the author.
Notes:

* Refusal rate refers to rejection of applications submitted by EU citizens and non-EU family members for residence and permanent residence documents. It includes applications which have been the subject of a formal refusal decision and applications rejected as being invalid.

** Refusal rate refers to rejection of applications submitted by third country family members for residence and permanent residence documents. It includes applications which have been the subject of a formal refusal decision and applications rejected as being invalid.

*** Refusal rate refers to rejection of applications submitted by non-EU family members for residence documents in cases claiming the benefit of family reunification under the *Surinder Singh* ruling (C-370/90) following the exercise of free movement rights by the EU relative.

(1) Data on refusal rate in *Singh* cases relates to applications made in first half of 2012.
(2) Data only refers to number of successful applications.
(3) Data only available for 2011.
(4) Low number of applications may be explained by voluntary registration system for EU citizens.
(5) Data only relates to application made by third country national family members.
(6) Yearly average based on applications lodged in period 2007–2013.
(7) Data only relates to number of successful applications made by EU citizens.
(8) Refusal data only relates to applications by EU citizens.

While the average rate of rejection of applications for residence documents by EU citizens and their family members is around 7% across the EU, the statistics indicates the existence of significantly high rates of rejection in several Member States. The rejection rates for all EU residence applications are considerably higher in Spain (13%), Sweden (22%) and the UK (43%).[9] In absolute terms, this means that in 2012 over 7,000 residence applications were turned down in Sweden, 15,000 applications were refused in Spain and 36,000 residence applications were rejected in the UK.

The situation of third-country national family members is even bleaker. A detailed examination of applications by non-EU family members reveals that rejection rates are even higher in a significant number of Member States: Cyprus (30%), Hungary (31%), Ireland (37%), Spain (34%), Sweden (29%) and

9 Refusal rates refer to the rates of rejection of applications submitted by EU citizens and non-EU family members for residence and permanent residence documents. The rates include applications which have been the subject of a formal refusal decision and applications rejected as being invalid.

the UK (65%).[10] This compares with an average refusal rate of 20% in respect of applications for residence documents submitted by non-EU family members across the Member States.

These high refusal rates are of serious concern. Given that the EU free movement rules provide 'a largely rights-based legal framework', a relatively high rate of rejection of applications in a Member State is likely to indicate that 'something is lacking, namely either the quality of information provided to applicants or the quality of decision-making in the first instance.'[11] Indeed, the Commission's Single Market Scoreboard confirms that EU citizens and their family members encounter significant problems with residence formalities in all Member States with high refusal rates.[12]

There is little data to determine the quality of decision-making by the national authorities in EU free movement cases. A useful proxy to measure the quality of national decisions would be to look at the outcome of appeals filed

---

10 Refusal rates refer to the rate of rejection of applications submitted by third-country family members for residence and permanent residence documents. These include applications which have been the subject of a formal refusal decision and applications rejected as being invalid.

11 J. Shaw and N. Miller, 'When Legal Worlds Collide: An Exploration of What Happens when EU Free Movement Law Meets UK Immigration Law' (2013) 38 *EL Rev*, 137–166, 164.

12 Single Market Scoreboard, Feedback and Concerns, available at http://ec.europa.eu/internal_market/scoreboard/feedback/concerns/index_en.htm (last accessed on 31 July 2015). The following concerns are noted: Cyprus: 'Third-country nationals who are family members of EU citizens report serious delays in obtaining residence cards'; Hungary: 'EU citizens complain that official foreign documents are not always accepted by Hungarian authorities'; Ireland: 'EU citizens report about delays regarding their application for residence cards. Difficulties are reported by some citizens whose application for a permanent residence card was refused without any grounds'; Spain: 'Citizens frequently face delays and administrative burdens when trying to obtain a residence card in Spain'; Sweden: 'EU citizens report as a problem the refusal of a "personal number" if they cannot show the S1 form. No other portable form is accepted nor is proof of private insurance. Without a personal number, a citizen cannot undertake important activities like opening a bank account, renting property, attending Swedish courses, filing with the unemployment agency, entering an agreement with an employer, subscribing to a fixed telephone or mobile phone or television. A personal identity number is also the key to basic health care in Sweden. Students, retired persons (EU citizens and even Swedes having lived abroad) and their family members report that health insurance is refused'; UK: 'EU citizens complain about excessive delays and formalities in processing residence cards for their family members from third countries. Problems are reported concerning the acquisition of the right to permanent residence in the UK. Problems are reported stating that the authorities often retain key personal documents including passports or original documents for long periods (sometimes over six months). This creates additional problems for both, the third-country national and the EU spouse, to lead a normal life, to proof [sic] their right to reside in the UK and to work and to travel to the home country of the EU citizen. Students and inactive EU citizens and their spouses complain that they are required to have Comprehensive Sickness Insurance (CSI). This is a breach of Directive 2004/38 and Regulation 883/04 and means that social security benefit is refused on the grounds that the inactive EU citizen (or family member) does not have the right to reside, given that he/she does not have CSI.' For a closer examination of the situation in the UK, see A. Valcke, 'Five Years of the Citizens Directive in the UK' (2011) 25 *Journal of Immigration, Asylum and Nationality Law*, 217–244 and 331–357.

against decisions relating to EU residence rights. Regrettably, the UK is the only Member State for which data on appeals is available as shown in Table 3.

Table 3. Appeals against EU residence decisions in the UK and appeal outcomes (2010–2014)

Year	Total EU residence applications	Total EU residence refusals	Refusal rate	Appeals (as % of applications)	Appeals (as % of refused applications)	Successful appeals before First Tier Tribunal (FTT)	Appeals refused by FTT, but appealed to Upper Tribunal (UT)	Successful appeals before UT of appeals refused by FTT
2010	81,984	17,288	20.89	7%	33%	38%	7%	31%
2011	97,982	29,170	29.77	6%	20%	37%	6%	30%
2012	83,644	36,232	43.32	9%	21%	33%	6%	21%
2013	102,088	40,807	40.00	11%	28%	31%	4%	19%
2014	100,667	38,280	38.03	9%	24%	14%	1%	7%
		Five-year average	**34.04%**	8%	25%	31%	5%	22%

Source: UK Home Office, with additional research by the author.

The data casts doubt on the quality of decision-making by the UK Home Office in EEA residence cases. Over the period 2010–2014, the average rate of refusal in EEA residence cases by the UK authorities reached 34%.[13] During this time, roughly a quarter of refusal decisions have been appealed to the First Tier Tribunal. In 31% of cases, EU citizens and their family members obtained a successful outcome to their appeal. In 5% of cases where the first-level appeal failed, a further appeal was lodged before the Upper Tribunal. In these second-level appeals, a further 22% of cases were resolved in favour of EU citizens and their family members. This would seem to suggest that roughly 10% of decisions are decided wrongly by the UK administrative authorities and subsequently overturned by the courts. The proportion of wrongly decided cases might be even higher, given that the withdrawal of legal aid in immigration cases in 2013[14] may have deterred EU citizens and their family members from appealing against a refusal by the UK authorities to issue them residence documents.

As regards the situation of family members of EU citizens returning home after exercising free movement rights, Denmark and Ireland are the only countries to provide information on refusal rates in so-called *Surinder Singh*

13 This compares with an average rate of refusal of EU residence applications by the UK authorities in the period 2004–2014 of 21.09%. The increase in refusal rates above this average witnessed since 2010 coincides with the change in UK government.

14 For a discussion, see S. York, 'The End of Legal Aid in Immigration – A Barrier to Access to Justice for Migrants and a Decline in the Rule of Law' (2013) 27 *Journal of Immigration, Asylum and Nationality Law*, 106–138.

cases.[15] These cases concern applications for family reunification by non-EU family members of EU citizens returning home after exercising free movement in another Member State. The data suggest almost two-thirds of applications by non-EU family members were refused in Denmark, while Ireland refused such applications in 96% of cases.

3. DATA ON ABUSE OF RIGHTS BY EU CITIZENS AND THEIR FAMILY MEMBERS

Under Article 35 of Directive 2004/38, Member States retain the power to refuse or withdraw residence documentation to EU citizens who engage in fraud or abuse of rights. Recital 28 of the Directive specifically cites 'marriages of convenience or any other form of relationships contracted for the sole purpose of enjoying the right of free movement and residence' as an example of such abuse. This power has been confirmed by the Court of Justice on several occasions,[16] although so far there has been no case in which a Member State has been able to successfully invoke it as a justification for restricting the free movement rights of EU citizens and their family members.

One of the abuses that is often cited by EU Member States as justifying a call for imposing further restrictions on the free movement of EU citizens concerns marriages of convenience,[17] whereby an EU citizen enters into a sham marriage with a non-EU national for the sole purpose of enabling the latter to benefit from the free movement rules.

In the recent *McCarthy* case,[18] the UK government referred to its powers under Article 35 of the Directive in seeking to justify their long-standing policy not to recognise family residence cards issued by the Member States under Article 10 of Directive 2004/38 which should exempt non-EU family members from the need for a visa when entering a Member State pursuant to Article 5(2) of the Directive. The UK authorities argued that the '"systemic problem" of abuse of rights and fraud by third-country nationals' and the 'palpable risk that a

15 In the Netherlands these are called 'Belgian route' cases and in Norway 'Swedish route' cases due to the preference of destination of the EU citizens to exercise their free movement rights in those Member States.

16 Case C-370/90, *Surinder Singh*, EU:C:1992:296, para. 24; Case C-109/01, *Akrich*, EU:C:2003:491, paras. 55–57; Case C-456/12, *O. and B.*, EU:C:2014:135, para. 58; and Case C-202/13, *McCarthy*, EU:C:2014:2450, paras. 43–58.

17 It will be recalled that in April 2013, the Ministers of four EU Member States – the UK, Austria, Germany and the Netherlands – wrote to the Irish Presidency of the European Council on the matter of free movement of persons within the Union. The letter specifically concerned the issue of 'benefits tourism' but also fraud, such as marriages of convenience, available at http://docs.dpaq.de/3604-130415_letter_to_presidency_final_1_2.pdf (last accessed on 31 July 2015).

18 Case C-202/13, *McCarthy*, EU:C:2014:2450, paras. 26–27.

significant proportion of those engaged in the "business of sham marriages" will use fake residence cards for the purpose of gaining illegal access to the United Kingdom' justified a blanket policy to refuse entry to the UK to family members holding a residence card issued by another Member State.[19] However, the Court did not agree with the UK's contention and ruled that Article 35 could not be used to adopt general measures of prevention without engaging in a specific assessment in each individual case.[20]

Despite such claims of 'systematic abuse',[21] few EU countries routinely collate statistics on cases of fraud or abuse in connection with the free movement rules. According to the European Migration Network,[22] only six Member States systematically collate data on suspected marriages of convenience.[23] In addition, following a request from the Council, a number of other Member States have provided data to the Commission on suspected cases of marriages of convenience.[24] Table 4 provides an overview of published data on EU residence cases involving a marriage or registered partnership of convenience.

Table 4. Data on marriages of convenience (data for 2012 unless otherwise stated)

Member State	Suspected cases	Identified case	Total FM applications	% suspected cases	% identified cases
Belgium	990	n/a	8,561	11.6%	n/a
Bulgaria	3	n/a	857	0.4%	n/a
Cyprus(1)	n/a	58	1,004	n/a	5.8%
Czech	n/a	51	2,402	n/a	2.1%
Denmark	n/a	8	3,939	n/a	0.2%

19 Case C-202/13, *McCarthy*, EU:C:2014:2450, para. 27.

20 Case C-202/13, *McCarthy*, EU:C:2014:2450, paras. 55–57.

21 This is the term used in by the Austrian, British, Dutch and German Ministers in their letter to the Irish Presidency of the European Council, available at http://docs.dpaq.de/3604-130415-letter-to-presidency-ral-1-2.pdf (last accessed on 31 July), 2–3.

22 European Migration Network, Study on Misuse of Family Reunification Study, June 2012, available at http://ec.europa.eu/dgs/home-affairs/what-we-do/networks/european_migration_network/reports/docs/emn-studies/family-reunification/0a_emn_misuse_family_reunification_study_final_june_2012_en.pdf (last accessed on 31 July 2015). See also European Migration Network, Ad Hoc Query on Marriages of Convenience, 18 May 2011, available at http://ec.europa.eu/dgs/home-affairs/what-we-do/networks/european_migration_network/reports/docs/ad-hoc-queries/family-reunification/303_emn_ad-hoc_query_marriage_of_convenience_18mar2011_wider_dissemination_en.pdf (last accessed on 31 July 2015); European Migration Network, Ad Hoc Query on Marriages of Convenience, 27 August 2013, available at http://ec.europa.eu/dgs/home-affairs/what-we-do/networks/european_migration_network/reports/docs/ad-hoc-queries/family-reunification/491_emn_ahq_marriage_of_convenience_8jul2013_en.pdf (last accessed on 31 July 2015).

23 The Member States concerned are Belgium, Bulgaria, Cyprus, Estonia, Finland, Latvia, Poland and the UK.

24 Communication from the Commission to the European Parliament, the Council, the European Economic and Social Committee and the Committee of the Regions, 'Free movement of EU citizens and their families: Five actions to make a difference', COM(2013) 837.

Estonia	38	0	342	11.1%	0.0%
Finland (visas)[(2)]	n/a	10	650	n/a	1.5%
Finland (residence)[(3)]	250	n/a	2,910	8.6%	n/a
Germany	250	n/a	7,700	3.2%	n/a
Ireland[(4)]	n/a	9	2,338	n/a	1.4%
Latvia[(5)]	5	n/a	319	1.6%	n/a
Netherlands[(6)]	92	61	n/a	n/a	n/a
Poland	145	2	153	94.8%	1.3%
Portugal[(1)]	n/a	48	5,616	n/a	0.9%
Sweden	n/a	30	26,546	n/a	0.1%
UK (EEA Family Permits)	256	176	12,800	2.0%	1.4%
UK (residence cards)	1,891	n/a	32,192	5.9%	5.9%[(7)]
			EU average	**15.5%**	**1.9%**

Sources: COM (2013) 837, EMN ad hoc query 27 August 2013, ICF GHK/Milieu 2013 study, and EMN Report June 2012, with additional research by the author.

Notes:

(1) Yearly average based on total cases reported 2010–2012.

(2) Identified cases are in connection with 'visa applications'.

(3) Suspected cases are in connection with application for documentation submitted by all third-country nationals, including EU residence applications.

(4) Identified cases reported in 2010; residence applications based on yearly average 2006–2013.

(5) Cases reported in 2011.

(6) Yearly average based on total cases reported 2010–2012.

(7) Figure is an estimate based upon the findings of the Independent Chief Inspector's sample of 60 cases in which a residence card was refused in Oct. 2013–Jan. 2014. This figure was calculated by multiplying the percentage of sampled refused residence card applications involving an identified marriage of convenience (20%) with the refusal rate for residence card applications in 2012 (32.5%). The resulting estimate has been reduced from 6.5% to 5.9% to ensure identified cases do not exceed suspected cases.

Based on the information provided by the Member States, it would appear that across the EU approximately three out of twenty residence applications are suspected of involving a relationship of convenience. However, the number of cases in which a finding of a marriage of convenience is made by the national administrative authorities is much lower. Cases in which residence documentation is refused or withdrawn on the basis of a marriage of convenience account for less than 2% of EU residence applications.

Nonetheless, there are shortcomings in this data that prevents it from being considered as conclusive evidence of the prevalence of marriages of convenience in the Member States concerned. Firstly, often the data on suspected marriages is not sufficiently disaggregated to distinguish suspected sham marriages which involve EU citizens from those involving nationals and resident non-EU citizens. As a result, it is by no means certain that all or even a majority of these cases necessarily involved EU citizens. Some of these cases may involve nationals of the country concerned particularly where family reunification rules for own nationals are not unduly restrictive. For example, this is the case in Belgium, where the published data on identified cases of marriages of convenience is not fully disaggregated by nationality.[25] The official data does not identify any cases in which EU citizens might have been involved.

Secondly, the data often only concerns cases in which the administrative authorities have a suspicion that a marriage is one of convenience ('% suspected cases' in Table 4). The data also indicates that only a fraction of suspected cases turn out to be confirmed following an administrative investigation (column '% identified cases' in Table 4). Indeed, the data would suggest that only about one in eight suspected cases of marriage of convenience result in an administrative decision to refuse or withdraw residence rights on the grounds that the non-EU family member's relationship with an EU citizen is not genuine. The only notable exception is the UK, where it would appear that most cases in which a relationship is suspected of being a sham usually result in an administrative finding that the relationship is fraudulent.[26]

In addition, no data is available to confirm whether any of these decisions were appealed and, if so, whether they were upheld by the judicial authorities. This represents a significant gap in trying to obtain an accurate picture of the prevalence of marriages of convenience and other sham relationships in EU residence cases.

Moreover, there is some anecdotal evidence[27] that suggests the national authorities may be misusing the powers of Article 35 by requiring non-EU

25 The Immigration Office's annual reports only identify the top two nationalities involved in marriages of convenience, namely Turkish and Moroccan nationals in the period 2009–2013. In 2013, the annual report reveals that no EU citizens were involved in identified cases of marriages of convenience.

26 This is based upon an estimate of applications refused on the basis of being a marriage of convenience reported in Independent Chief Inspector of Border and Immigration 'The Rights of European Citizens and their Spouses to Come to the UK: Inspecting the Application Process and the Tackling of Abuse – October 2013 – January 2014' (June 2014), 19 and 23, available at http://icinspector.independent.gov.uk/wp-content/uploads/2014/06/European-Casework-Report-Final.pdf (last accessed on 31 July 2015). The estimate is based upon the findings of the Independent Chief Inspector's sample of 60 refusal cases decided in October 2013–January 2014, which found that 20% of cases involved an identified marriage of convenience, multiplied by the rate of refusal in EU residence applications for 2012 (32.5% – this does not include refusals in permanent residence applications or applications rejected as invalid). The resulting estimate has been reduced from 6.5% to 5.9% to ensure identified cases do not exceed suspected cases.

27 See for example, X. Le Den and J. Sylvest, 'Understanding Citizens' and Businesses' Concerns with the Single Market: a View from the Assistance Services' (Ramboll, May 2011); http://ec.europa.eu/internal_market/strategy/docs/20concerns/feedback_report_en.pdf (last accessed on 31 July 2015). The study mentions the '[n]on-recognition of marriages due to presumption of abuse or fraud' as constituting a specific example of Member States applying the law incorrectly: 'The authorities suspect sham marriages and therefore do not grant the family right sought. These cases concern marriages with third-country nationals, most of which have taken place outside the EU.'

family members who apply for a residence card to prove they are in a genuine relationship, thereby reversing the burden of proof contrary to the Commission's guidance on investigating marriages of convenience.[28] The data would suggest that in Poland almost all residence applications submitted by non-EU spouses are suspected of being fraudulent. In addition, the practice of the Cypriot and the UK authorities is also questionable. Both Member States have noticeably higher rates of decisions to refuse the issue of residence documentation based on the existence of marriages of convenience (5.8% and 5.9%[29] respectively) when compared to the EU average (1.9%). Furthermore, the reliability of the UK's data has been questioned by the House of Lords and the House of Commons Joint Committee on Human Rights.[30]

Aside from fraudulent marriages and other unions, Belgium is the only country that regularly identifies cases in which persons have fraudulently claimed to be EU citizens using false identity cards or passports. This concerned on average 0.1% of applications during the period 2010–2014. Some information is also available for the UK. In a sample of 120 refusal cases relating to applications by EEA nationals and their family members, a report by the UK's Independent Chief Inspector of Borders and Immigration[31] found that fraudulent identity documents had been used in four applications for residence documentation.[32] If this holds true across all EU residence applications, it would mean around 0.5%[33] of EU residence applications involve attempts to use fraudulent evidence of EEA nationality in the UK.

---

28 European Commission Staff Working Document, *Handbook on addressing the issue of alleged marriages of convenience between EU citizens and non-EU nationals in the context of EU law on free movement of EU citizens*, SWD (2014) 284 final.

29 See footnote 26.

30 When the recent Immigration Act 2014 proceeded through Parliament, the Committee drew attention to 'the questionable strength of the evidence relied on by the Government to demonstrate the necessity for legislating to supplement the powers that already exist to combat sham marriages [...] Asked about the criteria the Government proposes to use to identify suspect marriages or civil partnerships, the Government says that the referral [of a suspect marriage or civil partnership for investigation] will be assessed against intelligence/ evidence based risk profiles and factors to identify whether it is at high risk of being a sham marriage or civil partnership, e.g. that one or both parties 'is of a nationality at high risk of involvement in a sham, on the basis of objective information and intelligence about sham cases': Joint Committee on Human Rights, *Legislative Scrutiny: Immigration Bill (eighth report)* (2013–14, HL 102, HC 935), 117 and 122.

31 Independent Chief Inspector of Border and Immigration, 'The Rights of European Citizens and their Spouses to Come to the UK: Inspecting the Application Process and the Tackling of Abuse – October 2013 – January 2014' (June 2014), 19 and 23, available at http://icinspector.independent.gov.uk/wp-content/uploads/2014/06/European-Casework-Report-Final.pdf (last accessed on 31 July 2015).

32 Three cases concerned applications by a family member for a residence card and one case concerned an application for a registration certificate.

33 This is an estimate based upon the findings of the Independent Chief Inspector's sample of 90 refusal cases decided in October 2013 – January 2014. The estimate was calculated by multiplying the percentage of sampled refusal cases involving applications by both EEA

4. DATA ON THE EXPULSION OF EU CITIZENS AND THEIR FAMILY MEMBERS

Belgium, France and the UK are the only Member States that regularly publish statistics on the expulsion of EU citizens and their family members. In addition, some limited official data is also available for the Netherlands, as a result of information released in parliament.[34]

Figure 1 provides a comparison of the number of EU citizens and their family members who received an order to leave the national territory in the four Member States concerned, irrespective of whether the expulsion was enforced. For the UK, the figures also include refusals at the border.

Figure 1. Expulsion of EU citizens and their family members (2004–2014)

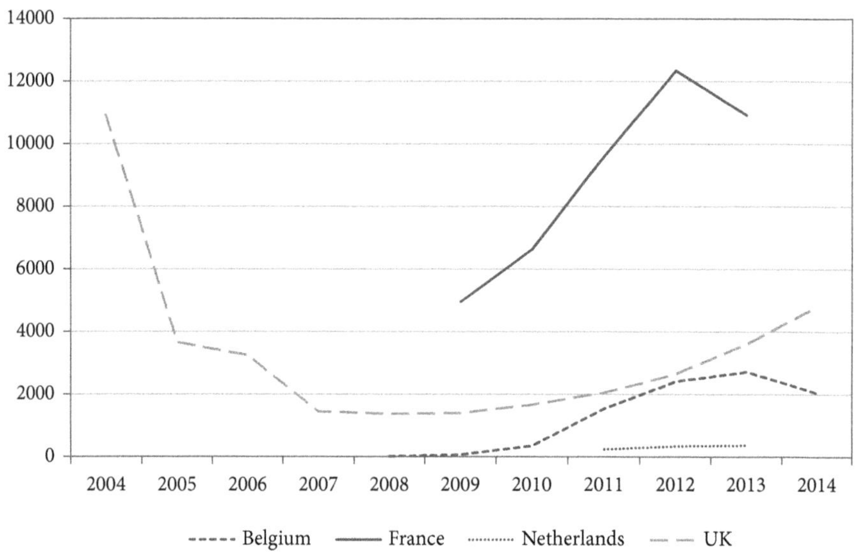

These expulsions should be seen in context. To put these figures into perspective, it is therefore more useful to compare these expulsion rates by reference to the size of the resident EU population. Table 5 provides a comparison of number of

nationals and non-EEA family members which involved an attempt to use fraudulent travel document (3%) with the total refusal rate for residence documentation in 2012 (16.9% – this does not include refusals in permanent residence applications or applications rejected as invalid).

34 The figures are quoted in S. Braaksma and T. Westra, 'De sociale zekerheid van MOE-landers in Nederland', in C. Huinder, A. Odé, K. de Vries, S. Bonjour, L. Coello Eertink and J. Dagevos (eds.), *Open grenzen, nieuwe uitdagingen: arbeidsmigratie uit Midden- en Oost-Europa* (Amsterdam: Amsterdam University Press, 2015), 105–124 (with thanks to G. Vonk).

expulsions affecting EU citizens and their family members as a proportion of the resident EU population.

Table 5. Expulsion of EU citizens (2011–2013)

Member State	2011			2012			2013		
	Total expulsions	Proportion of EU resident population	Most affected nationality	Total expulsions	Proportion of EU resident population	Most affected nationality	Total expulsions	Proportion of EU resident population	Most affected nationality
Belgium	1,542	0.21%	Bulgaria (16%)	2,407	0.31%	Romania (16%)	2,712	0.34%	Romania (30%)
France	9,608	0.71%	Romania	12,331	0.89%	Romania	10,915	0.77%	n/a
Netherlands	230	0.04%	n/a	330	0.06%	n/a	360(1)	0.06%	n/a
UK	2,052	0.08%	Romania (21%)	2,651	0.10%	Romania (24%)	3,601	0.13%	Romania (32%)

Sources: Belgian Immigration Office, Belgian Ministry of the Interior, French Ministry of the Interior, Institut national de la statistique et des études économiques, Centraal Bureau voor de Statistiek, Braaksma & Westra (2015, n. 33), UK Home Office, Office of National Statistics, with additional research by the author.
Notes:
(1) Estimate based on number of expulsions Jan.-Jun. 2013

This shows that over the period 2011–2013, the French authorities served expulsion orders on more EU citizens as a proportion of the resident EU population than Belgium, the Netherlands and the UK combined. By calculating the ratio of expulsions in the Netherlands, Belgium, the UK and France over this three-year period (1:2:6:16), this cancels out differences between the size of each country's EU resident population. This exercise illustrates that for each EU citizen whose expulsion was ordered by the Netherlands, the UK expelled two EU citizens, Belgium ordered the expulsion of six EU citizens and France served expulsion orders on 16 EU citizens.

Throughout this period, Romanian nationals were the most affected by expulsion measures in Belgium and the UK and comprised about one-third of EU citizens affected by expulsion orders. In the case of France, the proportion is likely to be even higher, since 29.7% of all foreigners (EU and non-EU) expelled from France were from Romania. The French Ministry of the Interior has reported that in the period 2009–2012, Romanian citizens held the unenviable title of being the most prominent national group to be expelled from France.[35] According to a consortium of non-governmental organisations, a substantial

[35] Ministère de l'Intérieur, *Les Etrangers en France: Dixième rapport établi en application de l'article L.111-10 du Code de l'entrée et du séjour des étrangers et du droit d'asile* (2012), 73.

proportion of Romanian citizens who were expelled from the French state during this period identified themselves as belonging to the Roma community.[36]

The sheer scale of expulsions from France and the questionable circumstances in which these took place have generated much controversy.[37] The European Commission launched an investigation into the actions of the French authorities for suspected breaches of Directive 2004/38,[38] spurred by the filing of complaints by migrants' rights organisations.[39] The case was closed at the informal stage of the investigation[40] following concessions made by the French government that supposedly 'led to the full incorporation in the French legislation of the safeguards established by EU law'.[41] Despite these commitments, expulsions from France almost doubled between 2010 (6,620) and 2012 (12,331). In 2013, expulsion measures taken against EU citizens by the French authorities (10,915) were still 65% higher than in 2010. Given the concerns that remain about the circumstances in which these expulsions continue to be carried out against EU

36 La Cimade and others, *Centres et locaux de rétention administrative*, Annual reports 2011, 8, available at www.lacimade.org/publications?category=Rapports+sur+la+r%C3%A9tention+administrative (last accessed on 31 July 2015).

37 See for example, S. Carrera and A. Faure Atger, 'L'Affaire des Roms: A Challenge to the EU's Area of Freedom, Security and Justice', CEPS Papers in Liberty and Security in Europe (September 2010); S. Carrera, 'Shifting Responsibilities for EU Roma Citizens: The 2010 French Affair on Roma Evictions and Expulsions Continued', CEPS Papers in Liberty and Security in Europe No. 55 (June 2013); J.S. Gehring, 'Roma and the Limits of Free Movement in the European Union', in W. Maas (ed.), *Democratic Citizenship and the Free Movement of People* (Leiden-Boston: Martinus Nijhoff Publishers, 2013), 143–174; J.M. Markham-Cameron, 'The EU and the Rights of the Roma: How Could the EU have Changed the French Repatriation Program of 2010?' (Claremont-UC Undergraduate Research Conference on the European Union, 2013); S. Carrera, 'The Framing of the Roma as Abnormal EU Citizens', in E. Guild, C. Gortázar Rotaehe and D. Kostakopolou (eds.), *The Reconceptualization of European Union Citizenship* (Leiden-Boston: Brill/Nijhoff, 2014), 33–63; A. Çağlar and S. Mehling, 'Sites and Scales of the Law: Third-Country Nationals and EU Roma Citizens', in E.F. Isin and M. Saward (eds.), *Enacting European Citizenship* (Cambridge: CUP, 2014), 155–177.

38 European Commission Press Release, *European Commission assesses recent developments in France, discusses overall situation of the Roma and EU law on free movement of EU citizens*, IP/10/1027, 29 September 2010.

39 European Roma Rights Centre, *Submission in Relation to the Analysis and Consideration of Legality Under EU Law of the Situation of Roma in France* (27 August 2010), available at www.errc.org/cms/upload/file/france-ec-legalbrief-27-august-2010.pdf (last accessed on 31 July 2015); Groupe d'information et de soutien des immigrés and others, *Plainte contre la France pour violation du droit communautaire en matière de libre circulation des personnes* (22 October 2010), available at www.gisti.org/IMG/pdf/cedh_plainte-roms_2010-10-22.pdf (last accessed on 31 July 2015).

40 European Commission Press Release, *Statement by Viviane Reding, Vice-President of the European Commission, EU Commissioner for Justice, Fundamental Rights and Citizenship, on the recent developments concerning the respect for EU law as regards the situation of Roma in France*, MEMO 10/502, 19 October 2010.

41 European Commission, *Report from the Commission to the European Parliament, the Council and the European Economic and Social Committee under Article 25 TFEU: On progress towards effective EU Citizenship 2011–2013*, COM (2013) 270 final, 5.

citizens and their family members by the French authorities, the matter has now been brought before the European Parliament following the lodging of a petition by the same rights organisations that had originally complained to the Commission in 2010.[42]

Likewise, the questionable nature of the expulsion of EU citizens by the Belgian authorities has also been the subject of a complaint by civil society organisations[43] alleging breaches of Directive 2004/38 and Regulation 883/2004.[44] This is the subject of an ongoing investigation by the European Commission.[45]

5. CONCLUSION

At present, the availability of data on the practical application of Directive 2004/38 by the Member States is mostly left to the discretion of the Member States. Aside from the collection of annual statistics on EU residents, migration flows and the acquisition of citizenship,[46] there is presently no harmonised approach on the compilation of statistics on the residence rights of EU citizens and their family members across Member States.

On the contrary, EU law imposes an obligation on the Member States to collate much more detailed data on the migration of non-EU citizens.[47] As a result, this leads to the paradoxical situation in which statistical information is much more readily available concerning the migration of non-EU nationals in the EU than the free movement of EU citizens.

---

42 European Roma Rights Centre, GISTI and others, Petition, *Pétition au Parlement européen relative à l'éloignement et à l'enfermement des citoyens européens* (25 February 2015), available at www.gisti.org/IMG/pdf/saisine_pe_2015-02-25_fr.pdf (last accessed on 31 July 2015).

43 INCA CGIL, ABVV-FGTB, EU Rights Clinic and Bruxelles Laïque, *Expulsions de citoyens européens de Belgique. Violation des articles 7 et 14 de la Directive 2004/38 sur le droit de séjour des citoyens UE et des articles 4 et 61 du Règlement n° 883/2004 sur la coordination de la sécurité sociale* (4 November 2014), available at www.osservatorioinca.org/section/image/attach/Lettre_CE_2014_11_04.pdf (last accessed 31 July 2015).

44 Regulation (EC) 883/2004 of the European Parliament and of the Council of 29 April 2004 on the coordination of social security systems, OJ 2004, L 200/1.

45 It will be recalled that this is not the first time that the expulsion of EU citizens by the Belgian authorities has been the subject of investigation by the EU institutions. In Case C-408/03, *Commission v Belgium*, EU:C:2006:192, paras. 68–72, the Court of Justice found that the Belgian practice to serve expulsion orders automatically on EU citizens who had failed to provide documentary proof of their right to reside in Belgium within the prescribed time period breached the EU free movement rules.

46 Article 3 Regulation 862/2007.

47 Article 4 Regulation 862/2007 requires the collation of statistics on persons having applied for or benefiting from international protection; Article 5 covers statistics on illegal entry and stay; Article 6 concerns the issue of residence permits to third-country nationals; Article 7 relates to statistics on return; Articles 8 and 9 provide for further details on the compilation of statistics.

Serious consideration should therefore be given to imposing obligations on the Member States to collate comprehensive data on the exercise of residence rights by EU citizens and non-EU family members.[48] This could be achieved relatively easily by amending Regulation 862/2007, which applies to all 28 Member States. This should allow for the more accurate monitoring of the application of Directive 2004/38 by the national authorities and facilitate enforcement by the Commission. It would also help to minimise the ability of governments to make claims about the effect of the EU rules on free movement which are not substantiated by empirical evidence.

48 The obligation to collate data should ideally extend to the numbers of registration certificates and residence card issued annually, rates of applications rejected as incomplete or invalid, the average time taken to process applications, the rates of refusals, revocations and deportations disaggregated by category. These would include refusals, revocations, deportations and entry bans based on public policy, public security and public order, as well as those based on other grounds, such as citizens being a burden on the social assistance system and the abuse of free movement rights, including relationships of convenience and the use of false travel documents. Finally, the obligation should also extend to judicial appeals against decisions restricting free movement rights, including outcomes.

CHAPTER 8

CIVIC INTEGRATION EXAMS IN EU IMMIGRATION LAW

What Integration is Not in European Law

Sergio CARRERA*

1. INTRODUCTION

The relationship between integration policies and EU migration law has taken unprecedented forms in the last decade of European integration. During the negotiations over the first pieces of EU secondary legislation covering the conditions of entry and residence of third-country nationals (TCNs) in the EU in the early 2000s, a new approach to integration made its way into Directives 2003/109 on the status of third-country nationals who are long-term residents[1] and 2003/86 on the right to family reunification.[2] This approach makes use of integration policies as criteria for access to EU rights and freedoms by TCNs. Integration functions as a legal requirement or migration control tool over socio-economic inclusion, security of residence, and family reunification. The academic literature has qualified this mutation as a 'paradigm shift' from past normative approaches to integration developed since the 1970s in EU law and policy.[3] Indeed, integration policies used to mainly focus on the facilitation of

* The author would like to thank Prof. Elspeth Guild and Dr Ricky van Oers for their comments on a previous draft of this chapter.

1 Council Directive 2003/109 concerning the status of third-country nationals who are long-term residents, OJ 2004, L 16/44 (hereinafter referred to as 'Directive 2003/109' or 'LTR Directive').

2 Council Directive 2003/86 on the right to family reunification, OJ 2003, L 251/12 (hereinafter referred to as 'Directive 2003/86').

3 S. CARRERA, *In Search of the Perfect Citizen? The Intersection between Integration, Immigration and Nationality in the EU* (Martinus Nijhoff: Leiden, 2009). See also: D. KOSTAKOPOULOU, S. CARRERA and M. JESSE, 'Doing and Deserving: Competing Frames of Integration in the EU', in E. GUILD, K. GROENENDIJK and S. CARRERA (eds.), *Illiberal Liberal States: Immigration, Citizenship and Integration in the EU* (Ashgate: Farnham, 2009); S. CARRERA and A. WIESBROCK, *Civic Integration of Third Country Nationals: Nationalism versus Europeanisation in the Common EU Immigration Policy* (Brussels: CEPS Liberty and

mobility through non-discrimination, respect for family life and security of residence. Lately, however, integration has become a new ground for exclusion of foreigners in the EU's management of human mobility and identity.[4]

Two novel formulations of this control-oriented approach to integration can now be found in Directives 2003/109 and 2003/86, i.e. 'integration conditions' and 'integration measures'. Integration conditions are used in Article 5 Directive 2003/109 for the acquisition of long-term resident status,[5] while integration measures are present in Article 15(3) Directive 2003/109 (which specifies the conditions for residence in a second Member State),[6] and Article 7(2) Directive 2003/86 (stipulating the requirements for the exercise of the right to family reunification).[7] The scholarly debate has engaged with the meaning and differences between the scope of integration 'conditions' and 'measures' in the Directives and EU immigration law more generally. It has also paid attention to the legality of EU Member States' integration policies implementing them into their respective legal systems through the use of mandatory integration programmes, tests/exams and contracts.[8] A key controversy in scholarly and policy debates has been the extent to which EU Member States could lawfully

Security in Europe Series, 2009) and K. Groenendijk, 'Integration of Immigrants in the EU: The Old or the New Way', in Y. Pascouau and T. Strik (eds.), *Which Integration Policies for Migrants? Interaction between the EU and its Member States* (Nijmegen: Wolf Legal Publishers, 2012).

4 E. Guild and S. Carrera, 'Are Integration Tests Liberal? The "Universalistic Liberal Democratic Principles" as Illiberal Exceptionalism', in R. Bauböck and C. Joppke (eds.), *How Liberal Are Citizenship Tests?*, EUI Working Paper No. 41, 2010.

5 Article 5 states that 'Member States may require third-country nationals to comply with integration conditions, in accordance with national law'. The notion of 'integration conditions' also appears in the Directive 2003/86 in Article 4(1), which states that 'where a child is aged over 12 years and arrives independently from the rest of his/her family, the Member State may, before authorising entry and residence under this Directive, verify whether he or she meets a condition for integration provided for by its existing legislation on the date of implementation of this Directive'.

6 Article 15 stipulates that 'Member States may require third-country nationals to comply with integration measures, in accordance with national law. This condition shall not apply where the third-country nationals concerned have been required to comply with integration conditions in order to be granted long-term resident status, in accordance with the provisions of Article 5(2). Without prejudice to the second subparagraph, the persons concerned may be required to attend language courses.'

7 Article 7(2) reads as follows: 'Member States may require third-country nationals to comply with integration measures, in accordance with national law. With regard to refugees and/or their family members, the integration measures foreseen in this provision may only be applied once the persons concerned have been granted family reunification.'

8 See for instance R. Van Oers, E. Ersbøll and D. Kostakopoulou (eds.), *A Re-Definition of Belonging? Language and Integration Tests in Europe* (Leiden: Martinus Nijhoff Publishers, 2010); E. Guild, K. Groenendijk and S. Carrera (eds.), *Illiberal Liberal States: Immigration, Citizenship and Integration in the EU* (Ashgate: Farnham, 2009); Y. Pascouau and T. Strik (eds.), *Which Integration Policies for Migrants? Interaction between the EU and its Member States* (Nijmegen: Wolf Legal Publishers, 2012) and S. Morano-Foadi and M. Malena (eds.), *Integration for Third-Country Nationals in the European Union: The Equality Challenge* (Cheltenham: Edward Elgar, 2012).

apply obligatory civic integration programmes conditioning access and/ maintenance of EU rights by TCNs to passing an exam on knowledge of the receiving country's language and 'societal values'.

More than ten years after the adoption of these Directives, this discussion moved to the Court of Justice of the European Union (CJEU) in Luxembourg. In early 2015 the CJEU gave its judgment in two cases dealing with the lawfulness of civic integration programmes in the Netherlands. This country has been one of the pioneers in applying 'in full' the concept of civic integration conditions (both language and knowledge of society) in the following two forms, one outside and another inside its territory: first, as a mandatory requirement for TCNs to be granted a visa and lawful entry into the country for the purposes of family reunification (civic integration test abroad); and second, a similar integration test for TCNs to acquire permanent residence status inside the country.[9] The relevant cases are *P. and S. v Commissie Sociale Zekerheid Breda*[10] and *Zaken v K. and A.*[11] The two judgments need to be read in conjunction.[12] In both instances the legality of the transposition in Dutch national legislation of integration 'measures' and 'conditions' envisaged in the LTR Directive and Directive 2003/86 constituted a key aspect of the main proceedings. The cases attracted a fair degree of expectations from those in the academic literature who had followed this discussion for about a decade. Would the CJEU find the Dutch civic integration tests unlawful altogether? One of the cross-cutting issues at stake, which the CJEU had not previously addressed and where further clarity was clearly sought, was the parameters which would determine the legality of obligatory civic integration exams (in-country and abroad) from the perspective of European immigration law and the EU Charter of Fundamental Rights. Interestingly, the Advocates General in each of the cases reached divergent conclusions in their Opinions as regards the ways in which the Luxembourg Court should handle this sensitive matter. The judgments, which were respectively published in June and July 2015, reached interesting findings, yet left also open a number of fundamental questions.

---

9 For an assessment of the Dutch case see S. Carrera and A. Wiesbrock, *Civic Integration of Third Country Nationals: Nationalism versus Europeanisation in the Common EU Immigration Policy* (Brussels: CEPS Liberty and Security in Europe Series, 2009); L.F.M. Besselink, 'Integration and Immigration: The Vicissitudes of Dutch "Inburgering"', in E. Guild, K. Groenendijk and S. Carrera (eds.), *Illiberal Liberal States: Immigration, Citizenship and Integration in the EU* (Farnham: Ashgate, 2009); S. Bonjour, 'Between Integration Provision and Selection Mechanism. Party Politics, Judicial Constraints and the Making of French and Dutch Policies of Civic Integration Abroad' (2010) 12 *EJML*, 299–318; and T. Strik, A. Böcker, M. Luiten and R. Van Oers, 'The INTEC Project: Synthesis Report – Integration and Naturalisation Tests: The New Way to European Citizenship', in Y. Pascouau and T. Strik (eds.), *Which Integration Policies for Migrants? Interaction between the EU and its Member States* (Nijmegen: Wolf Legal Publishers, 2012).

10 Case C-579/13, *P. and S.*, EU:C:2015:369.

11 Case C-153/14, *Zaken*, EU:C:2015:453.

12 The cases were examined during a similar time period (first half of 2015) by the same rapporteur and members of the Second Chamber of the Court.

This chapter examines the lawfulness of mandatory civic integration exams in the scope of EU law, in particular when they play a role of derogations or exceptions to EU rights and fundamental freedoms of TCNs as envisaged in EU law. It assesses this matter in light of the above-mentioned *P. and S.* and *Zaken* CJEU judgments of 2015. The following questions are specifically explored: First, to what extent and under which conditions are obligatory civic integration requirements in compliance with EU law? What can be learned in light of these recent CJEU judgments? Second, in what ways has EU Member States' discretion been affected when applying integration programmes as a condition derogating or restricting access by TCNs to EU status of long-term residence, the EU right to family reunification and other fundamental rights envisaged by the EU Charter of Fundamental Rights? Third, when normatively delineating the criteria assessing 'the societal link' or integration between a TCN and a Member State, what are the rule-of-law boundaries or standards now inscribed in EU law?

The chapter starts by taking stock of the two cases by looking at their facts and the questions at stake, the main differences and points of convergence in the Opinions issued by AGs Szpunar and Kokott, and the conclusions finally reached by the CJEU (sections 2 and 3). Section 4 examines the challenges raised by the conditions for integration in the Dutch civic integration test in light of EU law and the findings reached by the Luxembourg Court. The following three challenges are in particular highlighted: First, the use of obligatory civic integration exams blurs the distinction between integration 'measures' and 'conditions' in EU immigration law, according to which integration measures cannot impose an obligation to pass an exam affecting the granting or maintenance of EU LTR status or the right to family reunification when otherwise. Second, integration 'conditions' also have a difficult relationship with the EU right to family reunification foreseen in Directive 2003/86 and the right to private and family life enshrined in Article 7 EU Charter of Fundamental Rights. These exams do not allow for an individual and personalised (case-by-case) assessment. Third, integration as a condition can challenge the effectiveness of EU immigration law and the rights foreseen therein due to its indeterminate legal nature, in particular in what concerns the civic societal values aspects of the exam.

The chapter argues that it is regrettable that the CJEU did not take these two cases as an opportunity to bring further legal certainty as regards the distinction between integration measures and conditions in EU immigration law, the role played by obligatory civic integration exams as a migration-control tool, and the specificity of certain EU rights enjoyed by TCNs in European secondary law in conjunction with the EU Charter when studying the lawfulness of national implementing measures. What was perhaps more at stake in these two cases was for the Luxembourg Court to ensure a consistent degree of protection of TCNs regarding specific EU rights envisaged in EU immigration law *in combination with* fundamental rights foreseen in the EU Charter, i.e. the EU right to family reunification. The line of argumentation used by the Luxembourg Court in the *Zaken* judgment when testing the lawfulness of the Dutch civic integration policy in the context of family reunification is also surprising when read along the CJEU Opinion 2/13 on the non-accession by the EU to the European Convention of Human Rights and Fundamental Freedoms (ECHR). One could have well expected that a logical result of Opinion 2/3 would inevitably be for the Luxembourg Court to increasingly adopt the role of a 'fundamental rights Court'. If that would have been the case, the interpretation and validity of Member States' implementing legislation, such as that at issue in the proceedings, would have been examined by paying particular attention to their compatibility with the set of rights which are specific to EU secondary law (e.g. family reunification or long-term residence) in combination with the fundamental rights foreseen in the EU Charter. This approach was however absent in the cases under scrutiny in this chapter, with the CJEU not functioning as a 'fundamental rights adjudicator'.

That notwithstanding, the CJEU has confirmed in these two judgments that the inclusion of integration 'conditions' or 'measures' as criteria in EU immigration law means that their national interpretation and domestic application is now subject to supranational rule of law and fundamental rights scrutiny. This is the case irrespective of the commonly accepted mantra that 'integration policies' remain within the remit of Member States' national competences in the Union legal system. Supranational accountability and legal standards cover not only the ways in which integration measures and conditions are applied or *the means* which are devised in their implementation across the national arenas so as not to affect negatively the effectiveness of the specific set of EU right granted to TCNs by European law. They also profoundly affect the boundaries within which Member States can legally frame and administratively apply 'integration exams', both in their linguistic and 'societal knowledge' aspects, as an exception or derogatory criterion to the EU status and rights of TCNs stipulated in EU law. The *P. and S.* and *Zaken* judgments can therefore be seen as a timid first step towards the development of common EU standards defining what is not permissible in the scope of EU law as regards the use of civic integration exams ('what integration is not in EU law') when EU Member States restrict the EU rights and freedoms of TCNs.

2. CIVIC INTEGRATION AND LONG-TERM RESIDENCE STATUS

Directive 2003/109 has been subject to few CJEU rulings since 2012.[13] The legality of civic integration conditions for TCNs to benefit from the common EU

[13] See for instance Case C-469/13, *Tahir*, EU:C:2014:2094; Case C-40/11, *Iida*, EU:C:2012:691; Case C-502/10, *Singh*, EU:C:2012:636; Case C-508/10, *Commission v Netherlands*, EU:C:2012:243; and Case C-571/10, *Kamberaj*, EU:C:2012:233.

status of LTR has not attracted much judicial attention so far. This was one of the key issues of controversy in the recent CJEU ruling in *P. and S.* This section examines the facts and key questions of this case, the main arguments delivered by the AG's Opinion and the direction chosen by the Luxembourg Court in its ruling of 4 June 2015.

2.1. FACTS AND QUESTIONS REFERRED

The two applicants (one holding US nationality and another from New Zealand) had legally resided in the Netherlands and acquired long-term EC resident status in 2008 and 2007 respectively. Following the entry into force of the new Civic Integration Law (*Wet Inburgering*) in January 2010, they received a notification from the Dutch authorities telling them about their obligation to pass a civic integration exam including oral and written proficiency in the Dutch language and sufficient knowledge of Dutch society. While they would not lose their pre-existing long-term resident status or the rights deriving from it, failing to fulfil this obligation would result in a financial penalty. P. and S. challenged the lawfulness of the Dutch decisions on the basis of two arguments: first, as beneficiaries of long-term EC resident status they should be treated equally to Dutch citizens and should not be required to meet an additional integration obligation. Second, the application of the obligation was contrary to the objective of Directive 2003/109 and its Article 5(2) and (11)(1). In brief, the main controversy in the proceedings was the extent to which a Member State could impose *ex post* an integration condition obliging a TCN who already holds long-term resident status to pass an exam on linguistic and societal knowledge, and if that Member State had the competence to apply a sanction in the form of a fine in the event of non-compliance. The CJEU was not asked to interpret the legality of a national integration conditions *ex ante* the granting of the LTR status, but rather the application of integration conditions *after* the TCN has already acquired that status and has not exercised mobility to a second Member State.

2.2. AG SZPUNAR'S OPINION

The Opinion issued by AG Szpunar on 28 January 2015[14] examined the following. First, is the civic integration obligation in compliance with long-term EC resident status envisaged in Directive 2003/109? Second, to what extent does European law limit the discretion enjoyed by EU Member States to define the actual content and the implementation of this requirement? As regards the first question, Article 5(2) Directive 2003/109 (which deals with the conditions

[14] Opinion of Advocate General Szpunar in Case C-579/13, *P. and S.*, EU:C:2015:39.

for acquiring long-term residence status) expressly foresees the possibility of applying 'integration conditions, in accordance with national law'. As AG Szpunar acknowledged, the Directive does not however specify the extent to which it is possible to impose an integration condition *after* the status is acquired.

The Opinion highlighted that when assessing 'the link' between the person and the state this Directive 2003/109 is clear as regards the most relevant connecting factor:[15] the length of residence. The Directive was founded on the idea that the ties (*arraigo* or *l'ancrage de la personne dans la société*) between person and state are the result of legally and continuously residing in a Member State for a period of five years. This, in his view, does not exclude the possibility for Member States to apply integration programmes to long-term residents. Yet these programmes must take due account of the fundamental difference between the concepts of 'integration conditions' and 'integration measures' as used by Directive 2003/109, in particular Article 5(2) which envisages 'integration conditions', and Article 15(3) which foresees the application of 'integration measures'. The LTR Directive and Directive 2003/86 establish a distinction between integration programmes (*actions d'intégration*), defined as 'conditions' to acquire or exercise certain rights, and those defined as 'measures', which should have facilitating the integration of persons as their ultimate goal.[16]

Crucially, he argued, national provisions making the maintenance of long-term resident status or the exercise of the rights foreseen in the Directive subject to conditions would be contrary to Articles 5(2), 9 and 15(2), which only allows for the application of integration 'measures'.[17] Directive 2003/109 does not prevent Member States from imposing 'integration measures' on TCNs who have acquired long-term EU resident status *as long as* these measures have facilitating integration as their main public intended goal and do not constitute an express or hidden (*de facto* or *de jure*) condition for maintaining this status or for the exercise of the corresponding rights.[18] In his view, the fact that the EU LRT TCNs have not exercised mobility to another EU Member State should not change the fact that the state at hand cannot apply integration conditions after the acquisition of that status. The Opinion underlined that it is not relevant whether the integration condition was applied to the person before or after s/he acquired the status of long-term resident, and 'if the Member State did not establish this kind of obligation as a condition for obtaining the status of long-term resident, after it cannot reconsider this decision requiring to those already enjoying this status, a condition for maintaining this status or for the exercise of corresponding rights.'[19]

---

15 Opinion of Advocate General Szpunar in Case C-579/13, *P. and S.*, EU:C:2015:39, para. 41.

16 Opinion of Advocate General Szpunar in Case C-579/13, *P. and S.*, EU:C:2015:39, para. 47.

17 Opinion of Advocate General Szpunar in Case C-579/13, *P. and S.*, EU:C:2015:39, para. 54.

18 Opinion of Advocate General Szpunar in Case C-579/13, *P. and S.*, EU:C:2015:39, paras. 58–59.

19 Opinion of Advocate General Szpunar in Case C-579/13, *P. and S.*, EU:C:2015:39, para. 59.

AG Szpunar went a step further and underlined the need to examine whether integration conditions undermine the scope and efficacy of EU law, the principle of proportionality and the EU Charter of Fundamental Rights. While EU Member States enjoy a margin of appreciation when applying national law, they cannot apply domestic legislation which may endanger the fulfilment of the objectives pursued by a Directive and prevent its *effet utile* (the general EU principle of effectiveness).[20] According to AG Szpunar, even though the provisions envisaged in the Directive related to integration measures/conditions refer to national law, these must also comply with the EU Charter.[21] These national provisions fall within the scope of Union law and Article 51(1) of the EU Charter.[22] As regards the proportionality test of civic integration programmes in the Netherlands, AG Szpunar concluded that 'the obligation to integrate' must not make the exercise of the rights derived from the status excessively difficult in practice.[23] These measures must also comply with the right to private and family life envisaged in Article 7 of the EU Charter.[24]

The next question addressed in his Opinion was the extent to which the Dutch national provisions on civic integration could be interpreted as 'integration measures' or 'integration conditions' in light of Directive 2003/109. While the Directives do not expressly envisage or develop the distinction, 'integration measures must be considered less restrictive than integration conditions'.[25] According to AG Szpunar 'integration measures – unlike integration conditions – are intended solely to facilitate a particular person's integration into the economic and social life of the State in question and under no circumstances may they serve as an instrument for selecting immigrants or for controlling migration'.[26] The key distinguishing factor is that 'integration measures' should not impose an obligation to pass an integration exam before a given deadline. Instead they should aim at facilitating adaptation to (or at assisting socialisation in) the society and not establish requirements or 'qualifying conditions' for legal residence in the country.[27] In his view, the distinction between integration measures and conditions 'are especially important for the application of Directive 2003/86. Treating an integration exam as an absolute "condition" for obtaining an entry permit for a family member undermines the very essence of

20 Opinion of Advocate General Szpunar in Case C-579/13, *P. and S.*, EU:C:2015:39, here reference was made to Case C-508/10, *Commission v Netherlands*, EU:C:2012:243, paras. 64–65.

21 Opinion of Advocate General Szpunar in Case C-579/13, *P. and S.*, EU:C:2015:39, para. 76. Here reference was made to the Case C-571/10, *Kamberaj*, EU:C:2012:233, in para. 81.

22 Opinion of Advocate General Szpunar in Case C-579/13, *P. and S.*, EU:C:2015:39, para. 78.

23 Opinion of Advocate General Szpunar in Case C-579/13, *P. and S.*, EU:C:2015:39, para. 81.

24 Opinion of Advocate General Szpunar in Case C-579/13, *P. and S.*, EU:C:2015:39, para. 83.

25 Opinion of Advocate General Szpunar in Case C-579/13, *P. and S.*, EU:C:2015:39, para. 85.

26 Opinion of Advocate General Szpunar in Case C-579/13, *P. and S.*, EU:C:2015:39, para. 86.

27 Opinion of Advocate General Szpunar in Case C-579/13, *P. and S.*, EU:C:2015:39, para. 90.

the right to family reunification'.[28] He concluded that it was difficult to see how an obligatory exam would facilitate a TCN's participation in society.[29]

2.3. THE *P. AND S.* JUDGMENT

The Luxembourg Court delivered its judgment on 4 June 2015. It examined the preliminary questions in light of two general considerations: first, the fact that the 'civic integration obligation' in the main proceedings did not constitute a condition for acquiring or preserving long-term EU resident status, but rather exclusively consisted on a financial sanction or fine; and second, the relevance granted by the EU legislature to integration measures in Recital 4 of the Preamble in Directive 2003/109 which states its decisive function in fostering economic and social cohesion.

The Luxembourg Court first concluded that the imposition of a fine could not be considered as an 'integration condition' within the scope of Article 5(2) of the Directive. Moreover, it held that this provision neither requires nor precludes EU Member States from applying an 'integration measure' such as that at issue in the proceedings.[30] From the wording expressed in these paragraphs of the judgment it would appear as if the CJEU would be implicitly acknowledging the relevance of distinguishing between integration 'measures' and integration 'conditions' in Directive 2003/109. We will come back to this issue in section 3.1 below. The CJEU additionally held that the non-application of a civic integration obligation did not jeopardise the principle of equal treatment to which TCNs who are long-term residents are entitled in Article 11(1) of the Directive. However, it concluded that 'the means of implementing that civic integration obligation must not undermine the principle of non-discrimination' in those areas listed in this same provision of the Directive.[31] When assessing the legality of the 'civic integration obligation', the Court distanced itself somewhat from AG Szpunar's Opinion on the question whether an obligatory exam on language and 'societal values' would in fact facilitate the participation of a TCN in Dutch society by ruling that:

> 'it cannot be disputed that the acquisition of knowledge of the language and society of the host Member State greatly *facilitates communication* between third-country nationals and nationals of the Member State concerned and, moreover, *encourages interaction and the development of social relations* between them. Nor can it be contested that the acquisition of knowledge of the language of the host Member State

---

28 Opinion of Advocate General Szpunar in Case C-579/13, *P. and S.*, EU:C:2015:39, para. 46.

29 Opinion of Advocate General Szpunar in Case C-579/13, *P. and S.*, EU:C:2015:39, paras. 89–92.

30 Case C-579/13, *P. and S.*, EU:C:2015:369, para. 38.

31 Case C-579/13, *P. and S.*, EU:C:2015:369, paras. 42–43. On the non-discrimination obligation see para. 44 of the judgment.

> makes it less difficult for third-country nationals to access the labour market and vocational training'[32] (emphasis added).

The CJEU concluded that 'such an obligation does not, by itself, jeopardise the achievement of the objectives pursued by Directive 2003/109, but may on the contrary contribute to their achievement'.[33] That notwithstanding, it also underlined the central importance of carefully examining 'the means' by which such an examination would be implemented on the ground, which could be liable to jeopardise the Directive's objectives. Here the Court's views were closer to AG Szpunar's Opinion and held that particular attention should be paid to:

> 'the level of knowledge required to pass the civic integration examination, to the accessibility of the courses and material necessary to prepare for that examination, to the amount of fees applicable to third-country nationals as registration fees to sit that examination, or to the consideration of specific individual circumstances, such as age, illiteracy or level of education.'[34]

As regards the lawfulness of applying a fine to those TCNs with EU LTR status who had not passed a 'civic integration examination', the CJEU held that this does not as such undermine the effectiveness of the Directive or the achievement of its objectives. However, it expressed concerns about the nature of the fine, in particular the following four aspects: first, the maximum amount was very high (€1,000); second, a fine could be imposed every time that the period prescribed had expired without any limit; third, the fine would be imposed irrespective of whether the TCNs never sat that examination or did so several times; and fourth, the registration fees involved in sitting the examination and the costs incurred in the preparation are fully borne by the TCN (€230) each time they sit the examination. In light of these considerations, the Court reached the conclusion that the imposition of the fine was not the only negative effect suffered by TCNs and held that:

> 'the payment of a fine penalising failure to comply with the obligation to pass the civic integration examination, in addition to payment of the costs incurred in relation to the examinations sat, is liable to jeopardise the achievement of the objectives pursued by Directive 2003/109 and, therefore, deprive it of its effectiveness.'[35]

Ultimately, the CJEU left it to the referring national tribunal to determine whether 'the actual means' of implementing the obligation to pass a civic integration examination are in fact not liable to jeopardise the achievement of the

---

32 Case C-579/13, *P. and S.*, EU:C:2015:369, para. 47.
33 Case C-579/13, *P. and S.*, EU:C:2015:369, para. 48.
34 Case C-579/13, *P. and S.*, EU:C:2015:369, para. 49.
35 Case C-579/13, *P. and S.*, EU:C:2015:369, para. 54.

objectives of Directive 2003/109, irrespective of whether the EU LTR status was acquired before or after the obligation to pass a civic integration examination.[36]

3. CIVIC INTEGRATION AND FAMILY REUNIFICATION

Directive 2003/86 has been the focus of various CJEU rulings since 2006.[37] The *Zaken v K. and A.* raised some expectations of gaining a better understanding of two main aspects: first, the exact scope of the integration requirements envisaged in the Directive for TCNs to enjoy the EU right to family reunification; and second, the question whether the Dutch civic integration exam could in fact be deemed to be in compliance with the principle of proportionality and the EU Charter of Fundamental Rights. AG Kokott's Opinion in the case was issued on 19 March 2015, which was then followed by the publication of the CJEU ruling on 9 July 2015.

3.1. FACTS AND QUESTIONS REFERRED

The applicants were Azerbaijani and Nigerian nationals wishing to enter the Netherlands and join their family members who were already residing there. They asked for exemption from the civic integration examination based on physical and mental difficulties, which was however rejected by the Dutch authorities. The central question was the extent to which a TCN could be obliged to pass an exam on the language and culture and society of the receiving Member State as a condition for entry in the context of family reunification and under the regime envisaged in Directive 2003/86. In other words, is 'integration abroad' a permissible 'integration measure' within the material scope of Directive 2003/86?

The following three preliminary questions were sent to Luxembourg by the national court. First, can the notion of integration measures foreseen in Article 7(2) Directive 2003/86 be interpreted as meaning that Member States authorities can require the sponsor's family to demonstrate their knowledge of the official language at an A1 level and basic knowledge of the society before authorising entry and residence in the Netherlands? Second, is it relevant when assessing the proportionality of the national provisions to consider the ways in which the special individual circumstances of the individual are taken into

36 Case C-579/13, *P. and S.*, EU:C:2015:369, para. 56.

37 Case C-338/13, *Noorzia*, EU:C:2014:2092; Case C-138/13, *Dogan*, EU:C:2014:2066; Case C-513/12, *Ayalti*, EU:C:2013:210; Case C-356/11, *O. and S.*, EU:C:2012:776; Case C 578/08, *Chakroun*, EU:C:2010:117; and Case C-540/03, *Parliament v Council*, EU:C:2006:429.

consideration? And third, does the Directive preclude applying a fee of €350 per attempt for the examination and costs of €110 for the pack to prepare for the examination?

3.2. AG KOKOTT'S OPINION

When examining the Dutch civic integration examination from the perspective of Directive 2003/86, AG Kokott was of the view that 'integration measures' must be interpreted autonomously, as they have now become a concept of EU law.[38] In her opinion, while there is not a commonly established definition of what 'integration measures' precisely mean in EU immigration law, the term measure is sufficiently broad to encompass an integration test. Kokott continued by arguing that:

> 'it is not inconceivable, either conceptually, systematically or teleologically, that an integration measure within the meaning of the Family Reunification Directive should encompass an examination that is used in order to demonstrate that an integration-related condition of family reunification has been met [...] Nor can any compelling argument be derived from the Directive on long-term residents – on which consultation took place at the same time as on the Family Reunification Directive – as to why integration measures within the meaning of the Family Reunification Directive should not be associated with the passing of an examination'.[39]

A key point of divergence between AG Szpunar's Opinion in *P. and S.* and that of AG Kokott in the present case is that she did not agree with the need to interpret or apply a similar cross-cutting distinction on the scope of the notions of 'integration measures and conditions' in both the Family Reunification Directive (FRD) and Directive 2003/109. In her view a parallel interpretation is not possible because the circumstances governing each of these two Directives are not analogous. Directive 2003/109, and the distinction which it foresees between 'integration conditions' and 'integration measures' in Articles 5 and 15 respectively, aim at guaranteeing that TCNs who hold a right of permanent residence and have already passed an 'integration examination' in one Member State are not subject to a similar exam when moving to a second Member State. On the other hand in her view, Directive 2003/86 is however concerned about the first entry of family members in the EU, and therefore the use of integration measures/conditions have a different quality altogether when compared to Directive 2003/109. AG Kokott argued that 'there was no danger of integration

---

38 Opinion of Advocate General Kokott in Case C-153/14, *Zaken*, EU:C:2015:186, para. 19.

39 Opinion of Advocate General Kokott in Case C-153/14, *Zaken*, EU:C:2015:186, paras. 24–26.

measures having to be complied with afresh after integration conditions had already been complied with elsewhere'.[40]

AG Kokott concluded that 'notwithstanding the terminology of the Directive on long-term residents', the Dutch civic integration examination falls within the concept of 'integration measure' within the meaning of Article 7(2) FRD. She then assessed the proportionality of the civic integration examination. Here she agreed with the Dutch government's argument in the proceedings that the Dutch law intended to improve 'the starting-point of those coming to the Netherlands' and emphasised that it 'pursues a legitimate objectives aimed at integrating the person coming to join the family' and 'uses appropriate means to do so'.[41] She underlined that:

> 'language proficiency not only improves the prospects of third country nationals in the labour market, but also enables them to seek help in the host country independently in emergencies. Basic knowledge of a country also ensures that the person coming to join the family is familiar with important fundamental rules of co-existence, which can help to avoid misunderstanding s and breaches of the law[42] [...] it is, moreover, logical that the person intending to join his family should be required to have studied essential aspects of the host State and its rules in advance, particularly since this is not only in the interest of the host State but also in the interest of the person coming to join his family.'[43]

One issue where both AG Szpunar and AG Kokott reached somewhat a similar conclusion is that the Dutch legislation on civic integration would not be appropriate 'if individual circumstances are not taken sufficiently into account when the legislation is being applied' or where 'there are grounds on which family reunification should be granted notwithstanding the failure to pass the examination'. As we will explore further in section 4.2 below, this argument, which follows what is outlined in Article 17 Directive 2003/86,[44] is of central importance when testing the legality of civic integration examinations. AG Kokott expressed the view that it is for the national court to determine

40 Opinion of Advocate General Kokott in Case C-153/14, *Zaken*, EU:C:2015:186, paras. 29–30.

41 Opinion of Advocate General Kokott in Case C-153/14, *Zaken*, EU:C:2015:186, paras. 33–34.

42 Opinion of Advocate General Kokott in Case C-153/14, *Zaken*, EU:C:2015:186, paras. 34–38.

43 Opinion of Advocate General Kokott in Case C-153/14, *Zaken*, EU:C:2015:186, para. 37. It is interesting to note that here the AG makes express reference in footnote 16, to the point 4 of the Common Basic Principles for Immigrant Integration Policy in the EU, according to which 'basic knowledge of the host society's language, history and institutions is indispensable for integration', and footnote 17 to the Commission Communication on 'European Agenda for the Integration of Third Country Nationals', COM (2011) 455 final, 5.

44 Article 17 stipulates that 'Member States shall take due account of the nature and solidity of the person's family relationships and the duration of his residence in the Member State and of the existence of family, cultural and social ties with his/her country of origin where they reject an application, withdraw or refuse to renew a residence permit or decide to order the removal of the sponsor or members of his family.'

whether the domestic legislation at issue is in conformity with this obligation.[45] Finally, she pointed out a risk that the fees are disproportionate as they can represent 'a significant financial burden in many parts of the world, in view of the per capita there', and therefore could prevent the person intending to join his family from exercising the right to family reunification.[46]

3.3. THE *ZAKEN* JUDGMENT

The ruling was published on 9 July 2015. The CJEU held that the requirement to pass a 'civic integration examination' does not undermine the aims of family reunification envisaged in the FRD.[47] Similarly to *P. and S.*, and as we will see in section 4 below controversially, the CJEU reiterated its opinion that 'it cannot be disputed that the acquisition of knowledge of the language and society of the host Member State greatly facilitates communication between third-country nationals and nationals of the Member State concerned and, moreover, encourages interaction and the development of social relations between them'.[48] The Court concluded that Article 7(2) Directive 2003/86 allows Member States to require TCNs to pass a 'civic integration examination' consisting of an assessment of a 'basic knowledge' both of the language and society of the state, and which may entail the payment of various costs, 'before authorising that national's entry into and residence in the territory of the Member State for the purposes of family reunification'.[49]

Notwithstanding, it provided a toolbox of legal standards for testing the compliance of such an integration examination with the principle of proportionality in paragraphs 56–58 of the judgment. The following three were in particular highlighted: first, the conditions for its application would exceed 'what is necessary to achieve those aims' in cases where that requirement would 'systematically prevent family reunification of a sponsor's family member where, despite having failed the integration examination, they have demonstrated their willingness to pass the examination and they have made every effort to achieve that objective';[50] second, the integration measures should not aim at filtering

45 Opinion of Advocate General Kokott in Case C-153/14, *Zaken*, EU:C:2015:186, paras. 41–45 – here she sets out some criteria for testing the legality.

46 Opinion of Advocate General Kokott in Case C-153/14, *Zaken*, EU:C:2015:186, para. 53. In her view a possible way to deal with this would be introducing measures 'for the granting of a dispensation or deferral.'

47 Case C-153/14, *Zaken*, EU:C:2015:453, para. 55.

48 Case C-153/14, *Zaken*, EU:C:2015:453, para. 54 – the Court held that '[f]rom that perspective, the requirement to pass a civic integration examination at a basic level is capable of ensuring that the nationals of third countries acquire knowledge which is undeniably useful for establishing connections with the host Member State.'

49 Case C-153/14, *Zaken*, EU:C:2015:453, para. 71.

50 Case C-153/14, *Zaken*, EU:C:2015:453, para. 56.

those persons aimed at exercising the right to family reunification 'but at facilitating the integration of such persons within the Member States'; and third, 'specific individual circumstances' should be taken into consideration when exempting certain family members from the requirement of passing an exam, including 'age, illiteracy, level of education, economic situation or health'.[51]

The CJEU held that if these 'proportionality standards' are not taken duly into account, an integration requirement would constitute an unlawful obstacle in making the right to family reunification effective in light of the Directive.[52] This interpretation, the CJEU ruled, complies with Article 17 Directive 2003/86, which obliges EU Member States to examine the criteria for granting the right to family reunification on a case-by-case basis.[53] When assessing the Dutch legislation, the Court stated that in the proceedings at issue it was only where the 'hardship clause' stipulated in Article 3.71a(2)(d) of the 2000 Vb (Decree on foreign nationals, *Vreemdelingenbesluit*) applied that the request for authorisation of entry/residence could not be rejected by the Dutch authorities. Moreover, only in those cases where the applicant for family reunification is permanently unable to pass that examination would the hardship clause lifting the obligation apply. The CJEU concluded in paragraph 63 that:

> 'the hardship clause [...] is not capable of dispensing the members of the sponsors' family concerned, in the light of the individual circumstances of their situations, from the requirement to pass the civic integration examination in all possible cases where maintaining that requirement would make family reunification impossible or excessively difficult.'

Concerning the issue of the fees applicable to the examination, the Court provided further details when examining their legality in relation to the principle of proportionality, to see whether these costs would jeopardise the objectives of the Directive. The level of the costs should not aim, or have the effect of, making family reunification impossible or excessively difficult in practice, which would be the case if the fees were excessive in light of their 'significant financial impact' on TCNs. The Court took a similar approach to the *P. and S.* case when examining this aspect. It held that in the proceedings at issue the family members were under the obligation to pay the course and preparation fees, which consisted of €110 for the preparation pack and €350 for the course.[54] Those who do not pay the course fees are not allowed to take the examination. The Court concluded that 'the amount of the fees relating to the civic integration examination at issue is capable of making family reunification impossible or extremely difficult'.[55]

---

51 Case C-153/14, *Zaken*, EU:C:2015:453, para. 58.
52 Case C-153/14, *Zaken*, EU:C:2015:453, para. 59.
53 Case C-153/14, *Zaken*, EU:C:2015:453, para. 60.
54 Case C-153/14, *Zaken*, EU:C:2015:453, paras. 66–67.
55 Case C-153/14, *Zaken*, EU:C:2015:453, para. 69.

In light of the above, the CJEU held that the Netherlands could not require TCNs to pass the civic integration examination at hand in so far as it does not allow 'regard to be had to special circumstances objectively forming an obstacle to the applicants passing the examination and in so far as they set the fees relating to such an examination at too high a level', and therefore those conditions make the exercise of the right to family reunification impossible or excessively difficult.[56]

4. THE CHALLENGES OF OBLIGATORY CIVIC INTEGRATION EXAMS TO EU LAW

This section examines the following challenges which civic integration tests pose to European law: first, the distinction between integration conditions and integration measures in EU immigration law, and the relevance of the mandatory and sanction-driven approach to integration policies; second, the relevance of the EU Charter of Fundamental Rights in conjunction with EU immigration law rights when assessing the proportionality of integration conditions; and third, the indeterminate nature of the notion of civic integration, in particular its component related to 'societal knowledge or values'.

4.1. INTEGRATION CONDITIONS *AND/OR* MEASURES?

A key point of controversy which emerged in the two cases under examination in this chapter was the relevance and scope of the difference between the notions of 'integration conditions' and 'integration measures', and whether they have a consistent and cross-cutting meaning in both the LTR Directive and Directive 2003/86. AG Kokott and AG Szpunar fundamentally disagreed on this point. AG Kokott argued that they differ, and therefore that EU Member States could apply 'integration conditions' (including both knowledge of language and society) abroad as a requirement for TCNs to have access to the EU right of family reunification. She emphasised that 'integration measures' could mean passing a mandatory test and that obligatory 'civic integration exams abroad' still conform to the EU notion of 'measures'.

AG Szpunar presented a completely different reading of these notions. He was of the opinion that they are in fact to be interpreted similarly and consistently when reading both EU legal instruments. This would have meant that the Dutch civic integration condition for family reunification would be unlawful in light of EU immigration law because only 'integration measures' (and not 'conditions')

56 Case C-153/14, *Zaken*, EU:C:2015:453, para. 71.

are permitted by Directive 2003/86. He based his argument on the negotiations of the Directives and their provisions at stake (Articles 5 and 15 Directive 2003/109). Indeed, during the *travaux préparatoires* several EU Member States proposed to substitute the expression 'conditions' for 'measures' in Article 15, which did not finally survive the negotiations.[57] AG Szpunar stressed that the provisions envisaged in Directive 2003/86 also show the need to distinguish between integration measures and conditions. Similarly to the wording of Article 15(3) Directive 2003/109, Article 7(2) of this Directive makes reference to 'integration measures'.[58]

The distinction between the notion of measures and conditions is in his view of particular relevance in the scope of Directive 2003/86, and in his opinion 'to consider the integration exam as a condition, indispensable for obtaining an authorization to enter the territory by a family member violates the very essence of the right to family reunification.'[59] AG Szpunar stated that the distinction between measures and conditions plays also a fundamental role in the scope of Directive 2003/109 because:

> 'integration measures imposed to long-term residents benefiting from a right of residence in another Member State cannot constitute "conditions", meaning that they cannot become nor *de iure* neither *de facto* an instrument/tool for the selection of persons or immigration control. On the contrary, this integration actions could jeopardise the right of free movement inside the EU, which is a fundamental aspect of the legal status derived from Directive 2003/109.'[60]

Importantly, he added that:

> 'in my view, this does not mean that integration measures cannot impose obligations to long-term residents. However, the obligations cannot imply the need to prove a predetermined level of linguistic skills and knowledge about the society through an exam or an aptitude test.[61] I would like to highlight that the doctrine has expressed a similar opinion, according to which integration measures cannot include obligations of results like the obligation to pass an exam.'[62]

---

57 Opinion of Advocate General SZPUNAR in Case C-579/13, *P. and S.*, EU:C:2015:39, para. 44.

58 Opinion of Advocate General SZPUNAR in Case C-579/13, *P. and S.*, EU:C:2015:39, para. 45.

59 Opinion of Advocate General SZPUNAR in Case C-579/13, *P. and S.*, EU:C:2015:39, reference was here made in footnote 16 to Opinion of Advocate General MENGOZZI, para. 59 (see also para. 51) and some documents presented by the European Commission referred to in note 52 of the same Conclusions, as well as to the Opinion of the European Committee on Social Rights in Working Document of 15 July 2014 titled '*La relation entre le droit de l'union européenne et las Charte sociale européenne*', para. 76.

60 Opinion of Advocate General SZPUNAR in Case C-579/13, *P. and S.*, EU:C:2015:39, para. 47.

61 Opinion of Advocate General SZPUNAR in Case C-579/13, *P. and S.*, EU:C:2015:39.

62 Opinion of Advocate General SZPUNAR in Case C-579/13, *P. and S.*, EU:C:2015:39, paras. 95–96. He made reference to E. BRIBOSIA and S. GANTY, 'Arrêt "Dogan": quelle légalité pour les tests d'intégration civique? (2014) *Journal de droit européen*, 378, and added that '[s]ome authors argue that the concept of integration measures, unlike "integration conditions" which

The relevance of distinguishing between integration measures and conditions in both Directives was previously discussed by AG Mengozzi in his Opinion delivered on 30 April 2014 in Case C-138/13 *Naime Dogan v Federal Republic of Germany*. When assessing the precise scope of the notion of 'integration measures', AG Mengozzi underlined the need to consider the concept of integration measures with that of integration conditions which in his view 'was undoubtedly at the forefront of the legislature's mind' during the *travaux préparatoires*.[63] The legislator deliberately used a different concept to 'integration conditions' in Article 15 Directive 2003/109 in the context of the acquisition of certain EU rights. In his view, the concepts are rather different and not synonymous. When referring to 'condition for integration' the AG said that 'it is clear that, once again, we are dealing with a notion which connotes the idea of a prerequisite which must be proven by the interested party'.[64] AG Mengozzi was of the view that 'it is nonetheless clear that "integration measures" must be regarded as less onerous than "integration conditions"' and argued that:

> 'the integration measures referred to in Article 7.2 cannot pursue the aim of *selecting* the persons who may exercise their right of reunification, as such selection is the aim of the criteria and conditions laid down in Article 7.1. On the contrary, the integration measures in Article 7.2 must essentially be intended to *facilitate* integration in the Member States.'[65]

While the CJEU did not directly consider Mengozzi's point in its judgment issued on July 2014,[66] the ruling in *Dogan* is also of significance for *Zaken*. When assessing the lawfulness of the mandatory German 'integration abroad' of family members of Turkish nationals (which unlike the Dutch version does not include a civic dimension but exclusively an linguistic one), the CJEU held that family reunification represents an 'essential way of making possible the family life of Turkish workers [...] and contributes both to improving the quality of their stay and to their integration'.[67] The Court considered that the German integration test abroad made family reunification more difficult or impossible. Therefore, Turkish nationals would find themselves obliged to choose between their activity in the EU and their family life in Turkey. The judgment concluded that

are binding and are subject to penalties, may also mean that they may not include mandatory conditions or penalties', when referring to S. Carrera, 'Integration of Immigrants in EU Law and Policy', in L. Azoulai and K. De Vries (eds.), *EU Migration Law: Legal Complexities and Political Rationales* (Oxford: OUP, 2014).

63 Opinion of Advocate General Mengozzi in Case C-138/13, *Dogan*, EU:C:2014:287, para. 51.

64 Opinion of Advocate General Mengozzi in Case C-138/13, *Dogan*, EU:C:2014:287, para. 54.

65 Opinion of Advocate General Mengozzi in Case C-138/13, *Dogan*, EU:C:2014:287, paras. 52–53.

66 Case C-138/13, *Dogan*, EU:C:2014:2066.

67 Case C-138/13, *Dogan*, EU:C:2014:2066, para. 34.

the German law constituted a 'new restriction' in the context of the EC–Turkey Additional Protocol and therefore was unlawful.[68]

The positions held by AG Szpunar and AG Mengozzi as regard the relevance of distinguishing integration measures and conditions in EU immigration law have been shared by the European Commission. In the Communication on guidance for application of Directive 2003/86 on the right to family reunification COM (2014) 210 of 3 April 2014, the Commission emphasised that while Member States have a margin of appreciation when requiring TCNs to comply with 'integration measures', these should comply with the following requirements: first, they should facilitate the integration of family members as their main purpose, so 'if integration measures are in effect used to limit family reunification, this would amount to an additional requirement for family reunification'; and second, they should respect the principle of proportionality, in particular in respect of their accessibility, design and organisation. The Commission also expressly acknowledged the difference between 'integration measures' and 'integration conditions' by saying that:

> 'in contrast, Article 7.2 allows Member States to require third country nationals to comply with integration measures. *Member States may require family members to make a certain effort to demonstrate their willingness to integrate*, for instance, by requiring participation in language or integration courses, prior to or after arrival. Since these measures are meant to help facilitate the integration process, this also implies that the way in which Member States conceive this possibility cannot be unlimited' (emphasis added).[69]

Differently from AG Kokott's Opinion, the Communication continued by saying that while the verification of the willingness to integrate by the TCN may take the shapes of an examination, these integration measures 'cannot result in a performance obligation that is in fact a measure that limits the possibility of family reunification. The measures must, on the contrary, contribute to the success of family reunification.'[70]

The academic literature has supported AG Szpunar, AG Mengozzi and the Commission's interpretations of the difference between integration measures and conditions in the scope of all EU migration-related Directives. Groenendijk has argued that 'integration conditions' would allow Member States to impose more far-reaching obligations on the TCN such as passing an integration test. On the contrary, 'integration measures' would only permit Member States to require TCNs to make a certain effort by participating in language or

---

68 Case C-138/13, *Dogan*, EU:C:2014:2066, paras. 35–36.

69 European Commission, 'Communication on guidance for application of Directive 2003/86 on the right to family reunification', COM (2014) 210, 15–16.

70 European Commission, 'Communicationon guidance for application of Directive 2003/86 on the right to family reunification', COM (2014) 210, 15–16.

integration courses.[71] In his opinion, it is certain that the distinction between measures and conditions is central for the legitimacy of the national framework under which the normative understanding of integration provided by these Directives can be implemented. When looking at the legislative work predating their formal adoption inside the Council, Groenendijk has also pointed out how a large number of EU Member States shared the view that the two notions were not identical in scope and nature, and that 'integration conditions would put a greater burden on migrants than integration measures'.[72] In his view 'if integration criteria were an overarching term covering both integration conditions and integration measures, there would have been no need to use the two terms in the Blue Card Directive'.[73]

In my PhD dissertation I followed a similar understanding of these two different concepts and expressed the view that an additional feature distinguishing these two notions is the mandatory or binding nature subsumed in using integration conditions. The non-facultative nature or 'conditionality' inherent in the notion of integration conditions – *the conditionality of integration* – constitutes a core distinguishing feature between this term and that of integration measures across the EU immigration law spectrum.[74] When looking at the relevant provisions in both Council Directives 2003/109 (Article 5(2)) and 2003/86 (Article 4(1)), the expression 'integration conditions' has offered Member States the possibility of applying integration as a binding requirement which, in the event of non-fulfilment, would justify non-access to or withdrawal of the security of residence provided by long-term EC resident status and/or the EU right to family reunification. It also implies the possibility for national authorities to apply penalties to the applicant, including the refusal of a permanent residence permit and family reunion, non-renewal of a temporary residence permit and eventual expulsion from the country. Therefore, one could conclude that the reference to integration measures in Article 7(2) Directive 2003/86 and Article 15(3) Directive 2003/109 would prevent Member States from introducing mandatory integration conditions and applying disciplinary measures against TCNs.[75]

The three AGs made reference to the negotiations of the LTR Directive and/or Directive 2003/86 in an attempt to support some of their argumentations. These

71 K. Groenendijk, 'Family Reunification as a Right under Community Law' (2006) 8 *EJML*, 215–230.

72 K. Groenendijk, 'Integration of Immigrants in the EU: The Old or the New Way?', in Y. Pascouau and T. Strik (eds.), *Which Integration Policies for Migrants? Interaction between the EU and its Member States* (Wolf Legal Publishers: Nijmegen, 2012).

73 K. Groenendijk, 'Integration of Immigrants in the EU: The Old or the New Way?', in Y. Pascouau and T. Strik (eds.), *Which Integration Policies for Migrants? Interaction between the EU and its Member States* (Wolf Legal Publishers: Nijmegen, 2012), 10.

74 S. Carrera, *In Search of the Perfect Citizen? The Intersection between Integration, Immigration and Nationality in the EU* (Leiden: Martinus Nijhoff Publishers: 2009).

75 S. Carrera, 'Integration of Immigrants in EU Law and Policy', in L. Azoulai and K. De Vries (eds.), *EU Migration Law: Legal Complexities and Political Rationales* (Oxford: OUP, 2014).

took place during a period when the Justice and Home Affairs Council was the sole legislative actor with the ownership and ultimate decision (on unanimous vote by all its members) on the destiny of any legislative proposal in the area of 'legal immigration'. The role played by a small group of representatives from the Ministries of Interior of certain EU Member States, and that of the EU Presidency itself, was decisive in order to understand the final outputs of these measures, as well as the agreement which was reached on the framing of integration as a 'condition' and a 'measure'.[76] The differentiation between integration measures and conditions is indeed clear when looking at the Council negotiations, where a small group of EU Member States (Austria, Germany and the Netherlands) called for the introduction of this 'new approach to integration' – integration criteria – and when asked during the discussions about what these integration conditions actually meant, their answer was that it would actually mean the need to pass an integration programme as the condition for granting common EU LTR status, which would include sufficient knowledge of the country.[77]

As studied in section 2 of this chapter, regrettably the CJEU did not directly or expressly enter into the discussion on the relevance of distinguishing between integration 'measures' and 'conditions' when assessing the Dutch implementing legislation in the scope of the LTR Directive and Directive 2003/86. This can be seen as a missed opportunity by the Court to bring further legal clarity and consistency in the application of EU Member States' civic integration programmes when acting within the remit of EU immigration law. However, the Court did offer some food for legal thought. The Court reached the conclusion in the *P. and S.* case that the application of a fine *ex post* the acquisition of EU LTR status did not constitute an 'integration condition' within the meaning of Article 5(2) Directive 2003/109, but rather an 'integration measure'. As highlighted in section 2.3 above, one can argue that the CJEU implicitly acknowledged the relevance of the measure–condition distinction in the framework of this specific Directive; a determining factor for this distinction in the case under consideration being that the failure to pass the exam was not decisive when granting or losing pre-existing EC LTR status and security of residence in the country, but only as regards the application of a financial sanction.

The Second Chamber of the CJEU did not duly consider however the extent to which a similar interpretation could be applied in the scope of Directive 2003/86 in the *Zaken* judgment. Here the Court concluded that the Dutch civic integration test abroad was generally in compliance with the aims of Directive

76 S. Carrera, 'Integration of Immigrants in EU Law and Policy', in L. Azoulai and K. De Vries (eds.), *EU Migration Law: Legal Complexities and Political Rationales* (Oxford: OUP, 2014).

77 Council, 12217/02, 23 September 2002, page 2.

2003/86. Controversially, the Court held that the integration abroad text fell within the scope of Article 7(2) Directive 2003/86, which only speaks of 'integration measures' and not 'conditions'. Accordingly, the Netherlands could – under certain conditions – lawfully require TCNs to pass such an examination as a 'condition' for granting lawful entry and residence in the country. One could be inclined to conclude that the judges were somewhat persuaded by AG Kokott's rather unsatisfactory Opinion that the distinction between 'measures' and 'conditions' was not relevant in the context of Directive 2003/86, but only when applying Directive 2003/109.

It is striking that the Court decided to follow that route, and distance itself from the Opinions previously issued by AG Szpunar and Mengozzi, the one by the European Commission and the majority of the legal doctrine on the centrality inherent in that distinction. The *Zaken* judgment can be also seen as a step backwards from what the Court ruled in the above-mentioned *Dogan* case. As has been referred to above, here the CJEU concluded that the mandatory German 'integration abroad' of family members of Turkish nationals was unlawful as it constituted a 'new restriction' in the context of the EC–Turkey Additional Protocol. Contrary to this line of jurisprudence, the Court seems to now accept a new or additional criterion or restriction (in the form of a performance obligation) on the access to family members of TCNs to the EU right to family reunification before entering the European territory. Furthermore, accepting a directive-by-directive interpretation of the scope and material reach of 'integration measures' and 'conditions' may well lead to an obscure and rather fragmented framework of laws and meanings leading to legal uncertainty, to the detriment of the effectiveness and consistent application by EU Member States of the EU rights, administrative guarantees and safeguards stipulated in EU immigration law.

That notwithstanding, and as previously referred to in section 3.2, among the set of legal standards developed by the Court in the *Zaken* ruling when determining the lawfulness of the Dutch integration test abroad, one which is of particular relevance following the doctrinal distinction between integration 'measures' and 'conditions' is contained in paragraph 56 of the judgment. Here the CJEU got closer to AG Szpunar's Opinion and the Commission's view and held that the conditions for its application would be disproportionate in those cases where the civic integration requirement would 'systematically prevent family reunification of a sponsor's family member where, despite having failed the integration examination, they have demonstrated their willingness to pass the examination and they have made every effort to achieve that objective'.[78] One could interpret this paragraph as a hint given by the Luxembourg Court to the Dutch national tribunal that failing the integration test abroad should not constitute a migration-control tool systematically preventing family

78 Case C-153/14, *Zaken*, EU:C:2015:453, para. 56.

reunification. Inherent in this point, one could argue, is the indirect acceptance by the CJEU of the distinction between integration measures and conditions also within the scope of Directive 2003/86. In fact, mere willingness to pass the test and making 'every effort' should suffice. The extent to which the Dutch civic integration test abroad meets this standard remains disputed.

4.2. THE 'SPECIFICITY' OF EU RIGHTS AND THE LUXEMBOURG COURT AS A FUNDAMENTAL RIGHTS ADJUDICATOR

Sections 2 and 3 of this chapter have illustrated that one of the starting points for the Court in both judgments in determining the compliance of Dutch integration programmes with EU law was the assumption that these aimed at facilitating the integration of TCNs. The CJEU uncritically accepted in both judgments, without any supporting evidence of the practical application and effects on the rights of individuals affected, that the national policies under scrutiny met the Directives' aims of facilitating participation of TCNs in Dutch society, and facilitated communication, 'interaction and the development of social relations between them'.[79] The CJEU's opinion that these assumptions 'cannot be disputed' reminds us of AG Kokott's Opinion in the *Zaken* case, which concurred with the Dutch government argument in the proceedings that the Dutch law aimed to ameliorate 'the starting-point of those coming to the Netherlands'.

It is however this particular point that the Court should not have just assumed, but rather more meticulously examined. In fact, it is precisely the extent to which the Dutch civic integration policy actually fosters or facilitates access by TCNs to EU rights that was the most determining factor when testing the lawfulness of the Dutch integration policy. The Court could have considered more carefully the extent to which the Dutch civic integration tests at home and abroad actually aim at facilitating integration or rather at controlling immigration, especially in practice. It is striking that both the CJEU and AG Kokott accepted so easily the arguments put forward by the Dutch government without effectively investigating and gathering sufficient information on the actual public policy purposes of these policies as well as their actual implementation on the ground.

The selective or control-driven rationale of the Dutch civic integration policy is an issue which has been well documented and amply discussed by the literature. Already in 2009 we provided evidence proving that behind the Dutch public official justification of facilitating the integration process of newcomers, the Integration

[79] Case C-579/13, *P. and S.*, EU:C:2015:369, para. 47; Case C-153/14, *Zaken*, EU:C:2015:453, para. 54.

Abroad Act (*Wet inburgering in het buitenland*) pursued a more implicit objective of restricting the number of family immigrants to the Netherlands.[80] A key objective was to reduce the number of applicants willing to undertake the effort and financial risk (fees) in taking the exam.[81] A clear proof of this rationale was the decision taken by the Dutch government back in 2008 to increase the level/difficulty of the test as too many candidates were considered to be successful.[82] More recent studies have confirmed and further elaborated on this finding.[83]

It is welcomed that the CJEU insisted on the general principle of proportionality when assessing the obligatory civic integration examinations in both the *P. and S.* and *Zaken* cases. Testing the legality of integration conditions includes their compliance with the EU general principles, and the extent to which civic integration exams are proportionate is of central importance to determine their compatibility with EU law. This had been clearly stated by the Commission in the above-mentioned Communication on guidance for application of Directive 2003/86 on the right to family reunification COM (2014) 210. The Commission was also here clear when stating that 'the automatic refusal of family reunification as a result of a failed integration examination could amount to a violation of Article 17, Article 5.5 and Article 8 ECHR'.[84] This followed the opinion previously held by the CJEU in judgments like *Chakroun* C-578/08 of March 2010,[85] where the Court ruled that when interpreting Directive 2003/86 due consideration should be given to its Article 17, which requires 'an individual examination of applications for family reunification'.[86] Similarly, in paragraph 55 of the Opinion in *Dogan* of 30 April 2014, AG Mengozzi underlined that:

> 'conceding the possibility of making admission into the Member State concerned conditional on passing a test for which it's not actually possible to prepare [...] *is*

80 We argued that: 'It follows from the explanatory memorandum to the Integration Abroad Act that the requirement to pass an integration exam abroad is intended to stimulate potential immigrants to carefully consider whether it is worth applying for admission to the Netherlands.' See 'Memorie van Toelichting', *Kamerstukken II*, 2003–2004, 29 700 nr. 3.

81 S. Carrera and A. Wiesbrock, *Civic Integration of Third Country Nationals: Nationalism versus Europeanisation in the Common EU Immigration Policy* (Brussels: CEPS Liberty and Security in Europe Series, 2009).

82 The decision was taken on 15 March 2008 on the basis of an assessment conducted in 2007 showing that candidates had a higher level of language proficiency than expected and a majority of applicants passed the exam. Refer to *Kamerstukken II*, 2006–07, 29 700, nr. 40. See also P.F. Sanders, 'Onderzoek naar de kwaliteit van het inburgeringsexamen buitenland', TNO-rapport TNODV 2007 (Arnhem: Research Center voor Examinering en Certificering, Cito en Universiteit Twente, 2007).

83 Cf. T. Strik, A. Böcker, M. Luiten and R. Van Oers, 'The INTEC Project: Synthesis Report – Integration and Naturalisation Tests: The New Way to European Citizenship', in Y. Pascouau and T. Strik (eds.), *Which Integration Policies for Migrants? Interaction between the EU and its Member States* (Nijmegen: Wolf Legal Publishers, 2012).

84 See footnote 55 in page 16 of the Communication.

85 Case C-578/08, *Chakroun*, EU:C:2010:117.

86 Case C-578/08, *Chakroun*, EU:C:2010:117, para. 48.

in practice, tantamount to making it impossible to exercise the right to reunification provided for in the directive. Likewise, *legislation which does not allow account to be taken of difficulties*, even of temporary nature, relating to the health *of the family member concerned or his/her personal circumstances*, such as age, illiteracy, disability and level of education, would undermine the effectiveness of Directive 2003/86' (emphasis added).[87]

One of the key challenges characterising mandatory integration exams is that they make it extremely difficult to consider the personal and family circumstances of the person involved. The focus on the actual results prevents a personal assessment being taking into consideration of the consequences of excluding someone from EU migration law rights and her/his private and family life enshrined in Article 7 of the EU Charter. This is a point where both AG Kokott and AG Szpunar reached a similar conclusion in their Opinions when testing the appropriateness of integration exams. Both suggest that the legality of the Dutch obligatory civic integration exams would be at stake if EU rights were not granted on the merely automatic basis of failing to pass the test. It is the 'automatism' characterising testing the integration of TCNs which makes its compatibility with EU law more at stake.

The CJEU followed a similar interpretation in both judgments. It underlined that when evaluating the means used by the Dutch national authorities in the implementation of civic integration exams special attention should be paid to the extent to which these allow for consideration of the specific individual circumstances, such as age, illiteracy or level of education.[88] In the *Zaken* judgment the Court held that the national policy at issue should allow for dispensing certain family members from the obligation to pass the exam for reasons related to 'age, illiteracy, level of education, economic situation or health'.[89] Here too, both rulings show a rather poor understanding and knowledge of the practical issues inherent in the application of civic integration exams on the ground, particularly those affecting the integration abroad test. If the CJEU had duly considered these aspects, the legality of the Dutch civic integration exams could have been expected to fall altogether. It is nonetheless welcome that the CJEU held that the 'hardship clause' stipulated in Article 3.71a(2)(d) of the 2000 Vb was not capable of exempting the members of the sponsors' family concerned, in the light of their individual circumstances, from the requirement of passing the civic integration examination in all possible cases and therefore making the exercise of the right to family reunification impossible or excessively difficult.

The inherently difficult relationship between mandatory civic integration policies and a personalised assessment, and ways to go about it, have been

87 Opinion of Advocate General Mengozzi in Case C-138/13, *Dogan*, EU:C:2014:287, paras. 57–59.

88 Case C-579/13, *P. and S.*, EU:C:2015:369, para. 49.

89 Case C-153/14, *Zaken*, EU:C:2015:453, para. 58.

issues addressed by the academic literature. Acosta has for instance proposed a 'personalised proportionality', which would mean that 'whenever there is any testing imposed in order to acquire long-term residence, Member States should have not only exemptions for specific groups of people but also clauses providing for the granting of long-term residence in other cases.'[90] Similarly van Oers, Ersbøll and Kostakopoulou have argued that:

> 'it is doubtful whether there is "a reasonable relationship of proportionality" between integration tests as a condition for family reunification, a permanent residence permit and/or citizenship and the aim of improving immigrants' integration if groups of immigrants with a poor education, low income, etc., remain unable to meet the conditions and are thus excluded from access to family reunification, a permanent residence permit and/or citizenship [...] Therefore, language-learning facilities should be made available for immigrants, fees should not pose insurmountable barriers and language and societal knowledge testing, if any, should only test immigrants' relative competence. If testing at a fixed level is maintained, provision should be made for exemption for groups of people who, through no fault of their own, will not pass the test.'[91]

However, some of these practical options present a whole series of inherent limitations. First, they assume or still leave open the overall legitimacy of applying integration conditions/tests abroad in the context of EU immigration law, which as we have seen above remains contested. Second, they also presume that integration tests can be designed in ways that could overcome these deficits. As Guild, Groenendijk and Carrera have argued, the use of computers in the examination process may well constitute an insurmountable obstacle for less educated people. This aspect becomes ever more challenging to apply in practice in light of the 'privatisation' processes surrounding integration exams, where private companies and educations institutions are those ultimately in charge of administering the tests through computer programmes.[92]

AG Szpunar also went a step further in his Opinion and argued about the need for EU Member States to comply with the EU Charter of Fundamental Rights, and more precisely its Article 7 on the right to private and family life. The judgments could have also paid particular attention to existing evidence on the actual effects of this migration-control tool over the *effet utile* of the LTR

---

90 D. Acosta, '"En Attendant Godot" or the EU Limits to Integration Conditions', in Y. Pascouau and T. Strik (eds.), *Which Integration Policies for Migrants? Interaction between the EU and its Member States* (Nijmegen: Wolf Legal Publishers, 2012).

91 R. van Oers, E. Ersbøll and D. Kostakopoulou, 'Mapping the redefinition of belonging in Europe', in R. van Oers, E. Ersbøll and D. Kostakopoulou (eds.), *A Re-Definition of Belonging? Language and Integration Tests in Europe* (Leiden: Martinus Nijhoff Publishers, 2010).

92 E. Guild, K. Groenendijk and S. Carrera (eds.), *Illiberal Liberal States: Immigration, Citizenship and Integration in the EU* (Farnham: Ashgate, 2009).

status and the EU right to family reunification in combination with Article 7 of the EU Charter. This is one central aspect which is by and large overlooked by AG Kokott's Opinion and missing from both CJEU rulings. The Recital 2 Directive 2003/86 is clear in this regard. It states '*that measures concerning family reunification should be adopted in conformity with the obligation to protect the family and respect family life enshrined in many instruments of international law. The increasing relevance of the EU Charter of Fundamental Rights in conjunction with the specific set of EU rights envisaged in European secondary law on immigration should not be underestimated for future cases before the Court dealing with the lawfulness of national restrictions and exceptions*'.

A realist doctrinal assessment of EU Member States actions interfering with 'family reunification' would inaccurately attribute more value to the contributions by the European Court of Human Rights (ECtHR) and apply a narrow understanding of TCNs constitutional status in European law.93 Such an approach would not take due account of the 'specificity' which EU rights of TCNs have progressively adopted in the European legal system.[94] As the CJEU has reminded us in its Opinion 2/13 of December 2014,[95] which concluded that the draft EU accession treaty to the ECHR did not comply with EU law,[96] the very nature of EU law is one with very specific characteristics that are intrinsically linked to the autonomy of the EU legal order.[97] The EU judicial system is aimed at ensuring consistency and uniformity in the interpretation of European law. It is for the Luxembourg Court to ultimately ensure the judicial protection of individuals' right in the scope of EU law.[98] The specificity of rights enjoyed by TCNs in the Union legal system is well exemplified by the EU right to family reunification, which, in combination with Article 7 EU Charter, can be seen to have taken the human right to family life enshrined in the ECHR towards new legal venues and fora. Indeed, Directive 2003/86 has been said to establish for the first time a right to family reunion by family members of TCNs in the EU. This Directive attaches to this EU right a set of administrative guarantees and protections which have direct effect and which have been said to compose a new 'subjective' and *sui generis* right in the EU legal system.[99]

---

93 See further on this issue the chapter of D. Thym elsewhere in this book.

94 See for instance E. Guild, *The Legal Elements of European Identity: EU Citizenship and Migration Law* (The Hague: Kluwer Law International, 2004); C. Murphy, *Immigration, Integration and the Law: The Intersection of Domestic, EU and International Legal Regimes* (Farnham: Ashgate, 2013; K. Groenendijk, 'Family Reunification as a Right under Community Law' (2006) 8 *EJML*, 215–230; A. Wiesbrock, *Legal Migration to the European Union* (Leiden: Martinus Nijhoff, 2010), 169–207.

95 Opinion 2/13, EU:C:2014:2454.

96 Opinion 2/13, EU:C:2014:2454, para. 258.

97 Opinion 2/13, EU:C:2014:2454, paras. 166, 170, 172–174.

98 Opinion 2/13, EU:C:2014:2454, para. 175.

99 K. Groenendijk, 'Family Reunification as a Right under Community Law' (2006) 8 *EJML*, 215–230; S. Iglesias Fernández, 'El Valor de la Directiva 2003/86/CE sobre Reagrupación

CJEU Opinion 2/13 is of central relevance in this discussion. One could have expected the CJEU to uphold more vigorously and actively the consistency and uniformity of TCNs' rights across EU law, including of course when reading them in conjunction with those envisaged in the EU Charter. This however has not been the case in either of the two judgments under examination in this chapter. On the contrary the Court would have examined the Dutch civic integration policy from the perspective of its practical impacts over the set of rights specific to EU secondary law (e.g. family reunification or long-term residence) in combination with the fundamental rights foreseen in the EU Charter. We have explored elsewhere that the CJEU is yet to function as a proper fundamental rights tribunal in the Area of Freedom, Security and Justice (AFSJ).[100] This opinion has been shared by de Búrca, who has rightly argued that there will be a growing demand for the Luxembourg Court to perform the role of a fundamental rights adjudicator, which will increasingly put into question its so far 'self-referential, formulaic and often minimalistic style' of judicial reasoning.[101] Chiefly, it will increasingly require it to expand its expertise and adapt its procedures for having due regard to the actual impact of EU Member States' practices on EU rights.

4.3. INTEGRATION AS AN INDETERMINATE LEGAL CONCEPT: WHAT INTEGRATION IS NOT

The above-mentioned challenges take an even more prominent form when considering the uncertainties inherent in the notion of integration. 'Integration' is an indeterminate legal concept which leaves Member States' discretion too large when applying exceptions to EU rights. The legal uncertainty inherent in the concept of 'integration' becomes particularly great when it comes to 'civic integration'; that is exams not only consisting of linguistic requirements but also the testing of knowledge on 'societal values' or 'knowledge of the

Familiar a la Luz de los Derechos Fundamentales y de la Sentencia del TJCE en el Asunto 540/03' (2007) 26 *Revista de Derecho Comunitario Europeo*, 125–153.

100 S. Carrera, M. De Somer and B. Petkova, *The Court of Justice of the European Union as a Fundamental Rights Tribunal: Challenges for the Effective Delivery of Fundamental Rights in the Area of Freedom, Security and Justice* (Brussels: CEPS Liberty and Security in Europe Series, 2012), 19–20. Here we have argued that 'the CJEU should give due consideration to the procedural law tools and standards that have been developed by the ECtHR in Strasbourg. Improving the accessibility of third-party interventions and ensuring a proactive use of interim relief measures accommodated to fundamental rights cases would tremendously ease the difficulties inherent to the conversion of the EU Charter from "law on the books" into a justiciable document having tangible effects for vulnerable individuals, i.e. into "law in practice"'.

101 G. De Búrca, 'After the EU Charter of Fundamental Rights: The Court of Justice as a Human Rights Adjudicator?' (2013) 20 *MJ*, 168–184.

country'. One aspect characterising the very term 'integration' is the high level of discretion that it grants to the State for its understanding, interpretation and applicability.[102] Integration into 'what'? Is there a definition provided by the law about the 'way of life' or of the 'receiving society'? The civic dimension of integration tests has found that fundamental disagreement and lack of consensus exist, and that a consistent definition of 'what' precisely those values and 'way of life' actually are remains contested.

Kostakopoulou has highlighted that the very concept of integration is an empty shell and cannot be understood without a subjective understanding and framing of the 'society' within which someone is to be 'integrated'.[103] In her view 'it is very doubtful whether this is an objective and value-free presupposition, as it carries within it traces of a certain ideological configuration which associates foreignness with "objective deficiencies" in need of remedy'.[104] There is a direct relationship between a biased framing of 'the receiving society' and that of the integration standard developed in the test or exam. Civic integration starts from the ideological premise of a static society template within which all TCNs will disappear. Because these understandings lack an individual or personalised understanding of the 'receiving society', one can argue that 'integration conditions' are destined to fail when putting into practice an individualised or personalised. Any attempt to conceptualise national identity is open to widely subjective interpretations of 'us' and 'our' supposed identity and societal values, in our view of what is 'normal' and what is 'abnormal'.[105] Any vision of unity or any discourse advocating for perfectly integrated receiving societies is an illusion.

The insistence on 'basic knowledge of a country' goes along with a hierarchical understanding of societies according to which some Western 'countries' have 'fundamental rules of co-existence' which are not shared by 'non-Western others' who are in this way indirectly portrayed as inferior or 'less developed' – they are asked to learn superior rules of coexistence than those of where they are coming from. This raises issues of discrimination now prohibited in EU secondary law and the EU Charter. As the CJEU concluded in the *P. and S.* judgment, the means of implementing a civic integration obligation 'must

---

102 S. Carrera, *In Search of the Perfect Citizen? The Intersection between Integration, Immigration and Nationality in the EU* (Martinus Nijhoff: Leiden, 2009).

103 D. Kostakopoulou, 'Introduction', in R. Van Oers, E. Ersbøll and D. Kostakopoulou (eds.), *A Re-Definition of Belonging? Language and Integration Tests in Europe* (Leiden: Martinus Nijhoff Publishers, 2010).

104 D. Kostakopoulou, 'Introduction', in R. Van Oers, E. Ersbøll and D. Kostakopoulou (eds.), *A Re-Definition of Belonging? Language and Integration Tests in Europe* (Leiden: Martinus Nijhoff Publishers, 2010), 7.

105 S. Carrera, 'Integration as a Process of Inclusion for Migrants? The Case of Long-term Residents in the EU', in H. Schneider (ed.), *Migration, Integration and Citizenship: A Challenge for Europe's Future* (Maastricht: Forum Maastricht, 2005).

not undermine the principle of non-discrimination' in those areas listed in Article 11(1) Directive 2003/109.[106]

There is also a difficult relationship between civic integration and the 'in accordance to the law' test developed by the ECtHR in cases of states' interferences with fundamental human rights such as Article 7 of the EU Charter. One of the most important standards developed by the ECtHR when assessing the 'in accordance with the law' test has been the extent to which the law is accessible and sufficiently clear and whether the consequences are foreseeable for the individual involved.[107] The law needs to be formulated with sufficient precision to enable them to foresee the consequences of a given action. These ultimately relate to the quality of the law itself and aim at preventing disproportionate arbitrariness by national authorities when applying restrictions to fundamental human rights.

AG Szpunar's Opinion comprehensively highlighted that the argument that integration policies fall within the scope of EU Member States' exclusive competence cannot be used to conclude that EU Member States have full freedom in this matter. The exercise by EU Member States of their competences, as long as these affect conferred and protected rights in the EU legal system, can be also subject to EU scrutiny in light of EU law.[108] Indeed, integration measures and conditions are now exceptions to EU rights envisaged by EU immigration Directives. As such they need to be interpreted restrictively and EU Member States' transposition and practical implementation are now subject to European scrutiny. Particular focus is here paid to the means through which these integration policies are applied and their compatibility with the EU general principles such as proportionality and the EU Charter.

The *P. and S.* and *Zaken* judgments provide in this respect a timid step towards what the role of CJEU should be in this domain of law: to set clear legal standards on what 'integration is not' in the scope of EU rights specific to the EU legal system. Common EU standards on what is not permissible in the scope of European immigration law as regards the use of mandatory civic integration exams should include the following:

- integration policies cannot pursue a migration control/selection public intended goal to limit family reunification, otherwise they would unlawfully constitute an additional restriction;
- integration policies need to facilitate and promote family reunification;

---

106 Case C-579/13, *P. and S.*, EU:C:2015:369, paras. 42–43. On the non-discrimination obligation refer to para. 44 of the judgment.

107 See for instance ECtHR, 18 May 2010, *Kennedy v United Kingdom*, no. 26839/05; ECtHR, 10 February 2009, *Iordachi and Others v Moldova*, no. 25198/02; ECtHR, 1 July 2008, *Liberty and Others v United Kingdom*, no. 58243/00; and ECtHR, 6 December 2007, *Liu and Liu v Russia*, no. 42086/05.

108 Opinion of Advocate General Szpunar in Case C-579/13, *P. and S.*, EU:C:2015:39, para. 48. Reference was here made to Case C-135/08, *Rottmann*, EU:C:2010:104.

- integration policies need to allow for an individualised/personal assessment of the circumstances and must comply with the EU Charter, in particular (yet not exclusively) with Article 7;
- restrictions must be interpreted restrictively and must not made the exercise of the rights too difficult in practice;
- proportionality test criteria related to accessibility, design and organisation; and
- integration measures are not the same as integration conditions in EU immigration law, not only in the EU Directive 2003/109.

5. CONCLUSIONS

This chapter has examined the challenges of civic integration tests pose to EU immigration and fundamental rights law. It has studied the main findings and implications of Cases C-579/13 *P. and S. v Commissie Sociale Zekerheid Breda* and C-153/14 *Zaken v K. and A.* Civic integration exams pose three main challenges from the perspective of EU law: first, they blur the fundamental distinction between the notions of integration conditions and measures in the LTR Directive and Directive 2003/86; second, they also have a difficult relationship with specific EU rights such as the EU right to family reunification; and third, they challenge the effectiveness of EU immigration law and the rights foreseen therein due to its indeterminate legal nature.

There has been a large degree of consensus regarding the need to distinguish the notion of integration measures from that of integration conditions in the scope of EU immigration law, and its cross-cutting or consistent interpretation across all relevant immigration Directives. Independently of the formal distinction between 'integration conditions' and 'integration measures', the chapter has argued that a point which the CJEU could have more carefully examined is the extent to which the restrictions inherent in the Dutch civic integration test abroad in practice makes family reunification more difficult or even impossible in ways which directly violate the proportionality principle. The CJEU should have played a more active role as a fundamental rights adjudicator and not just assume that the Dutch integration policy aims (*de jure* or *de facto*) at facilitating the integration of TCNs. Rather the Court could have critically examined the actual practical impact or repercussions of the use of these exams in light of existing evidence.

Notwithstanding, both judgments demonstrate that EU Member States' interpretation and use of integration programmes in the scope of EU immigration law is increasingly subject to supranational rule of law and fundamental rights scrutiny and standards. These also include most importantly the EU Charter of Fundamental Rights. Supranational accountability covers not only the ways in which measures and conditions are formulated and implemented; it also extends towards the ways in which Member States legally frame and administratively apply the notion of 'integration' itself as an exception to EU statuses and rights of TCNs. The CJEU has provided a limited yet welcome step forward when setting the rule-of-law standards on what is not permissible by EU Member States in the use of civic integration exams (what integration is not). One could only expect the Luxembourg Court to increasingly play the role of fundamental rights adjudicator in future judgments assessing the lawfulness of obligatory civic integration exams in the scope of EU immigration law.

CHAPTER 9

I STUDY HERE, AND THUS I BELONG? Mobile Students in the European Union

Alexander HOOGENBOOM

1. INTRODUCTION

In the light of the theme of the seminar organised, this chapter seeks to address the question 'where do I belong' for Europe's mobile students.[1] With over 650,000 students leaving their countries of origin to study elsewhere in the European Union, and this number growing more or less steadily over the last few years,[2] this question is indeed of particular significance in the context of both a changing higher education landscape and the recent debates on free movement. The former is mainly visible in the trend of the progressive internationalisation of higher education[3] and the trend towards commodification.[4] Such internationalisation is set to further encourage student mobility flows which puts into greater focus the question of 'who pays for what'. In addition, the introduction of economic principles and thinking into higher education policy necessitates, as will be argued later on in this chapter, re-evaluating some of the established principles in EU free movement law.

As regards the latter, it is true that students are not directly among those most frequently mentioned in some of the anti-free movement rhetoric that

---

1 The focus here will be on students with a nationality of one of the 28 Member States of the European Union, rather than those students who have a nationality from a third country.

2 Http://ec.europa.eu/eurostat/tgm/refreshTableAction.do?tab=table&plugin=0&pcode=tps00064&language=en (last accessed on 31 January 2016).

3 See e.g. P. ALTBACH, *Trends in Global Higher Education: Tracking an Academic Revolution* (UNESCO, 2009), 23 *et seq.*

4 See e.g. E. HACKL, 'Tensions in the Policy Objectives of the European Higher Education Area? Public Good and Public Responsibility Versus Service Liberalisation: Equality Versus Institutional Diversity', in A. CURAJ *et al.* (eds.), *European Higher Education at the Crossroads: Between the Bologna Process and National Reforms* (Dordrecht: Springer, 2012), 89–91 and M. MCKELVEY and M. HOLMÉN, 'Introduction', in M. MCKELVEY and M. HOLMÉN (eds.), *Learning to Compete in European Universities: From Social Institution to Knowledge Business* (Cheltenham: Edward Elgar, 2009), 1.

is currently quite a popular pastime among certain European leaders: that dubious honour is instead primarily reserved to persons of independent means, jobseekers, and workers seeking to claim certain benefits.[5] However, indirectly, restrictions proposed on labour market access and the like[6] will also affect the decision of the student considering a study period abroad as job prospects play an important role as a 'mobility determinant'.[7] Consider further that promised crackdowns on migration have in the past in particular hurt students,[8] and that mobile European students are increasingly portrayed as if they were somehow abusing the system at the cost of taxpayers.[9]

Nevertheless, mobility of students is usually identified as a crucial pivot in the European Union 'dash for growth',[10] and the phenomenon is habitually attributed a wide range of economic and civic benefits.[11] As such, a certain ambiguity in terms of desirability can be said to surround this type of mobility in the European Union.

In that context, the purpose of this chapter is twofold. Firstly, it seeks to clarify and bring a degree of coherence to some forty years of case-law[12] and to derive the principles that apply to the question 'where do I belong' as a mobile student. In that context, it will be shown that the case-law may be grouped around two main strands:

(1) *Access to education*, which addresses discriminatory conditions imposed by Member States that hamper the enrolment into a course of study or otherwise impede acquisition of student status.[13]

---

5 See e.g. David Cameron's immigration speech, available at www.bbc.com/news/uk-politics-30250299 (last accessed on 31 January 2016) and L. Asscher and D. Goodhart, 'Code Oranje voor vrij werkverkeer binnen EU', Volkskrant of 17 August 2013.

6 See for an overview: S. Peers, 'The nine labours of Cameron: Analysis of the plans to change EU free movement law', available at http://eulawanalysis.blogspot.nl/2014/11/the-nine-labours-of-cameron-analysis-of.html (last accessed on 31 January 2016).

7 See e.g. C. van Mol, *Intra-European student mobility in international higher education circuits (*Palgrave MacMillan, 2014), 56–60, 123–124 and literature cited.

8 See The Guardian, 'Immigration crackdown deterring foreign students, says universities chief', available at www.theguardian.com/education/2013/jan/08/immigration-foreign-students-universities (last accessed on 31 January 2016).

9 S. Bird, 'How foreign students are fleecing Britain: Taxpayers are owed £46 billion in outstanding student loans. So why are foreigners being allowed to vanish with no intention of paying their debts?', Daily Mail of 14 December 2013; K. Kildegaard Sørensen, 'Borgerlige partier åbner for brugerbetalte uddannelser', Berlingske of 10 June 2013; De Standaard, 'Nederlanders halen diploma op Vlaamse kosten', of 17 September 2012; and E. Heuts, interview with Ferdinand Mertens (ex-public servant at the Ministry for Education, Culture and Science), Transfer 10 April 2011.

10 See the flagship initiative 'Youth on the move' in COM (2010) 2020, Europe 2020: A European strategy for smart, sustainable and inclusive growth, of 3 March 2010, 3, 11.

11 Report of the High Level Expert Forum on Mobility, June 2008, available at http://ec.europa.eu/education/doc/2008/mobilityreport_en.pdf (last accessed on 31 January 2016).

12 Starting with Case C-9/74, *Casagrande*, EU:C:1974:74.

13 Case C-357/89, *Raulin*, EU:C:1992:87, para. 34.

(2) *Conditions under which the free movement of students is exercised: access to study-facilitating benefits.* This legal regime covers discriminatory conditions attached to social assistance[14] designed to facilitate higher education attendance, such as study grants and loans,[15] or travel arrangements allowing students to benefit from reduced public transport fees.[16]

Secondly, this chapter seeks to critically engage with these principles as developed by the Court of Justice, in which in particular it is suggested that the EU must engage in a balancing act between on the one hand the overall objective of promoting student mobility, while at the same time recognising that student mobility may have consequences for the autonomy and capacity of Member States in the organisation of their higher education systems.

2. RULES APPLYING TO THE FREE MOVEMENT OF STUDENTS: ACCESS TO EDUCATION AND BELONGING

The question of 'where do I belong' is intimately tied up with the question of solidarity. There is a tension between individual choice and movement and access to community-provided benefits and advantages conditional on a form of membership. Interestingly, where it concerns 'access to education' this tension is largely resolved in favour of the autonomy of the mobile student. Fancy a Bachelor of Laws from the London School of Economics or a degree from Lund University? The mobile Union citizen can exercise his or her free movement rights and enrol at a higher education institutes under equal terms with host Member State nationals. These equal terms are defined quite broadly in this context, which means that the mobile student has the opportunity to challenge a wide range of restrictions and obstacles related to the acquisition of the status of student.

This includes, on the one hand, financial obstacles and restrictions such as discriminatory tuition or enrolment fees. Legislation which imposed on foreign Union citizens with a foreign nationality a higher fee than students with the host Member State nationality was found to violate Article 18 TFEU in the *Gravier* case.[17] The prohibition is wide-ranging, and also includes indirect ways by which Member States might seek to introduce an unlawful distinction: any contributions or financing options granted to host Member State nationals

14 See for a definition, Case C-140/12, *Brey*, EU:C:2013:565, para. 61.

15 With the exception of those grants/loans designed to cover the payment of tuition or enrolment fees, see Case C-357/89, *Raulin*, EU:C:1992:87.

16 Case C-75/11, *Commission v Austria*, EU:C:2012:605.

17 Case 293/83, *Gravier*, EU:C:1985:69.

to cover such tuition fees must also be extended to foreign Member State nationals.[18] Moreover, Member States may not use the 'carrot and stick' of higher education funding granted to higher education institutes to induce or force them to prefer host Member State nationals over foreign Member State nationals.[19] A second set of cases, on the other hand, concerns administrative or technical restrictions. Attempts by Member States to impede students from enrolling through quotas favouring students resident in the host Member State over non-resident students[20] or diploma requirements favouring the enrolment of the domestically educated students over those educated abroad[21] equally fall foul of Article 18 TFEU.

These equal treatment rights as regards the conditions relating access to education are innate rights of Union citizens: that is to say, the student is not required to show a degree of connection or genuine link with the host Member State to benefit from these equal treatment rights. In other words, Member States have little opportunity to define conditions for membership of the community which would entitle a person to higher education-related benefits: instead these benefits (such as supply-side higher education subsidies covering the difference between the tuition fee paid and the actual cost of education a student per year) must be provided virtually without further issue. Member States' attempts to justify discriminatory financial or administrative measures are treated with great suspicion. First, the Court habitually rejects grounds for justifications relating to financial or budgetary concerns;[22] it is indeed questionable whether it regards such grounds as capable of justifying restrictive measures at all in this context.[23] Where Member States invoke more noble concerns, such as the danger that the influx of foreign students could affect the quality of education and the public health sector (as invoked in the case of *Bressol*), limits again apply: such claims are subject to high evidentiary requirements and Member States must do their homework to show that the risk claimed actually materialises, and to what extent.[24] Moreover, even if this is established, the Court insists on a strict application of the principle of proportionality: the national concerns must be weighed against the fact that access to education constitutes the very essence of the free movement of students.[25] Member States must indeed ensure that 'sufficiently wide access [for students coming from other Member States] to

18 Case 197/86, *Brown*, EU:C:1988:323, paras. 14–19.
19 Case 42/87, *Commission v Belgium*, EU:C:1988:454, para. 8.
20 Case C-73/08, *Bressol*, EU:C:2010:181.
21 Case C-147/03, *Commission v Austria*, EU:C:2005:427.
22 Case C-73/08, *Bressol*, EU:C:2010:181, paras. 49–51.
23 See the unsuccessful attempt to rely on this type of argument already in Case 293/83, *Gravier*, EU:C:1985:69, para. 12. See also: Opinion of Advocate General Sharpston in Case C-73/08, *Bressol*, EU:C:2009:396, paras. 87–99.
24 Case C-73/08, *Bressol*, EU:C:2010:181, paras. 66–74.
25 Case C-73/08, *Bressol*, EU:C:2010:181, para. 79.

higher education'[26] is not impeded. Finally, it should be noted that apart from in *Bressol*, the Court has never upheld attempts by the Member States to justify their restrictions in this context.[27]

The overall message is clear: Union citizens are in principle free to choose from educational opportunities open to them on the basis of their academic merit. In exercising that freedom, it should not matter whether the higher education institute offering the particular course of study is located in the Member State of nationality of that Union citizen or rather abroad. At this stage, the student 'belongs' wherever he or she chooses to go and the host Member State must show solidarity with the Member State nationals from abroad. This is, moreover, not an insignificant requirement: most Member States of the European Union have relatively limited tuition fees,[28] from which it follows that each higher education place is heavily subsidised by the State.[29]

3. STUDY FACILITATING BENEFITS AND BELONGING

The question of 'belonging' requires a much more detailed answer under this heading. Under this regime, the margin of appreciation left to the Member State is greater and the scrutiny of the Court less intense: Member States, while obliged to show a *certain* degree of financial solidarity[30] as regards the provision of study facilitating benefits, need only provide benefits falling under this category to Union citizens who can demonstrate a degree of integration (a 'genuine link').[31] This is a relatively complex area of EU law, in which the discussion as regards the boundaries of solidarity is held more openly and explicitly than where it concerns the benefits falling under the regime of 'access to education'.

Two types of study facilitating benefits have so far been recognised: the 'classic' study grants and/or loans that address subsistence directly, and travel arrangements for students, allowing them to benefit from reduced (public) transport fees. For the latter benefits, the picture is relatively clear: all Union citizens enrolled in a higher education situated in the territory of the Member

26 Case C-73/08, *Bressol*, EU:C:2010:181, para. 79.

27 Case 152/82, *Forcheri*, EU:C:1983:205; Case 293/83, *Gravier*, EU:C:1985:69; Case 309/85, *Barra*, EU:C:1988:42; Case 24/86, *Blaizot*; EU:C:1988:43; Case 42/87, *Commission v Belgium*, EU:C:1988:454; Case C-47/93, *Commission v Belgium*, EU:C:1994:181; Case C-65/03, *Commission v Belgium*, EU:C:2004:402; and Case C-147/03, *Commission v Austria*, EU:C:2005:427.

28 Eurydice, *National Student Fee and Support Systems in European Higher Education* (EACEA, 2014), available at http://eacea.ec.europa.eu/education/eurydice/documents/facts_and_figures/fees_support.pdf (last accessed on 31 January 2016).

29 Key Data on Education in Europe (EACEA P9 Eurydice, 2012), 87–93.

30 Case C-184/99, *Grzelczyk*, EU:C:2001:458, para. 44.

31 Case C-209/03, *Bidar*, EU:C:2005:169, para. 56.

State are to be considered sufficiently connected, by that reason only, to that Member State in order to receive the benefit in question.[32] For the former type of benefits, a more extensive discussion is warranted.

The basic point of departure is Union citizen A, who would like to study in Member State X. Assume, as a conceptual point of departure, that Union citizen A has no Member State nationality (or that that nationality is unknown).[33] From which Member States, and under what conditions, could he potentially claim financial support in the form of study grants and/or loans?

Two options present themselves: financial support can either be provided by the Member State of study (Member State X) or Union citizen A may be able to claim financial support provided by a third Member State, such as Member State Y, for studies abroad (portable financial aid for studies). The conditions under which Union citizen A is entitled to financial support on equal terms with the nationals of the relevant Member State (Member State X or Y) have been set out by the Court in the course of its long jurisprudence on the matter.[34]

3.1. UNION CITIZEN A SEEKING TO CLAIM FINANCIAL SUPPORT FROM MEMBER STATE X IN ORDER TO PURSUE A COURSE OF STUDY IN THAT SAME MEMBER STATE[35]

The default position. In the absence of any particular links with a Member State (e.g. resident family members) or a particular status (such as e.g. worker), a Union citizen is deemed to be sufficiently connected if he has lawfully resided in a Member State for a period of time. The case of *Förster* allows Member States to hold that the requisite degree of integration for the purpose of claiming maintenance aid for study purposes is only attained after five years of prior residence.[36]

---

32 Case C-75/11, *Commission v Austria*, EU:C:2012:605, para. 64. See further the ongoing Case C-233/14, *Commission v the Netherlands,* lodged on 11 July 2014. However, AG Sharpston recently argued in her Opinion in the latter case that this distinction between study grants and/or loans and travel accommodations for students is fallacious. Instead, she posits that such arrangements should be subsumed under the legal regime as developed for access to 'regular' study grants and/or study loans to be discussed below. See Opinion of Advocate General Sharpston in Case C-233/14, *Commission v the Netherlands*, EU:C:2016:50, para. 91 *et seq.*

33 See also the point of departure in Case C-46/12, *L.N.*, EU:C:2013:97, para. 11.

34 It should be noted, of course, that this presupposes that there is a financial aid system in place; Member States have, as a matter of their educational policy, discretion as to the organisation of their higher education system and thus also as to the issue of whether to create such a system of financial support for studies. This freedom is also emphasised in Articles 165 and 166 TFEU.

35 The following section draws upon an earlier article: A. Hoogenboom, 'Mind the Gap: Mobile Students and their Access to Study Grants and Loans in the EU' (2015) 22 *MJ*, 96.

36 Case C-158/07, *Förster*, EU:C:2008:630, paras. 49–58. See also Article 24(2) jo. 16 of Directive 2004/38 on the right of citizens of the Union and their family members to move and reside

The student-worker position. Insofar as Union citizen A is economically active in the Member State where he seeks to claim the study grants and/or loans, the picture changes. If he qualifies as a worker (> eight hours of remunerated employment per week)[37] or a self-employed person,[38] he has immediate access to financial support as such persons must be presumed to have a genuine link.[39]

The student-family member. Here the basis for claiming financial assistance for studies lies in a family relationship: a close such relationship allows Union citizen A to derive a genuine link with Member State X from e.g. a parent or spouse who is economically active in that Member State.

Where Union citizen A resides in Member State X and enrols in education there while his parent is engaged in an economic activity as a Union worker,[40] Article 10 of Regulation 492/2011 provides for immediate entitlement to study grants and/or loans.[41] The picture is slightly different if Union citizen A is not resident in Member State X but is still seeking to study there. Suppose that Union citizen A resides in Member State Z with his parent, who is engaged as a frontier worker in Member State X. In such circumstances, Article 7(2) of Regulation 492/2011 provides the legal basis for a claim of equal treatment concerning study grants and/or loans for Union citizen A in Member State X: the award of study grants and/or loans to children of workers constitutes a social advantage for the worker under that Article (even where such financial support is granted directly to the student).[42] A similar reasoning applies where Union citizen A is not a child, but rather another form of family member[43] (e.g. a spouse) of a Union worker or self-employed person active in Member State X: here too Article 7(2) Regulation 492/2011 provides for access to study grants and/or loans.[44]

---

freely within the territory of the Member States, OJ 2004, L 158/77 (hereinafter referred to as 'Directive 2004/38').

37 Case C-444/93, *Megner*, EU:C:1995:442, paras. 18–20.

38 Case C-337/97, *Meeusen*, EU:C:1999:284, paras. 26–30.

39 Case C-46/12, *L.N.*, EU:C:2013:97, paras. 46–50; Case C-542/09, *Commission v the Netherlands*, EU:C:2012:346, paras. 65–66.

40 Similar principles should apply, *mutatis mutandis*, to self-employed persons following Case C-337/97, *Meeusen*, EU:C:1999:284, paras. 26–30.

41 Moreover, once obtained the child continues to enjoy a right of equal treatment even if the original conditions for acquisition (for example a working parent) are no longer present: Case C-413/99, *Baumbast*, EU:C:2002:493, paras. 50–52, 54, 68–74.

42 Case C-3/90, *Bernini*, EU:C:1992:89, paras. 24–25. See also Case C-337/97, *Meeusen*, EU:C: 1999:284, paras. 19–24. However, for Article 7(2) of Regulation 492/2011 to remain active, the worker-parent must continue to support the student and retain the status of worker in the state of employment. It is true that family members of ex-workers can in some circumstances rely on the right of equal treatment as regards social advantages where these are intrinsically linked with the ex-worker's prior worker status. However, study grants and/or loans do not seem to be among that category of social advantages: see Case C-33/99, *Fahmi*, EU:C:2001:176, paras. 33–47.

43 Here, reference may be made to the concept of family member as elaborated in Articles 2 and 3 of Directive 2004/38.

44 Classically, see Case 32/75, *Cristini*, EU:C:1975:120. As with the child, the worker-spouse from whom the right is derived probably needs to continue to have the status of a worker (although the requirement of dependency cannot be applied to the spouse and/or partner).

3.2. UNION CITIZEN A SEEKING TO CLAIM FINANCIAL SUPPORT FROM MEMBER STATE Y IN ORDER TO PURSUE A COURSE OF STUDY IN MEMBER STATE X

It should be noted at the outset that Member States are not required, as a matter of EU law, to provide for portable financial aid for studies.[45] However, where a Member State has nonetheless introduced the option of export of study grants and/or loans in its domestic legislation, the specific conditions attached to eligibility for such export must comply with EU law.

The default position. For the default position, nothing really changes. Similar to Member State X, Member State Y could require Union citizen A to have resided for up to five years on its territory before becoming granting access to financial aid for studies (including access to portable grants). As the case-law stands, there is no reason to assume that Member States are allowed to apply stricter or more elaborate genuine link requirements where it concerns eligibility for portable maintenance aid.

The student-worker position. There is also no real change for the student-worker: the classic case-law suggests that where the student is a worker, or has retained the status of worker,[46] he is to be considered sufficiently connected to the Member State of employment (here Member State Y) for the purpose of claiming portable study grants and/or loans.[47]

The student-family member position. Access of family members to portable study grants and/or loans has recently become more complex. Discussing the position where Union citizen A is the child of a worker or self-employed person first, it is prudent, following the ruling in *Giersch*, to distinguish several gradations. At the top of the 'hierarchy' stands the situation where the family (worker-parent + child) as a whole, lives in the Member State Y in which the child applies for a portable study grant (in order to study in Member State X). Where the conditions for the application of Article 10 of Regulation 492/2011 have been fulfilled (see above), the child seems to be sufficiently connected to the Member State for the purposes of claiming portable study grants.[48]

The intermediate position is the situation of a 'frontier-family', in which all members live in Member State Z, but with a worker-parent engaged in Member State Y. If in such a situation the child applies for a portable study grant in Member State Y (with a view to study in Member State X), the legal basis for this claim will be Article 7(2) of Regulation 492/2011 (see the attached conditions above). Where, in addition to the link through the worker-parent the child can

---

45 Case C-275/12, *Elrick*, EU:C:2013:684, para. 25; and Case C-220/12, *Meneses*, EU:C:2013:683, para. 25.

46 The same reasoning should again apply, *mutatis mutandis*, to self-employed persons.

47 Case 235/87, *Matteucci*, EU:C:1988:460, para. 12 *et seq.*

48 Case C-20/12, *Giersch*, EU:C:2013:411, paras. 72–76, in particular para. 75; and Case C-308/89, *di Leo*, EU:C:1990:400, para. 15.

also show other links with Member State Y (such having completed a period of schooling there), the ruling in *Giersch* suggests that the child can be considered sufficiently connected.[49]

Finally, in the circumstances of a 'pure frontier-family', where the only link of Union citizen A with Member State Y is the link of employment of a worker-parent, the Court has suggested that Member States can require a certain strength to that link, as evidenced by a minimum period of prior employment of the economically active parent of five years.[50]

Regarding the position of the 'other family member', in particular the spouse and/or (registered) partner, the reasoning set out above should apply in principle *mutatis mutandis*, although the legal basis for the claim will in that case always be Article 7(2) of Regulation 492/2011.

3.3. PECULIARITIES AND TRENDS

In order to complete the picture, two further issues should be noted. First, for the default position, it is no longer clear whether the *Förster* rule, whereby Member States can require five years' prior residence before being eligible for study grants and/or loans, is still good law. On the one hand, recent case-law suggests that Member States can no longer rely exclusively on only one ' genuine link indicator' (such as residence) to establish the requisite link.[51] Rather, a broader view must be taken as to the different ways an individual may demonstrate his or her degree of integration, such as for example resident family members, past employment, past schooling and the ability to speak the language of the Member State in question.[52] On the other hand, Directive 2004/38 explicitly mandates that Member States may withhold eligibility for study grants and/or loans until the person in question has obtained a right to permanent residence – which is normally acquired after five years of legal residence.[53] The case of *Dano* indirectly seems to resolve the debate in favour of the maintaining the status quo, as that case seems to give absolute priority to Directive 2004/38 in terms of defining the limits and scope of the principle of non-discrimination on grounds of nationality.[54]

---

49 Case C-20/12, *Giersch*, EU:C:2013:411, paras. 72–76.

50 Case C-20/12, *Giersch*, EU:C:2013:411, paras. 78–80.

51 Starting with Case C-224/98, *D'Hoop*, EU:C:2002:432, para. 39. See more recently in particular Case C-503/09, *Stewart*, EU:C:2011:500, para. 95; Case C-367/11, *Prete*, EU:C:2012:668, para. 3; and Joined Cases C-523/11 and C-585/11, *Prinz and Seeberger*, EU:C:2013:524, para. 37. For this point see also, P. Neuvonen, 'In search of (even) more substance for the "real link" test: comment on *Prinz and Seeberger*' (2014) 39 *EL Rev*, 125.

52 Joined Cases C-523/11 and C-585/11, *Prinz and Seeberger*, EU:C:2013:524, para. 38.

53 See Article 16 of Directive 2004/38.

54 Case C-333/13, *Dano*, EU:C:2014:2358, paras. 61–64.

A second point is the curious situation that the Court seems to allow 'nationality' to matter – that is to say Member States can favour their own nationals directly, in a discriminatory fashion. As AG Sharpston has put it, direct discrimination arises when:

> 'the category of those receiving a certain advantage and the category of those suffering a correlative disadvantage coincide exactly with the respective categories of persons distinguished only by applying a prohibited classification.'

In *Förster*, the Court seemed to uphold the Dutch system which provides immediate access to study grants and loans to Dutch nationals (on the simple fact of possession of nationality), but makes eligibility of Union citizens with a nationality of another Member State subject to additional criteria (e.g. worker status, five years of residence).[55] Similarly, in *Prinz and Seeberger*,[56] the Court ruled that:

> 'although the existence of a certain level of integration may be regarded as established by the finding that a student has resided in the Member State where he may apply for an education or training grant for a certain period, a sole condition of residence, such as that at issue in the main proceedings, risks [...] excluding from funding students who, despite not having resided for an uninterrupted period of three years in Germany immediately prior to studying abroad, are nevertheless sufficiently connected to German society. That *may be the case where the student is a national of the State concerned* and was educated there for a significant period or on account of other factors such as, in particular, his family, employment, language skills or the existence of other social and economic factors'[57] (emphasis added).

So not only *can* Member States privilege their own nationals in study grant and loan matters, but they *must* in fact privilege them, as nationality is to be held as an independent connecting factor by which a Union citizen can establish a genuine link with a Member State of the EU. This raises interesting questions, both as regards the future of normally strictly prohibited direct discrimination on grounds of nationality as well as regards the nature of Union citizenship. Indeed, as regards the latter, the Court seems to take the Union citizen, as a construct, as the point of departure, and then considers the various ways to which it may be connected to one of the territorial units of the EU; a conceptual reversal of Article 20 which states that Union citizenship is meant to be additional to national citizenship.[58]

---

55 See Article 2.2 *Wet Studiefinanciering* 2000 jo. *Besluit Studiefinanciering* 2000.

56 Which concerned two German nationals who challenged the requirement set out by the *Bundesausbildungsförderungsgesetz* to have resided in Germany for two years in the five years preceding an application for portable study grants as incompatible with Article 21 TFEU.

57 Joined Cases C-523/11 and C-585/11, *Prinz and Seeberger*, EU:C:2013:524, para. 38.

58 See also the facts underlying Case C-46/12, *L.N.*, EU:C:2013:97 in which the nationality of the applicant was unknown and was rather simply described as a Union citizen.

4. EVALUATING STUDENT BELONGING IN THE EUROPEAN UNION

After now having set out the 'state of affairs' as regards the belonging of the mobile student in the European Union, this section seeks to critically inquire into the principles that have been developed by the Court. As a point of departure, it is submitted here that the law so developed must engage in an a balancing act, between one hand the commitment of the European Union, and the Member States,[59] to promoting student mobility,[60] and on the other the need to respect the Member States' competence in developing their higher education policy and organising their higher education sector.[61]

The former commitment flows from that the fact that Union citizens have the right to move and reside in another Member State for the purpose of study[62] and for that purpose can rely on the principle of non-discrimination on grounds of nationality.[63] Article 165(2), second indent, TFEU moreover provides specifically that this species of Union citizens' mobility is to be promoted, and the Court of Justice in *Bressol* was clear that the 'free movement of students' constitutes a principle to be respected by the Member States.[64] Finally, there also non-blackletter law reasons for supporting such mobility. It has been argued that there exists a nexus between student mobility and future highly skilled mobility, the optimal allocation of which among the Member States of the EU generates significant economic benefits and enhanced EU competitiveness.[65] Moreover, the 'mobility experience' is a learning experience in itself, and promotes the acquisition of a number of hard and soft skills valued by the labour market.[66] A final important point is the idea, largely confirmed by research,[67] that the mobility experience is also an important transformative

59 In the context of the Bologna process, which is, strictly seen, not an EU programme: see www.ehea.info/Uploads/Declarations/BOLOGNA_DECLARATION1.pdf (last accessed on 31 January 2016).

60 See Articles 165(2), second indent TFEU. See further also Article 166(2), third indent TFEU.

61 Article 165(1) TFEU.

62 Article 21 TFEU jo. 7(1)(c) Directive 2004/38; see also Case C-357/89, *Raulin*, EU:C:1992:87, paras. 34–40.

63 Case C-73/08, *Bressol*, EU:C:2010:181, paras. 30–33.

64 Case C-73/08, *Bressol*, EU:C:2010:181, para. 79.

65 A. Hoogenboom, 'Mobility of Students and the Financial Sustainability of Higher Education Systems in the EU: A Union of Harmony or Irreconcilable Differences?' (2013) 9 *Croatian Yearbook of European Law and Policy*, 44–47.

66 A. Hoogenboom, 'Mobility of Students and the Financial Sustainability of Higher Education Systems in the EU: A Union of Harmony or Irreconcilable Differences?' (2013) 9 *Croatian Yearbook of European Law and Policy*, 47–49.

67 R. King and E. Ruiz-Gelices, 'International Student Migration and the European "Year Abroad": Effects on European Identity and Subsequent Migration Behaviour' (2003) 9 *International Journal of Population Geography*, 229; K. Oborune, 'The impact of the Erasmus programme on fostering European Identity in Latvia', Proceedings of the International Scientific Conferences of the Faculty of Social Sciences of Daugavpils University (2011),

experience from a citizenship perspective: mobile students tend to identify more strongly as European and/or as Union citizens, which, in the context of the ongoing debate about the democratic deficit of the EU, would seem a very valuable benefit.[68]

The need to respect the competence and (relative) freedom of the Member State in the organisation of higher education equally flows from the Treaties; Article 6(e) jo. 165(1) TFEU clearly attributes the primacy for policy development in this field with Member States rather than the Union level. Moreover, provision and organisation of education is a core State task and intimately bound up with national identity,[69] as has also been recognised by the Court.[70] Article 4(2) TEU requires the Union to respect such sensitive affairs and to protect the diversity of the Member States in this regard, which in particular comes into play where pressures generated by the application of free movement rules become so large as to force upon Member States a certain education policy choice which conflicts with their domestic preferences. As such, Article 4(2) functions in this context not so much as a general derogation possibility that may be invoked to justify any incursion on free movement, but rather as a sort of ultimate safeguard, with a commensurately high threshold, against interference that would go against the basic core competence of the Member States in the area of higher education.

The question that the following section will be addressing is whether this balancing act is reflected in the principles set out by the Court, and examining whether the principles so developed reveal an authentic commitment to the two aspects, as well as form a coherent whole.[71]

available at http://du.lv/files/0000/5976/krajums.pdf#page=57 (last accessed on 31 January 2016); B. Streitweiser, 'Erasmus Mobility Students and Conceptions of National, Regional and Global Citizenship Identity', Buffet Center Working Paper No. 11/01 (2011), 5–6; K. Mitchell, 'Student Mobility and European Identity: Erasmus Study as a civic experience?' (2012) 8 *Journal of Contemporary European Research*, 490; C. van Mol, 'Intra-European Student Mobility and European Identity: A Successful Marriage?' (2012) 19 *Population, Space and Place*, 209; and K. Mitchell, 'Rethinking the "Erasmus Effect" on European Identity' (2014) *Journal of Common Market Studies*, 15–17.

68 Such identification might contribute to input legitimacy: F. Scharpf, *Governing in Europe: Effective and Democratic?* (Oxford: OUP, 1999), 6–12.

69 See CONV 375/1/02 REV 1, The European Convention: Final Report of Working Group V on Complementary Competencies, 10–11. See further e.g. E. Gellner, *Nations and Nationalism* (Oxford: Blackwell Publishing, 2006), 26–37; and A. Smith, 'National Identity and the Idea of European Unity' (1992) 68 *International Affairs*, 63–65, 72–73. See also BVerfG, 2 BvE 2/08 ('Lisbon-Urteil') of 30 September 2009, para. 249.

70 See e.g. Case C-473/93, *Commission v Luxembourg*, EU:C:1996:263, paras. 32–35; Case C-379/87, *Groener*, EU:C:1989:599, paras. 18–20; and Case 263/86, *Humbel*, EU:C:1988:451, para. 18.

71 Authenticity and coherency are the two basic principles, argued by Dworkin, that should govern a set of ethical, moral and legal principles: R. Dworkin, *Justice for Hedgehogs* (Cambridge (US): HUP, 2013), 37–39, 107–109.

4.1. ACCESS TO EDUCATION

It was already alluded to above that when it comes to 'student belonging' in this area, the Court employs a simple principle: the host Member State, however chosen and even in the absence of any prior interaction between that State and the (prospective) student, bears the responsibility to ensure that all Union citizens have access to higher education offered on its territory on equal terms.

Qualifying such access as the 'very essence' of the free movement of students, coupled with very limited and circumscribed possibilities for derogation by the Member States shows a strong commitment to promoting such study mobility. Indeed, financial and administrative barriers applied 'at the door' are capable of having a significant chilling effect on student mobility.[72]

Of course, the same could be said about the non-access to study grants and loans. Indeed, it is not immediately obvious why the two regimes should be treated differently/be subjected to different legal principles, since a student's decision to go abroad is influenced by the overall financiability of his stay abroad – an issue that will be affected by tuition fees as well the possibilities in obtaining a form of financial support for subsistence. From the perspective of the Member State, both the subsidising of places at higher education institutes and the provision of financial support in the form of a grant or loan weigh on the public purse.[73]

Nonetheless, it is submitted here that such a difference can still be justified. Sangiovanni submits that the Member States of the European Union, by creating a European Union and setting out the preambular goal of promoting wide access to education of all (Union) citizens and the Treaty objective of encouraging student mobility, accepted and committed themselves between them to a degree of reciprocity consisting of a mutual opening up of their educational systems.[74] This also seems to underlie the Court's judgment in *Gravier*, where it held that:

> 'it is [...] necessary to define precisely the nature of the problem. In the first place, the questions referred concern neither the organization of education nor even its financing, but rather the establishment of a financial barrier to access to education for foreign students only [...].'[75]

---

72 See ESU, *Bologna with Student Eyes 2012* (ESU, 2012), 31–36; and Eurydice, *The European Higher Education Area in 2012: Bologna Process Implementation Report* (EACEA P9 Eurydice, 2012), 165 *et seq.*

73 See also G. Davies, 'Higher Education, Equal Access and Residence Conditions: Does EU Law Allow Member States to Charge Higher Fees to Students Not Previously Resident?' (2005) 12 *MJ*, 229–235.

74 A. Sangiovanni, 'Justice and the Free Movement of Persons: Educational Mobility in the EU and the US', in D. Hicks and T. Williamson (eds.), *Leadership and Global Justice* (London: Palgrave MacMillan, 2012), 148.

75 Case 293/83, *Gravier*, EU:C:1985:69, para. 18.

As such, the issue of access to education on equal terms is decoupled from the financial and organisational context of the Member State – it is more akin to an innate right of free moving Union citizens that forms part and parcel of the European integration project in a fundamental sense. The mutual opening up takes the form of a guarantee of a Union citizen to 'become' a student (acquire student status), allowing him or her to challenge financial or administrative barriers to this goal – but it does not extend so far as to mean that student is also automatically and innately entitled to active support from the host Member State community to pursue this goal, in the form of grants and/or scholarships.[76]

The distinction also finds a degree of commonality with the human rights tradition, which emphasises access on equal terms as a core State obligation[77] but does not require that all particular educational pursuits must of necessity be financially support by a State.[78] Indeed, the wording used in *Gravier* echoes that of the European Court of Human Rights. Whereas Article 2 of Protocol 1 to the European Convention on Human Rights 'lays down no specific obligations concerning the extent of these means and the manner of their organisation or subsidisation', Contracting Parties must nevertheless secure the right to education to everyone within its jurisdiction without discrimination.[79] Also in *Bressol*, the Court held that its interpretation of Article 18 jo. 21 TFEU essentially implements, within the European Union context and for Union citizens, Article 13(2)(c) International Covenant on Economic, Social and Cultural Rights: 'as is apparent from the wording of Article 13(2)(c) [ICESCR], the Covenant pursues in essence the same objective as Articles 18 and 21 TFEU, that is to ensure that the principle of non-discrimination is observed in relation to access to higher education.'[80]

For the reasons given above, it would follow that the legal regime applying to access to education should be student-friendly, and harsh on Member States seeking to justify restrictions. The balancing act referred to above is, however, still respected. The case of *Bressol* shows that where Member States can make a well-substantiated case that the influx of students threatens fundamental education objectives (in *casu*: the nexus between education and the continued

76 The choice for this *quasi*-constitutional settlement, it has been argued elsewhere, has a certain intelligibility to it when considered from the European philosophical tradition: in the cosmopolitan tradition Kant distinguished between the *besuchsrecht*, which is the right to associate, and the *gastrecht*, a relationship entitling one to certain rights and support based on perceived membership of the foreigner of the host community.

77 F. Coomans, 'In Search of the Core Content of the Right to Education', in S. Russell (ed.), *Core Obligations: Building a Framework for Economic, Social and Cultural Rights* (Antwerp: Intersentia, 2002), 225.

78 ECtHR, 23 July 1968, *relating to certain aspects of the laws on the use of languages in education in Belgium v Belgium*, no. 1474/62, 1677/62, 1691/62, 1769/63, 1994/63, 2126/64, 'Interpretation adopted by the Court', para. 3.

79 ECtHR, 23 July 1968, *relating to certain aspects of the laws on the use of languages in education in Belgium v Belgium*, no. 1474/62, 1677/62, 1691/62, 1769/63, 1994/63, 2126/64, 'Interpretation adopted by the Court', paras. 3–5.

80 Case C-73/08, *Bressol*, EU:C:2010:181, para. 86.

provision of specialised forms of healthcare in the French Community), the Court seems willing to allow the Member State some leeway, in line with the requirements imposed by Article 4(2) TEU. Having reviewed the evidence, the Belgian Constitutional Court did find the requirement to be justified for a few of the courses to which the quota applied.[81] Considering that the threshold for invoking Article 4(2) TEU should be relatively high, the current balancing act that the Court conducted in *Bressol* seems appropriate in this context.

4.2. STUDENT TRAVEL BENEFITS

This category is a curious one. Whereas the Court has qualified these benefits as a form of maintenance aid,[82] it equally held that they could not be considered study grants or a study loan.[83] The category, in the view of this author, thus does not benefit from the derogation in Article 24(2) that allows Member States to withhold such benefits until the person in question is either economically active or has obtained a right to permanent residence.[84] In fact, the Court limited the freedom of Member States to design their own genuine link criteria, and held that the appropriate criterion would be to check if the Union citizen claiming the benefit was enrolled (full-time) in a higher education institute of the host Member State.[85]

So in fact, travel benefits form a hybrid category. While designated a form of maintenance aid, in practice the room for manoeuvre of the Member States is so limited that access to the benefit is akin to access for, say, loans that are designed to cover tuition fees: in practical terms, both are premised on enrolment in a higher education institute for the right to be 'active'. As such, access to this benefit is better analysed, from a coherency point of view, from the perspective that it belongs to the 'access to education' regime. In that context, there seem to be no real issues with the position of the Court; it is difficult to see how the extension of a travel accommodation to foreign students *ab initio* could jeopardise the Member States' higher education sector, and their freedom to organise it in accordance with domestic preferences.

As such, the basic principles developed by the Court in this regard raise little issue. A further point that needs to be elaborated upon is, however, the position of the Netherlands in the pending case C-233/14, *Commission v the Netherlands*. In *Commission v Austria*, the benefit claimed was a benefit provided to students separately from the study grant/loan system in place.[86] The Netherlands

---

81 Belgian Constitutional Court, 31 May 2011, no. 89/2011, paras. B.8.1–B.8.8.5 (concerning the bachelor in veterinary sciences and bachelor physiotherapy and physiotherapy and rehabilitation).

82 Case C-75/11, *Commission v Austria*, EU:C:2012:605, paras. 42–43, 55.

83 Case C-75/11, *Commission v Austria*, EU:C:2012:605, para. 55.

84 Case C-75/11, *Commission v Austria*, EU:C:2012:605, para. 55.

85 Case C-75/11, *Commission v Austria*, EU:C:2012:605, para. 65.

86 Case C-75/11, *Commission v Austria*, EU:C:2012:605, paras. 9–10.

is seeking to rely on that fact to submit that their system is different: the *studentenreisproduct* provided to students (choice of free travel during the week *or* at the weekend with a discount for the other days) is integrated into the study finance system – thereby making it a 'study grant/loan' in the domestic system as it is subject to similar conditions as the subsistence allowance.[87] AG Sharpston has followed that reasoning in her Opinion.[88]

It is submitted here that this line of reasoning should have had little chance of succeeding. The Court was quite clear in *Commission v Austria* that the formal qualification is not determinative, referring also to the case of *Vatsouras*[89] in that context.[90] The constitutive elements of the so-called *studentenreisproduct*, when analysed in terms of its nature and purpose are, of course, similar to the benefit at issue in *Commission v Austria*: in the end, it is about promoting actual attendance at classes and the like at a higher education institute and for that purpose, just like in Austria,[91] the Netherlands negotiates and concludes an agreement with the Dutch public transport providers.[92] The place in the domestic legal system is not relevant in that context.[93] Nonetheless, the Court decided differently in Case C-233/14, *Commission v the Netherlands*.[94] It ruled that the student travel benefits at issue could be considered to fall within the derogation of Article 24(2) of Directive 2004/38.[95] This suggests that the legal qualification of such travel benefits under EU law depends on their position in the national legal context,[96] a conclusion quite contrary to what the Court usually rules.

4.3. STUDY GRANTS AND LOANS

As seen above, the Court allows Member States greater freedom where it comes to restricting the circle of beneficiaries of study grants and/or loans, apparently convinced that unlimited access to such systems could jeopardise their overall financial sustainability and, ultimately, existence to the detriment of all persons seeking to attend higher education.[97] Nonetheless, it will be submitted here that some of the principles of the Court's current case-law should be re-evaluated,

87 Articles 3.6 jo. 3.7 jo. 5.3 *Wet studiefinanciering* 2000, *Stb.* 2000, 286.

88 Opinion of Advocate General SHARPSTON in Case C-233/14, *Commission v Netherlands*, EU:C:2016:50, para. 91 *et seq.*

89 Joined Cases C-22/08 and C-23/08, *Vatsouras*, EU:C:2009:344, paras. 38–45.

90 Case C-75/11, *Commission v Austria*, EU:C:2012:605, para. 63.

91 Case C-75/11, *Commission v Austria*, EU:C:2012:605, para. 10.

92 See the references to the '*overeenkomst tussen de vervoersbedrijven en de Staat in verband met de uitvoering van het reisrecht*' in the *Regeling Studiefinanciering* 2000, *Stcrt.* 2000, 169.

93 Joined Cases C-22/08 and C-23/08, *Vatsouras*, EU:C:2009:344, para. 45.

94 Due to deadline for the going to press of this book, a full discussion of the judgment is not possible.

95 Case C-233/14, *Commission v the Netherlands*, EU:C:2016:396, para. 90.

96 Case C-233/14, *Commission v the Netherlands*, EU:C:2016:396, para. 88.

97 Case C-209/03, *Bidar*, EU:C:2005:169, para. 56.

both in the name of ensuring a coherent legal framework, but also because the current system takes the commitment towards promoting student mobility insufficiently seriously.

4.3.1. *Solidarity, Economic Opportunity and Domestic Changes*

A first point can be simply put: in the case of certain categories of study *loans*, a Member State should be precluded from applying a genuine link criterion as a precondition for eligibility (for mobile Union citizens). Indeed, the reasoning of the Court in this area can be summarised in the following three step scheme:

(1) Study facilitating benefits are a form of social assistance;[98] benefits are provided predicated on an idea(l) of solidarity within a community.
(2) *Grzelczyk* confirms that Member States must also extend a certain degree of financial solidarity to Union citizens (non-nationals).[99]
(3) However, this type of solidarity need not be extended to all Union citizens, but only to those who can show that they have obtained a degree of integration with that Member State (genuine link).[100]

Whereas the focus of the Court has been to clarify, on the basis of the various references by national courts, the conditions under which students are to be regarded as sufficiently connected with the host Member State in order to be able to claim (portable) study grants and/or loans, it is submitted here that recent developments in higher education policy warrant a closer look at this scheme already at an earlier stage: the issue of (the degree of) solidarity.

The concept of 'solidarity' in Europe is notoriously undefined[101] but the different conceptions seem to coalesce around two main elements:[102]

(1) It denotes a group, with a degree of cohesion and common purpose: a community characterised by a 'we-feeling'.[103]
(2) This in turn provides the basis for a pooling of resources among the members to insure each other against social risks and to pursue the production of certain collective goods.[104]

---

98 Case C-209/03, *Bidar*, EU:C:2005:169, paras. 55–56.

99 Case C-184/99, *Grzelczyk*, EU:C:2001:458, para. 44.

100 Case C-209/03, *Bidar*, EU:C:2005:169, paras. 55–56.

101 V. Hatzopoulos, 'The concept of "economic activity" in the EU Treaty: from ideological dead-ends to workable judicial concepts', College of Europe Research Paper in Law 06/2011, 10–11.

102 S. Stjernø, 'The idea of solidarity in Europe' (2011) 3 *European Journal of Social Law*, 168–169.

103 See also K. Deutsch *et al.*, 'Political Community and the North Atlantic Area', in B. Nelsen and A. Stubb (eds.), *The European Union: Readings on the Theory and Practice of European Integration* (Boulder (US): Lynne Rienner Publishers, 2003), 123–124, 129, 133–136.

104 See further A. Sangiovanni, 'Solidarity in the European Union' (2013) 33 *Oxford Journal of Legal Studies*, 213.

This concept of solidarity, and its two founding elements, may be usefully contrasted with transactions in the economic sphere (although the relationship between them is more of a scale rather than two fixed points). First, solidarity is in principle always bounded (because dependent on a community), in contrast to economic transactions which in principle have no such inherent limit: the latter can be engaged in by any two parties while maintaining complete independence from each other (the 'arm's length principle'). Secondly, the degree of interdependence between two or more persons, which underpins solidarity, generates a commitment to the common weal, and transfer of resources in its name, that goes beyond 'rational reciprocity' – that is to say beyond a transaction characterised by a *quid pro quo* nature as such, which lies at the basis of and forms the essence of an economic transaction (cfr. Opinion of Advocate General Fennelly in *Sodemare*: solidarity as an inherently uncommercial act[105]).[106]

At this stage the reader may wonder how this short theoretical excursion relates to the subject matter at hand. The main point is this: Union citizens enjoy the right not to be discriminated against on grounds of nationality. In principle, therefore, they should have access to the same economic opportunities and the same social welfare institutions that the nationals of any of the Member States of the European Union have. As regards the former, the main thrust of the Treaties is strongly in favour of the principle that a Union citizen is not to be deprived of economic opportunities offered abroad. As regards access to (some of)[107] these social welfare institutions, however, the Court has set limits. The *Bidar* line of case-law is meant to protect these institutions, and their financial and social sustainability, by holding that only if a Union citizen can be held to be part of the community that sustains the institutions is he or she entitled to the benefits thereof (the genuine link test). For the 'economic opportunities' side no such inherent restrictions exist: a Union citizen should be able to take up any form of employment he or she desires, or set up a business abroad;[108] no genuine link requirements may be imposed and no restrictions which relate to economic or budgetary concerns are allowed.[109] This freedom to contract across borders is moreover further (indirectly) safeguarded by the rules of EU competition law.[110] As such, whether the *Bidar* rules apply (let us call these the

105 Opinion of Advocate General Fennelly in Case C-70/95, *Sodemare*, EU:C:1997:55, para. 29.

106 G. Marks, 'Europe and Its Empires: From Rome to the European Union' (2012) 50(1) *Journal of Common Market Studies*, 1.

107 Indeed, as seen, where it concerns access to education and related benefits no such limits are allowed.

108 Subject to the Treaty derogations.

109 V. Brisimi, *The Interface between Competition and the Internal Market: Market Separation under Article 102 TFEU* (Oxford: Hart Publishing, 2014), 81.

110 Which militates against trade restrictions introduced by undertakings that have as their purpose to insulate Member States, see: SWD (2014) 198 final, Commission Staff Working Document Guidance on restrictions of competition 'by object' for the purpose of defining which agreements may benefit from the De Minimis Notice, of 26.06.2014, 7–8.

'social welfare rules'), or the rules governing 'economic opportunity', depends on the context.[111]

With the progressive commercialisation of education, it is arguable that this policy field is moving from away from being a 'social welfare institution' to one related more closely to 'economic opportunity'. This can well be illustrated with the reforms that took place in the United Kingdom (England).

In essence, the 2012 higher education reforms in England, United Kingdom, had to main effects. First, it introduced high tuition fees – set at some £9,000 per academic year (about €11,200) for course leading to a bachelor's degree[112] and removed a fee limit on postgraduate courses altogether, in line with the suggestions made in the Browne Review.[113] Secondly, it extended its system of income-contingent loans, in what are now the Education (Student Support) Regulations 2011 (hereafter the Regulations).[114] These Regulations provide to eligible persons a basic support package that may be claimed during undergraduate studies, consisting of a tuition fee loan designed to cover the full tuition charged by the higher education institute in England[115] and a maintenance loan,[116] which may be claimed by eligible students under the age of sixty as long as the degree in connection with which the loan is requested is not equivalent or lower to a degree the student already possesses.[117] The maximum amount of the maintenance loan per academic year varies from £4,418 to £7,751 (€5,500–9,655) depending on which category (A–D) the student belongs to.[118]

The loan so obtained is a so-called income-contingent loan: students borrow, in essence, against their future income with the state acting as a bank. The interest accrual on the loans taken out stands at the inflation index increased by up to 3% (3.9% total for the academic year 2015/2016).[119] Annual repayment, after completion of the studies under the current post-2012 reform system takes

---

111 An analysis also supported by the need to have regard to the nature and purpose of a particular benefit: Case C-75/11, *Commission v Austria*, EU:C:2012:605, para. 63.

112 Section 4 Higher Education (Higher Amount) (England) Regulations 2010, no. 3020.

113 J. Browne, Securing a sustainable future for higher education: An independent review of higher education funding and student finance (URN 10/1208), 55, available at https://www.gov.uk/government/uploads/system/uploads/attachment_data/file/31999/10-1208-securing-sustainable-higher-education-browne-report.pdf (last accessed on 31 January 2016).

114 SI 2011, no. 1986. See also Section 22 of the Teaching and Higher Education Act 1998 (c. 30).

115 Section 23(2) Education (Student Support) Regulations 2011.

116 In certain circumstances a maintenance *grant* is made available to students whose household income is below a certain threshold: See Section 76 Education (Student Support) Regulations 2011.

117 Section 69(1)(a) Education (Student Support) Regulations 2011. Exceptions exist where the designated course leads to certain qualifications (such social worker) as mentioned in Section 69(2) Education (Student Support) Regulations 2011.

118 See Section 76 Education (Student Support) Regulations 2011.

119 See www.slc.co.uk/services/interest-rates.aspx (last accessed on 31 January 2016).

place at a rate of 9% of every pound earned over £21,000. If the loan is not repaid after thirty years, it is written off.[120]

The focus of the analysis here lies on the part of the loan that is a contribution towards the subsistence of the student during his or her studies (rather than the tuition fee loan which is subject to a different regime under free movement rules, see above). Currently, access to such a maintenance loan is subject to a genuine link test: either the Union citizen is economically active, or a family person of such a person,[121] or he or she has been ordinarily resident in England on the first day of the first academic year of the course, and has been ordinarily resident in the UK for a three-year period immediately preceding that first day.[122] It is submitted here that such genuine link requirements may not be imposed in the situation of the English maintenance loan.

In essence, under an income-contingent loan system, the student is seen as a self-investor: given that obtaining a higher education degrees generally leads to a significant increase in lifetime earnings (even when factoring in opportunity costs),[123] a student would rationally chose to obtain a loan to enable him or her to pursue such studies as long as the costs for doing so remain below the benefit provided by the degree. The role of the state is to act as a bank providing the loan – necessary because the market for study loans suffers from adverse selection (banks would tend to choose rich students over poor, future accountants over musicians, etc.), leading to inefficient outcomes.[124]

Such a system in essence functions as a form of consumption smoothing: redistribution of the income of an individual earned in a particular lifetime period (adult working life) to an earlier stage (the study).[125] It is not dissimilar to a pension system, in which incomes of individuals from their working life are redistributed towards their future retirement.[126] What does this mean in the context of the above analysis as regards solidarity? It will be recalled that the interest accrual on the loans under the Education (Student Support) Regulations 2011 stands at the inflation index increased by up to 3% (3.9% total for the academic year 2014/2015):[127] it is thus a loan taken out against *market* interest rates. In such a context, Barr and Johnston estimate that the system

---

120 See C. Crawford and W. Jin, *Payback time? Student debt and loan repayments: what will the 2012 reforms mean for graduates?*, The Institute for Fiscal Studies Report R93 (2014), 7. See also https://www.gov.uk/student-finance/repayments (last accessed on 31 January 2016).

121 Paragraph 6 Schedule 1 to the Education (Student Support) Regulations 2011.

122 Section 10(1)(a)–(c) Schedule 1 to the Education (Student Support) Regulations 2011.

123 OECD, *Education at a Glance 2014: OECD Indicators* (OECD Publishing, 2014), 154–155.

124 See M. Friedman, 'The Role of Government in Education', in R. Solo (ed.), *Economics and the Public Interest* (New Brunswick (US): Rutgers University Press, 1955).

125 J. Le Grand *et al.*, *The Economics of Social Problems* (London: Palgrave Macmillian, 2008), 70–75.

126 N. Barr, 'Higher Education Funding' (2004) 20 *Oxford Review of Economic Policy*, 270.

127 See www.slc.co.uk/services/interest-rates.aspx (last accessed on 31 January 2016).

should be largely self-financing in nature:[128] that is to say, the students pay their own way (individual accounts) and there is no transfer of public funds from *outside* the system *into* the system. In that light, it is submitted here that the question of access to such a system by Union citizens should by governed by the 'economic opportunity' regime rather than the 'social welfare' rules: immediate access for all Union citizens rather than after a waiting period.[129] After all, there is no or very little solidarity in such a system which warrants the application of the *Bidar* rule. It follows that the rules operated under the Education (Student Support) as regards access of Union citizens to maintenance loans (prior residence requirements, requirement to be economically active, etc.) arguably violate EU law.

Four counter-arguments will now be considered. First, it may be submitted that while the system is mostly based on a system of individualised accounts (individual loan, and individual repayment), the system nonetheless contains an element of redistribution. Given that repayment is income contingent, it follows that that some students who end up in lower paying jobs may never repay in full – which is exacerbated by the fact that taxation does not start until one earns more than £21,000 pounds, and that loans are written off after thirty years. However, this is insured for by means of a risk premium inherent in the market interest rate charged on the loans:[130] from such a setup it follows that students who do repay in full contribute more to the system than they received, whereas students who not repay in full receive more than they contributed. However, this is not redistribution in the solidarity sense – it is rather inherent in any market-based insurance scheme and constitutes a risk shared by all participants in the system. There is also no transfer from individuals outside the system to those within the system (as it is, as seen, in principle self-financing). In other words, the existence of such an insurance premium does not bring the scheme beyond what may be expected from the rational reciprocity of market participants.

Secondly, it could be held that in the short term the system does generate costs for the public purse: after all, the repayment of the loan is not immediate but takes place over a number of years. As such, during the maturing process, there is a direct and upfront solidarity on the part of the British taxpayers with the participants in the system. This argument also does not convince. In the context of the economic freedoms the Court has never accepted short-term economic or budgetary expense as a ground for justification in the light of the

---

128 A. Johnston and N. Barr, 'Student loan reform, interest subsidies and costly technicalities: lessons from the UK experience' (2013) 35 *Journal of Higher Education Policy and Management*, 175–176.

129 Indeed, the Court has always connected the pursuit of education with (future) labour market access or as a means to ameliorate one's position on that market: See e.g. Case C-413/01, *Ninni-Orasche*, EU:C:2003:600, para. 35; and Case 293/83, *Gravier*, EU:C:1985:69, para. 24.

130 See also, N. Barr, *The Welfare State as Piggy Bank: Information, Risk, Uncertainty and the Role of the State* (Oxford: OUP, 2001), chapter 12.

overall long-term benefits of free factor movement in a common market.[131] Also in *Bidar*, the Court referred to an 'unreasonable burden which could have consequences for the overall level of assistance'[132] – an analysis that takes the long-term effects as its point of departure. Finally, such reasoning taken more generally would make every loan provided charity/a grant until the point of repayment – even though there are fundamental differences between the two.[133] Overall, therefore, this argument can also not serve as a ground for excluding Union citizens from immediate access to maintenance support under the Education (Student Support) Regulations 2011.

Thirdly, it may be submitted that the return of the mobile Union citizen 'back home' (to his or her Member State of origin) makes repayment less likely, as his or her financial situation cannot be easily monitored nor debts enforced. As such, granting loans to Union citizens which lack sufficient connection to the UK (England), and are thus likely to return home, constitutes an inherently higher risk than those who do have a genuine link – thereby justifying the operation of such genuine link requirements. This argument too must be rejected. First, in legal terms, in *Byankov* the Court suggested that restrictions on free movement on grounds of possible non-repayment of debts could not be justified, in particular in the light of the 'existence of EU law a body of legal rules that are capable of protecting creditors' rights without necessarily restricting the debtor's freedom of movement', referring in particular to Council Regulation 44/2001 of 22 December 2000 on jurisdiction and the recognition and enforcement of judgments in civil and commercial matters.[134] In the light of such legislation which facilitates cross-border collection and enforcement of debts, there seems to be little scope for this argument under EU law as it stands. Secondly, the argument in fact also fails: of those students currently in arrears as regards repayment to the Student Loan Company the great majority are British.[135]

Finally, it could be argued that Article 24(2) of Directive 2004/38 allows Member States to refuse access to maintenance aid for studies 'consisting in student grants or student loans' of those individuals who have not yet obtained a right to permanent residence, or are economically active (or a family member of such a person). The case of *Dano* seems to confirm the hegemony of the Directive over an argument on the basis of Article 18 TFEU (and relevant case-law such as *Bidar*).[136] It is submitted here, however, that this argument too cannot hold. The exception laid down in Directive 2004/38 for study loans should be reserved to study loans which contain a strong element of state subsidy; it should not cover

131 See by analogy Case 238/82, *Duphar*, EU:C:1984:45, para. 23.

132 Case C-209/03, *Bidar*, EU:C:2005:169, para. 56.

133 See W. Schmidt, 'The Economics of Charity: Loans versus Grants' (1964) 72 *Journal of Political Economy*, 387.

134 Case C-249/11, *Byankov*, EU:C:2012:608, para. 45.

135 Comptroller and Auditor General, Student loan repayments, Session 2013–14, HC 818, p. 21.

136 Case C-333/13, *Dano*, EU:C:2014:2358, paras. 61–62.

systems whereby the loans are taken out against market interest rates. After all, the Court insists on evaluating benefits, and the appropriate genuine link criterion to be applied as a result, in the light of their *nature and purpose.*[137] In that light, it would stand to reason that a Member State cannot simply designate its support system as a 'study loan', thereby benefiting from the exception, despite the underlying nature being one of a market transaction.

Overall, therefore, it is submitted here that in a system such as that created by Education (Student Support) Regulations 2011, maintenance loans should be provided to all Union citizens on the basis of Article 18 TFEU without the UK (England) being allowed to impose genuine link requirements as a condition for eligibility. Moreover, the reasoning above could be applied, *mutatis mutandis*, to any systems applied by the Member States that relies on study loans taken out against market interest rates. This interpretation is commensurate with promoting further student mobility; after all, broader access to such loans gives more mobile Union citizens the opportunity to finance their studies. At the same time, the interpretation does not violate the 'no-go zone' of educational autonomy of the Member State: as seen above, 'more customers' for the study loan system does not in principle affect the public purse and/or the financial sustainability of the system.

4.3.2. *The Lack of Coordination and Legal Certainty*[138]

A second important point was elaborated elsewhere: a coordination gap. The current system lacks clear rules by which a Member States is designated as financially responsible (in terms of having to provide study grants and/or loans under its domestic system) for the mobile student. This gap is noticeable in a few cases.

First, for the 'default position', the 'no right to export' rule means that the student in question cannot require a Member State to which he or she is sufficiently connected to provide financial aid if the education is pursued abroad. At the same time, the durational residence requirements that the host Member State may impose following *Förster* means that that same student can also be excluded from receiving such support in the state of study: a classic situation of falling through the cracks.

Similarly, for the 'family member position', the *Giersch* ruling may lead to similar issues. Where a frontier-family is residing in Belgium, with the parents working in Luxembourg and the student-child seeking to study in the Netherlands, none of the three Member States is as such obliged to provide study

---

137 Joined Cases C-22/08 and C-23/08, *Vatsouras*, EU:C:2009:344, paras. 41–42; and Case C-75/11, *Commission v Austria*, EU:C:2012:605, para. 63.

138 The following section draws upon an earlier article: A. Hoogenboom, 'Mind the Gap: Mobile Students and their Access to Study Grants and Loans in the EU' (2015) 22 *MJ*, 96.

grants and/or loans *ab initio*. There is no economic link with either Belgium or the Netherlands; and thus the default position (five years' prior residence) applies. Luxembourg, following *Giersch*, can equally deny financial responsibility if the parents have not yet been employed there for a period of five years.

Three points are made here in particular. First, there is nothing inherent in the nature of study grants and/or loans that should preclude a right to export. If the main principle is that students should be free to choose their education, constrained only by their academic abilities, then study grants and/or loans should support that endeavour whether undertaken 'at home' or abroad. This does not undermine the financial sustainability of such systems – if the allowance amount remains the same, it is from a systemic point of view neutral whether the student is enrolled domestically or abroad. Nor is it likely that the introduction of portable financial aid will *in itself* attract more users/'social tourists' than without it,[139] as a Member State retains the possibility of imposing relatively extensive genuine link requirements (even considering the proposed re-evaluation to be discussed below) for preliminary access. As such, the balancing act to be undertaken, described above, comes out in favour of revisiting this principle of EU law.

Secondly, it is submitted here that the insistence, in *Förster,* on five years' prior residence as the sole indicator before being considered sufficiently connected to the host Member State is both too restrictive and incongruent. Admittedly, this position is upheld, or even strengthened by *Dano*: if Article 24 Directive 2004/38 is indeed determinative for the scope of Article 18 TFEU, only persons with a right to permanent residence have a right to receive study grants and/or (subsidised) loans under the same conditions as host Member State nationals. Considering the narrow interpretation of the Court as to what constitutes 'legal residence' in the context of Article 16 of Directive 2004/38,[140] this can be considered an even further step back.

This is problematic. In the light of the overall aim of promoting student mobility, allowing Member States to maintain a criterion which in practice excludes *tout court* the possibility of students to claim study grants and/or (subsidised) loans seems to go against the very spirit of the objective set out in Article 165 TFEU. After all, there are few courses of study that last more than five years, making the idea of access to such grants or loans within the 'study lifetime' of the student practically void of any meaning. Indeed, the truly mobile and independent student (bachelor's degree in one Member State, master's in another)

---

139 Indeed evidence for social tourism is limited: See *A fact finding analysis on the impact on the Member States' social security systems of the entitlements of non-active intra-EU migrants to special non-contributory cash benefits and healthcare granted on the basis of residence* (ICF GHK and Milieu Ltd, 2013), available at http://ec.europa.eu/social/BlobServlet?docId=10972&langId=en (last accessed on 31 January 2016).

140 Joined Cases C-424/10 and C-425/10, *Ziolkowski and Szeja*, EU:C:2011:866.

has the least capabilities of obtaining financing for his or her endeavours,[141] whereas the student who has been statically residing in a Member State, and/or is in a state of dependency (e.g. because supported by an economically active mobile Union citizen), has the most opportunities for funding. Secondly, the insistence on 'residence only' as a measure of the degree of integration is incoherent with the development in *Prinz and Seeberger*, as well as a host of other cases,[142] of the requirement imposed on Member States to engage in a more sophisticated analysis: it risks disregarding evidence of a very real degree of connection that a student may demonstrate with regard to a particular Member State.

Overall, therefore, both the *degree* of genuine link that a student must show as well as the *means* by which he or she can demonstrate that link seem unduly restrictive as matters stand. It is submitted here that a return to a *Grzelczyk*-style analysis is a more attractive alternative: the question should be whether access to study grants and/or loans in the light of the legal, social and economic integration history of a Union citizen-student, would constitute an unreasonable burden on the part of the Member State. This would require the Member State, unlike what is currently the case, to carry out a more sophisticated analysis as to who can be considered sufficiently connected (the entitlement to solidarity), while at the same time substantiate more extensively the threat to the financial equilibrium that underlies the study grant and/or loan system that comes with including or excluding certain categories of students (degree of solidarity actually claimed).

In that context it is also crucial to note that students' claims are for the most part finite in time and less open-ended than say the benefits at issue in the case of *Brey*.[143] Finally, this issue takes on particular importance in the light of recent research that indicates that Member States can derive substantial benefits from being a net importer of students. Indeed, for the Netherlands the Central Planning Agency finds that the benefits linked to the mobile EU student generates a net benefit of some €652 million a year;[144] a more extensive study commissioned by the DAAD which includes an examination of Austria, Germany, Poland, Spain and Switzerland concludes that in the middle to long

---

141 A student may not always be able to work sufficient hours alongside their studies to qualify as a worker for a variety of personal or academic reasons, or because the host Member State labour market is not forthcoming.

142 See e.g. Case C-359/13, *Martens*, EU:C:2015:118, para. 37; Case C-367/11, *Prete*, EU:C:2012:668, para. 31; Case C-503/09, *Stewart*, EU:C:2011:500, para. 95; Joined Cases C-11/06 and C-12/06, *Morgan and Bucher*, EU:C:2007:626, paras. 34–46; and Case C-258/04, *Ioannidis*, EU:C:2005:559, para. 31 *et seq.*

143 Which concerned a supplement to a retirement pension Case C-140/12, *Brey*, EU:C:2013:565.

144 Calculated from CPB Notitie of 18 April 2012, *The economische effecten van internationalisering in het hoger onderwijs*, Report for the Ministry for Education, Culture and Science, available at www.rijksoverheid.nl/bestanden/documenten-en-publicaties/rapporten/2012/05/16/de-economische-effecten-van-internationalisering-in-het-hoger-onderwijs/de-economische-effecten-van-internationalisering-in-het-hoger-onderwijs.pdf (last accessed on 31 January 2016).

term the beneficial effects of student mobility for each of these countries far exceed the initial burden on the public purse caused by tuition fee subsidies and the provision of grants.[145]

5. CONCLUSION

This chapter started with the question of 'where do I belong' as applied to mobile students in the European Union. The answer is a complicated one: whereas there is a clear allocation rule (as regards financial responsibility) in access to education matters, access to financial support in the form of study grants and/or loans is a much more complicated whole. In the latter case, there is much to be said for re-evaluating some of the principles that have been developed in the Court's case-law, including the 'no right to export' rule, the strict application of *Förster* and the non-application of a genuine link test to study loans taken out at market interest rates. Nonetheless, it may in the end be questioned whether the Court can, as a judicial institution, sufficiently address problems which in part stem from Member States' failure to coordinate. Moreover, even if such a coordination system was in place, some issues would remain: if it were determined in a given situation that Romania, for example, is the competent Member State to provide study grants to the mobile student, the amount of such grants may not suffice for a student to effectively take up studies in a Member State where the cost of living is higher. In such a context, there is perhaps a need for an EU instrument to fill the gap and make student mobility a realistic (from a financial point of view) alternative to studies at home. To an extent, the new Erasmus programme seeks to pilot such an instrument,[146] but this only applies to master's studies abroad, and the ambitions of the programme have been scaled back quite substantially from the original proposal.[147]

---

145 I. Pfeiffer and M. Böhmer, *Studentische Mobilität und ihre finanzielle Effekte auf das Gastland* (Prognos, 2013), 87–89, available at https://eu.daad.de/medien/eu/publikationen/erasmus/1_prognos-studie.pdf (last accessed on 31 January 2016).

146 See Article 20 of Regulation 1288/2013/EU of the European Parliament and of the Council of 11 December 2013 establishing 'Erasmus+': the Union programme for education, training, youth and sport and repealing Decisions No. 1719/2006/EC, No. 1720/2006/EC and No. 1298/2008/EC, OJ 2013, L 347/50.

147 N. Barr *et al.*, 'Feasibility Study on Student Lending' (EAC/47/2009 Report to the European Commission: Directorate-General for Education and Culture, 2011).

CHAPTER 10

BEING ECONOMICALLY ACTIVE: HOW IT STILL MATTERS

Herwig VERSCHUEREN

1. INTRODUCTION

The classic way for migrating Union citizens to claim rights in the host State is to be economically active. Ever since the Rome Treaty of 1957, economic migration between the Member States is one of the cornerstones of the process of economic integration through the internal market. The original Article 48 EEC (now Article 45 TFEU) secured the freedom of movement for workers, which entails the right to move freely within the territory of the Member States for the purpose of employment, the right to stay and remain in the host Member State as well as the prohibition of any discrimination on grounds of nationality between the workers of the Member States in terms of employment, pay and working conditions. Article 52 (now 49 TFEU) guaranteed unrestricted freedom of establishment for self-employed persons in the Member States and equal treatment with nationals of the host State and Article 59 (now 56 TFEU) prohibited restriction to the freedom to provide services across the border.

After more than fifty years of European integration economic activity still is the central connecting factor between migrating EU citizens and the legal order of host Member States. This chapter proceeds as follows. It first recapitulates the rights economically active EU migrants have under EU law (section 2). Next it examines three questions. In section 3 it questions if and why it is still important for a person to be qualified as economically active or to be considered as a family member of such a person. Relevant questions indeed, because since the introduction of European citizenship the application of the general prohibition of discrimination on grounds of nationality, is now also triggered in situations where the migrant person is economically inactive (Articles 18, 20 and 21 TFEU). In section 4 the question which persons can rely on the status of 'worker' will be examined. Are all 'working' activities sufficient to qualify a person as a worker and what are the problems of applying the definition of worker in secondary law and in the CJ's case-law? Finally, the chapter examines whether it is enough to be qualified as a 'migrant worker' or as a member of his/her family to claim rights in the host Member State. It seems indeed that the most recent case-law of the CJ has cast some doubt on this question (section 5). In section 6 we offer some concluding remarks.

2. THE RIGHTS OF ECONOMICALLY ACTIVE EU MIGRANTS

The right to free movement and to equal treatment for economically active EU migrants, as laid down in the Treaty, has further been implemented in secondary law, such as Regulation 1612/68[1] (now replaced by Regulation 492/2011).[2] These regulations include the prohibition of discrimination on grounds of nationality in Article 7, not only for employment and working conditions but also for social and tax advantages and vocational training. Equal treatment is also guaranteed regarding membership of trade unions (Article 8) and housing (Article 9) as well as regarding the migrant workers' children access to education (Article 10, formerly Article 12 Regulation 1612/68). Equal treatment with the nationals of the host State also applies to social security benefits within the meaning of Regulation 883/2004[3] (Article 4). Furthermore, for the economically active and the members of their family the right to reside on the territory of the host State and to remain there is formulated in more detail in Directive 2004/38.[4] Their family members may also claim such a right in the Member State where the EU citizen worked before when they continue their education there[5] or even in the Member State where the worker resides while working in another Member State.[6]

In particular equal treatment as far as 'social advantages' are concerned has created a large body of CJ case-law.[7] For the CJ, this principle should not

1 Regulation (EEC) 1612/68 of the Council of 25 October 1968 on freedom of movement within the Community, OJ 1968, L 257 (hereinafter referred to as 'Regulation 1612/68').

2 Regulation (EU) 492/2011 of the European Parliament and of the Council of 5 April 2011 on freedom of movement for workers within the Union, OJ 2011, L 141/1 (hereinafter referred to as 'Regulation 492/2011').

3 Regulation (EC) 883/2004 of the European Parliament and the Council of 29 April 2004 on the coordination of social security systems, OJ 2004, L 200/1 (hereinafter referred to as 'Regulation 883/2004').

4 Article 7(1)(b) and (d) of Directive 2004/38/EC of the European Parliament and of the Council of 29 April 2004 on the right of citizens of the Union and their family members to move and reside freely within the territory of the Member States, OJ 2004, L 158/77 (hereinafter referred to as 'Directive 2004/38').

5 Case C-413/99, *Baumbast*, EU:C:2002:493; Case C-310/08, *Ibrahim*, EU:C:2010:80; Case C-480/08, *Teixeira*, EU:C:2010:83; and Case C-529/11, *Alarape and Tijani*, EU:C:2013:290. According to this case-law, the primary carers of these family members also maintain the right to reside.

6 Case C-457/12, *S. and G.*, EU:C:2014:136, para. 41.

7 This chapter does not deal with the CJ's case-law on the prohibition of discrimination regarding 'fiscal advantages'.

be interpreted restrictively It is not only applicable to all employment and working conditions, but also to all the advantages which, whether or not linked to a contract of employment, are generally granted to national workers.[8] The CJ considered, *inter alia*, the following 'social advantages' to fall within this meaning: reduced public transport fares,[9] maintenance grants for students supported by a migrant worker,[10] social assistance,[11] funeral allowances,[12] pre-retirement benefits,[13] the tide-over allowance for young people seeking their first employment,[14] as well as social security benefits in general.[15] The social advantages in question may also be advantages granted to family members supported by the migrating worker, such as financial support for students[16] or housing assistance, even if the 'worker' him/herself has left the host State.[17]

This case-law does not only protect workers against direct discrimination on grounds of nationality but also against indirect discrimination.[18] Residence clauses are the most typical example of this kind of indirect discrimination.[19] They were systematically brushed aside by the Court, in the case of frontier workers as well.[20] However, a migrant worker who has ended his/her working life and does not reside or has left the Member State where he/she was last employed, can no longer derive rights from his/her former status as a worker,[21] unless the

8 Case C-310/91, *Schmid*, EU:C:1993:221, para. 18; Case C-57/96, *Meints*, EU:C:1997:564, para. 39; Case C-85/96, *Martínez Sala*, EU:C:1998:217, para. 25; and Case C-542/09, *Commission v Netherlands*, EU:C:2012:346, para. 65.

9 Case 32/75, *Cristini*, EU:C:1975:120.

10 See *inter alia* Case C-3/90, *Bernini*, EU:C:1992:89; Case C-337/97, *Meeusen*, EU:C:1999:284; and Case C-542/09, *Commission v Netherlands*, EU:C:2012:346, para. 34.

11 Case 249/83, *Hoeckx*, EU:C:1985:139; Case 316/85, *Lebon*, EU:C:1987:302; Case 139/85, *Kempf*, EU:C:1986:223.

12 Case C-237/94, *O'Flynn*, EU:C:1996:206.

13 Case C-35/97, *Commission v France*, EU:C:1998:431.

14 Case C-278/94, *Commission v Belgium*, EU:C:1996:321.

15 Case C-310/91, *Schmid*, EU:C:1993:221; Case C-43/99 *Leclere*, EU:C:2001:303; Case C-137/04, *Rockler*, EU:C:2006:106; and Case C-185/04, *Öberg*, EU:C:2006:107.

16 Case 316/85, *Lebon*, EU:C:1987:302; Case 235/87, *Matteucci*, EU:C:1988:460; Case C-3/90, *Bernini*, EU:C:1992:89; Case C-337/97, *Meeusen*, EU:C:1999:284; Case C-542/09, *Commission v Netherlands*, EU:C:2012:346.

17 As in Case C-310/08, *Ibrahim*, EU:C:2010:80; Case C-480/08, *Teixeira*, EU:C:2010:83; and Case C-529/11, *Alarape and Tijani*, EU:C:2013:290.

18 In most cases the Court was confronted with indirect forms of discrimination which the CJ identified as forms of discrimination which, through the application of other criteria of differentiation, lead in fact to the same result as overt discrimination on grounds on nationality. See, *inter alia*, Case C-237/94, *O'Flynn*, EU:C:1996:206, para. 18; Case C-57/96, *Meints*, EU:C:1997:564, para. 44; Case C-542/09, *Commission v Netherlands*, EU:C:2012:346, para. 37; and Case C-20/12, *Giersch*, EU:C:2013:411, para. 41.

19 See, *inter alia*, Case C-224/97, *Ciola*, EU:C:1999:212, para. 14; Case C-382/08, *Neukirchinger*, EU:C:2011:27, para. 34; Case C-542/09, *Commission v Netherlands*, EU:C:2012:346, para. 38; and Case C-20/12, *Giersch*, EU:C:2013:411, para. 44.

20 Case C-57/96, *Meints*, EU:C:1997:564; Case C-337/97, *Meeusen*, EU:C:1999:284; and Case C-287/05, *Hendrix*, EU:C:2007:494.

21 Case C-43/99, *Leclere*, EU:C:2001:303, para. 59; and Case C-345/09, *van Delft*, EU:C:2010:610, para. 90.

advantage is intrinsically linked with the employment relationship or a worker's working life.[22]

In addition, workers are not only protected against direct or indirect discrimination on grounds of nationality. The CJ's case-law also protects them against all measures which, even though applicable without discrimination on grounds of nationality, are capable of hindering or rendering less attractive the exercise by Union nationals of the fundamental freedom of movement as a worker.[23] Consequently, migrant workers may claim benefits invoking this notion of 'obstacle', not only from the host State,[24] but also from the home State when leaving it[25] or upon returning to it.[26]

Indirect discrimination or obstacles to free movement are prohibited unless they are objectively justified. In order to be justified they must be appropriate with a view to securing the attainment of a legitimate objective and must not go beyond what is necessary to attain that objective (*rule of reason*').[27] But in the cases of migrant workers it has proved to be very difficult for Member States or private parties to convince the Court that a measure was duly justified.

In other words, workers, former workers and members of their families are granted equal treatment and protection against obstacles to their free movement in a lot of situations and cases. These principles also apply horizontally.[28] They aim at facilitating the mobility of the migrant worker and his/her family[29] and are seen as a means of their integration into the host society.[30] Yet more recent case-law, which we will discuss in section 5, would seem to depart from this approach.

22 Case C-57/96, *Meints*, EU:C:1997:564, para. 41; Case C-43/99, *Leclere*, EU:C:2001:303, paras. 56–57; Case C-35/97, *Commission v France*, EU:C:1998:431; and Case C-228/07, *Petersen*, EU:C:2008:494.

23 Case C-415/93, *Bosman*, EU:C:1995:463, and more recently Case C-379/09, *Casteels*, EU:C:2011:131, para. 22; Case C-212/06, *Gouvernement de la Communauté française and Gouvernement wallon*, EU:C:2008:178, para. 45; and Case C-202/11, *Las*, EU:C:2013:239, para. 20.

24 Case C-212/06, *Gouvernement de la Communauté française and Gouvernement wallon*, EU:C:2008:178; and Case C-202/11, *Las*, EU:C:2013:239.

25 Case C-109/04, *Kranemann*, EU:C:2005:187; Case C-287/05, *Hendrix*, EU:C:2007:494; Case C-18/95, *Terhoeve*, EU:C:1999:22; and Case C-325/08, *Olympique Lyonnais*, EU:C:2010:143.

26 Case C-19/92, *Kraus*, EU:C:1993:125; Case C-370/90, *Singh*, EU:C:1992:296; and Case C-291/05, *Eind*, EU:C:2007:771.

27 See, *inter alia*, Case C-325/08, *Olympique Lyonnais*, EU:C:2010:143, para. 38; Case C-20/12, *Giersch*, EU:C:2013:411, para. 46; and Case C-542/09, *Commission v Netherlands*, EU:C:2012:346, para. 55.

28 Case C-415/93, *Bosman*, EU:C:1995:463, para. 82; Case C-325/08, *Olympique Lyonnais*, EU:C:2010:143, para. 30; Case C-281/08, *Angonese*, EU:C:2000:296, para. 31; and Case C-94/07, *Raccanelli*, EU:C:2008:425, paras. 41–45.

29 Case C-207/78, *Even*, EU:C:1979:144.

30 Joined Cases 389/87 and 390/87, *Echternach and Moritz*, EU:C:1989:130, para. 35.

3. IS IT STILL IMPORTANT TO BE AN 'ECONOMICALLY ACTIVE' PERSON?

Meanwhile, one could wonder whether legally speaking it is still relevant to be an 'economically active' person to be entitled to benefits or advantages from the host State or even the home State. Indeed, the CJ stated that, since the introduction of European citizenship by the Maastricht Treaty, non-economic migration between Member States also triggers the application of the Treaty prohibition of discrimination on grounds of nationality in the host State (now Article 18 TFEU).[31] The Court confirmed that this also applies to the entitlement to social assistance benefits[32] as well as to other non-contributory benefits, such as student maintenance grants.[33] Moreover, economically inactive Union citizens may not be subjected to measures creating an unjustified, but non-discriminatory, restriction on the right to move and reside within the territory of the Member States, more specifically when leaving their home State to live[34] or study in another Member State.[35]

However, the Court did not grant economically inactive migrants unconditional access to the welfare benefits of the host State. Depending on the case, the applicant should 'not become an unreasonable burden on the public finances',[36] 'have a genuine link with the employment market of the State concerned',[37] or 'need to demonstrate a certain degree of integration into the society of the host State'.[38] Requiring a genuine link with the host Member State could, for the Court, represent a legitimate objective and justify restrictions on the right to move and reside freely in the territory of the Member States.[39] Moreover, in respect of economically inactive EU migrants the CJ confirmed that Member States enjoy broad discretion to decide which criteria are to be used

31 See for the first time Case C-85/96, *Martinez Sala*, EU:C:1998:217, recently confirmed in Case C-333/13, *Dano*, EU:C:2014:2359, para. 59.

32 Case C-184/99, *Grzelczyk*, EU:C:2001:458; and Case C-456/02, *Trojani*, EU:C:2004:488.

33 Case C-209/03, *Bidar*, EU:C:2005:169.

34 Case C-499/06, *Nerkowska*, EU:C:2008:300; Case C-406/04, *De Cuyper*, EU:C:2006:491; and Case C-192/05, *Tas-Hagen and Tas*, EU:C:2006:676.

35 Joined Cases C-11/06 and C-12/06, *Morgan and Bucher*, EU:C:2007:626; Joined Case C-523/11 and C-565/11, *Prinz and Seeberger*, EU:C:2013:524; Case C-220/12, *Thiele Meneses*, EU:C:2013:683; and Case C-359/13, *Martens*, EU:C:2015:118.

36 Case C-184/99, *Grzelczyk*, EU:C:2001:458, para. 44 and Case C-75/11, *Commission v Austria*, EU:C:2012:605, para. 60.

37 Case C-138/02, *Collins*, EU:C:2004:172, paras. 67–69; and Joined Cases C-22/08 and C-23/08, *Vatsouras* and *Koupatantze*, EU:C:2009:344, paras. 38 and 39.

38 Case C-209/03, *Bidar*, EU:C:2005:169, para. 57. See also Case C-258/04, *Ioannidis*, EU:C:2005:559, para. 30 *et seq.*; Case C-158/07, *Förster*, EU:C:2008:630, para. 54; and Case C-103/08, *Gottwald*, EU:C:2009:597, para. 32 *et seq.*

39 Case C-359/13, *Martens*, EU:C:2015:118, para. 36; Case C-220/12, *Thiele Meneses*, EU:C:2013:683, para. 34; Case C-224/98, *D'Hoop*, EU:C:2002:432, para. 38; Case C-192/05, *Tas-Hagen and Tas*, EU:C:2006:676, para. 35; Case C-499/06, *Nerkowska*, EU:C:2008:300, para. 37; and Case C-103/08, *Gottwald*, EU:C:2009:597, para. 32.

when assessing the extent of the connection between the recipient of a benefit and the Member State concerned with regard to benefits that are not governed by EU law.[40]

In addition, for economically inactive migrant persons the right of residence for more than three months and the retention of that right for up to five years is conditional upon them having sufficient resources for themselves and their family members, so as not to become a burden on the social assistance system of the host Member State, as well as sickness insurance.[41]

In the light of these provisions and case-law it would seem more than ever important for a person to be qualified as a worker or as a member of a worker's family. Indeed, being economically active seems for the CJ to constitute a sufficient link of integration, *inter alia*, because migrant workers also contribute to the financing of the social policies of the host State by paying taxes.[42] In *Commission v Netherlands* the Court of Justice was quite clear on this point. The CJ recognised that Member States may also require migrant workers to show proof of a certain degree of integration in their societies if they want to receive social advantages (such as, in this case, financial assistance for the education of their children). However, for the Court a residence requirement to prove the required degree of integration is, in principle, inappropriate when the persons concerned are migrant workers or frontier workers. The CJ added that, as regards migrant workers and frontier workers, the fact that they have participated in the employment market of a Member State establishes, in principle, a sufficient link of integration into the society of that Member State, allowing them to benefit from the principle of equal treatment, as compared with national workers, as regards social advantages. The link of integration arises from, *inter alia*, the fact that, through the taxes which he/she pays in the host Member State by virtue of his/her employment, the migrant worker also contributes to the financing of the social policies of that State and should profit from them under the same conditions as national workers.[43]

In the same vein, in *Caves Krier*,[44] the CJ noted that a condition of residence is, as a rule, inappropriate as regards migrant workers and frontier workers since, having participated in the employment market of a Member State, they have in principle established a sufficient link of integration into the society of that State, allowing them to benefit from the principle of equal treatment, as compared with, respectively, national workers and resident workers. The CJ

40 Case C-103/08, *Gottwald*, EU:C:2009:597, para. 34; Case C-220/12, *Thiele Meneses*, EU:C:2013:683, para. 37; and Case C-359/13, *Martens*, EU:C:2015:118, para. 38.

41 Article 7(1)(b) Directive 2004/38. See further on these conditions and on the right of economically inactive EU migrants to equal treatment for social benefits the chapter of P. Minderhoud in this volume.

42 Case C-542/09, *Commission v Netherlands*, EU:C:2012:346, paras. 63–66.

43 Case C-542/09, *Commission v Netherlands*, EU:C:2012:346, para. 66.

44 Case C-379/11, *Caves Krier*, EU:C:2012:798.

repeated that the link of integration arises, in particular, from the fact that, through the taxes which they pay in the host Member State by virtue of their employment there, migrant and frontier workers also contribute to the financing of the social policies of that State.[45] The CJ also confirmed that the objective of avoiding an unreasonable financial burden cannot be regarded as an overriding reason relating to the public interest, capable of justifying the unequal treatment of workers from other Member States as compared with workers of the host State.[46] Yet in *Giersch* the CJ seems to have accepted that for frontier workers integration in the host State may not be sufficient to claim equal treatment for certain benefits[47] (see further on this issue in section 5).

The presumption that 'work' constitutes a sufficient link with the host Member State is also confirmed in Directive 2004/38. In order to obtain the right to reside in the host State it is sufficient to be a worker (or a self-employed person). There can be no resources requirement *vis-à-vis* citizens of other Member States who can prove that they are working as employed or self-employed persons falling within the scope of the CJ's case-law. The same applies to their family members.[48] Moreover, Union citizens who are no longer workers or self-employed persons retain, under certain circumstances, this status[49] In addition, the derogation in Article 24(2) of this Directive, to equal treatment regarding social assistance for the first three months (or even longer for jobseekers) of residence or for maintenance aid for studies in the first five years, does not apply to workers, self-employed persons, persons who retain such a status or their families.

It follows from this analysis that, despite the introduction of European citizenship and the right to move and reside freely within the Member States for economically inactive Union citizens as well, it continues to be important for a person claiming rights from the host Member State or even from his/her home Member State, to be regarded as an economically active person within the meaning of EU law, or as a person retaining such a status. 'Economic activity serves as a sort of "master key" that unlocks redistributive arrangements in the host State for migrants', which is justified by their participation in the employment market of that State.[50]

---

45 Case C-379/11, *Caves Krier*, EU:C:2012:798, paras. 51–53; and Case C-20/12, *Giersch*, EU:C:2013:411, para. 63.

46 Case C-542/09, *Commission v Netherlands*, EU:C:2012:346, para. 57–58; and Case C-20/12, *Giersch*, EU:C:2013:411, paras. 51–52.

47 Case C-20/12, *Giersch*, EU:C:2013:411, paras. 64–65.

48 See Article 7(1)(a) and (d) and Article 14(4)(a) of Directive 2004/38.

49 Article 7(3) Directive 2004/38. See further in section 4.6 on this category.

50 F. De Witte, 'Who funds the mobile student? Shedding some light on the normative assumptions underlying EU free movement law: *Commission v Netherlands*' (2013) 50 *CML Rev*, 209. In the same vein C. O'Brien, 'Social Blind Spots and Monocular Policy Making: The ECJ's Migrant Worker Model' (2009) 46 *CML Rev*, 1111–1113.

4. WHO IS TO BE CONSIDERED AS BEING 'ECONOMICALLY ACTIVE'?

4.1. THE CONCEPT OF 'WORKER' UNDER FREE MOVEMENT LAW

So, within the concept of European citizenship, the distinction between economically active persons and those who are not remains crucial for determining the claim these persons may have on rights *vis-à-vis* Member States. Therefore, the definition of these categories of persons and the delineation of their personal scope continue to have a decisive impact on their rights under EU law.

As regards the concept of 'worker', the CJ has given a very broad interpretation. It is indeed settled case-law that within the meaning of Article 45 TFEU this concept has an autonomous meaning which is specific to European Union law and must not be interpreted narrowly.[51] The main reason for the CJ to adopt an autonomous meaning for the concept of 'worker' in EU law on the free movement of workers, is to prevent Member States from modifying the meaning of this concept and from eliminating at will the protection afforded by the Treaty to these category of persons.[52] Any person pursuing economic activities which are real and genuine, to the exclusion of activities on such a small scale as to be regarded as purely marginal and ancillary, must be regarded as a 'worker'.[53] This

51 Case 53/81, *Levin*, EU:C:1982:105; Case 66/85, *Lawrie-Blum*, EU:C:1986:284, para. 16; Case 197/86, *Brown*, EU:C:1988:323, para. 21; Case C-3/90, *Bernini*, EU:C:1992:89, para. 14; and Case C-413/01, *Ninni-Orasche*, EU:C:2003:600, para. 23; and Case C-46/12, *L.N.*, EU:C:2013:97, para. 39.

52 Case 75/63, *Hoekstra*, EU:C:1964:18. However, the concept of 'worker' does not always have an autonomous meaning within EU law. There is no single definition of worker in European Union law: it varies according to the area in which the definition is to be applied (Case C-85/96, *Martínez Sala*, EU:C:1998:217, para. 31; and Case C-256/01, *Allonby*, EU:C:2004:18, para. 63; Case C-393/10, *O'Brien*, EU:C:2012:110, para. 30). In some areas an EU concept of 'worker' must be applied, such as in the field of equal treatment for male and female workers (see Case C-366/99, *Griesmar*, EU:C:2001:648, para. 31) or for the implementation of Working Time Directive 2003/88/EC (see Case C-151/02, *Jaeger*, EU:C:2003:437, paras. 58–59) and the Collective Redundancies Directive 98/59 (see Case C-229/14, *Balkaya*, EU:C:2015:455, para. 33). In other areas, regard must be had solely to the definition of worker laid down in national legislation, such as in the case of Directive 77/187/EEC on transfers of undertakings (see Case 105/84, *Danmols Inventar*, EU:C:1985:331, paras. 26–28) or Posting of Workers Directive 96/71 (Article 2 and Article 4(5) of Enforcement Directive 2014/67/EU). Moreover, the social security coordination of Regulation 883/2004 refers, for the implementation of its provisions, to the definition of employed or self-employed activity as defined in the Member States' social security legislation (see Article 1(a) and (b) Regulation 883/2004 and Case C-340/94, *De Jaeck*, EU:C:1997:43, para. 34; Case C-221/95, *Hervein and Hervillier*, EU:C:1997:47, para. 22; and Case C-137/11, *Partena*, EU:C:2012:593, para. 50).

53 For early statements of this rule, see Case 53/81, *Levin*, EU:C:1982:105, para. 17; Case 139/85, *Kempf*, EU:C:1986:223, para. 13; and Case 66/85 *Lawrie-Blum*, EU:C:1986:284, para. 16. See more recent Case C-413/01, *Ninni-Orasche*, EU:C:2003:600, para. 23; Case

concept must be defined in accordance with objective criteria which distinguish the employment relationship by reference to the rights and duties of the persons concerned. The essential feature of an employment relationship is that, for a certain period, a person performs services for and under the direction of another person (subordination), in return for which he/she receives remuneration.[54] The nature of the legal relationship between the employee and the employer, for instance public or private, is not decisive,[55] neither is the sector, for instance sports.[56]

The origin of the funds from which the remuneration is paid or the limited amount of that remuneration does not impact on a person's status as a 'worker'.[57] The fact that the income from employment is lower than the minimum required for subsistence does not prevent an employed person from being regarded as a 'worker'.[58] This is also the case when the person in question seeks to supplement that remuneration by other means of subsistence, such as financial assistance drawn from the public funds of the State in which he/she resides.[59] The rather low productivity of the person concerned is not relevant either.[60] Furthermore, regarding the duration of the activity pursued, the fact that the employment is of short duration does not exclude in itself this kind of employment from the scope of Article 45 TFEU.[61] Moreover, in the Court's view, the income can also consist of an indirect contribution, such as board and lodging.[62] Still, these elements may be taken into account by the national court

C-228/07, *Petersen*, EU:C:2008:494, para. 45; Joined Cases C-22/08 and C-23/08, *Vatsouras and Koupatantze*, EU:C:2009:344, para. 26; and Case C-46/12, *L.N.*, EU:C:2013:97, para. 39.

54 See Case 66/85, *Lawrie-Blum*, EU:C:1986:284, para. 17; Case C-94/07, *Raccanelli*, EU:C:2008:425, para. 33; Case C-413/01, *Ninni-Orasche*, EU:C:2003:600, para. 24; Joined Cases C-22/08 and C-23/08, *Vatsouras and Koupatantze*, EU:C:2009:344, para. 26; Case C-46/12, *L.N.*, EU:C:2013:97, para. 40; and Case C-270/13, *Haralambidis*, EU:C:2014:2185, para. 34.

55 Case 344/87, *Bettray*, EU:C:1989:226, para. 16; Case C-357/89, *Raulin*, EU:C:1992:87, para. 10; and Case C-270/13, *Haralambidis*, EU:C:2014:2185, para. 40.

56 Case C-415/93, *Bosman*, EU:C:1995:463; Case C-325/08, *Olympique Lyonnais*, EU:C:2010:143; and Case C-519/04, *Meca-Medina and Lajcan*, EU:C:1006:492.

57 Case 66/85, *Lawrie-Blum*, EU:C:1986:284, para. 21; Case 344/87, *Bettray*, EU:C:1989:226, para. 15; Case C-3/90, *Bernini*, EU:C:1992:89, para. 16; Case C-10/05, *Mattern and Cikotic*, EU:C:2006:220, para. 22; Case C-46/12, *L.N.*, EU:C:2013:97, para. 41; and Case C-316/13, *Fenoll*, EU:C:2015:200, para. 34.

58 Case 53/81, *Levin*, EU:C:1982:105, para. 15–16; and Case C-317/93, *Nolte*, EU:C:1995:438, para. 19.

59 Case 139/85, *Kempf*, EU:C:1986:223 para. 14; and Case C-444/93, *Megner & Scheffel*, EU:C:1995:442, para. 18.

60 Case C-188/00, *Kurz*, EU:C:2002:694, para. 32; and Case C-316/13, *Fenoll*, EU:C:2015:200, para. 34.

61 Case C-3/90, *Bernini*, EU:C:1992:89, para. 16; Case C-444/93, *Megner & Scheffel*, EU:C:1995:442, para. 18; Case C-413/01, *Ninni-Orasche*, EU:C:2003:600, para. 25; Case C-109/04, *Kranemann*, EU:C:2007:187, para. 13; and Case C-229/14, *Balkaya*, EU:C:2015:455, para. 50.

62 Case 196/87, *Steymann*, EU:C:1988:475.

when assessing whether those activities are effective and genuine,[63] leaving some leeway to the Member States and their judiciary.

In addition, in order to assess whether employment makes it possible to confer the status of worker to a person within the meaning of Article 45 TFEU, factors relating to the conduct of the person concerned before and after the period of employment are not relevant. Such factors are not in any way related to the objective criteria referred to in the abovementioned case-law. This means that for the CJ the intentions the person involved had when he/she entered a Member State, such as to follow a course or study, does not preclude him/her from having the status of 'worker' within the meaning of Article 45 TFEU.[64] The right to freedom of movement of workers may not be made contingent on which objectives are being pursued by a national of a Member State applying to enter the territory of a host Member State, provided that he/she pursues or wishes to pursue effective and genuine employment activities. Once that condition has been satisfied, the motives which may have prompted a worker of a Member State to seek employment in another Member State are of no account and must not be taken into consideration.[65] The CJ also confirmed this approach when Member States invoked the risk of abuse, in particular resulting from the performance of short periods of employment solely for the purposes of obtaining certain social benefits[66] or the right to reside for family members.[67] In the case of migrant workers, the CJ is indeed very reluctant to qualify their migration as an abuse of rights, as long as they really perform work within the broad meaning the CJ applies to this concept.[68]

4.2. THE BLURRY NATURE OF THE CONCEPT OF 'WORKER'

Despite this abundant case-law, it is not always easy to draw the line between 'work' that falls under these definitions and 'work' that does not.[69] The growing

63 Case C-357/89, *Raulin*, EU:C:1992:87, para. 15. In this case the CJ had to deal with a so-called 'on-call' worker.

64 Case C-413/01, *Ninni-Orasche*, EU:C:2003:600, para. 28; and Case C-46/12, *L.N.*, EU:C:2013:97, para. 46.

65 Case 53/81, *Levin*, EU:C:1982:105, paras. 21–22; Case 39/86, *Lair*, EU:C:1988:32, para. 43; Case C-237/94, *O'Flynn*, EU:C:1996:206, para. 21; Case C-109/01, *Akrich*, EU:C:2003:491, para. 55; and Case C-46/12, *L.N.*, EU:C:2013:97, para. 47.

66 Case C-542/09, *Commission v Netherlands*, EU:C:2012:346, para. 68. Only in *Lair* the Court referred to the sole purpose of enjoying a benefit for students as being an abuse if it was claimed after a very short period of occupational activity: Case 39/86, *Lair*, EU:C:1988:32, para. 43.

67 Case C-109/01, *Akrich*, EU:C:2003:491; and Case C-127/08, *Metock*, EU:C:2008:449.

68 See on this discussion: K. Ziegler, '"Abuse of Law" in the Context of the Free Movement of Workers', in R. de la Feria and S. Vogenauer (eds.), *Prohibition of Abuse of Law* (Oxford; Hart Publishing, 2011), 295–314.

69 See also: C. O'Brien, 'Social Blind Spots and Monocular Policy Making: The ECJ's Migrant Worker Model' (2009) 46 *CML Rev*, 1107–1141.

importance of non-standard work in the Member States as a result of the emergence of atypical and hybrid working arrangements, has aggravated this issue.[70]

How many hours a week does a person have to work for his/her employment to be considered as 'real and genuine' and not as 'purely marginal and ancillary'? In *Kempf*, the CJ accepted 12 hours a week as sufficient, in *Megner and Scheffel* even ten hours.[71] In *Genc*, concerning the EEC–Turkey Association Agreement, the CJ did not rule out that 5.5 hours a week may be considered as 'real and genuine', following an overall assessment of the employment relationship in question.[72] Part-time working students,[73] trainees[74] or *au pairs*[75] could also be 'workers'. However, the low threshold the CJ applies may also lead to situations in which persons are very close to being economically inactive, as a result of which different rules on the right to reside and the right to equal treatment apply, leading to seemingly arbitrary outcomes.[76] Therefore, Member States may be tempted to apply a strict test and give a narrow interpretation to what is 'real and genuine' with a view to excluding certain migrants, such as part-time migrants, from the 'worker' status and hence from the rights which this entails.

The same goes for the concept of 'remuneration', which is also interpreted broadly by the CJ. In *Agegate* remuneration of fishermen on the basis of the proceeds of sale of their catches was accepted as such.[77] Chores in return for food, lodging and pocket money were considered remunerated work in *Steymann*.[78] But in *Trojani* the CJ had doubts on whether the work Mr Trojani did for the Salvation Army in return for which he received this type of 'remuneration' and which was part of the social integration programme of the 'employer', was sufficient to qualify him as a 'worker' and left the final judgment to the national court.[79] Volunteers seem to be excluded since they do not receive any remuneration, despite the fact that they may contribute to the host State's development.[80] The same goes for unremunerated care work, thus excluding for

70 See on the growing importance of non-standard work in the Member States the different contributions in: J. Buelens and J. Pearson (eds.), *Standard work: an anachronism?* (Antwerp-Cambridge: Intersentia, 2013) and N. Countouris, *The Changing Law of the Employment Relationship. Comparative Analyses in the European Context* (Ashgate: Farnham, 2007).

71 Case 139/85, *Kempf*, EU:C:1986:223; and Case C-444/93 *Megner & Scheffel*, EU:C:1995:442.

72 Case C-14/09, *Genc*, EU:C:2010:57, para. 28.

73 Case C-46/12, *L.N.*, EU:C:2013:97.

74 Case C-3/90, *Bernini*, EU:C:1992:89; C-109/04, *Kranemann*, EU:C:2005:187; and Case C-229/14, *Balkaya*, EU:C:2015:455, para. 50.

75 Case C-294/06, *Payir*, EU:C:2008:36.

76 D. Thym, 'The elusive limits of solidarity: residence rights of and social benefits for economically inactive Union citizens' (2015) 52 *CML Rev*, 43.

77 Case C-3/97, *Agegate*, EU:C:1989:650.

78 Case 196/87, *Steymann*, EU:C:1988:475.

79 Case C-456/02, *Trojani*, EU:C:2004:488.

80 See on the position of volunteers: C. O'Brien, 'Drudges, dupes and do-gooders. Competing notions of "value" in the Union's approach of volunteers' (2011) 1 *European Journal of Social Law*, 49–75.

instance persons who look after family members.[81] The fact that remuneration is an essential element in the CJ's definition of the concept of 'worker' could also mean that work performed in the context of unpaid work placement, education or vocational training or in the context of compulsory work activities as a condition to receive benefits, also falls outside its scope. Yet such activities might be valuable for the persons performing them as well as for the persons making use of them, the former as a step-up to economic activity and the latter for their economic value.[82]

Questions were also raised concerning the nature of publically subsidised work meant to promote the integration of the persons involved into society. Indeed, some Member States, e.g. Belgium, used the judgment in *Bettray*[83] as an argument (or pretext?) to exclude workers employed by public authorities in order to raise their chances of gaining access to the 'standard' labour market from the EU's worker's status. Subsequently, because these persons were said to depend on social assistance, an expulsion measure was taken against them.[84] In *Bettray*, the CJ refused to consider 'work merely as a means of rehabilitation and reintegration' as an economic activity since it was not 'employment under normal conditions'. Mr Bettray was a drug addict who was employed under the Dutch Social Employment Law. This law concerns employment with the purpose of enabling those persons, sooner or later, to recover their capacity to take up ordinary employment. This ruling could be understood because Mr Bettray's activities were 'merely' intended as a means of rehabilitation or reintegration and had very little or no economic value for the employer.[85] Indeed, later in *Birden* the CJ held that its position in *Bettray* did not follow the general trend of the case-law concerning the interpretation of the concept of 'worker' and that it could only be explained by the particular characteristics of that case.[86] In *Trojani* the CJ added that Mr Bettray could not be qualified as a 'worker' because he was a person who was unable, by reason of circumstances related to his situation, to work under normal conditions.[87] The *Birden* case concerned a programme intended to provide paid employment, on a temporary basis, to recipients of social assistance in order to enable, in particular, unemployed persons with no entitlement to

---

81 For a critical assessment of such exclusion and the ensuing difference in treatment: C. O'Brien, 'Social Blind Spots and Monocular Policy Making: The ECJ's Migrant Worker Model' (2009) 46 *CML Rev*, 1118–1123.

82 F. Van Overmeiren *et al.* (ed.), *The notions of obstacle and discrimination under EU law on the free movement of workers*, FreSsco, European Commission, December 2014, 34.

83 Case 344/87, *Bettray*, EU:C:1989:226.

84 Initially this was even confirmed by the Belgian judiciary, but subsequent to critical remarks of the European Commission both the competent authorities and the judiciary changed their position.

85 Opinion of Advocate General Geelhoed in Case C-456/02, *Trojani*, EU:C:2004:113, paras. 33–34. See also N. Rogers, R. Scannell, and J. Walsh, *Free movement of persons in the enlarged European Union* (London: Sweet & Maxwell, 2012), 103.

86 Case C-1/97, *Birden*, EU:C:1998:568, paras. 30–31.

87 Case C-456/02, *Trojani*, EU:C:2004:488, para. 19.

unemployment benefits to enter or re-enter the general labour market. For the CJ such a person must be regarded as a 'worker'. More recently in its judgment of 26 March 2015 in *Fenoll* the CJ explicitly confirmed that employment of severely disabled persons in a specialised centre for employment therapy could well be considered as not being purely marginal and ancillary and that such work could have some economic value, how limited it is.[88] Yet the Court, in *Trojani* as well as in *Fenoll,* left it to the national courts to 'ascertain whether the services actually performed [...] are capable of being regarded as forming part of the normal labour market. For that purpose, account may be taken of the status and practices of the hostel, the content of the social reintegration programme, and the nature and details of performance of the services'.[89]

So, doubts remain on what kind of work should be regarded as 'employment under normal conditions'. A strict interpretation would be difficult to reconcile with the notions of reasonable accommodation and positive action as regards disability discrimination and would exclude people with disabilities in adapted or sheltered work from the concept of 'worker'.[90]

Some new forms of labour and non-standard work could also run the risk of not being covered by the concept of 'worker'. This was illustrated by the *Raulin* case in 1992. In that case the CJ had to decide on the question whether a worker employed under a so-called 'on-call' contract (sometimes also called 'zero-hours' contracts) can be regarded as a worker. Such a contract is a means of recruiting workers in sectors where the volume of work is subject to seasonal or other variations. Under such a contract, no guarantee is given as to the hours to be worked and, often, the person involved works only a few days a week or hours a day. The employer is held to pay wages and grant social advantages insofar as the worker has actually performed work. Such contracts normally mean that there is no obligation for employers to offer work, or for workers to accept it. The CJ did not exclude that workers under such an 'on-call' contract could be regarded as migrant workers within the meaning of the Treaty. However, it also said that the national court may, when assessing the effective and genuine nature of the activity in question, take account of the irregular nature and limited duration of the services actually performed under a contract for occasional employment. The fact that the person concerned worked only a very limited number of hours in a labour relationship may be an indication that the activities exercised are purely marginal and ancillary.[91]

---

88 Case C-316/13, *Fenoll*, EU:C:2015:200, paras. 38–40.

89 Case C-456/02, *Trojani,* EU:C:2004:488, para. 24; and Case C-316/13, *Fenoll*, EU:C:2015:200, para. 42.

90 See Article 5 Directive 2008/78/EC. See on this issue also C. O'Brien, 'Social Blind Spots and Monocular Policy Making: The ECJ's Migrant Worker Model' (2009) 46 *CML Rev*, 1129–1134. See recently on this issue the Opinion of Advocate General Mengozzi in Case C-316/13, *Fenoll*, EU:C:2014:1753, paras. 35–47.

91 Case C-357/89, *Raulin*, EU:C:1992:87, paras. 11–14.

4.3. THE DISTINCTION BETWEEN 'WORKER' AND 'SELF-EMPLOYED PERSON' AND INTERMEDIATE CATEGORIES

Another issue is the subordination criterion the CJ uses and which it defines as performing work 'under the direction of another person'.[92] This concept could mean that, when the element of subordination is missing, other new forms of labour might also fall outside the scope of the worker's concept. In particular, the borderline between employees and self-employed persons is not always easy to establish. However, from a legal point of view this distinction between these two categories of economically active migrant persons could be relevant. Indeed, for those who are qualified as self-employed service providers within the meaning of EU law, Member States may not apply restrictions to the free movement of services or the freedom of establishment by imposing upon them rules of labour law or employment protection, which could be seen as an obstacle to their free movement.[93] Moreover, Articles 49, 56 and 57 TFEU do not require, in contrast to Article 45 TFEU, the host Member State to guarantee these self-employed persons to draw an income from their activities equal to that of its own nationals. Such a requirement would be 'irreconcilable with the free movement of services and the free establishment, which implies the freedom of self-employed persons to offer their services as cheaply as they can afford'.[94] The distinction between workers and self-employed persons is also important to define the scope of EU competition law, which applies to 'undertakings' (as self-employed persons may be) but not to 'workers'.

In its recent judgment of 4 December 2014 the CJ recognised the issue of the borderline between workers and self-employed persons for the implementation of, in this case, EU competition law.[95] The CJ acknowledged that in today's economy it is not always easy to establish the status of some self-employed contractors as 'undertakings'. For the Court a service provider can lose the status of independent trader if he/she does not determine independently his/her own position on the market and is entirely dependent on his/her principal, because

92 Case 66/85, *Lawrie-Blum*, EU:C:1986:284, para. 17; Case C-413/01, *Ninni-Orasche*, EU:C:2003:600, para. 24; Case C-268/99, *Jany and Others*, EU:C:2001:616, para. 34; Joined Cases C-22/08 and C-23/08, *Vatsouras and Koupatantze*, EU:C:2009:344, para. 26; Case C-46/12, *L.N.*, EU:C:2013:97, para. 40; and Case C-270/13, *Haralambidis*, EU:C:2014:2185, para. 28.

93 T. van Peijpe, 'EU Limits for the Personal Scope of Employment Law' (2012) 3 *European Labour Law Journal*, 39 and 42. Compare Case C-398/95, *Ypourgos Ergasias*, EU:C:1997:282; and Case C-255/04, *Commission v France*, EU:C:2006:401.

94 T. van Peijpe, 'EU Limits for the Personal Scope of Employment Law' (2012) 3 *European Labour Law Journal*, 44.

95 Case C-413/13, *FNV Kunsten Informatie en Media*, EU:C:2014:2411, in particular paras. 32–39. In this case the CJ had to decide on the application of EU competition law on a collective labour agreement, fixing minimum fees for self-employed substitutes who provide services to orchestras under a work or service contract.

he/she does not bear any of the financial or commercial risks arising from the latter's activity and operates as an auxiliary within the principal's undertaking.[96] The CJ held that the classification of 'self-employed person' under national law does not prevent that person from being classified as an employee within the meaning of EU law if his/her independence is merely notional, thereby disguising an employment relationship.[97] It follows, for the Court, that the status of 'worker' within the meaning of EU law is not affected by the fact that a person has been hired as a self-employed person under national law, for tax, administrative or organisational reasons, as long as that persons acts under the direction of his/her employer as regards, in particular, his/her freedom to choose the time, place and content of his/her work,[98] does not share in the employer's commercial risks[99] and, for the duration of that relationship, forms an integral part of that employer's undertaking, so forming an economic unit with that undertaking.[100]

Earlier, in *Jany and Others*, the Court had already applied rather strict conditions for the qualification of a person as self-employed by mentioning three cumulative criteria, more specifically that the activity must be carried out: (a) by the person providing the service outside any relationship of subordination concerning the choice of that activity, working conditions and conditions of remuneration; (b) under that person's own responsibility; and (c) in return for remuneration paid to that person directly and in full.[101] If this person does not fulfil these criteria cumulatively, he/she can be classified as a 'false self-employed' person and fall under the definition of 'worker' to which the employment protection of the host Member States would become applicable. But the final judgment on the implementation of these criteria rests with the national courts, which, however, must take into account the criteria mentioned in the CJ's case-law.[102] They must ascertain that, apart from the legal nature of the work or service contract, the relationship of the persons involved with the principal concerned is not one of subordination during the contractual relationship, meaning that they enjoy more independence and flexibility as regards the determination of the working hours, the place and manner of performing the tasks assigned than employees performing the same activity.[103] The Court also

96 See also Case C-217/05, *Confederación Española de Empresarios de Estaciones de Servicio*, EU:C:2006:784, paras. 43–44; and Case C-355/06, *Van der Steen*, EU:C:2007:615, para. 24.

97 See also Case C-256/01, *Allonby*, EU:C:2004:18, para. 71.

98 See also Case C-256/01, *Allonby*, EU:C:2004:18, para. 72.

99 See also Case C-3/87, *Agegate*, EU:C:1989:650, para. 36.

100 See also Case C-22/98, *Becu and Others*, EU:C:1999:419, para. 26.

101 Case C-268/99, *Jany and Others*, EU:C:2001:616, para. 70.

102 Case C-161/07, *Commission v Austria*, EU:C:2008:759, para. 39; and Case C-393/10, *O'Brien*, EU:C:2012:110, para. 43.

103 See also Case C-232/09, *Danosa*, EU:C:2010:674, para. 47. With regard to a member of the board of directors of a capital company the CJ recently confirmed that 'it is necessary to consider the circumstances in which the board member was recruited; the nature of the

held that 'the sui generis legal nature of the employment relationship under national law cannot have any consequences in regard to whether or not the person is a worker for the purposes of European Union law'.[104]

To a certain extent this case-law would seem to take account of new forms of a-typical employment and could become an important instrument against the undermining of employment protection through bogus self-employment. Indeed, in the context of economic competition within the EU internal market there is a growing tendency among people to enhance their competitive position by using the self-employment status rather than the worker's status, thus avoiding or circumventing a Member State's employment protection. The latter could increase the costs of the 'service' performed and hence jeopardise the competitive position of the persons involved (service provider and/or principal).[105]

Still, this case-law sticks to the traditional binary divide between employment and self-employment, between subordinated labour and independent or autonomous work. However, this divide has proved inadequate to describe the economic and social reality of work today, more specifically in the case of the intermediate category of the so-called 'economically dependent workers' whose work falls within the grey area between dependent work and self-employment.[106] In some Member States the personal scope of provisions of national employment law are (partly) extended beyond the traditional category of workers, more specifically to workers who are not in a subordinate position but who are, nevertheless, dependent on a single principal or client for their income.[107] It remains unclear if such persons could be regarded as 'workers' within the

duties entrusted to that person; the context in which those duties were performed; the scope of the person's powers and the extent to which he or she was supervised within the company; and the circumstances under which the person could be removed' and concluded that in this case the board member was in a relationship of subordination *vis-à-vis* the company: see Case C-229/14, *Balkaya*, EU:C:2015:455, paras. 38–41.

104 Case C-428/09, *Union Syndicale Solidaires Isère*, EU:C:2010:612, para. 30. See also Case C-229/14, *Balkaya*, EU:C:2015:455, para. 36.

105 See for a recent account of such phenomena: F. Muller, 'Cross-border mobility of "bogus" self-employed workers: a lack of legal framework coupled with protection of economic rights' (2014) 5 *European Labour Law Journal*, 306–308.

106 F. Rosioru, 'Legal acknowledgment of the category of economically dependent workers' (2014) 5 *European Labour Law Journal*, 280 and 282.

107 T. Van Peijpe, 'EU Limits for the Personal Scope of Employment Law' (2012) 3 *European Labour Law Journal*, 50 and F. Rosioru, 'Legal acknowledgment of the category of economically dependent workers' (2014) 5 *European Labour Law Journal*, 288–292. These authors refers to *'Arbeiterähnliche Personen'* in Germany and *'Parasubordinati'* in Italy or comparable para-subordinate workers in several other Member States. See for an in-depth analysis of the application of the EU definition of 'worker' on the latter category: L. Nogler, 'Rethinking the *Laurie-Blum* Doctrine of Subordination: A Critical Analysis Prompted by Recent Developments in Italian Employment Law' (2010) 26 *International Journal of Comparative Labour Law and Industrial Relations*, 83–101. See also on this issue: C. Barnard, *EU Employment Law* (Oxford: OUP, 2012), 144–154.

meaning of EU law on the free movement of workers, which still adheres to the binary divide between workers and self-employed persons.

Moreover, the qualification of the migrant person as a 'worker' under EU law, only guarantees equal treatment with the national workers of the home State in terms of employment protection. But Member States remain autonomous as far as the definition of the personal scope of their employment law is concerned, and more specifically, they are free to determine the criteria to distinguish 'workers' from 'self-employed persons'.[108] Consequently, if under the domestic law of the host State the type of relationship between the 'worker' and his/her principal/ client is not regarded as an employment relationship (as it may be under the law of the home State), the employment protection of the host State may well be inapplicable. This was, albeit in a different context, illustrated by *Raccanelli*. In this judgment, the CJ implicitly acknowledged the possibility that a migrant researcher who concludes, under the same conditions as national researchers of the host State, a grant contract with a research institute, is not regarded as a 'worker' for the implementation of national employment and social security law of that State.[109]

4.4. 'POSTED WORKERS' ARE NOT 'MIGRANT WORKERS'

'Posted workers' are not 'migrant workers'. Indeed, the CJ decided that a posted employee of a cross-border service provider is not a worker within the meaning of Article 45 TFEU and Regulation 492/1011.[110] The fact that these workers are excluded from the application of the Treaty provision on the free movement of workers has fundamental legal consequences. The question as to which employment protection scheme these workers can take recourse should, for the Court, be answered on the basis of the principles underlying the free movement of services, more specifically the right of these employees' employer to provide his/her services in another Member State without distinction in terms of nationality and without any other obstacles. In this legal context the application of the labour legislation of the host country has been regarded as an obstacle to the free movement of services by the employer concerned. In

---

108 This power can be limited by EU law, as was illustrated in some cases before the CJ. The latter held that in France the presumption of salaried status imposed upon performing artists is a disadvantage that may impede their activities as service providers, in particularly when the artists in question are recognised as service providers in their home State (Case C-255/04, *Commission v France*, EU:C:2006:401). The Greek rules imposing a legal framework of employment contracts between tourist guides and tourism and travel agencies, were also found to be in breach of the freedom to provide services as a self-employed person (Case C-398/95, *Ypourgos Ergasias*, EU:C:1997:282).

109 Case C-94/07, *Raccanelli*, EU:C:2008:425.

110 Joined Cases C-49/98 *et seq.*, *Finalarte and Others*, EU:2001:564, paras. 22–23 and subsequently confirmed in further case-law.

principle, he/she should have the right to continue to apply the labour law of the country of origin to his employees. In that case the possible application of the employment protection of the host State, should, since it can be an obstacle to the free movement of services, be justified for reasons of public interest and be proportional to this purpose (the so-called *rule of reason*).[111]

Thus the application of Regulation 1612/68 (now Regulation 492/2011) and of the prohibition of discrimination on grounds of nationality with regard to the pay and working conditions of Article 7 of these regulations was rendered inoperative, despite the fact that the fifth recital to these regulations explicitly refers to workers 'who pursue their activities for the purpose of providing services'.[112] The European legislator filled in this gap by adopting the Posting of Workers Directive 96/71.[113] The PWD does not impose the application of all of the labour law provisions of the receiving State, but only of those provisions that constitute the core of mandatory provisions for minimum protection (the so-called hard core).[114]

However, the CJ was not very consistent in excluding posted workers from the scope of the law on free movement of workers. Indeed, in *Hudzinski* and *Wawrzyniak*[115] the Court held that posted workers could invoke the Treaty provisions on the free movement of workers (Articles 45 to 48 TFEU) to receive social benefits (in this case family benefits) from the host State. The reason for this was the unlimited income tax liability of the posted workers in the host State (Germany) and the fact that in that State family benefits are financed by income tax.[116]

---

111 See, *inter alia*, Case C-43/93, *Vander Elst*, EU:C:1994:310, paras. 14 *et seq.*; Case C-272/94, *Guiot*, EU:C:1996:147, paras. 10 *et seq.*; Joined Cases C-369/06 and C-374/96, *Arblade and Leloup*, EU:C:1999:575, paras. 33 *et seq.*; Joined Cases C-49/98 *et seq.*, *Finalarte and Others*, EU:2001:564, paras. 28 *et. seq.*; Case C-165/98, *Mazzoleni*, EU:C:2001:162, paras. 22 *et seq.*; Case C-164/99, *Portugaia*, EU:C:2002:40, paras. 16 *et seq.*; Case C-60/03, *Wolff & Müller*, EU:C:2004:610, paras. 31 *et seq.*; Case C-346/06, *Rüffert*, EU:C:2008:189, para. 37; and Case C-319/06, *Commission v Luxembourg*, EU:C:2008:350, paras. 42–43.

112 For a previous detailed analysis of this issue, see: H. Verschueren, 'Cross-Border Workers in the European Internal Market: Trojan Horses for Member States' Labour and Social Security Law?' (2008) 24 *International Journal of Comparative Labour Law and Industrial Relations*, 171–177.

113 Directive 96/71/EC of the European Parliament and of the Council of 16 December 1996 concerning the posting of workers in the framework of the provision of services, OJ 1998, L 18/1 (hereinafter referred to as 'PWD').

114 More specifically (see Article 3(1)): maximum work periods and minimum rest periods; minimum number of paid annual holidays; minimum wages; conditions for the posting of employees, in particular by temporary employment agencies; health, safety and hygiene in the workplace; protective measures for special groups of employees (pregnant women, youngsters); provisions regarding equal treatment and non-discrimination.

115 Joined Cases C-611/10 and C-612/10, *Hudzinski and Wawrzyniak*, EU:C:2012:339.

116 See more on the position of posted workers in the chapter of M. Houwerzijl and A. van Hoek elsewhere in this volume.

4.5. FIRST-TIME JOBSEEKERS

In contrast, jobseekers come within the scope of the EU provisions on the right of free movement for workers. Article 45(3) TFEU also entails a person's right to move to a Member State in order to seek employment there, as confirmed by the CJ in *Antonissen* as early as 1991.[117] In this judgment the CJ also held that after six months Member States may require proof that the person is continuing to seek employment and has genuine chances of being engaged.[118] This judgment was taken over in Directive 2004/38 which guarantees the right to reside after the initial period of three months without any condition (Article 6) as long as the first-time jobseekers produce evidence that 'they are continuing to seek employment and that they have a genuine chance of being engaged' (Article 14(4)(b)).

Moreover, in *Collins*, the Court not only held that nationals of a Member State seeking employment in another Member State fall within the scope of Article 39 EC (now Article 45 TFEU) on the right to free movement for workers and jobseekers, but also that, therefore, they have the right to equal treatment.[119] This right also applies to financial benefits intended to facilitate access to employment on the labour market of a Member State. The CJ confirmed this approach in its subsequent case-law.[120] It thereby followed a strict interpretation of the exception provided for in Article 24(2) of Directive 2004/38 to the right to equal treatment for social assistance for economically inactive EU citizens in the first three months of their residence or for the longer period of job seeking in accordance with Article 14(4)(b). However, the Court considered it legitimate for a Member State to grant such an allowance only after a genuine link between the jobseeker and the labour market of that Member State has been ascertained.[121] The existence of such a link can be more specifically determined by establishing that the person concerned has genuinely sought work in the Member State in question for a reasonable period.[122] The Court has also acknowledged that residence within a Member State, and even family ties, could also ensure a real connection with the labour market of the host Member State.[123] So, an economically inactive person, such as a jobseeker, coming to a Member State

117 Case C-292/89, *Antonissen*, EU:C:1991:80. See also Articles 1–6 of Regulation 495/2011.

118 Case C-292/89, *Antonissen*, EU:C:1991:80, para. 21.

119 Case C-138/02, *Collins*, EU:C:2004:172, para. 56. The CJ overruled hereby its previous case-law in *Lebon*: Case 318/85, *Lebon*, EU:C:1987:302.

120 Case C-258/04, *Ioannidis*, EU:C:2005:559; Joined Cases C-22/08 and C-23/08, *Vatsouras and Koupatantze*, EU:C:2009:344, paras. 36–37; and Case C-367/11, *Prete*, EU:C:2012:668, para. 25.

121 Case C-138/02, *Collins*, EU:C:2004:172, para. 69; Case C-224/98, *D'Hoop*, para. 38; Case C-258/04, *Ioannidis*, para. 30; and Case C-367/11, *Prete*, EU:C:2012:668, para. 33.

122 Case C-138/02, *Collins*, EU:C:2004:172, para. 70; Joined Cases C-22/08 and C-23/08, *Vatsouras and Koupatantze*, EU:C:2009:344, paras. 38–39; and Case C-367/11, *Prete*, EU:C:2012:668, para. 46.

123 Case C-367/11, *Prete*, EU:C:2012:668, paras. 47–48. See also the opinion of Advocate General Wathelet in Case C-47/14, *Alimanovic*, EU:C:2015:210, para. 109.

with the intention of looking for a job may, when a sufficient link with the host Member State is present, invoke *vis-à-vis* that Member State provisions with regard to the prohibition of discrimination on grounds of nationality which were initially aimed at workers. This right to equal treatment can also refer to a social minimum benefit as in *Collins*, which concerned the means-tested jobseekers allowance in the UK, or in *Vatsouras* and *Koupatantze*, which concerned a dispute with regard to a German basic benefit in favour of jobseekers.

Yet first-time jobseekers are not fully equated with economically active Union citizens. Indeed, their right to reside depends on them providing evidence that they are continuing to seek employment and that they have a genuine chance of being engaged (Article 14(4)(b) of Directive 2004/38), in the absence of which their right to reside is subject, like for other economically inactive Union citizens, to them having sufficient resources. In addition, during this period they cannot claim equal treatment for social assistance in the host State. They have a Janus-faced status,[124] being on the one hand still considered as 'economically inactive', but benefitting from rights that normally belong to economically active EU citizens on the other. However, the debate on the type of benefits they could claim continues.[125] Furthermore, it is not always crystal clear how to determine whether a jobseeker has 'genuine chances of being engaged' or has a sufficient link with the host Member State's employment market,[126] which surely leads to disputable interpretations of this requirement.

4.6. RETENTION OF THE 'WORKER' STATUS

In certain circumstances an EU citizen can retain, *vis-à-vis* the Member States in which the citizen concerned had previously exercised economic activities, his/her status as an employee or self-employed person and the advantages linked to this status. This is confirmed in Article 7(3) Directive 2004/38, more specifically in the case where the Union citizen is temporarily unable to work as a result of illness or accident, or is in duly recorded involuntary unemployment[127]

---

124 F. Wollenschläger, 'The judiciary, the legislature and the evolution of Union citizenship', in P. Syrpis (ed.), *The judiciary, the legislature and the EU internal market* (Cambridge: CUP, 2012), 315 *et seq.*

125 See also Case C-67/14, *Alimanovic*, EU:C:2015:597.

126 D. Thym, 'The elusive limits of solidarity: residence rights of and social benefits for economically inactive Union citizens' (2015) 52 *CML Rev*, 42. See for an overview of the implementation of these rules by the Member States: F. Wollenschläger, 'Jobseekers' Residence Rights and Access to Social Benefits: EU law and its Implementation in the Member States' (2014) *Online Journal on Free Movement of Workers*, issue 7, 11–15.

127 The worker must have been employed for more than one year and register as a jobseeker with the relevant employment office. If he/she is in duly recorded involuntary unemployment after completing a fixed-term employment contract of less than a year or after having become involuntarily unemployed during the first twelve months, the status of worker shall be retained for no less than six months. This means that the host State is not obliged to consider

or embarks on vocational training.[128] In these circumstances the person concerned does not only retain the right to reside in the host State, but, on the basis of Article 24(1) of Directive 2004/38, can also claim the same treatment as the nationals of this host country with regard to all kinds of social benefits, including study finance grants for persons undergoing vocational training. Their family members can also rely indirectly on that status of 'worker'.

Moreover, the CJ has recently confirmed that the list in Article 7(3) of Directive 2004/38 containing the circumstances in which migrant workers who are no longer in an employment relationship may nevertheless continue to benefit from that status is not exhaustive. In *Saint-Prix*, the Court stated that a woman who gives up work or gives up seeking work because of the physical constraints of the late stages of pregnancy and the aftermath of childbirth retains the status of 'worker' within the meaning of Article 45 TFEU, provided she returns to work or finds a job within a reasonable period after the birth of the child.[129] The persons involved did not qualify for the retention of the worker's status under the circumstances covered by Article 7(3) of Directive 2004/38. This judgment is in line with the CJ's previous case-law which stated that the concept of 'worker' must not be interpreted narrowly and, as the AG submitted in this case, in accordance with the principle of prohibition of discrimination on grounds of sex.[130]

Therefore, being economically active does not appear to be an absolute prerequisite for entitlement to equal treatment with workers in the host State. Those who find themselves in an intermediate situation because they are (temporarily) unemployed or have started vocational training remain covered by the provisions applicable to migrant workers. However, this is not always true, as in the case of a voluntarily unemployed person who embarks on a training course which is not related to his/her previous employment. In addition, a number of situations are not (yet) explicitly covered by legislation or case-law, such as in the case of temporary interruption of the employment for caring obligations.[131] The implementation of the conditions for retaining the worker's status under Article 7(3) of Directive 2004/38 might also give rise to uncertainties and

---

him/her as a worker within the meaning of Directive 2004/38 after this period of six months. From the moment this person no longer enjoys that status, he/she will be considered as a first-time jobseeker under Article 14(4)(b) of Directive 2004/38 (see Case C-67/14, *Alimanovic*, EU:C:2015:597). Such a time limit may not be applied if the employment has lasted for more than one year.

128 Unless the person involved is involuntarily unemployed, the retention of the status of worker shall require the training to be related to the previous employment (Article 7(3)(d)). This provision was inspired by the case-law of the Court of Justice: see for instance Case 39/86, *Lair*, EU:C:1988:320; and Case C-413/01, *Ninni-Orasche*, EU:C:2003:600.

129 Case C-507/12, *Saint-Prix*, EU:C:2014:2007.

130 Opinion of Advocate General Wahl in Case C-507/12, *Saint-Prix*, EU:2013:841, paras. 33–35.

131 C. O'Brien, 'Social Blind Spots and Monocular Policy Making: The ECJ's Migrant Worker Model' (2009) 46 *CML Rev*, 1120–1123.

gaps or even inconsistencies. For instance, it remains unclear how one should determine the temporary nature of the interruption of the economic activity as a result of illness or accident or the extent to which a training course is sufficiently related to a person's previous employment. Some Member States have detailed provisions regarding the steps a person must take and the conditions they must fulfil in order to be 'duly' registered with an employment office. Moreover, the concept of being 'involuntarily unemployed' may lead to discussions as to under which circumstances the unemployment should be regarded as 'involuntary',[132] for instance when the unemployed person has rejected job offers from the employment services.[133] And what if the unemployed person did not register with the public unemployment agencies? Some Member States follow a strict interpretation of these provisions on the retention of the worker's status, thus limiting the right of EU migrants.[134] The required link between the training course and the previous employment in the case of voluntary unemployment also seems to be at odds with the 'rhetoric about occupational mobility'.[135]

Such strict interpretations may even lead to paradoxical situations. Under Article 7(3)(c) of Directive 2004/38 a worker who has become unemployed during the first twelve months of employment in the host State, may lose his/her status after six months of unemployment. Still, he/she may continue to be entitled to an unemployment benefit of the host State (pursuant to national law in combination with the provisions of social security Regulation 833/2004). Yet some Member States, such as Belgium, have taken expulsion measures against these persons. However, in such a situation they should continue to have to right to reside in the host State since they have sufficient resources not to become a burden on the social assistance system of the host State. Indeed, unemployment benefits are not social assistance benefits within the meaning of Directive 2004/38.[136] Moreover, jobseekers may not be expelled as long as they provide evidence that 'they are continuing to seek employment and that they have a genuine chance of being engaged' (Article 14(4)(b) of Directive 2004/38). In addition, expulsion would also lead to the loss of the unemployment benefit, since Regulation 883/2004 submits the retention of such a benefit to the residence in the competent Member State (Article 64). An expulsion measure would therefore have disproportional consequences for the persons involved and undermine the *effet utile* of Regulation 883/2004.

---

132 See also Case C-171/95, *Tetik*, EU:C:1997:31, paras. 38–39.

133 S. Mantu, 'Protecting EU workers in case of involuntary unemployment: retention of worker status' (2014) *Online Journal on Free Movement of Workers*, issue 7, 20–21.

134 S. Mantu, 'Protecting EU workers in case of involuntary unemployment: retention of worker status' (2014) *Online Journal on Free Movement of Workers*, issue 7, 20–24.

135 C. O'Brien, 'Social Blind spots and Monocular Policy Making: The ECJ's Migrant Worker Model' (2009) 46 *CML Rev*, 1126.

136 Joined Cases C-22/08 and C-23/08, *Vatsouras and Koupatantze*, EU:C:2009:344. See on the definition of 'social assistance': Case C-140/12, *Brey*, EU:C:2013:565, para. 61; and Case C-333/13, *Dano*, EU:C:2014:2359, para. 63.

5. IS BEING A 'WORKER' ALWAYS SUFFICIENT FOR ENTITLEMENT TO EQUAL TREATMENT?

The above analysis demonstrates that, despite the introduction of European citizenship, including for economically inactive persons, and the problems linked to the delineation of the concept of 'worker', exercising or having exercised an economic activity in another Member State, remains of paramount importance for the definition of the rights of EU migrants.

Yet there seem to be some cracks in the wall. Indeed, in more recent case-law the CJ seems to depart from the mechanical application of the equal treatment provisions concerning migrant workers' claims for social benefits. In *Geven*, the Court had to rule on the refusal of the competent German authorities to grant a child-raising allowance to a Dutch national who resided in the Netherlands and worked between three and 14 hours a week in Germany. The CJ did not contradict the national court's contention that Ms G.even had to be regarded as a worker within the meaning of Article 45 TFEU. Still, the Court accepted as appropriate the justification according to which the measure was intended to encourage the birth rate in Germany and that the benefit could be limited to migrant workers having a sufficient link with Germany. For the CJ, the fact that a non-resident worker does not have a sufficiently substantial occupation in the Member State concerned may constitute a legitimate justification for refusing to grant the child-raising allowance.[137]

More recently, in *Commission v Netherlands*,[138] the CJ confirmed that 'as regards migrant workers and frontier workers, the fact that they have participated in the employment market of a Member State establishes, *in principle*, a sufficient link of integration with the society of that Member State, allowing them to benefit from the principle of equal treatment, as compared with national workers, as regards social advantages' (para. 65; emphasis added). It continued that 'the link of integration arises from, inter alia, the fact that, through the taxes which he pays in the host Member State by virtue of his employment, the migrant worker also contributes to the financing of the social

---

137 Case C-213/05, *Geven*, EU:C:2007:438, para. 26. See also the reference to 'an occupation of more than minor extent' in Case C-212/05, *Hartmann*, EU:C:2007:437, para. 35. For a critical comment: C. O' Brien, 'Case C-212/05 Gertraud Hartmann v Freistaat Bayern; Case C-213/05 Wendy Geven v Land Nordrhein Westfalen; Case C-287/05 D.P.W. Hendrix v Raad van Bestuur van het Uitvoeringsinstituut Werknemersverzekeringen' (2008) 45 *CML Rev*, 499–514; S. O'Leary, 'Developing an Ever Closer Union between the Peoples of Europe? A Reappraisal of the Case Law of the Court of Justice on the Free Movement of Persons and EU Citizenship' (2008) *Yearbook of European Law*, 167–193; and P. Ploscar, *The Principle of Solidarity in EU Internal Market Law* (PhD, Department of Law, University of Antwerp, 2014), 237–240 and 317–318.

138 This was a case on the exportability of study grants finance for children of migrant workers which was subject to a condition of having been lawfully resident in the Netherlands during at least three out of the six years prior to enrolment.

policies of that State and should profit from them under the same conditions as national workers' (para. 66).

This position was repeated in *Caves Krier* and in *Giersch*.[139] In the latter judgment, which dealt with the residence clause in Luxembourg for the entitlement to study grants applied to children of a frontier migrant worker studying in another Member State, the CJ stated that 'with regard *inter alia* to frontier workers, the Court has allowed certain grounds of justification concerning legislation which distinguishes between residents and non-residents carrying out a professional activity in the State concerned, depending on the extent of their integration in the society of that Member State or their attachment to that State' (para. 64, emphasis added).[140] The CJ continued that a 'frontier worker is not always integrated in the Member State of employment in the same way as a worker who is resident in that Member State' (para. 65). The CJ suggested that Luxembourg could make the entitlement to a study loan or the non-reimbursement thereof subject to the condition that the students would return to that State after their studies (para. 79). It also stated that 'in order to avoid the risk of "study grant forum shopping", and to ensure that the frontier worker who is a taxpayer and who makes social security contributions in Luxembourg has a sufficient link with Luxembourg society, the financial aid could be made conditional on the frontier worker, the parent of the student who does not reside in Luxembourg, having worked in that Member State for a certain minimum period of time'. For the determination of that period the CJ referred to the five years' period laid down in Article 24(2) of Directive 2004/38 for maintenance aid for studies for economically inactive EU citizens.[141]

One may wonder whether the judgment in *Giersch* can be explained by the exceptional geographical position of Luxemburg, where approximately 70% of the work force is composed of frontier or migrant workers,[142] but it does not stand alone. Together with the other just mentioned rulings it constitutes a worrying departure from previous case-law on migrant workers and their rights *vis-à-vis* the State in which they are employed. Indeed, the CJ seems to indicate that migrant workers can no longer in all circumstances claim equal treatment in the Member State where they work and first have to demonstrate sufficient integration into the society of the host Member State before they can claim such a right. According to the CJ the mere fact of being economically active would

139 Case C-379/11, *Caves Krier*, EU:C:2012:798, para. 53; and Case C-20/12, *Giersch*, EU:C:2013:411, para. 63.

140 The CJ referred to earlier case-law in which it had already hinted at such a conclusion: Case C-212/05, *Hartmann*, EU:C:2007:437, para. 35; Case C-213/05, *Geven*, EU:C:2007:438, para. 26; and Case C-287/05, *Hendrix*, EU:C:2007:494, paras. 54–55.

141 Case C-20/12, *Giersch*, EU:C:2013:411, paras. 65–80. After this judgment the Luxembourg legislation was amended along this suggestion of the Court: S. O'Leary, 'The curious case of frontier workers and study finance: *Giersch*' (2014) 51 *CML Rev*, 617–618.

142 S. O'Leary, 'The curious case of frontier workers and study finance: *Giersch*' (2014) 51 *CML Rev*, 618–619.

seem 'in principle' only a sufficient element of integration. However, it appears to be a rebuttable presumption, or in *Giersch* even an opposite presumption, that frontier workers are not always sufficiently integrated into the Member State of employment.[143] Since the degree of integration might influence the implementation of the right to equal treatment, equal treatment seems no longer a means to integration.[144] The CJ seems to have introduced the 'integration model' it adopts in its case-law on economically inactive EU citizens[145] into its judgments on migrant workers, thus giving up the 'assimilation' model it previously accepted. Just being economically active might not be enough any longer. Either the occupation should be substantial or the migrant worker should have paid taxes or contributed to the financing of social security, or even have worked in the host State for a certain period more specifically up to five years as suggested in *Giersch*.

However, this case-law raises a number of questions. What if the migrant worker does not pay taxes in the host Member State (for instance because under the applicable bilateral tax agreement he/she pays taxes elsewhere) or is only liable to a small amount of taxes due to his/her low income or tax relief. And what if the migrant worker is not paying social security contributions in the Member State of employment because of Regulation 883/2004? The latter is for instance the case with frontier workers who work part-time in their home State and part-time in the neighbouring Member State. According to Article 13(1)(a) of this Regulation they are only subject to the social security legislation of the home State, including for their activities in the neighbouring host State. The reference in *Giersch* to the five years' residence condition in Article 24(2) of Directive 2004/38 as a source of inspiration for allowing a prior period of five years' employment in the host State before the frontier worker would be entitled to maintenance grants for his/her children, is particularly disquieting. In paragraph 80 of this judgment, the CJ almost literally took over the wording of this provision, but omitted to quote the final wording thereof, which says that it only applies to 'persons other than workers, self-employed persons, persons who retain such status and members of their families'. And why five years and not four or six or even ten? It also contrasts with earlier case-law in which the CJ rejected a condition linked to the duration of the work performed by the migrant worker.[146]

This case-law would amount to a spill-over of the 'genuine link' requirement, which the CJ has so far only applied to economically inactive migrants, and

143 S. O'Leary, 'The curious case of frontier workers and study finance: *Giersch*' (2014) 51 *CML Rev*, 610.

144 As stated in Joined Cases 389/87 and 390/87, *Echternach and Moritz*, EU:C:1989:130, para. 35.

145 D. Thym 'The elusive limits of solidarity: residence rights of and social benefits for economically inactive Union citizens' (2015) 52 *CML Rev*, 21, 36–37.

146 Case 39/86, *Lair*, EU:C:1988:32, para. 42; and Case 197/86, *Brown*, EU:C:1988:323, para. 22.

despite the fact that the CJ in *Commission v Netherlands* explicitly stated that the case-law on economically inactive EU migrants should not be applied to migrant workers.[147] The CJ seems to have (partially) given up the main distinction with regard to the prohibition of discrimination on grounds of nationality between citizens who can rely on the exercise of an economic activity (by themselves or by family members) and those who cannot. Some scholars submitted that the Court did not respect the boundaries between its case-law on workers and its case-law on citizenship.[148] Others called this 'cross-pollination' between the free movement of citizens and workers.[149] Anyway, this case-law threatens to introduce the problems of interpretation and implementation of the 'genuine link' requirement into the domain of free movement of workers. It adds to these difficulties the question of how to draw the line between the various categories of migrant workers (such as frontier workers), and how to take account of the nature of the benefits claimed or of the category of beneficiaries (such as benefits for family members).[150] It remains to be seen if the CJ will continue in this vein in its future case-law. However, we can predict that Member States will use the opportunities offered by this kind of case-law to limit the rights of EU migrant workers.

6. CONCLUSION

Despite the introduction of EU citizenship, including for economically inactive persons, those who are economically active continue to enjoy a stronger legal position under EU law compared to the rights of inactive persons. Being economically active clearly still matters. Mere citizenship continues to be a residual, inferior status. This demonstrates the resilience of the EU's market integration rationale and the dominance of 'mercantile' citizenship.[151]

It therefore remains to be important to be qualified as an 'economically active' migrant. However, the above analysis shows that the so-called 'autonomous'

---

147 Case C-542/09, *Commission v Netherlands*, EU:C:2012:346, paras. 58–67.

148 E. Guild, S. Peers, and J. Tomkin, *The EU Citizenship Directive* (Oxford: OUP, 2014), 227.

149 P. Ploscar, *The Principle of Solidarity in EU Internal Market Law* (PhD, Department of Law, University of Antwerp, 2014), 237–240.

150 F. De Witte, 'Who funds the mobile student? Shedding some light on the normative assumptions underlying EU free movement law: *Commission v Netherlands*' (2013) 50 *CML Rev*, 210–212.

151 See for a recent analysis: C. O'Brien, 'I Trade, Therefore I Am: Legal Personhood in the European Union' (2013) 50 *CML Rev*, 1643–1684. See also F. De Witte, 'Transnational Solidarity and Conflicts of Justice' (2012) 18 *ELJ*, 705–706; N. Nic Shuibhne, 'The Resilience of EU Market Citizenship' (2010) 47 *CML Rev*, 1597–1628; P. Ploscar, *The Principle of Solidarity in EU Internal Market Law* (PhD, Department of Law, University of Antwerp, 2014), 241–242; and D. Schiek, *Economic and Social Integration. The Challenge for EU Constitutional Law* (Cheltenham: Edward Elgar, 2012), 48–49.

meaning of the concept of 'worker' is unclear. The borderline between the categories of active and inactive EU citizens is still rather messy and subject to discussion and doubts, resulting in unpredictable qualifications and creating inconsistencies in the implementation by the Member States, their judiciary and even the Court of Justice. It does not take sufficient account of new forms of non-standard labour and of 'work' that does not fall under the EU definition of this concept, such as care work.[152] This has been partially solved by the creation of intermediate situations, such as those in which the status of 'worker' is retained or that of first-time jobseeker, the latter having, however, a limited number of rights. Still, even these positions are characterised by patchy definitions and disputable borderlines which may once again lead to various interpretations by the Member States and their judiciary, often strict ones intended to restrict the rights of the EU migrants concerned. In addition, this case-law sticks to the traditional binary divide between employment and self-employment, between subordinated labour and independent or autonomous work. As a consequence, it overlooks the economic and social reality of work today, more specifically in the case of the intermediate category of the so-called 'economically dependent workers' whose work falls within the grey area between dependent work and self-employment.

Moreover, even the status of economically active EU migrants does not guarantee full rights in the host State. Recent case-law seems to depart from the previous, almost mechanical, application of the right to equal treatment and to submit the economically active EU migrants to a 'genuine link' test as well, a test which is not always considered to be fulfilled, not even by those who qualify as 'workers'. This will undoubtedly induce Member States not only to implement the rights of migrant workers strictly, but also to support proposals to amend EU law with a view to limiting the rights of migrant workers who are not yet considered to be sufficiently integrated into the host Member State's society or of those not residing in that State, more specifically their family members.[153] Where do I belong remains a question to be answered, including for economically active EU migrants.

---

152 C. O'Brien, 'Social Blind Spots and Monocular Policy Making: The ECJ's Migrant Worker Model' (2009) 46 *CML Rev*, 1115, 1118, 1135–1136.

153 As happened in the context of the UK 'renegotiation' of its EU membership. See on the issue more in the chapter of J. Shaw in this volume.

CHAPTER 11

WHERE DO EU MOBILE WORKERS BELONG, ACCORDING TO ROME I AND THE (E)PWD?

Aukje van Hoek and Mijke Houwerzijl

1. INTRODUCTION

In this chapter we critically analyse criteria and concepts used by the EU legislator and the Court of Justice (CJ) in order to establish the place(s) where mobile EU workers 'belong' in relation to their labour law entitlements.[1] In this context the term 'belonging' refers to the fact that the mobile worker is included in the group that is covered by a given national system of labour law – either fully or partially. They are beneficiaries thereof and bound by it. Because of the private law character of the employment contract between employer and employee, the rules of private international law (PIL) play a central role in deciding which law applies to a given labour relationship with transnational elements. Nowadays, the law applicable to an employment contract is determined in all EU Member States by the PIL rules contained in Article 8 and 9 of the Rome I Regulation.[2]

---

1 This contribution draws on a combination of earlier work, in particular: A.A.H. van Hoek, 'Private international law: an appropriate means to regulate transnational employment in the European Union?' (2014) 3 *Erasmus Law Review*, 157–169; M.S. Houwerzijl, '"Regime shopping" across (blurring) boundaries', in S. Evju (ed.), *Regulating Transnational Labour in Europe: The quandaries of multilevel governance* (Oslo: Institut for privatrett, Skriftserie 196, 2014), 95–130 and A.A.H. van Hoek and M.S. Houwerzijl, '"Posting" and "posted workers" – The need for clear definitions of two key concepts of the Posting of Workers Directive', in C. Barnard, M. Gehring and I. Solanke (eds.), *Cambridge Yearbook of European Legal Studies* (Oxford: Hart Publishing, 2012), 419–451.

2 Regulation (EC) No. 593/2008 on the law applicable to contractual obligations (Rome I), OJ 2008, L 177/6 (hereinafter referred to as 'Rome I'). For the UK, see Commission Decision of 22 December 2008 on the request from the United Kingdom to accept Regulation (EC) No. 593/2008 of the European Parliament and the Council on the law applicable to contractual obligations (Rome I) (notified under document number C(2008) 8554) OJ 2009 L 10/22). Denmark is party to the Rome Convention of 1980, OJ 1998, C 27/34 (consolidated version). It should be noted though, that in the UK and the Scandinavian countries the law applying to the contract may have only a limited relevance for the actual protection of the

Additionally, the Posting of Workers Directive[3] (PWD) is of relevance in the specific situation of cross-border posting of workers. We will examine these legal instruments and their interpretation by the CJ from the perspective of 'belonging': why do the conflicts rules attribute a situation to the law of country A rather than country B? What underlying system of ordering is at work here? As will be shown, both in (the interpretation of) the relevant provisions of Rome I and in the PWD, several lines of ordering are visible, informed by the specific goals of labour law. These ordering lines may carry with them different types of 'belonging', attributing workers to legal systems on the basis of the territory and/or the branch of industry in which the work is performed, or the organisational framework of the employing company.

Our analysis is based on the assumption that both Rome I and the (E)PWD[4] may be seen as tools to strike a balance between the types of 'belonging' involved, in situations where this is necessary because they do not lead to the same applicable law. Striking the most suitable balance is not a 'static' exercise but rather an ongoing game where different weight may be given to the distinct lines of ordering depending on the specific circumstances of the individual case. The 'right' balance may also change over time in order to adapt to new political compromises and/or developments in society. In respect of the latter, it may be questioned whether in transnational employment relationships, based on the 'search of cheap labour' across the EU, the rules of Rome I and the (E)PWD still succeed in their aim to designate (together) the most suitable place(s) of belonging – and hence applicable labour law(s). The new European Commission led by Juncker seems to give a negative answer to this topical question, as regards the PWD, since a 'targeted review' of this Directive is part of its political priorities.[5] This then raises the question which adjustments could or should be made in order to restore the balance? We will reflect on this issue

---

worker. This is due to the special status of statutory protection in the UK and of collective agreements in the Scandinavian countries. See for the UK: U. Grušić, *The European Private International Law of Employment* (Cambridge: CUP, 2015), 13 and 179 *et seq.*; U. Grušić, 'The Territorial Scope of Employment Legislation and Choice of Law' (2012) 75 *Modern Law Review*, 722–751; L. Merrett, *Employment Contracts in Private International Law* (Oxford: OUP, 2011), 242 *et seq.*; and L. Merrett. 'The Extra-Territorial Reach of Employment Legislation' (2010) 4 *Industrial Law Journal*, 355–381.

3 Directive 96/71/EC concerning the posting of workers in the framework of the provision of services, OJ 1997 L 18/1 (hereinafter referred to as 'PWD').

4 'EPWD' refers to Directive 67/2014/EU on the enforcement of Directive 96/71/EC concerning the posting of workers in the framework of the provision of services and amending Regulation (EU) No. 1024/2012 on administrative cooperation through the Internal Market Information System ('the IMI Regulation'), OJ 2014 L 159/11.

5 Jean-Claude Juncker, 'Political guidelines for the next European Commission', available at http://ec.europa.eu/priorities/docs/pg_en.pdf, p. 12. On 8 March 2016 the official proposal was published. See COM (2016) 128 final. On 10 May 2016, parliamentary chambers from eleven EU Member States drew a 'yellow card', forcing the Commission to reconsider its proposal. These developments are not discussed below, since the text of this chapter was finalised in 2015.

towards the end of our chapter, taking into account the emerging discussion in academic literature about (the need for) 'transnational solidarity' based on European citizenship versus traditional notions of 'working-class solidarity', institutionalised in systems of national labour law.

We will start with a brief explanation of the ordering lines and 'types of belonging' that may underpin the formulation and interpretation of choice of law rules (section 2), followed by an overview of the relevant legal instruments for determining the applicable labour law in the EU context of free movement (section 3). Here, we also give our understanding of the interaction between Rome I and the PWD. Then, we turn to the (implications of the) relevant connecting factors enshrined in these legal instruments. We will look in particular at the way these factors operate in different situations of cross-border labour mobility within the EU (sections 4–8). Where apt, this will include discussing the goals behind the legal rules such as worker protection, legal certainty, '*Gleichlauf*', furthering fair competition and enhancing the free provision of services. Matters of compliance and enforcement will be touched upon in sections 8–9. Section 10 concludes.

2. LINES OF ORDERING AND TYPES OF 'BELONGING'

In the Rome I Regulation the individual contract of employment is treated as a weaker party contract. The choice of law rules of the Savignian system on which the Rome I Regulation is based aim to 'bring home' the international contract to the legal system in which it belongs.[6] But the special rules for contracts of employment contained in Article 8 thereof also aim to offer adequate protection to the individual worker. They do so *inter alia* by protecting the worker against a choice of law imposed by the employer (see below). However, it is not self-evident that the individual labour relationship with cross-border elements should be treated – purely – as a contract.[7] In many EU Member States, labour law is and was to a large extent public order legislation. Its purpose is largely regulatory –

6 See for example U. Grušić, *The European Private International Law of Employment* (Cambridge: CUP, 2015), 54: 'in other words, the protection of employees in private international law is primarily about finding and protecting the labour law system of the country or countries to which the employee "belongs", in whose labour market(s) he or she participates.'

7 I. Szaszy declared private international law to be unfit to deal with labour law. In the Netherlands, Koopmans was of a similar opinion. See T. Koopmans, *De internationaalrechtelijke aspecten van de arbeidsovereenkomst* (Baarn: Hollandia BV, 1966) and I. Szaszy, *International Labour Law. A comparative survey of the conflict rules affecting labour legislation and regulation* (Leiden: A.W. Sijthoff, 1968). This was however, fiercely opposed by Gamillschegg, one of the great spokesmen in favour of the contractual approach to employment: see F. Gamillscheg, *Internationales Arbeitsrecht (Arbeitsverweisungsrecht),*

it 'polices' the contract.[8] An important aspect of this regulatory function is that mandatory labour protection restricts competition based on differences in labour conditions, both between (groups of) workers amongst themselves and between employers, in their role of providers of goods and services. In the transnational context the term 'social dumping' may refer to both types of competition.[9] The regulatory goal of many labour law rules influences the scope of application thereof, often leading to territorial application. This territoriality is most often linked to the place of work, but can also be based on competition rationales – the decisive factor in that case being whether the contract affects competition between workers on the labour market or between providers of (goods and) services on the national markets. From another perspective the regulatory element of employment law can be seen as relating to the internal functioning of the undertaking. The worker becomes part of an organisation in which specific rules apply. Within this perspective, being embedded in the organisational structure of the undertaking, the *'Eingliederung'*, becomes the prominent characteristic of the employment contract and the location of the undertaking the relevant connecting factor.

These two lines of ordering, (1a) based on labour market competition, (1b) competition between providers of goods and services[10] and (2) based on organisational framework of the undertaking, are mirrored in the law and

---

Beiträge zum ausländischen und internationalen Privatrecht nr 27 (Berlin-Tübingen: Max-Planck-Institut für ausländisches und internationales Privatrecht, 1959).

8 The French term for such overriding mandatory provision with a territorial character is *'lois de police'*. See *inter alia* P. Mayer and V. Heuzé, *Droit International Privé* (Issy-les-Moulineaux: LGDJ, 2014), 99 and R. Callsen, *'Eingriffsnormen und Ordre public-Vorbehalt im Internationalen Arbeitsrecht – Ein deutsch-französicher Vergleich'*, Dissertation in internationaler Doppelbetreuung zur Erlangung des Dr. iur. Vorgelegt und öffentlich verteidigt am 13/12/2013 in Nanterre. See more in general on the regulatory function of private law in the EU *inter alia* H.W. Micklitz, 'Social Justice and Access Justice in Private Law' (2011) 2 *European University Institute Working Papers.* On the regulatory function of the choice of law rules in this area, see *inter alia* U. Grušić, *The European Private International Law of Employment* (Cambridge: CUP, 2015), 9, who refers to collective, public and systemic interests taking their place besides the interests of the parties to the contract.

9 See on the term 'social dumping' e.g. L.E. Berntsen, *Breaking the law? Varieties of social dumping in a pan-European labour market. Market expansion and social dumping in Europe* (London: Routledge, 2015); C. Barnard, 'Fifty Years of Avoiding Social Dumping? The EU's Economic and not so Economic Constitution', in M. Dougan and S. Currie (eds.), *50 Years of the European Treaties. Looking Back and Thinking Forward* (London: Hart Publishing, 2009); C. Joerges and F. Rödl, 'Informal Politics, Formalised Law and the Social Deficit' of European Integration: Reflections after the Judgments of the ECJ in Viking and Laval' (2009) 15 *ELJ.*

10 Within countries the line of ordering under 1a explains the system of extension of collective labour agreements; in the transnational context it is the rationale behind the equal treatment requisite in Article 157 TFEU (see judgment Case 43/75, *Defrenne*, EU:C:1976:56) and Article 45 TFEU (see judgment in Case 167/73, *Commission v France*, EU:C:1974:35). The main example of the line of ordering under 1b is the regulation of 'posting in *strictu sensu*' – see judgments Case C-113/89, *Rush Portuguesa*, EU:C:1990:142; and Case C-43/93, *Vander Elst*, EU:C:1994:310. Both distinct sublines have in common their aim to (partially) prevent

practice of collective negotiations where collective labour agreements may organise the entire labour force within a given territory, specific professions, specific sectors of the economy or a specific undertaking/company. Each of these may carry with them different types of 'belonging'. Finally, if labour law is taken as part of the fabric of the social welfare state, belonging may take on yet another meaning – (3) 'belonging' being determined by inclusion in the system of taxes and social security premiums. This interaction is very relevant in systems, as in most EU Member States, in which (collective) labour law protection and the social security and tax system form an inseparable whole. For instance, dismissal law protection and unemployment benefit schemes are often closely aligned. The same is true for rules on disability pensions and employer's liability for accidents at work.

So, in relation to the rationale behind PIL rules of bringing home the individual contract (while taking into account the weaker position of the individual worker), we distinguish three lines of ordering (informed by the specific goals of labour law), which may impact on the choice of connecting factors, which in turn determine applicable law. In (the interpretation of) the relevant provisions of Rome I and the PWD these different lines of ordering are visible, as will be shown below.

3. OVERVIEW OF THE RELEVANT LEGAL INSTRUMENTS AND THEIR INTERACTION

In the European Union, labour mobility and migration is part of the internal market. Both migration of workers and temporary posting of workers in the context of the cross-border provision of services are protected under the Treaty on the Functioning of the EU (TFEU). If EU nationals qualify as employees, they may move to another Member State for work by using their right enshrined in Article 45 TFEU. Employers based in the EU who post their employees to another Member State, may rely on Article 56 TFEU.

The right to free movement within the EU implies that administrative controls on (labour) migration are abolished. In contrast to situations of migration from third countries, rules of (national or European) migration law are not applicable to intra-EU situations of (labour) mobility and migration. As a result, free movement rights also remove the 'protective function' of migration law, for instance rules (existing in several countries) which may impose (as a minimum) the application of host state labour law as a condition for acquiring a work permit. Such rules are meant to prevent exploitation of migrant workers in low-skilled (and low-paid) jobs. In place of the protective function

competition on labour costs (also) in order to protect workers, by prescribing the territorial application of labour law (*lex loci laboris*).

of migration law, the free movement rules (and secondary EU law based on the freedoms) stipulate (partial) equal treatment between (migrant/posted) workers and domestic workers. However, the equal treatment rights which are granted to the workers exists only in interaction with and can in practice be limited by rules of private international law (PIL, also called 'conflict of laws') and the free movement rights of the employer in his role as service provider.

Article 8 of the Rome I Regulation harmonises the conflict rules in Europe on the law applicable to individual contracts of employment. In principle, parties are free to choose the law applicable to their employment contract. But Article 8(1) Rome I limits the effect of a choice of law since such a choice by the parties cannot deprive the employee of the protection afforded to him by mandatory provisions of the law applicable in absence of this choice (the 'objectively applicable law'). According to the majority opinion in literature, this means that the law chosen by the parties applies to the contract in full, except when mandatory rules of the otherwise applicable law would provide the worker better protection.[11] Hence, the employee will always be protected by the law which offers the better protection; if the employer and employee agree on better employment conditions than enshrined in the law applicable in the absence of choice, Article 8(1) Rome I prioritises the chosen law. But, if the parties agree on worse employment conditions than enshrined in the objectively applicable law, the latter law prevails. This '*favor* principle' is meant to prevent the employer from abusing his superior bargaining position.

Since the objectively applicable law acts as a 'floor', a minimum standard of protection, it is always relevant to ascertain the latter law, which can be done following the choice of law rules in Article 8(2)–(4) Rome I. According to Article 8(2) Rome I, the employment contracts is governed in principle by the law of the country in which or, failing that, from which the employee habitually carries out his work in performance of the contract – i.e. the habitual place of

11 Opinion of Advocate General Trstenjak in Case C-384/10, *Voogsgeerd*, EU:C:2011:564, para. 48 and Opinion of Advocate General Wahl in Case C-64/12, *Schlecker*, EU:C:2013:241, para. 24; O. Deinert, *Internationales Arbeitsrecht* (Tübingen: Mohr Siebeck, 2013), 96, 102 and 128; L. Merrett, *Employment Contracts in Private International Law* (Oxford: OUP, 2011), 215; P. Mankowski and O. Knöfel, 'On The Road Again oder: Wo arbeitet ein Fernfahrer? – Neues vom europäischen Internationalen Arbeitsvertragsrecht' (2011) 4 *Europäische Zeitschrift für Arbeitsrecht*, 524 and P. Winkler von Mohrenfels, 'Zur objektiven Anknüpfung des Arbeitsvertragsstatuts im internationalen Seearbeitsrecht: gewöhnlicher Arbeitsort, Flagge und einstellende Niederlassung (Rechtssache Voogsgeerd)' (2012) *Europäische Zeitschrift für Arbeitsrecht*, 371. The opposing view would grant a choice of law in a contract of employment only substantive effect – comparable to the effect of a choice of law in non-international contracts under Article 3(3). See *inter alia* L. Strikwerda, *Inleiding tot het Nederlandse internationaal privaatrecht* (Kluwer: Deventer, 2012), 175. This would mean that the chosen law only applies in as far as it does not deviate from mandatory provisions of the otherwise applicable law. The CJ has not taken up a clear position on this issue yet, see Case C-29/10, *Koelzsch*, EU:C:2011:151, para. 35; and Case C-384/10, *Voogsgeerd*, EU:C:2011:842, para. 28.

work. The country where the work is habitually carried out shall not be deemed to have changed if he is temporarily employed (posted) to another country. By referring to the *habitual* place of work, rather than the *actual* place of work, this provision stabilises the law applying to the employment contract: during a temporary posting, the law of the home state remains applicable. Article 8(3) Rome I contains an alternative reference rule in case the country where the work is habitually carried out cannot be identified. In that case the contract shall be governed by the law of the country where the place of business through which the employee was engaged is situated. Under Article 8(4) Rome I both pre-established connecting factors – habitual place of work and engaging place of business – may be set aside where it appears from the circumstances as a whole that the contract is more closely connected with another country, in which case the law of that other country shall apply.

However, Article 9(2) Rome I allows courts to apply domestic 'overriding mandatory' provisions (law of the forum), regardless of the (objectively) applicable law.[12] According to Article 9(1): 'Overriding mandatory provisions are provisions the respect for which is regarded as crucial by a country for safeguarding its public interests, such as its political, social or economic organisation, to such an extent that they are applicable to any situation falling within their scope, irrespective of the law otherwise applicable to the contract under this Regulation.' Many labour law rules have an overriding mandatory character, though the Member States traditionally draw the line between *lex causae*[13] rules and overriding mandatory provisions differently.[14] As a result,

12 Moreover, Article 9(3) Rome I allows the courts to give effect to overriding mandatory provisions of the country of performance, in so far as those overriding mandatory provisions render the performance of the contract unlawful. This provision is not considered in this chapter. However, it may be relevant in specific cases of transnational employment: on 25 February 2015, the German Federal Labour Court referred three questions relating to the interpretation of Articles 9 and 28 Rome I Regulation to the CJ. In the context of a wage claim made by a Greek national who is employed by the Greek State at a Greek primary school in Germany, the German Federal Labour Court faced the problem whether to apply the Greek Saving Laws No. 3833/2010 and 3845/2010 Laws as overriding mandatory provisions although the employment contract is governed by German law. See for a first analysis L. GÜNTHER, blog 25 April 2015, available at http://conflictoflaws.net/2015/german-federal-labour-court-on-foreign-mandatory-rules-and-the-principle-of-cooperation-among-eu-member-states (last accessed on 31 January 2016).

13 *Lex causae* is the law or laws chosen by a forum court from among the relevant legal systems to arrive at its judgment.

14 For a description of the different models of workers' protection in the EU Member States, see A.A.H. VAN HOEK and M.S. HOUWERZIJL, 'Comparative Study on the legal aspects of the posting of workers in the framework of the provision of services in the European Union' (2011) and 'Complementary study on the legal aspects of the posting of workers in the framework of the provision of services in the European Union' (2012) *Reports to the European Commission under contract VT/2009/0541* and *contract VC/2011/0096*, available at http://ec.europa.eu/social/main.jsp?catId=471&langId=en (last accessed on 31 January 2016). Also see A.A.H. VAN HOEK, 'Private international law: an appropriate means to regulate transnational employment in the European Union?' (2014) 3 *Erasmus Law Review*, 157–169. For a comparison between France and Germany with regard to overriding mandatory

Article 9 Rome I facilitates labour law systems which rely (sometimes heavily) on overriding mandatory law.

The PWD, aiming to reconcile the exercise of companies' fundamental freedom to provide cross-border services under Article 56 TFEU with the need to ensure a climate of fair competition and respect for the rights of workers (preamble, paragraph 5), uses in essence the same technique to achieve these aims. In Article 3, the PWD identifies which national mandatory rules of the host state must apply to posted workers. In this manner a hard core of clearly defined terms and conditions of work and employment for minimum protection of workers (laid down in Article 3(1)(a)–(g)) is established, that must be complied with by the service provider in the host Member State. According to the Preamble of the PWD (Recitals 7–11), the Directive thus makes the optional character of (now) Article 9 Rome I obligatory, by defining those subjects of employment law in which the national mandatory rules must be seen as 'overriding mandatory provisions'. Hence, the rules on mandatory protection laid down in the PWD can be understood to form an application of Article 9 Rome I.

In our view, the PWD can and should not be read in isolation from Article 8 Rome I. Indeed, from the perspective of the host state, the PWD fills in the 'gap'[15] that Article 8 Rome I would create for the territorial application of labour law. As is well known, 'the Directive, which was drafted in 1991, was partially intended to allay the fears of policymakers in high-wage economies that their markets would be flooded by increasing numbers of lower paid workers.'[16] Accordingly, Article 3(1) PWD states that: 'Member States shall ensure that, *whatever the law applicable to the employment relationship*, the undertakings referred to in Article 1(1) PWD guarantee workers posted to their territory the terms and conditions of employment covering the following matters [...]' (emphasis added). Thus, it is made clear that the law applying to the employment contract is regulated by PIL rules (currently Article 8 Rome I Regulation), but the PWD superimposes – if necessary – the minimum protection of the law of the host state upon the protection already offered under the law applying to the contract by virtue of Article 8 Rome I.

provisions, see R. Callsen, '*Eingriffsnormen und Ordre public-Vorbehalt im Internationalen Arbeitsrecht – Ein deutsch-französicher Vergleich*', Dissertation in internationaler Doppelbetreuung zur Erlangung des Dr. iur. Vorgelegt und öffentlich verteidigt am 13/12/2013 in Nanterre.

15 As pointed out above in section 3, Article 8(2) stipulates that the country where the work is habitually carried out shall not be deemed to have changed if a worker is temporarily employed (posted) in another country. See also below section 7.

16 A. Kennett and S. Nesbitt, 'The consequences of employing a mobile workforce – a patchwork of protections' (2000) 12 *International Company and Commercial Law Review*, 400. For the first draft of the PWD, see European Commission, 'Proposal for a Council Directive concerning the posting of workers in the framework of the provision of services' COM (1991) 230 final – SYN 346. See also M.S. Houwerzijl and F.J.L. Pennings, 'Double Charges in Case of Posting of Employees: The Guiot Judgment and its Effects in the Construction Sector' (1999) 1 *European Journal of Social Security*, 102.

An indication for the complementary character of the PWD in relation to Article 8 Rome I may also be found in Article 3(7) PWD. Article 3(7) first sentence PWD allows the *application* of better protection to posted workers than the minimum provided for by the Directive.[17] In the *Laval* and *Rüffert* judgments the CJ made it clear that this provision only refers to the more favourable terms and conditions of employment which those workers already enjoy pursuant to the law or collective agreements in the Member State of origin, or agreed voluntarily by the employer. Based on the legislative history of the PWD we support that reading.[18]

Some authors, however, seem to infer a home country control rule from said case-law, which would submit the posted worker to the laws of the country of establishment of his employer and disallow the application of more favourable provisions contained in the law applicable by virtue of Article 8 Rome I.[19] Admittedly, the reference to the 'country of origin' or 'home country' in the court's case-law may cause confusion if the Member State where the employee is recruited or where he will habitually perform his work is not the same as the Member State where the employer is established. However, in our view 'country of origin' or 'home country' should be read to refer to the country whose law is

---

17 Recital 17 of the PWD also refers to *application* of more favourable terms and conditions to posted workers. For the embodiment of the '*favor* principle' in pre-PWD case-law: see M.S. Houwerzijl and F.J.L. Pennings, 'Double Charges in Case of Posting of Employees: The Guiot Judgment and its Effects in the Construction Sector' (1999) 1 *European Journal of Social Security*, 102.

18 See Case C-341/05, *Laval*, EU:C:2007:809, paras. 79–81, 120; and Case C-346/06, *Rüffert*, EU:C:2008:189, paras. 32–34. Compare M.S. Houwerzijl, *De Detacheringsrichtlijn: over de achtergrond, inhoud en implementatie van Richtlijn 96/71/EG* (Deventer: Kluwer, 2005), 161. See, more in detail, also S. Evju, 'Posting Past and Present The Posting of Workers Directive – Genesis and Current Contrasts' (2009) *Formula WP 8*, 32: 'Initially it was clear from the wording of the proposed provision that it referred only to more favourable terms and conditions in a workers home state (under the law applicable to the contract of employment) (D 2, Parliament, COM-93 – ctr WG 11 – Council 1994h). There is no indication that the change of wording was intended to fundamentally depart from this. On the contrary, the subsequent concern was how to compare and the Statement in the Council Minutes on pay comparison (231/96) must be understood to presuppose that it is more favourable terms in the State of "the law applicable" that should be the yardstick.'

19 See e.g. F. Van Overbeeke, 'Over de interactie tussen het IPR en de bepalingen inzake het vrij verkeer, toegespitst op internationale arbeidsovereenkomsten' (2013) *Rechtskundig Weekblad*, 648 and M. Fornasier and M. Torga, 'The Posting of Workers: The Perspective of the Sending State – The Judgment of the Civil Chamber of the Estonian Supreme Court of 16 January 2013 No 3-2-1-179-12' (2013) 3 *Europäische Zeitschrift für Arbeitsrecht (EuZA)*, 364. Those authors draw a parallel between this situation and that of the eDate decision of Case C-509/09, *eDate Advertising and Others*, EU:C:2011:685 and Case C-161/10, *Martinez and Martinez*, EU:C:2010:656. However, we would submit there are crucial differences between the eDate scenario and the situation of discussed here. See in more detail (with references): A.A.H. van Hoek and M.S. Houwerzijl, '"Posting" and "posted workers" – The need for clear definitions of two key concepts of the Posting of Workers Directive', in C. Barnard, M. Gehring and I. Solanke (eds.), *Cambridge Yearbook of European Legal Studies* (Oxford: Hart Publishing, 2012), 419–451.

objectively applicable in light of Article 8 Rome I. This will most often be the country in which the work is normally or habitually performed, rather than the country of establishment of the employer.[20] Support for this reading may also be found in Article 4(1) of Directive 91/533 which, under the heading 'expatriate employees', gives rules on information requirements in situations where the employee is required to work in one or more countries other than *the Member State whose law and/or practice governs the contract or employment relationship abroad*' (emphasis added).[21]

In this section we sketched the relevant legal instruments and gave our understanding as to the interaction between the Rome I Regulation and the PWD. However, up until recently the CJ had no competence to interpret the existing choice of law instruments.[22] This enabled Member States to develop and/or maintain different interpretations of both the interaction between Article 8 and Article 9 of the Rome I Regulation and the interaction between the Rome I Regulation and the PWD. In the recently adopted EPWD, Article 4 makes reference to the Rome I Regulation with regard to the issue of applicable law.[23]

---

20 Compare A.A.H. Van Hoek and M.S. Houwerzijl, '"Posting" and "posted workers" – The need for clear definitions of two key concepts of the Posting of Workers Directive', in C. Barnard, M. Gehring and I. Solanke (eds.), *Cambridge Yearbook of European Legal Studies* (Oxford: Hart Publishing, 2012), 441–443. Employment conditions are specifically excluded from the coordinated field in the Services Directive: Directive 2006/123/EC of the European Parliament and of the Council of 12 December 2006 on services in the internal market, OJ 2006, L 376/36, Article 3(1)(a), 3(2) and recital 14.

21 Directive 91/533 was adopted a few months after the first draft was presented by the Commission for what has become the PWD. See COM (91) 230 final, 1 August 1990, Proposal for a Council Directive concerning the posting of workers in the framework of the provision of services. The interrelationship between Directive 91/533 and the PWD (Directive 96/71) was emphasised during the implementation process of the latter Directive. In the transposal stage, the Commission expressed its belief that compliance with the requirements laid down in Directive 91/533 (in particular Articles 2 and 4) should facilitate the implementation of the PWD and in particular the process of comparing the home state's and host state's provisions on minimum wages and paid holidays. See *Report of the Working Party on the transposal of the Directive concerning the posting of workers, Brussels*: European Commission, Employment & Social Affairs, 1999, 13. Also in case-law, the linkage between the two Directives has been at issue. See Joined Cases C-369/96 to C-376/96, *Arblade*, EU:C:1999:575, paras. 61, 65, 67–68 and 70, and Case C-319/06, *Commission v Luxembourg*, EU:C:2008:350, paras. 39–41.

22 The competence to interpret the predecessor of the Rome I Regulation, the Rome Convention, was established in a separate protocol which entered into force on 1 August 2004 (see Case C-29/10, *Koelzsch*, EU:C:2011:151, para. 30). The Rome I Regulation only applies to contracts concluded as from 17 December 2009: Corrigendum to Regulation (EC) No. 593/2008 of the European Parliament and of the Council of 17 June 2008 on the law applicable to contractual obligations (Rome I), OJ 2008, L 177.

23 The Commission proposal, COM (2012) 131 final, specifies in recital 6 that the PWD 'should not prejudice the application of the law which, under Article 8 of the Rome I Regulation, applies to individual employment contracts'. Interim solutions may be to call upon the Member State to jointly establish the applicable law to the contract, or introduce an assumption that in cases of 'non-genuine posting', the host state is the state in which the work is habitually performed under Rome I: see for example the Draft report, amendments tabled in committee PE500.574, nos. 90 and 119, procedure file 2012/0061/COD).

The exact implications of this latter position for the interpretation of Article 8 and 9 Rome I Regulation are yet unclear, though.

4. WHERE DO I BELONG? THE COUNTRY WHERE I HABITUALLY WORK?

Article 8(2) Rome I uses the habitual place of work as its primary connecting factor. Therefore, it is key to know how to interpret the concept 'habitual place of work'. In the absence of case-law on the interpretation of the Rome I Regulation, similar concepts and criteria in the Brussels I Regulation on jurisdiction[24] and the Rome Convention, the treaty which preceded the Rome I Regulation, may be of relevance. In its case-law the CJ has stressed the continuity between the different instruments as well as the cross-referential character of concepts used therein.[25] Hence, the interpretation of the concept 'habitual place of work' in the Rome Convention is also relevant for the interpretation of the same concept in the Rome I Regulation. In the same vein, the interpretation given in the context of the rules on jurisdiction is also relevant in the context of applicable law.[26]

So, how did the concept 'habitual place of work' evolve over time? In 1982 the CJ EU identified the contract of employment as a 'weaker party contract' meriting special protective PIL rules.[27] In a subsequent case the court specified that 'contracts of employment, like other contracts for work other than on a self-employed basis, differ from other contracts – even those for the provision of services – by virtue of certain particularities: they create a lasting bond which brings the worker to some extent within the organisational framework of the business of the undertaking or employer, and they are linked to the place

24 Council Regulation (EC) No. 44/2001 of 22 December 2000 on jurisdiction and the recognition and enforcement of judgments in civil and commercial matters (Brussels I), OJ 2001, L 12/1, Article 19, currently replaced by Regulation (EU) No. 1215/2012 of the European Parliament and of the Council of 12 December 2012 on jurisdiction and the recognition and enforcement of judgments in civil and commercial matters OJ 2012 L 351/1 (Brussels I recast), Article 21.

25 For an early reference, with regard to the continuity between the old case-law and the new text of Article 5(1) of the Brussels Convention, see Case C-383/95, *Rutten*, EU:C:1997:7, para. 21. For a cross-reference between the Brussels I and Rome I Regulations, see Case C-29/10, *Koelzsch*, EU:C:2011:151, para. 33.

26 See more extensively on this point V. Parisot, 'Vers une coherence verticale des textes communataires en droit du travail? Réflexion autour des arrêts Heiko Koelzsch et Jan Voogsgeerd de la Cour de justice' (2012) 139 *Journal de Droit International*, 597–645; A.A.H. van Hoek, 'Heiko Koelzsch tegen Groothertogdom Luxemburg' (2011) 60 *Ars Aequi*, 652 and the case note on the joined Cases C-585/08 and C-144/09, *Pammer and Hotel Alpenhof*, EU:C:2010:740 from A.A.H. van Hoek in (2012) 8 *European Review of Contract Law*, 93–107 with references. On the issue of the interpretation method, see also E. Pataut, 'Case note to Voogsgeerd' (2012) 101 *Revue Critique de Droit International Privé* 3, 658 with references to French literature.

27 Case 133/81, *Ivenel*, EU:C:1982:199.

where the activities are pursued, which determines the application of mandatory rules and collective agreements.'[28] Hence, in the court's reasoning we find the different types of ordering described above. In due course, the focus in the case-law on jurisdiction shifted however, from developing a bilateral[29] rule aimed at *Gleichlauf* – giving jurisdiction to a court which could apply its own system of labour law including the locally applicable collective agreements[30] – to the establishment of a unilateral rule offering the employee easy access to a nearby court.[31] To reach the desired protective result,[32] the 'habitual place of work' was interpreted in a factual manner, referring to the actual performance of the contract rather than the contractual arrangements.[33] Moreover, the CJ expanded the concept to also include cases in which the worker performed activities in more than one country. According to the case-law as it currently stands the habitual place of work does not only refer to the place *in which* the work is habitually performed, but also to the place *from which* the employee principally discharges his obligations towards his employer.[34]

In case of a sales representative working in different countries, the national court should try to determine in which place the employee has established the effective centre of his working activities.[35] When the employee carries out a large part of his work in the country in which he has established his office, that country is deemed to be the country *in or from which* the work is habitually performed. However, if a worker is sent to different locations to perform one and the same activity (cooking on oil rigs on the continental shelf for example), no such effective centre of working activities can be determined, nor can any qualitative criterion be used to determine the 'essential' part of the performance.

---

28 Case 266/85, *Shenavai*, EU:C:1987:11.

29 Available to both employee and employer.

30 See Case 133/81, *Ivenel*, EU:C:1982:199, paras. 12–15; Case 266/85, *Shenavai*, EU:C:1987:11, para. 16; Case 32/88, *Six Constructions Ltd*, EU:C:1989:68, para. 10; and Case C-125/92, *Mulox IBC Ltd*, EU:C:1993:306, para. 15.

31 Open for the employee only. See Case C-125/92, *Mulox IBC Ltd*, EU:C:1993:306, para. 19; and Case C-37/00, *Weber*, EU:C:2002:122, para. 40. It is interesting to note that these changes did not deter the CJ from referring to the old case-law for the interpretation of the current text.

32 On the protective character of the interpretation given to the rules on jurisdiction, see V. Parisot, 'Vers une coherence verticale des textes communautaires en droit du travail? Réflexion autour des arrêts Heiko Koelzsch et Jan Voogsgeerd de la Cour de justice' (2012) 139 *Journal de Droit International*, 620. For a critical analysis thereof, see U. Grušić, 'Jurisdiction in employment matters under the Brussels I Regulation: a reassessment' (2012) 61 *International and Comparative Law Quarterly*, 91–126.

33 See for example Case C-37/00, *Weber*, EU:C:2002:122, para. 58 and A. Winterling, *Die Entscheidungszuständigkeit in Arbeitssachen im europäischen Zivilverfahrensrecht* (Frankfurt: Peter Lang, 2006) 61–62.

34 See Case C-125/92, *Mulox IBC Ltd*, EU:C:1993:306, paras. 20 and 26. Compare Case C-437/00, *Pugliese*, EU:C:2003:219, para. 19 which refers to the place where or from which the employee in fact performed the essential part of his duties towards his employer. Neither the text of the Brussels Convention (as changed by the convention of 1989) nor the text of the Brussels I Regulation contain a reference to the place *from which* the work is habitually performed.

35 See Case C-383/95, *Rutten*, EU:C:1997:7, para. 23.

In that case, the relevant criterion for establishing an employee's habitual place of work is the place where he spends most of his working time engaged on his employer's business.[36] In principle the whole duration of the contract should be taken into account, unless there is a clear intention on the side of both parties to change the place of work, in which case only the most recent place of work will be relevant.[37]

In the *Koelzsch* and *Voogsgeerd* cases the CJ made clear that even in the case of a truck driver working in international transport (*Koelzsch*) or a sailor working on a seagoing vessel (*Voogsgeerd*) the national court should try to establish whether, based on the circumstances as a whole, a country can be identified where or from which the work is actually performed.[38] These cases were rendered in the context of the application of Article 6 of the Rome Convention, identifying the law applying to the employment contract. The CJ justifies this broad interpretation of the primary connecting factor by referring to the protective character of this provision. Hence, the provision: 'must be understood as guaranteeing the applicability of the law of the State in which [the employee] carries out his working activities [...]. It is [there] that the employee performs his economic and social duties and [...], it is there that the business and political environment affects employment activities. Therefore, compliance with the employment protection rules provided for by the law of that country must, so far as is possible, be guaranteed.'[39]

When ascertaining the place of work in case of international transport (including international shipping), the national courts must take account of all the factors which characterise the activity of the employee. These are, in particular, the place from which the employee carries out his transport tasks, receives instructions concerning his tasks and organises his work, and the place where his work tools are situated. Additionally, the court must determine the places where the transport is principally carried out, where the goods are unloaded and the place to which the employee returns after completion of his tasks.[40]

The habitual place of work is clearly not a connecting factor that is easily applied to so-called 'peripatetic employees'.[41] In the *Koelzsch* case, the Advocate

36 See Case C-37/00, *Weber*, EU:C:2002:122, para. 50.

37 See Case C-37/00, *Weber*, EU:C:2002:122, paras. 52–54.

38 See Case C-29/10, *Koelzsch*, EU:C:2011:151, paras. 47–49.

39 See Case C-29/10, *Koelzsch*, EU:C:2011:151, para. 42.

40 See Case C-29/10, *Koelzsch*, EU:C:2011:151, paras. 48–49; and Case C-384/10, *Voogsgeerd*, EU:C:2011:842, paras. 38–39.

41 'Peripatetic' employees (such as airline pilots, international management consultants, sales staff and so on) are in Great Britain distinguished as a category, next to 'expatriate' employees. For instance see L. Merrett. 'The Extra-Territorial Reach of Employment Legislation' (2010) 4 *Industrial Law Journal*, 367. Interestingly, Advocate General Bot uses the term in his Opinion of 11 June 2015 in the case *Tyco* (Opinion of Advocate General Bot in Case C-266/14, EU:C:2015:391, paras. 32 and 36) where he considers that 'peripatetic workers may be defined as being workers who are not assigned a fixed or habitual place of work. Such workers are therefore required to work at different premises every day.'

General refers to the need to study the duty roster (*Körselsrapport*) in order to assess the exact time and place of work for each individual employee. This does not only cause problems of proof, but may also lead to a more individualised protection of the workers involved. What might get lost in the process is the collective element of the employment relationship. The case-law discussed here contains several examples in which both the organisational framework of the employer and the system of collective agreements seem to point to a law other than that of the factual place of work. This raises the question of priority between the connecting factors; which of these connecting factors should prevail?

5. WHERE DO I BELONG? THE COUNTRY OF ENGAGEMENT?

In the *Koelzsch* and *Voogsgeerd* cases, the CJ stressed the priority of the habitual place of work over the place of establishment of the employer. This was innovative, as in many countries the employment contract of transport workers was deemed to be governed by the law of the place of establishment of their employer. This private international law rule was sometimes reinforced by the rules on admission to the sector by way of transport licensing.[42] However, in the two cases put before the CJ, the 'flag' of the company plays no role whatsoever. The court emphasises that the reference to the engaging place of business in the Rome Convention is strictly secondary.[43] Only when it is not possible to identify the country in or from which the work is habitually performed, recourse may be had to the second connecting factor, the engaging place of business.[44]

The identification of the habitual place of work in the *Koelzsch* and *Voogsgeerd* cases is left to the national courts. But in both cases it is clear from the facts that there was no relevant link between the actual performance of the contract by the employee and the country of establishment of the employer. The German truck driver Koelzsch operated from Germany, the Dutch sailor Voogsgeerd from

42 It is also interesting to note that in the *Voogsgeerd* case no mention is made of the flag(s) of the ships on which Voogsgeerd performed his work. Admittedly, the flag was not brought forward as a relevant connecting factor by any of the parties to the procedure. Neither was the connection to the habitual place of work, though. See on this issue P. Winkler von Mohrenfels, 'Zur objektiven Anknüpfung des Arbeitsvertragsstatuts im internationalen Seearbeitsrecht: gewöhnlicher Arbeitsort, Flagge und einstellende Niederlassung (Rechtssache Voogsgeerd)' (2012) *Europäische Zeitschrift für Arbeitsrecht*, 373–377; U. Grušić, 'Should the connecting factor of the engaging place of business be abolished in private international law?' (2013) 62 *International and Comparative Law Quarterly*, 180–181 and A.A.H. van Hoek, 'Het toepasselijk recht op arbeidsovereenkomsten in de zeevaart – Een commentaar op HvJ EU 15 december 2011, zaak C-384/10, Voogsgeerd/Navimer' (2014) 7 *Nederlands Tijdschrift voor Europees Recht*, 245–251.

43 See Case C-29/10, *Koelzsch*, EU:C:2011:151, paras. 48–49; and Case C-384/10, *Voogsgeerd*, EU:C:2011:842, paras. 34–35.

44 See Case C-384/10, *Voogsgeerd*, EU:C:2011:842, paras. 32–35.

Antwerp (BE); both were employed by a Luxembourg company. By focusing on the effective performance of the contract of employment as the connecting factor (which means priority of the habitual place of work over the place of establishment of the employer), the CJ prevents that a place without any real and relevant connection to the actual performance of the work is used to designate the objectively applicable law. In the context of the 'search for cheap labour', i.e. the application of the law of the country with the lowest labour standards, this approach of the CJ seems to counter the negative effects the employers' freedom of establishment and freedom to provide services may have on the protection of the employee. Cheap airlines are a case in point, but transport by road also gives rise to 'flags of convenience'. Moreover, by specifically denying any priority for the place of establishment of the employer, the court implicitly rejects the existence of a home country control rule with regard to contracts of employment.[45] Hence, from the first ordering perspective of preventing labour market competition (social dumping – see section 2 above), this line may be welcomed.

However, from the organisation of the business, designated as the second ordering perspective, the assessment is less positive. Due to the purely secondary relevance of the engaging place of business, it is no longer evident that all workers employed by a single transport company are covered by the same law.[46] In transport by road even a common base from which a group of workers (a 'crew') is employed, might be missing. The fact that the law applying to the employment contract (and hence employment conditions) has to be established on an individual basis, might seriously hamper the possibility for the workers to protect their interests by way of collective negotiations. But the individual character of the assessment may also make other, administrative and collective, modes of protection and enforcement more problematic.[47]

---

45 In line with the fierce resistance against the first proposal for what now is Directive 2006/123 (the Services Directive), but in contrast with the effect of the ruling of the CJ in Case C-438/05, *Viking*, EU:C:2007:772. See more extensively on this issue (with references): A.A.H. van Hoek and M.S. Houwerzijl, 'Looncuncurrentie als motor van de interne markt? Een tweeluik – Deel 1: De arresten Viking, Laval en Rueffert, verdragsaspecten' (2008) 14 *Nederlands Tijdschrift voor Europees Recht*, 190–205.

46 See L. Merrett, *Employment Contracts in Private International Law* (Oxford: OUP, 2011), 176 – describes the importance attached under English common law to the application of one and the same law to all workers employed by a single employer in a single location. This was deemed to be a matter of equality. Also the right to choose the applicable law to the individual contract is assessed critically against this need for equal treatment (at 214). The importance of a single law applying to the entire workforce of an undertaking is also mentioned specifically by P. Mankowski and O. Knöfel, 'On The Road Again oder: Wo arbeitet ein Fernfahrer? – Neues vom europäischen Internationalen Arbeitsvertragsrecht' (2011) 4 *Europäische Zeitschrift für Arbeitsrecht*, 525.

47 See for a more detailed discussion on the relevance of public law and collective methods of protection: A.A.H. van Hoek and M.S. Houwerzijl, 'Comparative Study on the legal aspects of the posting of workers in the framework of the provision of services in the European Union' (2011), 21, *Report to the European Commission under contract VT/2009/0541*, available

It is interesting to compare the situation in the transport sector to the facts in the cases decided under the Brussels Convention and Regulation. In the *Mulox* case, as in fact in *Ivenel* and *Rutten/Cross*, the worker was a sales representative having his base in a country other than the country of establishment of the employer. In the *Rutten* case it is clear from the facts of the case that the employee operated from his home base, rather than from an office employing several workers. Hence, this 'field worker' largely operated outside of any physical organisation. Also in these judgments the choice for the home base as the relevant connecting factor dislodges the employment contract from the organisational framework of the employer. Something similar is also happening in the *Weber* case. This case concerned a cook in the offshore industry. In that case, no centre of employment or base is deemed to be present as the worker is send to perform the same type of work in different locations. This description covers a variety of employment situations and in particular the construction worker or the temporary agency worker. In those cases the CJ focuses on the amount of time spent in a particular country. The organisational framework in which the employment contract finds its bedding seems to be largely irrelevant.

However, one should be careful not to jump to conclusions. In the case-law of the CJ, the place of work is deemed to be the primary connecting factor, with the place of engagement only filling a very subsidiary role. On closer inspection, the habitual place of work is a legal construct which includes elements of *Eingliederung* – embeddedness in an organisational framework. In the transport cases, in determining the habitual place of work, the CJ attached weight to the place where the worker receives instructions concerning his tasks and organises his work, as well as to the place where his work tools are situated. These criteria refer – at least in part – to the organisational structure of the employer. In the *Koelzsch* case there seems to have been some kind of collective presence in Germany (the country from which the work was performed) as the workers had established a works council there. In the *Voogsgeerd* case the worker reported to an office in Antwerp, where he received administrative briefings, as well as instructions for the performance of his work. So it could be argued that the CJ effectively conflated the organisational framework and the actual place of performance into a single connecting factor: the 'place where or from which the work is habitually performed'.

Taking into account the very broad interpretation of the 'habitual place of work' in Article 8(2) Rome I, it may seem as if there are hardly any situations that will be covered by Article 8(3) Rome I – referring to the place

at http://ec.europa.eu/social/main.jsp?catId=471&langId=en (last accessed on 31 January 2016). See on the impact of collective labour law on the choice of law position taken by individual authors, A.A.H. van Hoek, *Mobiliteit van werknemers* (The Hague: SDU, 2000), 226–227.

of engagement.[48] Nevertheless, the Court did clarify this concept in the *Voogsgeerd* judgment. As the elements related to the performance of the contract are already taken into account in determining the habitual place of work, the assessment of the place of engagement has a more formal character and focuses on the recruitment procedure: 'the courts should take into consideration not those matters relating to the performance of the work but only those relating to the procedure for concluding the contract, such as the place of business which published the recruitment notice and that which carried out the recruitment interview, and it must endeavour to determine the real location of that place of business.' Accordingly, this connecting factor does not establish a relevant link to the performance and the life line of the employment contract but is fixed at the very beginning thereof. The connecting factor serves to provide legal certainty in a case in which the primary connecting factor is not able to provide a clear link to any particular jurisdiction.[49] It is – in a sense – a home for the homeless.

6. WHERE DO I BELONG? A COUNTRY TO WHICH I AM MORE CLOSELY CONNECTED?

The possibility to use the 'escape clause', currently regulated in Article 8(4) Rome I, was the object of the most recent preliminary question regarding the law applying to individual employment contracts which was answered in the *Schlecker* case.[50]

The *Schlecker* case concerned a conflict between a German employee (Ms Boedeker) and her German employer (the Schlecker company), caused by the decision of the employer to terminate employment in the Netherlands and re-instate the employee in a different position in Germany. For the last 12 years (of a total of 27 years of service) the employee had been employed as manager of the Dutch division of the employer, supervising its 300 local branches. There was no contestation as to the fact that the Netherlands was (had become) the habitual place of work.[51] Ms Boedeker lodged a complaint in a Dutch court against her employer's unilateral decision to change her place of work. She relied on the application of Dutch law, which in this case offered her better protection than

48 However, the provision may remain of or regain relevance for the emerging group of 'hypermobile' workers.

49 See Case C-384/10, *Voogsgeerd*, EU:C:2011:842, para. 47. Furthermore, schematic interpretation of Article 6(2)(b) requires the – subsidiary – factor laid down in that provision to be applied when it is impossible to situate the employment relationship in a Member State. Consequently, only a strict interpretation of that subsidiary factor can guarantee the complete foreseeability of the law applicable to the contract of employment.

50 Case C-64/12, *Schlecker*, EU:C:2013:551.

51 Case C-64/12, *Schlecker*, EU:C:2013:551, para. 27.

German law. However, her employer Schlecker claimed that the contract was more closely related to Germany. Elements referring to Germany where *inter alia* the common nationality and place of domicile of both parties, the language and original currency of the contract, reference to provisions of German law in the contract and the fact that the employee was covered by German tax law, social security and additional pension schemes. Could the court in this case ignore the connection based on the place of work in favour of German law?

In the Dutch case which led to the preliminary question, Advocate General Strikwerda had stressed the protective character of using the habitual place of work as the primary connecting factor. Due to this specific character the Advocate General concluded that the escape clause based on a closer connection should be used sparingly when in competition with the habitual place of work.[52] In contrast, the Dutch government argued that applying the law of the habitual country of work, 'even where the circumstances as a whole point to another legal system would have the effect of rendering meaningless' the escape clause.[53]

In its judgment the CJ sides with the Dutch government. The habitual place of work does take priority over the engaging place of business, based on the protective character of the first connecting factor. No such hierarchy exists, however, with regard to the escape clause referring to the closest connection. Though the national court must first determine the applicable law by reference to the pre-established connecting factors, the national court may disregard these connecting factors and apply the law of another country, 'even where an employee carries out the work in performance of the contract habitually, for a lengthy period and without interruption in the same country', where it is apparent from the circumstances as a whole that the employment contract is more closely connected with that country.[54] Hence, both connecting factors are put on the same footing in this regard.

Furthermore, the CJ stresses that the closer connection test cannot be performed by simply counting connecting factors: not all connecting factors carry the same weight. According to the CJ 'among the significant factors suggestive of a connection with a particular country, account should be taken in particular of the country in which the employee pays taxes on the income from his activity and the country in which he is covered by a social security scheme and pension, sickness insurance and invalidity schemes. In addition, the national court must also take account of all the circumstances of the case, such as the parameters relating to salary determination and other working conditions.'[55] The content of the relevant laws is not decisive in this matter.

---

52 For a similar position, see L. Merrett, *Employment Contracts in Private International Law* (Oxford: OUP, 2011), 206 and 209. For the original judgment, see HR 3 februari 2012, ECLI:NL:HR:2012:BS8791, *NJ* 2012/90.

53 Case C-64/12, *Schlecker*, EU:C:2013:551, para. 21.

54 Case C-64/12, *Schlecker*, EU:C:2013:551, paras. 42, 35–36.

55 Case C-64/12, *Schlecker*, EU:C:2013:551, para. 41.

The *Schlecker* case brought to the fore that different agents may hold quite divergent views on the concept of 'adequate protection'. In the *Koelzsch* and *Voogsgeerd* cases, the CJ stressed that the rules on applicable law should submit the contract of employment to the law of the state in which the employee performs his economic and social duties because it is in this country that the business and political environment affects employment activities. In jurisprudence this mechanism, in which certain weaker parties are protected by applying the law of their social and economic environment, is referred to as the 'protection principle' or 'functional allocation'. This terminology is common in Dutch private international law,[56] which may explain the position of the Dutch Advocate General Strikwerda in the *Schlecker* case. In Dutch legal writing, the reference to the *locus laboris* in Article 8(2) Rome I Regulation is seen as the embodiment of the protective character of the choice-of-law rule. Accordingly, a deviation from the *locus laboris* rule in cases in which the social and economic environment of the employment can be clearly established, can be deemed to counteract the protective function of the rule.[57]

In his opinion before the CJ, Advocate General Wahl takes a totally different view on the protective character of Article 8 Rome I. According to Wahl, protection is given mainly by limiting the freedom of the parties to choose the applicable law.[58] If any protection is to be had from the choice of law rules that apply in absence of such a choice, it consists of a strict adherence to the proximity rule.[59] In this view, the employee is protected by applying the law that is most familiar to her. In the case of Ms Boedeker (the employee in the *Schlecker* case) this would be the law of her country of origin and domicile, rather than her country of work. Advocate General Wahl even argues that the protection of the employee is served by an extensive interpretation of the escape clause, because in that case the search for the closest connection is given precedence over legal certainty and predictability.

By giving a broad interpretation of the possibility to deviate from the law of the habitual place of work in favour of another law, the CJ seems – to a certain extent – to undo the effect of the decisions in *Koelzsch* and *Voogsgeerd*. The escape rule of Article 8(4) undermines the general applicability of the law of the habitual place of work and hence the territorial application of labour law.[60]

56 See in particular Th. M. de Boer, 'The Purpose of Uniform Choice of Law Rules: The Rome II Regulation' (2009) 56 *Netherlands International Law Review*, 298 and 316 and Th. M. de Boer, 'The EEC Contracts Convention and the Dutch courts: a methodological perspective' (1990) 54 *Rabels Zeitschrift*, 25–62.

57 This seems to be the French position as well, see O. Deinert, *Internationales Arbeitsrecht* (Tübingen: Mohr Siebeck, 2013), 156.

58 Opinion of Advocate General Wahl in Case C-64/12, *Schlecker*, EU:C:2013:241, para. 25.

59 Opinion of Advocate General Wahl in Case C-64/12, *Schlecker*, EU:C:2013:241, para. 26. However, he illustrates his point with reference to typical expat situations, such as posting to third countries with lower levels of protection.

60 See on this opinion *inter alia* U. Grušić, *The European Private International Law of Employment* (Cambridge: CUP, 2015), 26, who distinguishes the individualistic view on

Based on the criteria which are deemed to be relevant in establishing a closer connection, this other law will usually be the law of common origin.[61] In the context of the internal market, the rule established by the CJ in the *Schlecker* case may, *if* interpreted extensively, be quite similar to a home country control rule. Moreover, the importance attached to tax and social security shifts the attention to the rules applying to these fields of law. This furthers the alignment between applicable labour law and social security law, in line with the third line of ordering (see section 2 above). However, as Cornelissen points out in his contribution to this book, it may also open the door for possibilities to (mis)use *Schlecker*, especially in relation to a broad use of Article 16 of the Regulation 883/04 on coordination of social security within the EU.[62]

In this regard, we should not overlook that there are elements in *Schlecker* which may temper a very (or, from the perspective of preventing the undermining of the *lex loci laboris* principle, too) extensive interpretation of the escape clause.

Firstly, it is possible that the subject of the conflict, being the unilateral alteration of the employment contract by the employer, played a decisive role in the importance attached to the country of closer connection. While stating that the referring court must take account of all the elements which define the employment relationship and single out one or more as being, in its view, the most significant, the CJ adds – in line with the point of views of the Commission and the Advocate General (para. 66 of his Opinion) – that the referring court cannot *automatically conclude* to disregard the habitual place of work *solely* because, by dint of their number, the other relevant circumstances – apart from the actual place of work – would result in the selection of another country.[63]

Secondly, also in the Conclusion of AG Wahl, there are elements which allow for a less extensive reading of *Schlecker*. In para. 38 he seems to adhere to the point of view that 'the rules laid down in the Rome Convention are intended, in the first place, to prevent the creation, to the detriment of employees, of situations comparable to "law shopping" (before adding that they must not lead either to the creation, in favour of the worker, of an unlimited choice as regards

employment contracts which would underlie the position taken by Advocate General Wahl from a more systemic perspective which also takes into account the interest of the host state.

61 So in cases in which employer and employee do have a common origin. Cases of 'irregular posting' may not demonstrate this fact pattern. See A.A.H. van Hoek and M.S. Houwerzijl, 'Comparative Study on the legal aspects of the posting of workers in the framework of the provision of services in the European Union' (2011), 75, *Report to the European Commission under contract VT/2009/0541,* available at http://ec.europa.eu/social/main.jsp?catId=471&langId=en (last accessed on 31 January 2016).

62 See Regulation 883/2004, OJ 2004, L 166/1, Article 11(3)(a), 12(1) and 16(1). According to Article 16 'two or more Member States, the competent authorities of these Member States or the bodies designated by these authorities, may by common agreement provide for exceptions to Articles 11 to 15 in the interest of certain persons or categories of persons'. See on this issue the chapter of R. Cornelissen in this volume.

63 See Case C-64/12, *Schlecker*, EU:C:2013:551, para. 40.

the substantive provisions which he may regard as applicable and thus to the creation of significant uncertainty in determining the applicable law). And where he agrees with the Dutch government that, 'the prevailing principle in matters relating to affiliation to a social security scheme is, save in the specific case of the posting of the employee, that of *lex loci laboris*, which implies that an employee is subject to the social security scheme of the State in which he habitually works', and that 'by avoiding that rule, as the relevant basic legislation permits, the parties concerned sought to shift the centre of gravity of their relationship to another country', he also adds that, 'always with a view to providing adequate protection to the party regarded as economically and socially weaker, *it is appropriate to examine whether the connection to the social protection schemes was made by mutual agreement of the parties or whether it was imposed on the employee*' (para. 68; emphasis added). This remark might perhaps reassure Cornelissen a bit.[64]

Although it is too early to predict how extensively the CJ will interpret Article 8(4) Rome I in future cases, it is beyond dispute that with *Schlecker* the tax law and social security schemes applicable to the employee, have regained importance. As said, the weight attached to these factors in *Schlecker* do point to prioritising a different kind of belonging – not the labour market on which the employee performed her work was deemed to be decisive, but the social structure in which she was embedded through the system of social charges (the third line of ordering). Hence, the importance attached to tax and social security shifts the attention to the rules applying to these fields of law. Often, when an employment dispute reaches the courts, the relationship has been terminated. Since many court cases concern the rules on dismissals it might make sense to connect this specific element of employment law to the system of social security applicable to the worker concerned. This may impact on the way the courts handle the issue of applicable law. It can be questioned however, whether the same rationale is also valid for wages, working time, safety at work and all those other rules which influence the day to day performance of the contract. Do other types of belonging retain (or regain) relevance there? Inspiration may perhaps be drawn from the choices made with regard to cross-border posting of workers.

7. WHERE DO I BELONG WHILE POSTED ABROAD?

If one reads the case-law on the posting of workers in the context of the free provision of services from a lens of searching the applicable law to the contract between the parties involved, it seems as if the underlying assumption is that

64 See also the judgment in Case C-115/11, *Format*, EU:C:2012:606, where the Court emphasises the factual situation above the party intentions.

posted workers (always) ordinarily work in the country of establishment of their employer and therefore will be covered by the law of their (employer's) home state ('the country of origin').[65] However, the CJ never had to decide yet on the applicable law to the contract of a posted worker and this may explain why it never paid attention to the underlying contractual position of the parties. Until now, the case-law has focused on establishing whether the application of host state law during the period of posting would (disproportionally) infringe the free provision of services. In this respect, as is common ground, the posting of workers in the context of the free provision of services opposes the interests of host state employers and workers to the interests of the company performing the cross-border service (and – according to some[66] – even the interests of the posted workers themselves). But it also pitches the interests of high cost host states against those of low cost sending states.[67] This makes the topic highly controversial.[68]

By establishing a 'hard core' of minimum protection by mandatory law in the host state for posted workers, the PWD[69] tries to balance the interests involved. As is well known, this balance shifted towards the aim to further the provision of services, when the CJ interpreted the PWD in the notorious 'Laval-quartet' as to also limit the application of host state labour law to the areas mentioned in the Directive, unless the rule to be applied is considered to be part of public policy.[70] In other words: the PWD contains not only a minimum but also

---

65 Some authors infer a home country control rule from this case-law, see above section 3, footnote 19. For our, different, view see also section 3.

66 Often their employers, i.e. the service providers. For the first time this argument was put forward in Case C-49/98, *Finalarte and Others*, EU:C:2001:564. More recently, this (presumed) point of view of the workers from the new Member States is defended in literature by *inter alia* D. Leczykiewicz, 'Conceptualizing conflict between the economic and social in EU law after Viking and Laval', in M. Freedland and J. Prassl (eds.), *EU law in the Member States: Viking, Laval and beyond* (Oxford: Hart Publishing, 2015) and D. Kukovec, 'Hierarchies as law' (2014) 21 *Columbia Journal of International Law*, 142. An illuminating description of the different perspectives on justice contained in the different viewpoints is given by A. Somek, 'From Workers to Migrants, from Distributive Justice to Inclusion: Exploring the Changing Social Democratic Imagination' (2012) 18 *ELJ*, 711–726.

67 See M. Fornasier and M. Torga, 'The Posting of Workers: The Perspective of the Sending State – The Judgment of the Civil Chamber of the Estonian Supreme Court of 16 January 2013 No 3-2-1-179-12' (2013) 3 *Europäische Zeitschrift für Arbeitsrecht (EuZA)*, 358 and D. Leczykiewicz, 'Conceptualizing conflict between the economic and social in EU law after Viking and Laval', in M. Freedland and J. Prassl (eds.), *EU law in the Member States: Viking, Laval and beyond* (Oxford: Hart Publishing, 2015).

68 The controversial character may also be deduced from the large number of amendments (833) which were submitted for the draft report on the enforcement directive of the committee on employment of the EP (procedure file 2012/0061/COD). A similar lively discussion took place in the legislative procedure for the Services Directive. In the final version, employment conditions were specifically excluded from the home country control rule embedded therein: Directive 2006/123/EC of the European Parliament and of the Council of 12 December 2006 on services in the internal market, OJ 2006, L 376/36, Article 3(1)(a), 3(2) and recital 14.

69 Adopted in 1996, well before the accession to the EU of the post-communist countries.

70 The PWD also has an influence on the way the minimum level of protection should be established – e.g. by law or generally applicable collective agreement. Moreover, two

a maximum rule on application of host state law in the context of intra-EU provision of services. In the context of our quest to relevant concepts and criteria for 'belonging', it is of crucial interest to establish the rationale behind the delimitation of the package of host state law which must and may be guaranteed to the posted worker.

According to the Explanatory Memorandum: 'The national differences as to the material content of working conditions *and the criteria inspiring the conflict of law rules* may lead to situations where posted workers are applied lower wages and other working conditions than those in force in the place where the work is temporarily carried out' (emphasis added). 'This situation would certainly affect fair competition between undertakings and equality of treatment between foreign and national undertakings; it would from the social point of view be completely unacceptable'.[71] Consequently, Article 3(1) of the PWD includes in the hard nucleus of protection maximum work periods and minimum rest periods, minimum paid annual holidays and minimum rates of pay. These elements each have a distinct function in the overall protection of workers. However, they are closely correlated when considered from the perspective of fair competition. Especially when wages are calculated at the monthly or weekly rate, it is crucial to know how many hours a week/month the worker has to perform work in order to qualify for full pay. Likewise, holidays constitute direct wage costs and hence determine the actual cost per hour worked.[72] So, beyond doubt, the inclusion of minimum rates of pay, working time and paid holidays in the subjects regulated by the host country was seen as important to prevent unfair competition (our first line of ordering). Although health and safety rules were not addressed in the Explanatory Memorandum,[73] the character of these rules makes it difficult to opt for a non-territorial application.[74]

However, regarding minimum wages and paid holidays *unconditional* application of host state law would infringe the free provision of services and the

provisions allow for additional protection in case of employment through temporary work agencies.

71 COM(91)230 final, 11, under point 12. The last sentence seems to refer to the need to 'protect the workers concerned from practices which may develop within the international framework of an Increasing use of external work and employment resources', mentioned under point 19, fourth indent. See also tables 1–4 (pp. 5–8) which show 'considerable disparities and divergences' between the Member States regarding these subject matters.

72 Compare Case C-165/98, *Mazzoleni and ISA*, EU:C:2001:162, para. 39: 'Second, in order to ensure that the protection enjoyed by employees in the Member State of establishment is equivalent, they must, in particular, take account of factors related to the *amount of remuneration and the work-period to which it relates*, as well as the level of social security contributions and the impact of taxation' (emphasis added).

73 Nor the other items in the list included in Article 3(1), such as protection to specific (vulnerable) groups of workers, equal treatment m/f and provisions relating to conditions for hiring out of workers, in particular the supply of workers by temporary agencies.

74 Often the national rules do not apply to work performed outside the territory. The rules are enforced by public law bodies and may carry criminal sanctions in case of breach.

freedom of contract too much. Hence, if the applicable law to the employment contract offers equivalent or even better protection, there is no need to set aside the normal rule of conflict enshrined in Article 8 Rome I. This seems to be the rationale behind Article 3(7) PWD (first sentence)[75] which is also supported by the early pre-PWD case-law of the CJ on avoiding 'double burdens' for service providers in relation to their posted workers.[76]

Nevertheless, it is easier to pay lip-service to the favour-principle, than to operationalise it. For instance, how to interpret the minimum rates of pay in the host state and how to compare this with the level of wage actually paid by the service provider to his posted workers? While there is some case-law on the latter issue,[77] the first issue remained unclear for a long time. In this respect, the last sentence of Article 3(1) stipulates that the concept of minimum rates of pay referred to in paragraph 1(c) is defined by the national law and/or practice of the host state. Does this mean that Member States are entirely free in the way they define 'minimum rates of pay'?[78] Can the host state impose only a single (statutory or collectively agreed) minimum wage (flat rate)[79] or rather a set of rules determining the minimum rate of pay in the individual case (wage structure/job ladder)? The CJ confirmed the latter interpretation in his judgment in the Finnish preliminary reference case *Sähköalojen ammattiliitto*.[80] Notably, the CJ specifically points out that 'the minimum wage calculated by reference to the relevant collective agreements cannot be a matter of choice for an employer who posts employees with the sole aim of offering lower labour costs than those of local workers'.[81]

75 Elaborated upon in section 3 above, see footnotes 18 and 19.

76 See M.S. Houwerzijl and F.J.L. Pennings, 'Double Charges in Case of Posting of Employees: The Guiot Judgment and its Effects in the Construction Sector' (1999) 1 *European Journal of Social Security*, 91–112 and R. Giesing, 'Posting: Social protection of workers versus fundamental freedoms?' (2003) 40 *CML Rev*, 155.

77 Case C-341/02, *Commission v Germany*, EU:C:2005:220. Confirmed in Case C-522/12, *Isbir*, EU:C:2013:711.

78 Apart from the guidance provided in Article 3(1)(c) regarding overtime charges (which are explicitly deemed to form part of the 'minimum rates of pay' to be applied to posted workers) and contributions to supplementary pension schemes (which are specifically excluded from the minimum rates of pay).

79 For a long time, this seems to have been the prevailing opinion in Germany, which was codified in the German implementation Act of the PWD (AEntG) prior to its amendment in 2009. See more in detail about the German situation M. Kullmann, *Enforcement of Labour Law in Cross-Border Situations. A Legal Study of the EU's Influence on the Dutch, German, and Swedish Enforcement Systems* (PhD thesis) (Deventer: Kluwer 2015), 80.

80 Case C-396/13, *Sähköalojen ammattiliitto*, EU:C:2015:86, para. 43. Also, the Court clarified that host state rules may determine whether the calculation of the minimum wage must be carried out on an hourly or a piecework basis (para. 40) and that holiday pay constitutes part of the minimum wage (paras. 66–69).

81 Case C-396/13, *Sähköalojen ammattiliitto*, EU:C:2015:86, para. 41. The Court also seems to slightly restates the purpose of the PWD as well as the objective of a nucleus of mandatory rules for minimum protection guaranteed to posted workers. See paras. 28–30, emphasising the double aim of preventing unfair competition and ensuring the social protecting of the workers concerned.

Moreover, in this judgment the CJ gave a broad interpretation of the freedom for host states to include in the minimum rates of pay specific allowances such as a daily allowance intended to ensure the social protection of workers 'making up for the disadvantages' of the posting 'as a result of the workers being removed from their usual environment', and a compensation for daily travelling time.[82] Regarding the coverage of the cost of accommodation (as obliged in the Finnish collective agreement) and meal vouchers (in accordance with the contract of employment between service provider and posted worker) the CJ ruled that these should be regarded as compensation for expenses in line with Article 3(7) (second sentence), which does not permit such expenditure to be taken into account in the calculation of their minimum wage. Consequently, the service provider cannot take these costs into account when comparing the actual wage paid with the prescribed level of minimum rates of pay in the host country. Hence, if other host Member States would follow the example set by the Finnish collective agreement (on the conditions explicated by the CJ in *Sähköalojen ammattiliitto*), the status of the posted worker may (in some respects) eventually approximate the expat contract, which is (also) characterised by the special arrangements made to compensate for the expatriation of the worker, such as travel arrangements, housing facilities and expat allowances.[83]

But what about the other side of the coin? When and why may the law applicable to the employment contract continue to be adhered to in the case of cross-border posting? As explained in the Explanatory Memorandum to the first draft of the PWD, the designation and application of the mandatory rules to be observed by foreign service providers in the host state, had to be compatible with the temporary nature of the performance of work in the host country and consistent with the PWD's stated aims and objectives. Against that background, it was decided that 'mandatory rules concerning the form, suspension, alteration and termination of the contract of employment and workers' rights on information, consultation and participation are not dealt with'.[84]

Hence, the selection of said subject-matters which were kept outside the 'hard core' of Article 3(1) PWD, seems to be based either on considerations concerning the organisation of the work (second line of ordering), such as employee co-determination rights, or on considerations relating to the continuation of

---

82 Case C-396/13, *Sähköalojen ammattiliitto*, EU:C:2015:86, paras. 48–52, 54–56.

83 See on this issue *inter alia* C.M.E.P. van Lent, *Internationale intra-concernmobiliteit* (Deventer: Kluwer, 2000), 16.

84 COM (91) 230 final, p. 15, under point 25, third indent and p. 13 under point 19, third indent. It is interesting to note that in a study on international contracts of employment written by T Koopmans in 1966, the author already advocated a similar solution in case the place of work and the place of establishment were located in different countries. He would submit both working time and safety and health issues to the law of the actual place of work, whereas both organisational issues and contractual matters would be regulated by the law of the place of establishment of the employer: T. Koopmans, *De internationaalrechtelijke aspecten van de arbeidsovereenkomst* (Baarn: Hollandia BV, 1966).

the employment relationship, such as in the case of dismissal law (third line of ordering). Indeed, in genuine cases of (short-term) posting an overriding interest to apply host states' dismissal law is absent, since the labour market of the host country may be regarded as not-involved in such situations. In case of dismissal, a genuinely posted worker (with a habitual country of work) will usually fall back on the labour market in the home country. Likewise, the host state has no (or only a limited interest) in regulating the co-determination rights within the foreign company. From the perspective of internal market law, giving effect to mandatory host country rules on dismissal and co-determination rights may be seen as a violation of the free movement of services and of the freedom of contract, not justified by overriding interests of a public policy nature. Phrased in terms of 'belonging': neither the long-term effects of the contract nor the elements related to the organisation of the employer have close links with the country in which the work is temporarily employed.

Above, we examined the (temporary) dual belonging of (genuine) posted workers to host and 'home' country, depending on the subject matter of their labour law entitlements, as defined in Article 3(1) PWD. From the lens of 'belonging', the employment relationship of a (genuine) posted worker touches upon all different lines of ordering. Regarding wages, working time, safety at work and other (minimum) labour standards which influence the day to day performance of the contract, the 'belonging' of the posted workers is clearly determined in light of the first ordering line distinguished in section 2: prevention of social dumping. Here, preference is given to the actual place of work instead of the habitual one. The other types of belonging retain relevance in relation to organisational and contractual matters deemed to be more closely related to the continuing relationship between employer and posted worker.[85] So, for these subject matters including dismissal law, the posted worker continues to 'belong' to the labour market on which he habitually works. However, this preference of the habitual over the actual place of work is by definition 'finite': the precondition is that the posting should remain an exceptional circumstance of *limited duration* within a contract habitually performed in another country. Therefore, the PWD only covers workers who fulfil the definition of posted worker in Article 2 PWD. And it is to this we now turn.

8. WHEN DO I QUALIFY AS BEING POSTED ABROAD?

In order to avoid stretching the scope of application of the PWD (in interaction with the Rome I Regulation) to non-genuine situations of posting, the concepts of 'posting' and 'posted worker' are crucial.

85 According to the Explanatory Memorandum, this concerns 'the bulk of labour law' COM (91) 230 final, p. 13, under point 19, third indent.

With regard to the concept of 'posting', the PWD covers different types of posting which are described in Article 1 PWD and include service contracts in the context of subcontracting, intra-company transfers and temporary agency work. For the three situations of posting covered by the PWD, Article 1(3) states that there must be a link to a cross-border service provision that is temporary in nature. The requirement has two related aspects:

- The posting should be connected to provision (by the posted worker) of a cross-border service in the meaning of Article 56 of the TFEU (as defined in Article 1(1) of the PWD).
- In two of the three situations of posting there seems to be required a service contract between the employer and a recipient established or active in the country where the service is performed. This requirement is mentioned in Article 1(3)(a) and (c), but does not seem to be a prerequisite in case of intra-company postings (Article 1(3)(b) PWD).

In respect of the latter aspect, it is important to note that the provision of services is not the sole context in which posting (secondment) might take place. A worker may also be posted/seconded in the framework of a project for the account of his own employer. Here we may think of the activities of film crews, employees who are sent abroad on business trips, to attend seminars or perform harvesting activities.[86] As a result, instead of coming within the scope of the PWD, this group of seconded workers will be covered by Article 45 TFEU in interaction with Article 8 (and 9) of Rome I.

Apart from the fact that the PWD does not cover all cross-border postings, it should be noted that it doesn't contain a full coordination of cross-border services either.[87] Moreover, it does not even fully coordinate all employment in this context. For example, it would seem from the facts of the cases *Voogsgeerd* and *Koelzsch*, that neither Mr Voogsgeerd nor Mr Koelzsch were posted workers in the meaning of the PWD – even though their employer was a cross-border service provider.[88] Hence, the status of the employing company – as cross-border service provider – can and should be separated from the status of the worker – posted, migrant or otherwise.[89]

With regard to the concept of 'posted worker', in Article 2(1), the PWD defines the posted worker as a worker 'who, for a limited period, carries out

86 Article 4 Directive 91/533 seems to encompass both groups of posting. This is also true for the concept of posting.

87 The coordination of cross-border services is regulated (*inter alia*) by the Services Directive 2006/123. Labour law is specifically excluded from the fields coordinated by this Directive; see preamble paragraphs 14 and 86–87 and Article 1(6) of Directive 2006/123.

88 See for these facts section 5 above.

89 Compare in the context of the transitional period and migration law: Joined Cases C-307/09, 308/09 and C-309/09, *Vicoplus and Others*, EU:C:2011:64.

his work in the territory of a Member State other than the State in which he *normally* works' (emphasis added). This phrasing closely resembles Article 8(2) of the Rome I Regulation, although the PWD uses the word 'normally', whereas the Rome I Regulation refers to a 'habitual' country of work. For a long time it was unclear whether there is a difference in meaning between the two concepts; whereas the Rome I Regulation seems to focus on the habitual place of work *under the contract*, the concept of the PWD may also be applied when the work in the country of origin is performed for more than one employer. Thus, a purely literal reading of Article 2(1) PWD would fit with the posting rule with regard to social security: here, previous insurance in the country of origin is required, not necessarily previous engagement with the posting undertaking.[90] However, a contextual interpretation would be more in line with the aims of the PWD.

The difference between the two possible interpretations is important in the situation that workers are hired solely for the purpose of posting. In that case there will be no habitual place of work in the country of origin, at least not under the contract. So, according to the contextual interpretation of Article 2(1) PWD, such a situation would not qualify as a genuine posting within the meaning of the PWD.[91] We are in favour of this contextual approach, since, as explained above in section 3, in our view the PWD can and should not be read in isolation from Article 8 Rome I. After the implementation of the Enforcement Directive (due 18 June 2016), this issue may be solved: Article 4(3)(c) of the EPWD makes an explicit link between the concept of posting in the PWD and the 'habitual country of work' under the Rome I Regulation.[92]

A controversial issue neither solved nor clarified yet by the EPWD, is the interpretation of what is 'temporary' in Article 8 Rome I and the interpretation of 'a limited period' in Article 2(1) PWD. Some indications of the temporary/limited period of posting are included in recital 36 of the preamble of the Rome I Regulation,[93] which reads: 'As regards individual employment contracts, work carried out in another country should be regarded as temporary if the employee

90 See Article 12 Regulation (EC) 883/2004 as amended by Regulation (EC) 988/2009 and implemented by Regulation (EC) 987/2009, which came into force from 1.5.2010.

91 This approach was taken in a recent Dutch case (Rechtbank Midden Nederland 22 juli 2015, ECLI:NL:RBMNE:2015:5393) between Portuguese and English subsidiaries of the notorious Atlantco Rimec group on the one hand and the Dutch parties to the collective labour agreement in the construction industry on the other hand. The 'posted' workers involved were, according to their employment contracts, explicitly and solely hired for a specific construction project in the Netherlands. Therefore, according to the Dutch court, their 'habitual' country of work under the contract was the Netherlands. As a consequence, Dutch law was deemed to be objectively applicable to the employment contracts of the workers pursuant to Article 8(2) Rome I.

92 Albeit only as an indicative factor in the overall assessment of whether a posted worker temporarily carries out his or her work in a Member State other than the one in which he or she normally works.

93 In the Commission Proposal COM(2005)650 final the specifications were contained in the relevant Article itself, rather than in the preamble.

is expected to resume working in the country of origin after carrying out his tasks abroad. The conclusion of a new contract of employment with the original employer or an employer belonging to the same group of companies as the original employer should not preclude the employee from being regarded as carrying out his work in another country temporarily.' The second sentence actually expands the notion of posting. It can be traced to a proposal of the Groupe Européenne de Droit International Privé[94] and caters for expatriate employees who, for reasons of immigration, might enter into a contract with an establishment in the country of posting while maintaining their contractual link with the original employer in the home country. In contrast, the first sentence is meant to narrow down the concept. It again highlights the importance of economic activity in the country of origin (a place of work to return to), but does not contain any specific limits as to time and/or purpose of the posting.[95]

When approaching the temporary nature of the posting from an internal market perspective, it is remarkable that neither case-law nor legislation based on Article 56 TFEU gives a practicable definition of 'temporary'. In *Rush Portuguesa* the CJ stated that a service provider 'may move with its own work-force which it brings from its own Member State for the duration of the work in question'.[96] Hence, the temporary character of posting seems to be linked to the duration of the service abroad. So far, in this general case-law on services *no limitation in time* to the temporariness of a service provision has been accepted.[97] As stated in *Gebhard*, the temporary nature of the activities has to be determined in the light, not only of the duration of the provision of the service, but also of its regularity, periodical nature or continuity.[98] In *Schnitzer*,[99] application of these criteria made the CJ conclude that Article 56 TFEU includes services such as construction projects involving large building works which are provided over an extended period, up to several years. On the other hand, the CJ held in *Trojani* that an activity carried out on a permanent basis or without any foreseeable limit

94 The proposal was strongly supported by *inter alia* the German Max Planck institute in their comment on the Green Paper: Max Planck Institute for Foreign Private and Private International Law, 'Comments on the European Commission's Green Paper on the conversion of the Rome Convention of 1980 on the law applicable to the contractual obligations into a Community instrument and its modernization' (2003), 37, 65. See: http://ec.europa.eu/justice/news/consulting_public/rome_i/contributions/max_planck_institute_foreign_private_international_law_en.pdf (last accessed on 31 January 2016).

95 EuroISPA (European Internet Services Providers Association) Position Paper, 'Green Paper on the Conversion of the Rome Convention into a Community Instrument: COM (2002) 654' (2003), 36–37, available at http://ec.europa.eu/justice/news/consulting_public/rome_i/contributions/euroispa_en.pdf (last accessed on 31 January 2016).

96 Case C-113/89, *Rush Portuguesa*, EU:C:1990:142, paras. 17 and 19.

97 Case C-514/03, *Commission v Spain*, EU:C:2006:63, para. 22.

98 Case C-55/94, *Gebhard*, EU:C:1995:411, para. 27; and Case C-131/01, *Commission v Italy*, EU:C:2003:96, para. 22.

99 Case C-215/01, *Schnitzer*, EU:C:2003:662, para. 30.

would not be considered a service within the meaning of Article 56 TFEU.[100] Also, it was ruled by the CJ that a construction company exclusively focused on a different country than that of establishment cannot be considered a service provider.[101] Notably, the distinction between Article 56 and Article 49 is in reality difficult to operationalise. In the words of AG Léger in his Opinion to *Gebhard*: 'On the strictly legal level, this distinction is a tricky one, in so far as it is the upshot of a combination of criteria, closely depends on the factual circumstances in question and has never been precisely and systematically defined.'

So, both from an internal market perspective and from a PIL perspective the notion of temporariness is unclear and impractical. This also impacts on the distinction between situations falling within the scope of Article 45 TFEU *vis-à-vis* situations falling within Article 56 TFEU on the other hand, since the temporary nature of posting is often referred to as a key difference with the position of migrant workers, suggesting that the latter group is employed on a more continuous basis in the receiving state. But is that really and necessarily the case? As convincingly shown in the contribution to this book by Verschueren, this is not automatically true, on the contrary.[102] Nowadays many migrant and frontier workers are employed on fixed-term contracts. In case-law it is established that also part-time workers, on-call workers and trainees qualify as workers within the meaning of Article 45 TFEU, as long as their work is of an economic nature and is not (too) marginal or ancillary. In light of that case-law the fact that employment is of short duration cannot, in itself, exclude that employment from the scope of Article 45 TFEU. For instance, someone who has only worked on a temporary basis for two and a half months on the territory of another Member State than his state of origin, should be regarded as a worker within the meaning of Article 45 TFEU on condition that his activities were not purely marginal and ancillary. Clearly, what was once referred to as 'permanent' movement of migrant workers nowadays includes many cross-border movements with very much a temporary (fixed-term) nature.[103]

---

100 As shown by the very wording of Article 57 TFEU, in contradistinction to the permanent nature of the activity carried out by an economic operator who is established in a Member State (observation of AG Lèger, Opinion of Advocate General Lèger in Case C-55/94, *Gebhard*, EU:C:1995:194, para. 32).

101 This clearly follows from the judgment in Case C-404/98, *Plum*, EU:C:2000:607, situated in the context of what is now Regulation 883/2004.

102 See on the blurry nature of the concept of 'worker' in Article 45 TFEU, chapter of H. Verschueren in this volume. Also, M.S. Houwerzijl, '"Regime shopping" across (blurring) boundaries', in S. Evju (ed.), *Regulating Transnational Labour in Europe: The quandaries of multilevel governance* (Oslo: Institut for privatrett, Skriftserie 196, 2014).

103 Case C-413/01, *Ninni-Orasche*, EU:C:2003:600, paras. 25 and 32. See also Case C-169/03, *Wallentin*, EU:C:2004:203 and Case C-109/04, *Kranemann*, EU:C:2005:187 regarding trainees one of whom only worked abroad several weeks, as discussed by H. Verschueren, 'Cross-border workers in the European internal market: Trojan horses for Member States' labour

At first sight, a more distinctive criterion in demarcating Article 45 mobility from Article 56 mobility may be found in the notion of 'labour market access'. In the case *Rush Portuguesa*, the CJ made a distinction between migrant workers, who enter the labour market of the host state, and posted workers, who generally do not. The employer of a posted worker makes use of the free movement of services. The worker doesn't need to avail himself of the free movement of workers, because, according to the CJ, he does not seek access to the labour market of the host Member State, but will instead return to the state where he normally works once the service has been carried out. This passive movement (namely because the employer assigns him to) may be illustrated by the fact that the posted worker has concluded an employment contract with his employer governed by the law of the habitual country of work. Another indicator of passive movement, often used in the context of PIL, is the provision or reimbursement of travel, board and lodging costs by the employer.[104] Notably, in its recent judgment *Sähköalojen ammattiliitto*,[105] the CJ brought the status of the posted worker (in this respect) closer to the traditional expatriate employee, by ruling that such special arrangements should be regarded as compensation for expenses in line with Article 3(7) (second sentence) PWD.

The distinction based on labour market access is crucial in case the worker doesn't enjoy free movement himself, e.g. because he is covered by a transitional regime.[106] But the distinction between Article 45 mobility and Article 56 mobility also has an impact on the labour law protection of the workers involved. The PWD intends to provide a significant but not a full level of host state protection for posted workers, who may be vulnerable given their situation (temporary employment in a foreign country, difficulty in obtaining proper representation, lack of knowledge of local laws, institutions and language). As Kilpatrick observes:[107] 'Socially, it is not difficult to imagine that long-stretches of life in a (typically more expensive) host-state on a minimum skeleton of host-state labour standards can seem exploitative to posted workers and host-state inhabitants alike.'

---

and social security law?' (2008) 24 *International Journal of Comparative Labour Law and Industrial Relations*, 176.

104 This indicator is made explicit in Article 4(2)(d) of the EPWD. See in more detail A.A.H. van Hoek and M.S. Houwerzijl, '"Posting" and "posted workers" – The need for clear definitions of two key concepts of the Posting of Workers Directive', in C. Barnard, M. Gehring and I. Solanke (eds.), *Cambridge Yearbook of European Legal Studies* (Oxford: Hart Publishing, 2012).

105 See above footnote 80, elaborated upon in section 7.

106 This may be different when the worker is send abroad by a temporary work agency: see Joined Cases C-307/09, C-308/09 and C-309/09, *Vicoplus and Others*, EU:C:2011:64. For third-country nationals working and residing legally in a Member State the distinction makes it possible to post them to another Member State. See Case C-43/93, *Vander Elst*, EU:C:1994:310, recently confirmed in Case C-91/13, *Essent Energie Productie*, EU:C:2013:711.

107 C. Kilpatrick, 'British Jobs for British Workers? UK Industrial Action and Free Movement of Services in EU Law', LSE Legal Studies Working Paper No. 16/2009, 27.

The differences in labour costs attached to both 'avenues' for worker mobility seem to be used more and more strategically by firms (as a business model) in order to gain this 'comparative advantage'. Labour law is but one of the points to be taken into consideration; social security and tax law being at least as important. Intermediaries in other Member States are used with the sole purpose of turning (temporary or seasonal) migration into posting. When, for example, a TWA recruits Polish workers for jobs in Sweden, the actual circumstances may not change according to whether the TWA is Polish or Swedish, but the legal situation does. Therefore, blurring regulatory concepts and criteria also generate opportunities for non-compliance, resulting in violation of labour law and other (fundamental) rights of migrant workers.[108]

9. WHERE DO I BELONG WHEN I DO NOT (WANT TO) KNOW MY LEGAL STATUS?

The distinction between Article 45 and Article 56 mobility, stemming from *Rush Portuguesa*, is often poorly understood. In the popular press there is (almost) no awareness of the fact that there are different migration modalities, let alone that these are governed by different legal regimes.[109] This may be explained by the fact that all these modalities seem to lead to very similar actual work patterns and problems, such as underpayment, excessive deduction of costs for lodging and travel, violations of health and safety and working time regulation.

Contentious cases in the media often relate to situations which may not deemed to be 'proper' posting because the worker does not normally work in another state than the host state, because the employer is not genuinely established in another state or because an employment relationship between employer and worker is missing. Some cases relate to letter box companies opened only for the purpose of posting. The worker might actually be made to work under the direct supervision of the user undertaking, thus creating a situation of bogus subcontracting or illicit provision of manpower. The absence of genuine activities in the country of origin may be combined with repeated postings, in which the 'posted' worker is working in a specific Member State on an (almost) permanent basis. Other cases describe situations of rotational posting in which the worker is posted consecutively to different Member States or, with unpaid leave in between, to the same Member State again and again.

108 See more in detail M.S. Houwerzijl, '"Regime shopping" across (blurring) boundaries', in S. Evju (ed.), *Regulating Transnational Labour in Europe: The quandaries of multilevel governance* (Oslo: Institut for privatrett, Skriftserie 196, 2014).

109 See section 3 and Annexes I/II of our comparative studies commissioned by the European Commission, on the legal aspects of the posting of workers in the framework of the provision of services in the European Union 2011/12, available at http://ec.europa.eu/social/main.jsp?catId=471&langId=en (last accessed on 31 January 2016).

Anecdotal evidence from media is now confirmed and elaborated upon by research on the ground. Studies of (for example) Wagner and Berntsen based on interviews with workers situated at the building sites of the European Central Bank in Germany and the 'Eemshaven' in the Netherlands, as well as in workplaces in the meat sector and the supermarket distribution centres, clearly show that the workers concerned most often do not know their legal status.[110]

Hence, there is (reason for) clear concern about abuses of the freedoMs G.ranted by the EU internal market. Posting regulations are misused systematically and do create competition on wage levels in host state labour markets.[111] Especially in the area of provision of manpower, the problem of combating illegal activities is encountered. However, these forms of abuse are not specific to posting (nor for provision of manpower). The illegal temporary work agencies may be established both in the country of recruitment (leading to posting) or in the county of work (leading to migration). Several reported cases of abuse concerned migrant workers or even (bogus) self-employed.[112] These cases involve social dumping in its purest form – with no respect for either the protective system of the country of origin or that of the host country.

For trade unions and enforcement authorities it is difficult to trace and combat the situations mentioned above; the fluidity in the cross-border context, with firms often disappearing across borders or going bankrupt, complicate their efforts to enforce (and execute) local labour standards. Moreover, the employer-arranged migration context leads to isolation of migrants, as they often have

---

110 L.E. Berntsen, *Agency of labour in a flexible pan-European labour market: A qualitative study of migrant practices and trade union strategies in the Netherlands* (PhD thesis) (Groningen: University of Groningen, SOM Research School, 2015) and I. Wagner, *Posted Work and Deterritorialization in the European Union: A Study of the German Construction and Meat Industry* (PhD thesis) (Groningen: University of Groningen, SOM Research School, 2015). They conducted micro-level research (based on interviews) regarding migrant/posted workers strategies and union strategies at two big building sites, in the supermarkets branch and in the meat sector in the Netherlands and Germany. See also, for the UK: C. Barnard and A. Ludlow, 'Enforcement of Employment Rights by EU-8 Migrant Workers in Employment Tribunals', presented as a working paper at the LLRN conference 25–27 June 2015 in Amsterdam.

111 In the Netherlands, for instance, some Dutch truck drivers were given the choice of either accepting a reduction in their pay and other employment conditions, or accept pay rolling constructions via Cyprus, under threat of dismissal. See J. Cremers, 'Schijnconstructies in het internationale wegtransport' (2014) 25(1) *Zeggenschap*, 32–34.

112 See A.A.H. van Hoek and M.S. Houwerzijl, 'Comparative Study on the legal aspects of the posting of workers in the framework of the provision of services in the European Union' (2011) and 'Complementary study on the legal aspects of the posting of workers in the framework of the provision of services in the European Union' (2012) *Reports to the European Commission under contract VT/2009/0541* and *contract VC/2011/0096*, available at http://ec.europa.eu/social/main.jsp?catId=471&langId=en (last accessed on 31 January 2016). More recently, the European Agency on Fundamental Rights (FRA) called for 'zero tolerance for severe forms of labour exploitation', in its report on *Severe Labour Exploitation: Workers Moving within or into the European Union, States' Obligations and Victims' Rights* (Brussels, 2015).

limited knowledge of host state law and institutional structures. They are also segregated spatially and socially from their host surroundings because of the way they are housed near the place of work. And if trade unions and host state institutions succeed in reaching the workers, they experience enormous practical difficulties in establishing exactly which conditions (should) apply to a specific individual employment relationship, because the rules are so complicated in cross-border situations.[113]

A different, more ambiguous, situation arises when the employment conditions do conform (more or less) to the standards of the home state but not to those of the host. As becomes apparent from several empirical studies, in such cases the workers may not have an incentive to claim the extra rights awarded to them under the law of the host state. They seem to be happy with the job opportunity and do not want to put that in danger by claiming host state entitlements.[114] As Berntsen puts it: 'the commodified employment context tends to disempower migrants, at the same time it enables them to live better lives then they would if they opted not to participate in this European market context'.[115]

The harm of their passive attitude in claiming their rights is (felt to be) done to third parties, and – more abstractly – to the social structure of the host state, rather than to one of the parties to the individual contract. In extreme cases the workers will even operate in cohort with the employer to evade the law of the host state.[116] From our perspective on 'belonging', these persistent findings seems to point to a discrepancy or perhaps cognitive dissonance between the

113 See L.E. Berntsen, *Agency of labour in a flexible pan-European labour market: A qualitative study of migrant practices and trade union strategies in the Netherlands* (PhD thesis) (Groningen: University of Groningen, SOM Research School, 2015), 170–175; M. Kullmann, *Enforcement of Labour Law in Cross-Border Situations. A Legal Study of the EU's Influence on the Dutch, German, and Swedish Enforcement Systems* (PhD thesis) (Deventer: Kluwer, 2015), 211–225, 266–290 and I. Wagner, *Posted Work and Deterritorialization in the European Union: A Study of the German Construction and Meat Industry* (PhD thesis) (Groningen: University of Groningen, SOM Research School, 2015), 70–76.

114 See A.A.H. van Hoek and M.S. Houwerzijl, 'Comparative Study on the legal aspects of the posting of workers in the framework of the provision of services in the European Union' (2011) and 'Complementary study on the legal aspects of the posting of workers in the framework of the provision of services in the European Union', available at http://ec.europa.eu/social/main.jsp?catId=471&langId=en (last accessed on 31 January 2016), at section 4.5 on legal remedies.

115 L.E. Berntsen, *Agency of labour in a flexible pan-European labour market: A qualitative study of migrant practices and trade union strategies in the Netherlands* (PhD thesis) (Groningen: University of Groningen, SOM Research School, 2015), 171.

116 In the country reports for our PWD study commissioned by the European Commission, this was specifically mentioned by the Estonian expert. See A.A.H. van Hoek and M.S. Houwerzijl, 'Comparative Study on the legal aspects of the posting of workers in the framework of the provision of services in the European Union' (2011) and 'Complementary study on the legal aspects of the posting of workers in the framework of the provision of services in the European Union' (2012) *Reports to the European Commission under contract VT/2009/0541* and *contract VC/2011/0096*, available at http://ec.europa.eu/social/main.jsp?catId=471&langId=en (last accessed on 31 January 2016).

legal understanding of belonging (which is – at least – partly situated in the host state) and the 'feeling' of belonging (which seems to be situated in the 'home state' or 'wherever there is work').[117] In such cases the law of the host state will only be enforced if enforcement is entrusted to host state authorities or interested third parties (such as social funds or the unions in the host state). The EPWD facilitates and stimulates this in some respects, but asks for a real effort with budgetary implications and strong political will at the level of the host Member State.

10. SUMMARISING CONCLUSIONS

Above, we mapped and critically analysed criteria and concepts used by the EU legislator and the CJ in order to establish place(s) where mobile EU workers 'belong' in relation to their labour law entitlements. As was demonstrated, both in (the interpretation of) the relevant provisions of Rome I and in the PWD, several lines of ordering are visible, informed by the specific goals of labour law. These ordering lines may carry with them different types of 'belonging', attributing workers to legal systems on the basis of the territory and/or the branch of industry in which the work is performed, or the organisational framework of the employing company. Why do the conflicts rules attribute a situation to the law of country A rather than country B? And what underlying system of ordering is at work here? Above, these questions were in particular explored for so-called peripatetic employees, expatriate employees and posted workers, since case-law primarily dealt with these groups. Below, we summarise and conclude. Where apt, we give some food for thought from the lens of 'belonging'.

Notwithstanding the practical difficulties to apply the habitual place of work as a connecting factor to peripatetic employees, the CJ took this approach in the *Koelzsch* and *Voogsgeerd* cases. By stretching this concept very far, the CJ gave priority to the habitual place of work over the place of establishment of the employer. From the first ordering perspective of preventing labour market competition (social dumping), we welcomed this approach. However, from the organisation of the business, designated as the second ordering perspective, our assessment was at first sight less positive. However, on a closer inspection

117 In the PhD thesis of Berntsen, a long quotation from a Polish scaffolder, 28 years old, shows that the sense of belonging to the 'home country' may also be lost: 'I don't see my future in Poland. I see my future where there is work, because without work [...] you know how it is over there [in Poland], it is difficult to get a job', L.E. Berntsen, *Agency of labour in a flexible pan-European labour market: A qualitative study of migrant practices and trade union strategies in the Netherlands* (PhD thesis) (Groningen: University of Groningen, SOM Research School, 2015), 24. Home, and hence a sense of belonging, may be where ever there is work.

of the judgments, we argued that the CJ effectively conflated the organisational framework and the actual place of performance into a single connecting factor: the 'place where or from which the work is habitually performed'. Indeed, in its judgments the CJ attached weight to the place where the worker receives instructions concerning his tasks and organises his work, as well as to the place where his work tools are situated. These criteria refer – at least in part – to the organisational structure of the employer.

In contrast to its very broad interpretation of the 'habitual place of work', the CJ leaves little room for 'the place of engagement'. As clarified in *Voogsgeerd*, the latter connecting factor serves to provide legal certainty in a case in which the primary connecting factor is not able to provide a clear link to any particular jurisdiction. In absence of any further European case-law, it is difficult to predict for which category of (hyper-mobile) workers this connecting factor may act as a 'home for the homeless'.

More clarity has been obtained with regard to the escape clause referring to the country of closest connection. With regard to the situation of an expatriate employee, the CJ declared in *Schlecker*, the applicable law must first be determined by reference to the pre-established connecting factors. However, the national court may disregard these connecting factors and apply the law of another country, 'even where an employee carries out the work in performance of the contract habitually, for a lengthy period and without interruption in the same country', where it is apparent from the circumstances as a whole that the employment contract is more closely connected with that country. By giving such a broad interpretation of the possibility to deviate from the law of the habitual place of work in favour of another law, the CJ seems – to a certain extent – to undo the effect of the decisions in *Koelzsch* and *Voogsgeerd*. The escape rule undermines the general applicability of the law of the habitual place of work and hence the territorial application of labour law.

Although it is too early to predict how extensive the CJ will interpret the escape clause in future cases (and for other categories of workers), it is beyond dispute that with *Schlecker*, the tax law and social security schemes applicable to the employee have regained importance. The weight attached to these factors in *Schlecker* does point to prioritising a different kind of belonging – not the labour market on which the employee performed her work was deemed to be decisive, but the social structure in which she was embedded through the system of social charges (the third line of ordering). In conflicts concerning dismissal rules it might make sense to connect this specific element of employment law to the system of social security applicable to the worker concerned. It can be questioned however, whether the same rationale is also valid for wages, working time, safety at work and all those other rules which influence the day to day performance of the contract. Do other types of belonging retain (or regain) relevance there?

In the situation of posted workers the answer is yes. (Genuine) posted workers are deemed to belong to both host and 'home' country, depending on the subject matter of their labour law entitlements. From the lens of 'belonging', the employment relationship of a (genuine) posted worker touches upon all different lines of ordering. Regarding wages, working time, safety at work and other (minimum) labour standards which influence the day to day performance of the contract, the 'belonging' of the posted workers is clearly determined in light of the first ordering line: prevention of social dumping. The other types of belonging retain relevance in relation to organisational and contractual matters more closely related to the continuing relationship between employer and posted worker, situated in the habitual country of work (which in genuine posting situations will usually coincide with the country of common origin). So, for said subject matters including dismissal law, the posted worker continues to 'belong' to the labour market on which he habitually works. However, this preference of the habitual over the actual place of work is by definition 'finite': the precondition is that the posting should remain an exceptional circumstance of limited duration within a contract habitually performed in another country.

Therefore, it is important that the PWD only covers workers who fulfil the definition of posted worker in Article 2 PWD. For this purpose, the concepts of 'posting' and 'posted worker' are crucial, but currently unclear in several aspects. For instance, in situations that workers are hired solely for the purpose of posting there will be no habitual place of work in the country of origin, at least not under the contract. Based on the assumption that the PWD can and should not be read in isolation from Article 8 Rome I, such a situation should in our view not qualify as a genuine posting within the meaning of the PWD. After the implementation of the EPWD (due 18 June 2016), this issue seems to be solved: the EPWD creates an explicit link between the concept of posting in the PWD and the 'habitual country of work' under the Rome I Regulation. A controversial issue not solved nor clarified by the EPWD, is the interpretation of what is 'temporary' in Article 8 Rome I and the interpretation of 'a limited period' in Article 2(1) PWD. Both from an internal market perspective and from a PIL perspective the predominant notion of 'temporariness' is unclear and impractical: everything is left to an assessment on a case-by-case basis without any (rebuttable) limitations in time. Moreover, the blurriness of the concepts and criteria also generates opportunities for non-compliance, resulting in social dumping and violation of labour law and other (fundamental) rights of migrant and posted workers.

The politically difficult quest for effective remedies against social dumping and misabuse in transnational employment relationships based on 'the search of cheap labour', becomes even more complicated if the employment conditions do conform (more or less) to the standards of the home state. In such situations, the workers involved often seem to prioritise their job opportunities above claiming host state entitlements. Hence, the harm of their passive attitude in claiming their rights is (felt to be) done to third parties, and – more abstractly – to the social structure of the host state, rather than to one of the parties to the individual contract. In such situations, empirical research clearly demonstrates a discrepancy or perhaps cognitive dissonance between the legal understanding of belonging (which is – at least – partly situated in the host state) and the 'feeling' of belonging (which is allegedly situated in the 'home state'). Should that discrepancy lead to an adjustment of the balance between the distinct lines of ordering, prioritising the place of engagement or a country of closer connection, above the actual workplace? Recently, this stance, phrased as 'the point of view of the posted worker from post-communist states',[118] entered the academic debate.

Authors such as Kukovec and Leczykiewicz acknowledge that social dumping and 'a race to the bottom' may occur if the concept of territorial application of labour law would be replaced by a home country control rule. However, in their view these disadvantages, which mainly befall the wealthier 'central' Member States, are outweighed by the interests of the workers from the new, 'peripheral' Member States to use their one comparative advantage – the possibility to compete on the basis of lower labour costs.[119] Their argument can be placed in a discussion in which justice within the EU is mainly perceived as 'access justice': a theory in which justice is mainly concerned with the right of all citizens to participate in the benefits of the internal market.[120] This type of justice is contrasted with the more distributive role of the developed national welfare states that exist in (many of) the old Member States.[121] The system of distributive justice presupposes a more or less closed system of mutual rights and obligations. The narrative of 'belonging', while fitting nicely into the latter theory, does not seem to play any meaningful role in the former.

This is exemplified by Leczykiewicz where she states that 'employment opportunities on the Swedish and Finnish market in no way 'belong' to

---

118 Expressed in less ambivalent wording than by the interviewed workers in the studies of Berntsen and Wagner, see L.E. Berntsen, *Agency of labour in a flexible pan-European labour market: A qualitative study of migrant practices and trade union strategies in the Netherlands* (PhD thesis) (Groningen: University of Groningen, SOM Research School, 2015) and I. Wagner, *Posted Work and Deterritorialization in the European Union: A Study of the German Construction and Meat Industry* (PhD thesis) (Groningen: University of Groningen, SOM Research School, 2015).

119 See D. Leczykiewicz, 'Conceptualizing conflict between the economic and social in EU law after Viking and Laval', in M. Freedland and J. Prassl (eds.), *EU law in the Member States: Viking, Laval and beyond* (Oxford: Hart Publishing, 2015) and D. Kukovec, 'Hierarchies as law' (2014) 21 *Columbia Journal of International Law*, 142.

120 On the theory of 'access justice' versus 'social justice' see H. Micklitz, 'Social Justice and Access Justice in Private Law' (2012) 13 *European Journal of Comparative Law*, 233–266.

121 A. Somek, 'The social question in a transnational context' (2011) 39 *LSE 'Europe in question' Discussion Paper*, 31.

Swedish and Finnish workers.'[122] In her opinion this would also mean that the Finnish and Swedish workers are no longer legitimised to defend their system against underbidding by outsiders. Such a radical form of 'access justice' or 'transnational solidarity' by allowing workers to compete on wage levels runs counter to goals and underpinning of labour law, not only enshrined in the ordering lines we looked at above, but also in the EU Charter of Fundamental Rights (chapter on solidarity) and in Article 45 TFEU. Moreover, such forced openness from the part of the host state, would erode the basis for its national distributive institutions. All EU citizens may demand equal access to the national system, but who will build and maintain this system, if too many do no longer experience a sense of belonging (with the concomitant responsibility)? And, on a final note, one may wonder whether realisation of the ideal of 'access justice' would not turn into a trap, once the worker from the new Member State is for a longer period in the host Member State and actually becomes more embedded in this state (by starting a family life, hiring or buying a house, getting an accident, needing medical help etc.)? What type of belonging would s/he then prefer?

122 D. Leczykiewicz, 'Conceptualizing conflict between the economic and social in EU law after Viking and Laval', in M. Freedland and J. Prassl (eds.), *EU law in the Member States: Viking, Laval and beyond* (Oxford: Hart Publishing, 2015) 21, under footnote 48. In relation to posting her argument sits uneasily with the legal fiction that posted workers 'never' have access to the labour market of the host state and cannot deemed to be job seekers (and hence may not be seen as migrant workers).

CHAPTER 12

CONFLICTING RULES OF CONFLICT: SOCIAL SECURITY AND LABOUR LAW

Rob CORNELISSEN

1. INTRODUCTION

This chapter focuses on the consequences of the co-existence of two systems determining the applicable law for mobile workers, one in the field of social security and one in labour law.

The main principle of the rules determining the applicable legislation of the coordination regulation has always been the *lex loci laboris*. However, for some categories of workers, including posted workers and workers who normally are employed in the territory of two or more Member States, special rules have been created.

It follows from the Court's case-law that the provisions laid down in the EU regulations determining the legislation applicable form a complete system of conflict rules which are mandatory for Member States and *a fortiori* for the persons concerned.[1] The worker and his employer do not have the freedom to choose the applicable legislation.

The difference with the law applicable to individual employment contracts is striking. In accordance with private international law, the starting point for the system of conflict of law rules in matters of contractual relations between worker and employer is the parties' freedom to choose the applicable law. These rules are laid down in the 1980 Rome Convention on the law applicable to contractual obligations;[2] since the Amsterdam Treaty (1999) gave the Union

1 Judgments in Case C- 345/09, *Van Delft*, EU:C:2010:610, para. 52 and Case C-103/13, *Somova*, EU:C:2014:2334, paras. 54–59.

2 1980 Rome Convention on the law applicable to contractual obligations, OJ 1988, C 27.

the competence to do so,[3] Regulation 593/2008[4] was adopted replacing the 1980 Rome Convention.[5]

Posting of workers is a controversial issue in the EU. It follows from the case-law of the Court of Justice[6] that if an employer who is a cross-border service provider posts a worker, this worker is not to be considered covered by Article 45 TFEU and Regulation 492/2011.[7] This means that this worker cannot invoke the equal treatment principle regarding working conditions in comparison to nationals of the host Member State. In contrast, the freedom to provide services gives businesses the right to provide services in another Member State without being discriminated and/or discouraged by the authorities of the host Member State. To that end, they may post their own workers temporarily to the other Member State to carry out the work necessary to provide the services. In 1996 a Directive[8] was adopted in order to reconcile the exercise of this freedom to provide cross-border services under Article 56 TFEU with appropriate protection of the rights of workers temporarily posted abroad for that purpose. To this end the Directive sets out a nucleus of mandatory rules (to be laid down in law or in collective agreements which have been declared universally applicable) that must be applied to posted workers in the host Member State.

The co-existence of two systems of conflict of law rules could have as a result that a worker is subject to the social security legislation of one Member State and to labour law of another Member State. This chapter will show how this could lead to problems for the worker concerned.

---

3 Article 65 EC, currently Article 81 TFEU.

4 Regulation (EC) No. 593/2008 of the European Parliament and of the Council of 17 June 2008 on the law applicable to contractual obligations (Rome I), OJ 2008, L 177 (hereinafter referred to as 'Rome I').

5 Regulation Rome I applies to contracts concluded after 17 December 2009.

6 Judgments in Case C-113/89, *Rush Portuguesa*, EU:C:1990:142; Case C-43/93, *Van der Elst*, EU:C:1994:310; and Joined Cases C-49/98, C-50/98, C-52/98 to C-54/98 and C-68/98 to C-71/98, *Finalarte*, EU:C:2001:564.

7 This case-law has been criticised in literature; see in particular: H. Verschueren, 'Cross-border workers in the European Internal Market: Trojan horses for Member States' labour and social security law?' (2008) 24 *International Journal of Comparative Labour Law and Industrial Relations*, 167–199. The Court has actually not always been consistent on this point. Employees of agencies for the supply of manpower, e.g. may in certain circumstances be covered by Article 45 TFEU and Regulation 492/2011: Joined Cases C-307/09 to C-309/09, *Vicoplus*, EU:C:2011:64. In its judgment in Joined Cases C-611/10 and C-612/10, *Hudzinski and Wawrzyniak*, EU:C:2012:339, the Court referred to Article 45 TFEU in relation to posted workers.

8 Directive 96/71/EC of the European Parliament and of the Council of 16 December 1996 concerning the posting of workers in the framework of the provision of services, OJ 1997, L 18 (hereinafter referred to as 'Directive 96/71').

2. RULES OF CONFLICT IN EU SOCIAL SECURITY LAW

As the Court has underlined in its case-law, the EU Regulations on the coordination of social security systems[9] only coordinate the various social security schemes of Member States. They do not affect the competence of the Member States to regulate their social security systems.[10] In the absence of harmonisation at EU level, it is, in principle, for the legislation of each Member State to determine the categories of persons who are insured under its law.[11] However, Member States use different criteria to define these categories.

In order to prevent different national criteria leading to conflicts of law in situations where people cross the internal borders of the Union (negative conflict: a person would not be insured in any Member State; positive conflict: the person would be insured simultaneously in two or more Member States), the Regulations have, from the very beginning, contained uniform criteria for the determination of the legislation applicable.

2.1. THE BINDING CHARACTER OF THE CONFLICT OF LAW RULES

The rules determining the applicable social security legislation are binding. In fact, these rules would no longer make any sense if the Member State whose legislation has been determined as being applicable by the Regulation retained the right to determine, itself, under its own legislation, the personal scope of their social security system on the basis of territorial criteria. As the Court of Justice has emphasised in its case-law,[12] 'the provisions of Title II constitute a complete system of conflict rules the effect of which is to divest the legislature of each Member State of the power to determine the ambit and the conditions for the application of its national legislation so far as the persons who are subject thereto and the territory within which the provisions of national law take effect are concerned'.

---

9 Currently Regulation (EC) No. 883/2004 of the European Parliament and of the Council of 29 April 2004 on the coordination of social security systems, OJ 2004, L 166 (hereinafter referred to as 'Regulation 883/2004), lastly modified by Regulation (EU) No. 465/2012 of the European Parliament and of the Council of 22 May 2012 amending Regulation (EC) No. 883/2004 on the coordination of social security systems and Regulation (EC) No. 987/2009 laying down the procedure for implementing Regulation (EC) No. 883/2004, OJ 2012, L 149 (hereinafter referred to as 'Regulation 465/2012).

10 See, to that effect, Case C-282/11, *Salgado Gonzalez*, EU:C:2013:86, and the case-law cited.

11 Case C-103/13, *Somova*, EU:C:2014:2334, para. 34.

12 Case C-103/13, *Somova*, EU:C:2014:2334, para. 54.

The binding character of the rules on conflicts of law may lead to situations where persons residing in one Member State but working in another, are insured in the latter State, even if insurance in that State is conditional upon residence there. The effect of the conflict of law rules laid down in Regulation 883/2004 is that a provision of the applicable national legislation according to which coverage under the insurance scheme established by that legislation is conditional on residence in the Member State in whose territory the activity as an employed person is pursued may not be relied *vis-á-vis* such a person.[13] In practical terms it means that national affiliation conditions are overridden if their application is such as to deprive the conflict of law rule laid down in Union law of all practical effect. A person, for instance, residing in a Member State but working in another Member State, cannot be excluded from the scope of the social security scheme of the latter State for the sole reason of not residing there.

2.2. EXCLUSIVE EFFECT OF THE RULES

The exclusive effect means that you cannot be simultaneously subject to the legislation of two or more Member States.

Regulation No. 3,[14] applicable between 1959 and 1972, did not include an explicit provision prohibiting the simultaneous application of the legislation of two or more Member States. Article 12 of that Regulation simply stated that a worker employed on the territory of a Member State 'shall be subject of the legislation of that State'. The Court ruled[15] that Article 12 Regulation No. 3 did not prohibit Member States, other than the State whose legislation was applicable by virtue of the aforementioned article, from applying their social security legislation to migrant workers, if that simultaneous application led to a 'supplementary protection' of the worker concerned.

13 Case C-2/89, *Kits van Heyningen*, EU:C:1990:183; Case C-196/90, *De Paep*, EU:C:1991:381; Case C-347/10, *Salemink*, EU:C:2012:17; and Case C-106/11, *Bakker*, EU:C:2012:328. The recent judgment in Case C-179/13, *Evans*, EU:C:2015:12, concerned a UK national who, after having worked as an employed person in the UK and the Netherlands, had been a member of the consular staff of *a third country* (USA) in the Netherlands. In accordance with the Vienna Consular Convention Ms Evans had been granted a privileged status and did not pay social security contributions in the Netherlands while being a member of the consular staff of the USA. The Court ruled that, since Ms Evans, in accordance with the Vienna Consular Convention, had not been subject to the social security legislation of the Netherlands during the period that she was a member of the USA consular staff, she was not insured in the Netherlands during this period, even when she resided there. This judgment should be seen in the light of the applicability of the relevant provisions of the Vienna Consular Convention. It does not put into question the aforementioned case-law. On the contrary, in its judgment the Court explicitly reiterates its previous case-law on the binding effect of the conflict of law rules.

14 Regulation No. 3 on the social security for migrant workers, OJ 1958, 561/58 (hereinafter referred to as 'Regulation No. 3').

15 Case 92/63, *Nonnenmacher*, EU:C:1964:40; and Case 19/67, *Van der Vecht*, EU:C:1967:49.

In order to reflect more clearly the intention of the Community legislature in this respect,[16] it was decided when Regulation No. 3 was replaced by Regulation 1408/71,[17] to insert a provision[18] stipulating explicitly that persons to whom Regulation 1408/71 applied were subject to the legislation of a single Member State only.

Like its predecessor Regulation 1408/71, Regulation 883/2004 contains an explicit provision[19] that 'persons to whom this Regulation applies shall be subject to the legislation of a single Member State only'. The legislature decided even to insert a recital[20] in Regulation 883/2004 stating that 'the principle of unity of the applicable legislation is of great importance and should be enhanced'.[21]

The wording of Article 11(1) Regulation 883/2004, identical to that of Article 13(1) Regulation 1408/71, could not be clearer. And until a number of years ago, the Court indeed confirmed and even emphasised the exclusive effect of the conflict of law rules.[22] This case-law guaranteed the predictability of the conflict of law rules as well as legal certainty. However, despite the very clear wording of the conflict of law rule concerned, we know since the *Bosmann* judgment[23] that it is in some cases possible that a worker is also covered by the social security legislation of a Member State other than the one designated as the competent one by the Regulation. In those rather exceptional cases, we see, surprisingly, a similarity with the result of the rules determining the law governing the individual contract between worker and employer.

Ms Bosmann, a Belgian national, was a single mother living with her two children, students of 20 and 21 years old, in Germany. Under German law, all residents are entitled to family benefits for children of such ages who are students. In 2005 Ms Bosmann started to work as an employed person in the Netherlands. Her claim for family benefits in the Netherlands was rejected, because the legislation of the Netherlands only provides for family benefits for children until the age of 18. Her claim for German family benefits was rejected for the reason that she, being employed in the Netherlands, was subject to the legislation of the Netherlands. The German authorities referred

16 See the explanatory memorandum to the Commission's proposal, submitted to the Council in January 1966, COM (66) 8, 22.

17 Council Regulation (EEC) No. 1408/71 of 14 June 1971 on the application of social security schemes to employed persons, to self-employed persons and to members of their families moving within the Community, OJ 1974, L 149/2 (hereinafter referred to as 'Regulation 1408/71').

18 Article 13(1) first sentence of Regulation 1408/71.

19 Article 11(1) Regulation 883/2004.

20 Recital 18a Regulation 883/2004 as amended by Regulation 988/2009.

21 This is linked to the fact that Regulation 883/2004 no longer contains exceptions to the exclusive effect of the applicable social security legislation, as was the case under (Articles 14c and 14f of) the old Regulation 1408/71.

22 Case 302/84, *Ten Holder*, EU:C:1986:242; and Case 60/85, *Luyten*, EU:C:1986:307.

23 Case C-352/06, *Bosmann*, EU:C:2008:290.

to Article 13(2)(a) Regulation 1408/71 stipulating clearly: 'persons to whom this Regulation applies, shall be subject to the legislation of a single Member State only'. Ms Bosmann appealed against this decision and the case came finally before the Court.

In its judgment the Court emphasised that all provisions of the EU regulations on the coordination of social security systems must be interpreted in the light of Article 42 EC (currently Article 48 TFEU) which aims to prevent that workers who have made use of their right to free movement would be penalised in the field of social security.[24] In addition, the Court referred to the first recital of Regulation 1408/71[25] stating that the rules for coordination of national social security systems should contribute towards improving the standard of living and conditions of employment for people exercising their right of free movement. Therefore, the Member State of residence cannot be deprived of the right to grant family benefits to those who are resident within its territory. Even when it was denied,[26] by this judgment the Court overruled its previous case-law[27] on the matter. In the 1986 *Ten Holder* and *Luyten* judgments the Court emphasised that the exclusive effect of the rules on conflicts of law was not at variance with the *Petroni* principle, according to which the application of the Regulation cannot entail the loss of rights acquired exclusively under national legislation. The Court ruled in these 1986 judgments that that principle did not apply to the rules for determining the applicable legislation. In its *Bosmann* judgment, on the contrary, the Court implies[28] that the *Petroni* principle does apply to the rules determining the applicable social security legislation.

A couple of years later the Court went even further. Mr Hudzinski, a Polish national worked as a self-employed farmer in Poland where he lived with his family. In 2007 he worked as a seasonal worker in Germany and was, on that basis, subject to unlimited income tax liability there. Under German legislation non-residents who are subject to unlimited income tax liability are entitled to family benefits. However, by virtue of Regulation 1408/71 he continued, as a posted self-employed person, to be subject to Polish social security legislation,[29] even during the period where he worked in Germany. Mr Wawrzyniak was a Polish national residing with his family in Poland. He was as an employed worker in Poland covered by Polish social security legislation. In 2006 Mr Wawrzyniak was posted by his employer to work for almost a year in Germany in 2006. During that period he was also subject to unlimited tax liability in Germany. However, he continued, as a posted employed person, to

24 Case C-352/06, *Bosmann*, EU:C:2008:290, para. 29.
25 The first recital of Regulation 883/2004 is almost identical.
26 Case C-352/06, *Bosmann*, EU:C:2008:290, para. 32.
27 Case 302/84, *Ten Holder*, EU:C:1986:242; and Case 60/85, *Luyten*, EU:C:1986:307.
28 Case C-352/06, *Bosmann*, EU:C:2008:290, para. 29.
29 Article 14a(1)(a) Regulation 1408/7, corresponding to the current Article 12(2) Regulation 883/2004.

be subject to Polish social security legislation,[30] even during the period where he worked in Germany. Both Polish men referred to the *Bosmann* judgment when claiming German family benefits from the German institution for the period during which they worked in Germany. Their claims were rejected by the German institution because they were subject to Polish social security legislation during the periods where they worked in Germany.

In its judgment[31] the Court not only confirms the approach it took in its *Bosmann* judgment, but even enhances it. In fact, the *Hudzinski and Wawrzyniak* cases differ from the *Bosmann* case in two aspects. In the first place, Ms Bosmann's main argument was that she had suffered a legal disadvantage by reason of the fact that she had made use of her right to free movement. In fact, Ms Bosmann did not receive any family benefits at all from the Netherlands, the Member State to whose legislation she was subject by virtue of Regulation 1408/71. Mr Hudzinski and Mr Wawrzyniak continued to receive Polish family benefits while working in Germany. They did not lose any rights because they had exercised their right to free movement. In the second place, Ms Bosmann resided with her children in Germany, whereas the two Polish men and their children did not reside in Germany, but in Poland.

The Court repeated that the provisions of Regulation 1408/71, including the rules determining the applicable legislation, must be interpreted in the light of Article 48 TFEU which is to contribute to the establishment of the greatest possible freedom of movement for migrant workers. And again the Court underlined that the Regulation as a whole seeks to contribute to the improvement of the standard of living and conditions of employment of migrant workers, as it follows from its first recital. It would go beyond the objective of the Regulation based on Article 48 TFEU and exceed the purpose and scope of that article to interpret that Regulation as prohibiting a Member State from granting workers and members of their family broader social protection than that arising from the application of that Regulation. In this context the Court says explicitly that the *Petroni* principle also applies to the rules determining the applicable social security legislation:[32] EU legislation cannot be applied in such a way as to deprive a migrant worker of benefits granted solely by virtue of the legislation of a single Member State. Therefore, even when the two men are subject to Polish legislation, Germany cannot be denied the right to grant family benefits. Germany has this right, even if the men in question do not suffer any disadvantage for having made use of their right to free movement. In the *Bosmann* case the non-competent Member State which had the right to apply its national legislation was the State of residence. The *Hudzinski* judgment

30 Article 14(1)(a) Regulation 1408/71, corresponding to the current Article 12(1) Regulation 883/2004.

31 Joined Cases C-611/10 and C-612/10, *Hudzinski and Wawrzyniak*, EU:C:2012:339.

32 Joined Cases C-611/10 and C-612/10, *Hudzinski and Wawrzyniak*, EU:C:2012:339, para. 56.

clarified that the non-competent Member State which has the right to apply its national legislation is not necessarily the State of residence. It can be another Member State with which the worker has a close connection, like being subject to unlimited income tax liability.

This case-law is not limited to family benefits, but also concerns other branches of social security such as sickness benefits, including long-term care benefits, as the *Von Chamier* judgment[33] has clarified.

This case-law of the Court seems to justify the conclusion that a worker who fulfils the conditions for entitlement to benefits on the basis of national legislation of a State whose legislation is not the applicable one designated by Regulation 883/2004, but with whom he is closely connected, can claim a differential amount from this State, if the benefits provided by that State are more favourable than those provided by the Member State designated by the Regulation. Let us take as an example a pensioner who receives a pension from both Germany and Portugal and who resides in Portugal. Articles 23 and 29 Regulation 883/2004 determine Portugal as the Member State responsible for granting sickness benefits in cash to this pensioner. It is a conflict of law rule.[34] However, if the Portuguese benefits relating to the risk of reliance on care do not exist or are at a lower level than that of the benefits relating to that risk from Germany with whom the pensioner has a close connection,[35] he will be entitled to a topping-up of the benefit equal to the difference between the two amounts.[36] Although this case-law might be correctly perceived as filling a gap in the protection of the worker in the specific cases concerned, it does not necessarily serve legal certainty and the predictability of the conflict of law rules. In fact, there are still a number of question marks about the reach and limits of the *Bosmann* and subsequent case-law of the Court. According to this case-law a worker can also be covered by the social security legislation of a Member State other than the competent one designated by the Regulation, if there is a 'close connection' between the person concerned and the non-competent Member State. It is not always easy to determine whether or not such 'close connection' exists.

In a recent case concerning a Czech national the Court denied the non-competent Member State the right to grant family benefits on the basis of national law, because it did not have a sufficiently 'close connection' with the person concerned. The woman in question had lived in France with her husband for a number of years. Her husband worked in France, the family was covered by French health insurance, their child was born in France, and she had worked in France and had received maternity benefit and a specific family benefit in France.

---

33 Case C-208/07, *Von Chamier*, EU:C:2009:455.

34 Case C-345/09, *Van Delft*, EU:C:2010:610.

35 He draws a pension from that Member State and he is, under German law, voluntary insured with the German care insurance.

36 Case C-388/09, *de Silva Martins*, EU:C:2011:439.

As a 'post-active person' she was, by virtue of (Article 13(2)(f)) Regulation 1408/71 subject to French legislation. Once her entitlement to the specific French family benefit ceased, she applied for family benefits in the Czech Republic. In fact, it appeared from the file that according to Czech law any person who has registered as permanently resident in the Czech Republic is entitled to parental allowance. The case came finally before the Court which delivered a judgment without an opinion of the Advocate General.

The Court had to make a judgment on the question whether or not the non-competent Member State, was, under these circumstances, allowed to grant the woman family benefits. The Court noted that in this case there was not a sufficiently close link with the non-competent Member State, such as residence (as in the *Bosmann* case) or being subject to unlimited income tax (as in *Hudzinski*). The only connection she had with the Czech Republic was that she and her husband continued to have a home there and were still registered as residents in the Czech Republic, even when it appeared from all the facts and circumstances that their real residence (centre of interests) was in France. The Court ruled[37] that Article 13 Regulation 1408/71 (corresponding to Article 11 Regulation 883/2004) precluded the non-competent Member State from granting family benefits. The Court emphasised that the predictability and effectiveness of the application of the coordination rules should not be disproportionately affected. However, it cannot be deducted from this judgment that the *Bosmann* case-law is no longer valid. On the contrary, the Court clarified that if there are 'specific and particularly close connecting factors' between the person and the non-competent Member State, this Member State is allowed to grant workers and members of their family broader social protection than that arising from the application of the Regulation. This has recently been confirmed by the *Franzen* judgment (see below). It is up to the national courts to decide whether or not there is a sufficiently 'close connection' between the person and the non-competent State. In some cases, this might be a tedious exercise.

If indeed a 'close connection' exists, the question arises about the extent of the 'right' of the non-competent Member State to grant benefits. In the *Bosmann and Hudzinski* judgments the Court ruled that the Member State, not being the Member State designated by the Regulation, but that has a 'close connection' with the person concerned could not be denied the 'right' to grant family benefits. What does this mean? Can the non-competent Member State in question having a 'close connection' with the persons concerned introduce provisions in its legislation excluding such persons for the sole reason that they receive comparable benefits from another Member State? There is no doubt that such a provision would be considered by the Court as being incompatible with Articles 45–48 TFEU. In fact, the final question the Court had to deal with in the *Hudzinski* case was the following. By virtue of German law, a person who

[37] Case C-394/13, *B.*, EU:C:2014:2199.

has a close connection with Germany such as being subject to unlimited income tax there, and who fulfils all conditions for entitlement to family benefits is nevertheless excluded from these benefits if a comparable benefit is paid by another State. The Court was asked whether this provision was compatible with Union law. The Court replied that such legislation is likely to put migrant workers at a disadvantage compared with workers who have worked in only one Member State. A provision reducing the amount of foreign family benefits from the amount due under its own legislation would be acceptable, but it would be incompatible with Articles 45–48 TFEU to exclude the persons concerned from entitlement to such benefits. In other words, it follows from this case-law that a Member State, not being the competent Member State designated by the Regulation, has the 'right' to grant family benefits to a worker with whom it has a 'close connection' and who fulfils the conditions laid down in its legislation for entitlement to benefits. But in practical terms, this Member State is in such a situation actually obliged to grant such benefits to the workers concerned. Entitlement cannot be denied for the sole reason that the person receives a comparable benefit from another Member State.

Can the non-competent Member State which has a 'close connection' with the persons concerned introduce provisions in its legislation excluding such persons from its social security coverage for the sole reason that they are subject to the legislation of another Member State? This question has been submitted to the Court in the *Franzen*[38] case which was at the time of writing this chapter still pending. The case concerns a number of citizens who have the nationality of the Netherlands and who reside in the Netherlands. They were during some years engaged in minor employment in Germany. For this reason they were, in accordance with Article 11(3)(a) Regulation 883/2004, subject to German legislation. However, by virtue of German law, persons in minor employment are not covered by insurance concerning unemployment, family benefits and old age. Such persons are only insured against the risk of accidents at work and professional diseases. According to the legislation of the Netherlands everybody residing in the Netherlands is covered by insurance concerning family benefits and old age, except people who are subject to the legislation of another Member State. The persons concerned claimed family benefits and old-age pension in the Netherlands for the years that they were engaged in minor employment in Germany. The Dutch institutions based their refusal on the fact that during these periods they were, in accordance with Regulation 1408/71, subject to German and thus not to Dutch legislation. The Dutch court requested a preliminary decision of the Court about the important question whether in these circumstances Union law precludes the application of Dutch legislation which excludes residents in its territory from its social security coverage for the sole reason that they are subject to the legislation of another Member State. In

[38] Case C-382/13, *Franzen*, EU:C:2015:261.

his conclusions,[39] the Advocate General clarified that there was no doubt that the persons concerned were, during the periods in question, subject to German legislation. Therefore, in principle, the State of residence may exclude persons residing on its territory from its social security coverage for the sole reason that they are subject to the legislation of another Member State. The Advocate General continued his conclusions, however, by examining the final result of the application of the relevant rules for the persons concerned. He emphasised that the application of the conflict of law rules laid down in Regulation 1408/71 resulted in the persons concerned being subject to German legislation, which, on its turn resulted in the persons concerned being excluded from Dutch social security. The final result was that the persons concerned had lost their social protection concerning family benefits and old age guaranteed by their State of residence, without having obtained any comparable protection in the competent State. This result is incompatible with the objective pursued by Articles 45–48 TFEU, namely to prevent that persons would be penalised in the field of social security for having exercised their right to free movement of workers. In order to avoid such results, he proposes that the application of the legislation of the State of employment (competent State) should be suspended if the application of that legislation does not lead to any social protection concerning family benefits or old age. This temporary suspension should be limited to the periods during which the legislation of the State of employment continues to exclude the persons concerned from any protection concerning the aforementioned branches. During this period of suspension, the persons concerned should be subject to the legislation of the State of residence.

There are strong arguments for agreeing with the Advocate General that the final result of the relevant rules for the persons concerned is incompatible with Articles 45–48 TFEU. However, the way by which the Advocate General wants to avoid such result raises questions. In practical terms, he proposes that in circumstances such as in the present case, the level of protection should play a role for determining the applicable social security legislation.[40] It is up to the national courts to make the necessary findings. The task of the national court to make a comparison between the levels of social protection offered by any two States involved may in some cases prove to be an exercise which is particularly tedious, and in other cases profoundly uncertain. The Advocate General suggests furthermore that the suspension of the legislation of the State of employment only applies to the branches of social security for which the State of employment does not offer any protection.[41] In practical terms, he suggests that during the aforementioned period of suspension the persons concerned would be subject to

39 Opinion of Advocate General Szpunar in Case C-382/13, *Franzen*, EU:C:2014:2190.

40 Opinion of Advocate General Szpunar in Case C-382/13, *Franzen*, EU:C:2014:2190, para. 89.

41 Opinion of Advocate General Szpunar in Case C-382/13, *Franzen*, EU:C:2014:2190, para. 94 third sentence and para. 96(2) third sentence.

the legislation of two Member States at the same time: the State of residence for those branches for which the State of employment does not offer any protection and the State of employment for those branches for which it does offer sufficient protection (such as accidents at work). This suggestion too raises questions about legal certainty and predictability of the coordination rules.

In its judgment of 23 April 2015[42] the Court did not follow the opinion of the Advocate General on this point. Instead, the Court referred to the *Bosmann* case-law and repeated that a Member State which is not the competent one by virtue of Title II of the Regulation has nevertheless the power to grant, under certain conditions, benefits to a mobile worker under its own national law. By solving the case in this way, the Court actually avoided answering the third question raised by the referring court. The question was whether Union law precluded, in the circumstances of the present case, the application of the legislation of a Member State according to which its residents are excluded from the social security coverage of that Member State for the sole reason that they are subject to the legislation of another Member State.

2.3. MAIN PRINCIPLE: *LEX LOCI LABORIS*

The rules determining the applicable social security legislation do not pay attention to the content of the applicable law or to the law which would offer the most favourable benefits for the worker. However, the interests of the worker the EU social security regulations seek to protect are closely linked to the realisation of free movement of workers.[43] One of the main pillars of free movement of workers is the principle of equal treatment between migrant workers and national workers of the host State. This explains why the main principle of the rules determining the applicable social security legislation is the *lex loci laboris.*[44]

The *lex loci laboris* rule is based on the principle that a migrant worker should have the same rights as national workers in the host State.[45] This principle seeks to prevent unfair competition between employers who use migrant workers in a Member State and those who only use non-migrant workers.[46] The difference

42 Case C-382/13, *Franzen*, EU:C:2015:261.

43 Case C-212/06, *Walloon Government v Flemish Government*, EU:C:2008:178, para. 48.

44 S. Van Raepenbusch, 'Persons covered by Regulation (EEC) No. 1408/71 and European citizenship; from migrant workers to European citizens', in *25 years of Regulation 1408/71, a conference report* (Stockholm 1997), 69–90.

45 This idea is reflected in recital 17 of Regulation 883/2004. It is also underlined by the Court on numerous occasions: Case C-68/99, *Commission v Germany*, EU:C:2001:137, para. 23; Case C-249/04, *Allard*, EU:C:2005:329, para. 31; Case C-493/04, *Piatowski*, EU:C:2006:167, para. 19; and Case C-103/06, *Derouin*, EU:C:2008:185, para. 20.

46 H. Verschueren, 'Cross-border workers in the European Internal Market: Trojan horses for Member States' labour and social security law?' (2008) 24 *International Journal of Comparative Labour Law and Industrial Relations*, 167–199.

in social protection level between Member States, following the 2004, 2007 and 2013 enlargements has strengthened this objective even further.[47] It is only when the application of the law of the workplace would be either impossible or inappropriate because of the nature of the work performed, that the rules have, by way of exception, established other connecting factors for the determination of the applicable social security legislation.

2.4. POSTING

From the first coordination rules the law of the workplace did not apply in case a worker is sent by his employer for a short period to another Member State to work there on the employer's behalf. It would be a severe burden on workers, employers and social security institutions if the worker was required to be insured under the social security system of every Member State to which he was posted in the course of his employment, even if such posting was of very short duration.[48] However, in the *Manpower* and *Van der Vecht* judgments the Court has given a rather extensive interpretation of the term posting by deciding that the posting provisions also apply to a worker who is recruited with a view to being posted to another Member State.

The Court has, from the very beginning,[49] mentioned not only the interests of the worker but also those of the employer and of the social security institutions. The development in the Court's reasoning on the objective of the posting provisions in the field of social security is even more interesting. Initially, the objective of simplification was underlined. However, in its 2000 *Fitzwilliam* judgment,[50] the Court ruled that the purpose of the posting provisions is 'in particular, to promote freedom to provide services for the benefit of undertakings which avail themselves of it by sending workers to Member States other than that in which they are established'. The objective of simplification is mentioned only in the second place.

In labour law one of the connecting factors for determining the applicable law is the 'country in which or from which the employee habitually caries out his work in performance of the contract'.[51] The posting provisions in EU law on social security refer to 'a person who pursues an activity as an employed person in a Member State on behalf of an employer which normally carries out its activities there and who is posted by that employer to another Member State

47 However, the question arises whether the current rules of conflict of law are still appropriate. See the 2008 trESS Think Tank report: 'Towards a new framework for applicable legislation, new forms of mobility, coordination principles and rules of conflict'.

48 Case 19/67, *Van der Vecht*, EU:C:1967:49; and Case 35/70, *Manpower*, EU:C:1970:120.

49 Case 19/67, *Van der Vecht*, EU:C:1967:49; and Case 35/70, *Manpower*, EU:C:1970:120.

50 Case C-202/97, *Fitzwilliam*, EU:C:2000:75, repeated in Case C-404/98, *Plum*, EU:C:2000:607.

51 Article 8(2) Rome I.

to perform work on that employer's behalf'.[52] The decisive element here is not that the worker habitually caries out his work in the sending State, but that he is attached to an employer which normally carries out its activities in the sending State.

The application of the posting provisions is subject to a number of conditions to prevent the posting provisions from being used in cases for which they are not intended. Firstly, posting has to be temporary: Article 12 mentions a strict maximum time limit of 24 months. If the anticipated duration goes beyond 24 months, the posting provision does not apply at all. If, for reasons not foreseen, the duration of the work in the host State goes beyond 24 months, the worker will, after the expiration of this period, in principle be subject to the social security legislation of the host State, unless an Article 16 agreement is concluded between the competent authorities of the two States. Secondly, in order to avoid rotation of personnel performing the same activities, the worker may not be sent to replace a worker who has completed an earlier period of posting. Thirdly, in order to reflect the goal of achieving continuity in the affiliation of the worker to the social security system of the sending Member State, the worker must have been subject to the legislation of the sending State prior to the posting. Fourthly, the worker should continue to be under the authority of the employer which posted him: there must be a direct relationship between worker and employer during the whole duration of the posting.

Fears were expressed in the *Fitzwilliam* and *Plum*[53] cases that the application of the posting provisions by 'letter box' companies or by temporary employment agencies could lead to abuse. As a result, the Court[54] confirmed that there had to be a direct relationship between the undertaking providing temporary personnel and the posted worker. In addition, it imposed another condition on the use of posting arrangements by such agencies, namely that they must normally carry on their business in the territory of the State in which they are established. The latter condition means that the undertaking should habitually carry out significant activities in the sending State. By imposing the last condition, the Court wanted to prevent 'letter-box' firms from using the posting provisions. This case-law is now reflected in provisions laid down in Regulation 987/2009.[55]

Posting is a very sensitive issue. For some Member States and interest groups, the conditions are too strict and lead to protection of the market of the host State. For other Member States and interest groups, the application of the posting provisions leads to unfair competition and constitute a danger for the level of social protection in the host State.

52 Article 12(1) Regulation 883/2004.
53 Case C-404/98, *Plum*, EU:C:2000:607.
54 Case C-202/97, *Fitzwilliam*, EU:C:2000:75.
55 Article 14 Regulation 987/2009.

2.5. PURSUIT OF ACTIVITIES IN TWO OR MORE MEMBER STATES

For obvious reasons, the application of the law of the workplace is not suitable in cases where a person normally pursues activities in two or more Member States. For workers with such a working pattern, other connecting factors have been incorporated in special rules.

In labour law, the connecting criteria for determining the applicable law are either the 'country in which or, failing that, from which the employee habitually carries out his work' or, in the absence of such a place, that of the 'country where the place of business through which the employee was engaged is situated'. For social security the first connecting factor for determining the applicable law for workers normally working in two or more Member States is the notion 'substantial part' of the worker's activities. Workers who normally work in two or more Member States and who pursue a 'substantial part' of their work in their Member State of residence[56] are subject to the social security legislation of that State. 'Substantial part' means a quantitatively substantial part. Working time and/or remuneration constitute indicative criteria. A share of less than 25% of these criteria creates the presumption that there is no 'substantial part'.[57] When assessing these criteria the assumed future situation for the next twelve months has to be taken into account.[58] With the help of concrete examples, the Practical Guide[59] provides very useful guidance in order to clarify the notions used in Regulations 883/2004 and 987/2009 and also provides useful tools how to assess these notions for all kinds of specific groups, such as international transport workers.

In labour law, the second connecting factor, namely the 'country where the place of business through which the employee was engaged is situated', only plays a role when it is not possible for the court to determine the State in which the worker habitually carries our his work.[60] The approach in social security is similar, but slightly different. If the person concerned does not pursue a substantial part of his activity in the Member State of residence, then the decisive criterion is the 'registered office or place of business'[61] of the employer or of one

---

56 Since the entry into force of Regulation 465/2012, the requirement of pursuing a 'substantial part' of the work in the Member State of residence applies not only for workers having only one employer, but also for workers having two or more employers.

57 Article 14(8) Regulation 987/2009.

58 Article 14(10) Regulation 987/2009.

59 'Practical Guide on the applicable legislation in the EU, the EEA and in Switzerland', available at http://ec.europa.eu/social/BlobServlet?docId=11366&langId=en (last accessed on 31 January 2016).

60 Case C-29/10, *Koelzsch*, EU:C:2011:151.

61 '*Registered office or place of business*' refers to the registered office or place of business where the essential decisions of the undertaking are adopted and where the functions of its central

of the employers. The rules of Article 13(1)(b) Regulation 883/2004 are very detailed indeed.[62]

2.6. ARTICLE 16: A FLEXIBLE ARTICLE

Article 16 Regulation 883/2004 stipulates that two or more Member States may by common agreement provide for exceptions to the rules governing applicable legislation laid down in Articles 11–15. Article 16 is characterised by great flexibility. It allows Member States to adopt 'tailor-made' solutions for certain categories of people. In addition, it provides both a remedy and the only legal means for normalising complex situations. It creates the possibility to deal with specific situations that require the rules on determining applicable legislation to be adapted. The task of identifying such situations and of determining which legislation is applicable has been entrusted to the Member States involved. Member States enjoy a wide discretion in using Article 16.[63] In practice, Article 16 is often used in order to exempt workers from being subject to the legislation of the host State in situations where not all posting requirements are met. For example, if it is known that the anticipated duration of a posting will extend beyond 24 months, an Article 16 agreement can be concluded between the sending and host States in order to keep the worker(s) concerned under the legislation of the sending State. A number of Article 16 agreements relate to specific enterprises engaged in European projects, such as in the aerospace industry, or within the framework of cooperation between two Member States. Other agreements concern workers who are mobile within a corporate group.

There is only one condition for applying Article 16: the agreement shall be in the interest of the worker. If the only condition under which Article 16 may be applied is the worker's interest, great importance is obviously attached to the question of the criteria to be applied in deciding whether or not the agreement is indeed in the interest of the worker, but so far the Court has not passed a judgment on this matter. During the negotiations on the Commission proposal leading to Regulation 987/2009, the suggestion to include such criteria has been discussed in Council, but was not acceptable for several Member States. In other words, there is neither case-law nor a clarification in the implementing regulation on the question as to which criteria should be applied to assess whether or not an agreement is in the interest of the worker.

The issue of 'interest of the worker' is a rather sensitive one. By virtue of Article 18 Regulation 987/2009, a request for applying Article 16 Regulation

administration are carried out (Article 14(5a) Regulation 987/2009, inserted by Regulation 465/2012.

62 Further detailed rules are to be found in Article 14 of the Implementing Regulation 987/2009.

63 Case 101/83, *Brusse*, EU:C:1984:187.

883/2004 must be submitted by the employer or the worker, whenever possible in advance, to the competent authority of the Member State whose legislation is requested to be applied. Often such a request is signed by both the employer and the worker(s) concerned. But it seems to be premature to conclude that such a 'mutual' request automatically shows that the agreement requested would be in the interest of the worker(s). In fact, in a number of cases making such a request has been more or less imposed on the worker(s) concerned by the employer seeking to pay contributions in the State which is most favourable for him. This issue has become even more important since we know that after the *Schlecker* judgment[64] (see Houwerzijl and Van Hoek's chapter) the result of the rules determining the applicable social security legislation laid down in Regulation 883/20014, including its Article 16, may have an impact on the application of the rules determining the applicable labour law. Article 16 agreements can have retroactive effect. In fact, it follows from the spirit and scheme of Article 16 that an agreement within the meaning of that provision must also be capable, in the interest of the worker(s) concerned, of covering past periods.[65]

3. RULES OF CONFLICT IN LABOUR LAW

Contrary to the EU rules determining the applicable social security legislation, the worker and the employer have the freedom to choose the applicable labour law. If a choice has not been made, then the applicable labour law is determined in accordance with the criteria laid down in Article 8(2)–(4) Regulation 593/2008.[66]

It follows from Houwerzijl and Van Hoek's chapter that the freedom of choice as to which labour law is applicable has been curtailed to some extent, in order to protect the worker, being considered as the weaker party from a socio-economic point of view.[67] To this end, Articles 8 and 9 Regulation 593/2008 contain specific rules.

The content and functioning of these rules has been the subject of Prof. Houwerzijl's chapter. The same is true for the rules laid down in the Posting of Workers Directive guaranteeing minimum protection (Directive 96/71) and in Directive 2014/67 on the enforcement of Directive 96/71.[68]

---

64 Case C-64/12, *Schlecker*, EU:C:2013:551.

65 Case 101/83, *Brusse*, EU:C:1984:187; and Case C-454/93, *Van Gestel*, EU:C:1995:205.

66 Regulation (EC) No. 593/2008 on the law applicable to contractual obligations (Rome I), OJ 2008, L 177/6 (hereinafter referred to as 'Regulation 593/2008').

67 Case C-29/10, *Koelzsch*, EU:C:2011:151.

68 Directive 67/2014/EU on the enforcement of Directive 96/71/EC concerning the posting of workers in the framework of the provision of services and amending Regulation (EU) No. 1024/2012 on administrative cooperation through the Internal Market Information System ('the IMI Regulation'), OJ 2014 L 159/11 (hereinafter referred to as 'Directive 67/2014').

It follows from these rules that, unless it appears from the circumstances as a whole that the employment contract is more closely connected to another State,[69] the 'objectively applicable' law for workers who make use of their right to free movement, is the law of the host State where the work is actually performed. In fact, for such workers the host State is the State where the work is 'habitually carried out'. Such workers are entitled to equal treatment as national workers in respect of any conditions of employment and work. Any clause of a collective or individual agreement which violates this rule is null and void.

However, for posted workers, i.e. workers who are employed by an employer established in a Member State and who are temporarily sent by that employer to another Member State to provide services, the 'objectively applicable' law is the law of the sending State.[70] The notion of a 'posted worker' within the meaning of Directive 96/71 differs from that laid down in Regulation 883/2004. Contrary to Regulation 883/2004, Directive 96/71 does not stipulate a strict time limit, sometimes leading to complicated cases. Directive 96/71 in no way amends the law applicable to the employment contract, but only lays down a hard core of clearly defined protective rules that must be observed by the service provider notwithstanding the duration of the worker's posting. The application of the labour law of the host State in matters not listed in Article 3(1) can be seen as an obstacle to the freedom to provide services. This freedom may be restricted only by rules justified by overriding requirements relating to the public interest and applied in a non-discriminatory and proportionate way, in so far as that interest is not safeguarded by the rules to which the service provider is subject in the Member State of establishment.[71] It is incumbent on the host State to use the rule of reason to show that applying labour law of the host State is proportional and justified in the public interest.

4. PROBLEMS RESULTING FROM DIVERGING RULES DETERMINING THE APPLICABLE LEGISLATION

When a worker crosses an internal frontier within the Union in order to perform work in another Member State, he might be in a better or in a worse situation as regards his working conditions and his social protection. This is not, as such, incompatible with the Treaty.[72] In fact, there is hardly any Union law

---

69 Case C-64/12, *Schlecker*, EU:C:2013:551.

70 Unless, of course, it appears from the circumstances as a whole that the contract is more closely connected with another State.

71 Case C-319/06, *Commission v Luxembourg*, EU:C:2008:350, para. 43.

72 As regards social security, this has been underlined by the Court in Joined Cases C-393/99 and C-394/99, *Hervein*, EU:C:2002:182; Case C-68/99, *Commission v Germany*, EU:C:2001:137; Case C-493/04, *Piatowski*, EU:C:2006:167; Case C-208/07, *von Chamier*, EU:C:2009:455;

harmonising Member States' social systems. The more or less advantageous or disadvantageous situation for the worker can be seen as a logical consequence of the fact that Member States' systems in these fields are not harmonised.

For cross-border workers the situation becomes slightly more complicated when a branch of social protection, such as income compensation in case of sickness, is in some Member States dealt with primarily in labour law and only by way of a safety net in social security, whereas in other Member States, this risk is (almost) exclusively governed by social security legislation. For instance, when a worker in the Netherlands is unable to perform his work due to sickness, the employer has, by virtue of Dutch law, the obligation to continue to pay at least 70% of the wage during the first two years of the sickness. In other words, only in a very limited number of cases, by way of a safety net, the worker could be entitled to a statutory sickness benefit. This safety net is aimed at people for whom the obligation of the employer to continue to pay the salary does not apply.[73] Pay is undeniably part of labour law. But it can also be 'social security' within the meaning of Regulation 883/2004. In fact, since the *Paletta* judgment[74] we know that the continued payment of wage to the sick worker is a 'sickness benefit' within the meaning of the social security regulations.

Contrary to the Netherlands, in Belgium the obligation of the employer to continue to pay wages is limited to a period of one month. After that period, the worker is entitled to a sickness benefit[75] for a maximum period of one year. The amount of this sickness benefit is limited to 60% of the (ceiled) wage. After the end of that period, if the worker is still incapable of work, he will receive an invalidity allowance.

This difference in legislation between Belgium and the Netherlands will not cause problems, as long as Regulations 593/2008 and 883/2004 determine the same legislation as being applicable. A Dutch worker, for instance, who resides in the Netherlands, but who works as a frontier worker in Belgium, will be subject to Belgian legislation, both for social security and for labour law. Likewise, a Belgian worker who is posted by his Belgian employer for a period less than two years in the Netherlands will normally be subject to Belgian social security legislation by virtue of Article 12 Regulation 883/2004. Belgian law will normally also be the 'objectively applicable' law for labour law.[76] In case of sickness, this worker will be entitled to continue to receive his salary from

Case C-3/08, *Leyman*, EU:C:2009:595; Case C-345/09, *Van Delft*, EU:C:2010:610; and Case C-443/11, *Jeltes*, EU:C:2013:224.

73 For instance, because an employment contract no longer exists, such as unemployed workers who become unable to work because of sickness or people whose employment contract expires during sickness.

74 Case C-45/90, *Paletta*, EU:C:1992:236.

75 The terminology of the Belgian law is: 'primary incapacity allowance'.

76 Unless it appears from the circumstances as a whole that the employment contract is more closely connected to the Netherlands.

his Belgian employer for a period of one month and after that he will receive a Belgian sickness benefit.

However, problems can arise as a result from diverging rules determining the applicable legislation. As we have seen above, the EU rules determining the applicable social security legislation differ on several points from the EU rules determining the applicable labour law. This can lead to cross-border situations where a worker is subject to the social security legislation of Member State A and to labour law of Member State B. Workers who normally pursue an activity in two (or more) Member States as well as workers who are posted for a period longer than two years are easily confronted with this situation.

The following examples will illustrate the kind of difficulties a cross-border worker has to face when the EU rules in the fields of labour law and social security lead to the applicability of different national laws.

4.1. WORKERS WHO NORMALLY WORK IN TWO (OR MORE) MEMBER STATES

4.1.1. Workers Having One Employer

Let us start with the simple example of a worker who resides in the Netherlands but works for his employer, established in Belgium, for two days in the Netherlands and three days in Belgium. He is subject to Dutch social security, whereas Belgian law will probably be the 'objectively applicable' law within the meaning of Article 8 Regulation 593/2008,[77] since he performs the majority of the activities in Belgium.[78] If the worker falls ill, he will continue to receive his wage from his Belgian employer, but only for a period of one month. But what will happen after this month? His claim for a Belgian sickness benefit will be refused, since the worker is not subject to Belgian social security legislation. He turns to the Netherlands institution claiming a Dutch sickness benefit. This claim will also be refused by the Dutch authorities. As said before, in the Netherlands, the responsibility for income compensation in case of sickness of the worker has been shifted to the employer. The Dutch authorities will say that the (Belgian) employer has to continue to pay at least 70% of the salary to the worker for a maximum period of two years. Only if there is no longer any employer, the social security institution can intervene.[79] However, the Belgian employer will

---

77 Unless, of course, it appears from the circumstances as a whole that the contract has a closer connection with the Netherlands.

78 Case C-29/10, *Koelzsch*, EU:C:2011:151, para. 45.

79 S. Klosse and W. Rauws, 'Arbeidsrechtelijke aspecten van grensoverschrijdend werken', in H. Verschueren (ed.), *Werken over de grens België Nederlands* (Antwerp: Intersentia, 2011), 82–87. In its case-law the judiciary in the Netherlands has given a restrictive interpretation to Article 29(2) *Ziektewet*: ECLI:NL:CRVB: 2010:BN 2808 and 2809.

probably argue that Dutch law cannot impose on him an obligation to continue to pay at least 70% of the salary for a maximum period of two years, for which obligation no legal basis exists in Belgian law, which is the applicable legislation in accordance with Regulation 593/2008. The Dutch authorities will react by saying that Dutch law is the applicable one by virtue of Regulation 883/2004. The worker concerned is not in an enviable position. It is actually surprising that this practice of the Dutch social security institutions has, until now, not been challenged before national and European judiciary.

Could a claim for the continued payment of at least 70% of his salary by his Belgian employer be successful?

The worker could argue that, despite the fact that he 'habitually carries out' his work in Belgium, there is a closer connection between the employment contract and the Netherlands, leading to Dutch law governing the employment contract. However, taken into account the significant factors indicated by the Court in its *Schlecker* judgment, it is doubtful whether this claim would be successful. True, he pays his social security contributions in the Netherlands, but he pays taxes over the major part of his income (60%) in Belgium. The parameters relating to the other working conditions might also refer to Belgian law.

Could he challenge the refusal by the Dutch authorities to grant him a sickness benefit?

There is no doubt that Regulation 883/2004 applies to schemes relating to the obligations of an employer. Member States are free to organise their own social security systems, including the repartition of responsibilities for granting benefits. However, when exercising that power they have to comply with Union law.[80] The refusal of a Dutch sickness benefit is based on the assumption that the worker should get the continued payment of at least 70% of the wage from the Belgian employer. The employer has to respect the social security legislation of the Netherlands, such as the payment of social security contributions due under Dutch law. This is true even when the employer is established in another Member State.[81] But would it not go beyond a coordination of social security if the application of the EU rules determining the applicable social security legislation would result in intervening in the rights and obligations between employer and worker even in cases where there is no strong link between the employment contract and the Netherlands? The fundamental question arises whether Union law precludes the application of Dutch legislation according to which a claim for Dutch sickness benefit is refused in all cases where an employment contract exists, even when there is not a sufficiently strong link between the Netherlands and the employment contract.

---

80 Case C-227/03, *Van Pommeren*, EU:C:2005:431; Case C-212/06, *Walloon Government v Flemish Government*, EU:C:2008:178; and Case C-228/07, *Petersen*, EU:C:2008:494.

81 Article 21(1) Regulation 987/2009.

Identifying the Member State that has the closest connection with the employment contract is precisely the objective of Article 8 Regulation 593/2008. The rules laid down in Regulation 593/2008 guarantee that the obligation of the employer to continue to pay at least 70% of the wage if one of his workers is unable to work because of sickness, only exists where the Netherlands is the Member State having the closest connection with the relevant employment contract. In such cases the employer is, without any doubt, required to continue to pay at least 70% of the wage to the worker for a maximum period of two years in the situation where the worker falls ill. In cases where Dutch labour law is not applicable by virtue of Regulation 593/2008, it is doubtful whether the Dutch institutions are allowed to refuse a sickness benefit to a worker by referring to the obligation of the employer to continue to pay at least 70% of the salary, as foreseen by Dutch legislation, applicable by virtue of Regulation 883/2004. In the *De Paep* judgment[82] the Court underlined that the social security regulations do not contain conflict rules concerning the legislation applicable to the employment relationship existing between worker and employer. If indeed Belgium is the Member State having the closest connection with the contract between the employer and the worker, the obligations of the employer towards his workers are, in accordance with Regulation 593/2008, governed by Belgian and not Dutch law. In such situations, the social security legislation of the Netherlands, being competent in social security matters, cannot unilaterally shift the responsibility for social protection of a person covered by its system, either to the institution of another Member State, or to a private party (employer) bound by labour law of another Member State. The question seems to be legitimate whether such a shift would in these circumstances be compatible with the mandatory character of the EU rules determining the applicable legislation in social security.

In this context we should not forget that the objective of the provisions laid down in Article 13 of Regulation 883/2004 for workers normally working in two or more Member States is not to identify the Member State having the closest connection with the employment contract(s). On the contrary, the application of Article 13 leads to situations where a worker is subject to the social security legislation of a Member State having no connection at all with the employment contract(s)! A worker, for instance, who resides in the Netherlands and who works two days a week for one employer in Germany and three days a week for another employer in Belgium, is by virtue of Article 13(1)(iv)[83] subject to the social security legislation of the Netherlands, a Member State where he does not work at all.

---

82 Case C-196/90, *De Paep*, EU:C:1991:381, para. 13. In this context it is important to remember that already at that time Regulation 1408/71 stipulated in its Article 4(2) that it applied to 'schemes concerning the liability of an employer or ship owner in respect of the benefits referred to in paragraph 1'.

83 As modified by Regulation 465/2012.

Moreover, as the Court has underlined,[84] in making employed persons who pursue a professional activity in two Member States subject, with respect to the whole of their activities, to a single social security system, Regulation 883/2004 pursues a general objective which is to ensure free movement of workers and seeks to guarantee the equality of treatment of all workers employed in the territory of a Member State as effectively as possible and not to penalise workers who exercise their right to free movement. The Dutch provision leading to a refusal of a Dutch sickness benefit to the worker concerned after having received a continued payment of his employer for a limited period of one month is liable to hamper or to render less attractive the exercise of the fundamental freedom of movement of workers guaranteed by the Treaty. In its case-law the Court has underlined that while Member States are free to determine their own social security systems, they are nevertheless required to respect the spirit and principles of the regulations based on Article 48 TFEU, namely to ensure that a person is not penalised for exercising his right to free movement.[85] In its case-law the Court has not hesitated to declare the application of a provision of national law that hampers the exercise of free movement of workers as incompatible with Articles 45–48 TFEU.[86] Where the application of national legislation to a mobile worker in the same way as to a non-mobile worker leads to consequences incompatible with Articles 45–48 TFEU, the national authorities should interpret its own legislation in the light of the aims of Articles 45–48 TFEU and, as far as possible, prevent its interpretation from discouraging a mobile worker from actually exercising his right to freedom of movement. Where application in accordance with those requirements is not possible, the national authorities must fully apply Union law and protect the rights conferred on individuals, and where necessary not apply any national provision which, in the circumstances of the case, leads to a result contrary to Union law.[87] This obligation for the Member States is a consequence not only of Articles 45–48 TFEU, but also of the principle of sincere cooperation laid down in Article 4(3) TFEU.[88]

The mirror situation of the example may be less worrying for the worker. Let us assume that the worker resides in Belgium and that he works for one single employer established in the Netherlands. For this employer he works two days in Belgium and three days in the Netherlands. Since he pursues a 'substantial activity' in Belgium within the meaning of Article 14(8) Regulation 987/2009, he is subject to Belgian social security legislation. However, since the worker carries out the majority of his activities in the Netherlands, Dutch law will probably be the 'objectively applicable' law within the meaning of Article 8

84 Case C-249/05, *Allard*, EU:C:2005:329.

85 Case C-103/13, *Somova*, EU:C:2014:2334, paras. 35–38.

86 Case C-228/07, *Petersen*, EU:C:2008:494; Case C-212/06, *Walloon Government v Flemish Government*, EU:C:2008:178; and Case C-3/08, *Leyman*, EU:C:2009:595.

87 Case C 262/97, *Engelbrecht*, EU:C:2000:492.

88 Case C-165/91, *Van Munster*, EU:C:1994:359; and C-262/97, *Engelbrecht*, EU:C:2000:492.

Regulation 593/2008.[89] This means that if the worker falls ill, he will be entitled, in accordance with Dutch law, to continue to receive from his employer at least 70% of his salary for a maximum period of two years.

The mere fact that the Court has qualified the continued payment of the salary by the employer to the worker in case of sickness as a social security benefit within the meaning of the coordination regulation does not seem to affect this conclusion. True, the worker is subject to Belgian social security and the exclusive effect of the determination of the applicable social security legislation is explicitly stipulated by Article 11(1). However, the fact that the worker is subject exclusively to Belgian social security does not remove the obligation of his employer, based on applicable labour law of the Netherlands, to continue to pay at least 70% of the salary for a maximum of two years to his worker who is unable to work because of sickness. It would go beyond the objective of Regulation 883/2004 and exceed the purpose and scope of Article 48 TFEU to interpret that Regulation as prohibiting a Member State from granting workers broader social protection[90] than that arising from the application of that Regulation.[91]

4.1.2. Workers Having Two or More Employers

It is important to keep in mind that Regulation 883/2004 determines the applicable social security legislation in its entirety. If, in accordance with these rules, a worker who performs activities in Member State A and in Member State B, is subject to the legislation of Member State B, he is covered by the social security schemes of that State, including for his activities performed in State A. On the other hand, the applicable labour law has to be determined for each individual employment contract.[92] If the worker performs two activities, one in Member State A for employer A and one in Member State B for employer B, it is likely that the employment contract concluded with the first employer is governed by labour law of Member State A and the second contract by the law of Member State B.

Let us take the example of a worker, residing in the Netherlands, who works in Belgium for three days a week for employer B, established in Belgium, and for two days a week in the Netherlands for employer A, established in the

89 Unless, of course, it appears from the circumstances as a whole that the contract has a closer connection with Belgium.

90 Obviously, it is not possible for the worker to claim, in addition to his wage from his employer, sickness benefit from the Belgian social security institution, either on the basis of Belgian law (Article 103(1) *Wet 14 juli 1994 betreffende de verplichte verzekering voor geneeskundige verzorging en uitkeringen*), or on the basis of Regulation 883/2004 (Article 10); see also Case C-102/91, *Knoch*, EU:C:1992:303 concerning unemployment benefit.

91 Case C-208/07, *Von Chamier*, EU:C:2009:455; and Joined Cases C-611/10 and C-612/10, *Hudzinski*, EU:C:2012:339.

92 The heading of Article 8 Regulation 593/2008 is: 'Individual employment contracts'.

Netherlands. Since he performs a 'substantial part' of his overall activities in his country of residence, the Netherlands, he is covered by the social security schemes of the Netherlands. His employment contract concluded with his Dutch employer is probably governed by Dutch law and his employment contract with his Belgian employer by Belgian law. In case of sickness, there will be no problem as to the income compensation for his work performed in the Netherlands. He will continue to receive from his Dutch employer at least 70% of his wage for a maximum period of two years. His Belgian employer will continue to pay his wage for one month only. After that period, he has to claim sickness benefit from the Dutch social security institution. He probably will be confronted with a refusal for the same reasons as indicated above where the same worker has only one employer. The same reasoning for challenging that refusal as indicated above could be followed here.[93]

If the same person works in Belgium for four days a week for an employer established in Belgium, and for one day a week for an employer established in the Netherlands, he will be covered not by Dutch, but by Belgian social security. As in the previous example, his employment contract concluded with his Dutch employer is probably governed by Dutch law and his employment contract with his Belgian employer by Belgian law – nothing changes. In the event of sickness, he will continue to receive from his Dutch employer at least 70% of his Dutch wage for a maximum period of two years. His Belgian employer will continue to pay him his Belgian salary for a period of one month. Normally this should be immediately followed by a Belgian sickness benefit. In Belgium sickness benefits are calculated on the basis of previously earned wages. By virtue of Article 13(5) Regulation 883/2004, a person who pursues professional activities in two Member States is, with respect to the whole of their activities, subject to the social security legislation of a single Member State, which is in this case Belgium. This means that normally the Belgian sickness benefit should be based on the sum of the wages earned by the worker in the Netherlands and in Belgium together. However, by virtue of Belgian legislation[94] a sickness benefit cannot be granted if the worker is entitled to a wage over the same period. In my opinion, the Belgian institution could not use this provision laid down in Belgian law to refuse the worker the payment of any Belgian sickness benefit. In its case-law the Court has emphasised that while Member States are free to organise their own social security systems, they are nevertheless required, in exercising that power, to respect Union law. The application of the provision

93 Since the worker continues to receive at least 70% of his salary from his Dutch employer, the Dutch institution is allowed to restrict the amount of the Dutch sickness benefit by compensating only the loss of income earned with the Belgian employer, in line with Article 10 Regulation 883/2004 (see also Case C-102/91, *Knoch*, EU:C:1992:303, concerning an unemployment benefit).

94 Article 103(1) *Wet 14 juli 1994 betreffende de verplichte verzekering voor geneeskundige verzorging en uitkeringen* and Article 241(1) Royal Decree 3 July 1996.

in Belgian law leading to a refusal of any Belgian sickness benefit for the sole reason that the worker continues to receive, for a (very) small part of his work, a continued payment of his salary, is liable to hamper or to render less attractive the exercise of the fundamental freedom of movement of workers guaranteed by Articles 45–48 TFEU. For challenging the refusal of a Belgian sickness benefit the same reasoning could be followed as for challenging the refusal of a Dutch sickness benefit (indicated above under 4.1.1.). The obligation to grant a Belgian sickness benefit to the worker concerned, even if the Dutch employer continues to pay at least 70% of the Dutch wage during the sickness is a consequence not only of Articles 45–48 TFEU, but also of the principle of sincere cooperation laid down in Article 4(3) TFEU. However, the Belgian institution would be allowed to deduct the amount of the wage received by the Dutch employer from the sickness benefit due by the Belgian institution, in line with Article 10 Regulation 883/2004.[95]

4.2. WORKERS POSTED FOR MORE THAN TWO YEARS

Such workers are not considered as 'posted workers' within the meaning of Article 12 Regulation 883/2004. If, from the very beginning, the anticipated duration of the posting exceeds the maximum period of 24 months, Article 12 does not apply at all. If, for unforeseen reasons, the posting goes beyond the maximum period of 24 months, then the worker in question is, after the expiration of the maximum period, subject to the social security legislation of the State where the work is performed. A Belgian worker, for instance, who is posted by his Belgian employer to the Netherlands, is, after the expiration of the maximum period of two years, subject to the social security legislation of the Netherlands. However, Belgian labour law will probably still be the 'objectively applicable' law by virtue of Article 8 Regulation 593/2008. In case of sickness the worker will continue to receive his wage from his Belgian employer for the first month. But what will happen after this month? His claim for a Belgian sickness benefit will be refused, since the worker is not subject to Belgian social security legislation. His claim for Dutch sickness benefit will also be refused with a view to the obligation of the employer, under Dutch law, to pay sick pay. The Belgian employer will probably argue that for such obligation no legal basis exists in Belgian law, the applicable legislation in accordance with Regulation 593/2008. Could the worker's claim for the continued payment of at least 70% of his salary by his Belgian employer be successful?

---

95 This would also be in line with paras. 76–85 of Joined Cases C-611/10 and C-612/10, *Hudzinski* and *Wawrzyniak*, EU:C:2012:339, concerning family benefits.

This depends on the specific circumstances of the case.[96] If the worker could bring forward facts and circumstances showing that he no longer had the intention of going back to Belgium to work after the completion of the services for which he was posted, he can argue that after having been working in the Netherlands for more than two years, he had established the effective centre of his working activities[97] in the Netherland and that this State had become the State where he 'habitually carries out' his work within the meaning of Article 8(2) Regulation 593/2008.[98] This argument would be even stronger if, before having been sent to the Netherlands, he had worked only for a limited period of time in Belgium. Even if the parties had written in their employment contract that Belgian labour law would be the applicable one, it is probable that the worker could in such circumstances successfully demand the continued payment of his wage from his employer, thanks to Article 8(1) Regulation 593/2008.[99] The Belgian employer would be obliged to continue to pay at least 70% of the salary to the worker for a maximum period of two years and he would be bound in fact and in law by the medical findings made by the social security institution of the Netherlands concerning the commencement and duration of the incapacity for work, when he has not made use of his right[100] to have the worker examined by a doctor of his own choice. In its famous *Paletta* judgment,[101] the Court ruled that the employer, who continues to pay the salary in case of sickness of the worker, has to be treated as the 'competent institution' within the meaning of the EU regulations on social security.[102]

If the worker is not able to produce facts and circumstances showing that he did not have the intention to return to Belgium after the completion of his work in the Netherlands, he could use another way to try and claim the continued payment of his salary by his Belgian employer. If, notwithstanding the fact that he 'habitually carries out' his work in Belgium, the worker can produce facts and circumstances showing that there is a closer connection between the employment contract and the Netherlands, then Dutch labour law should be applied by virtue of Article 8(4). In its *Schlecker* judgment, the Court identified as one of the more significant factors for this assessment the country where

---

96 S. Klosse and W. Rauws, 'Arbeidsrechtelijke aspecten van grensoverschrijdend werken', in H. Verschueren (ed.), *Werken over de grens België Nederland* (Antwerp: Intersentia, 2011), 85–86.

97 Case C-383/95, *Rutten*, EU:C:1997:7; and Case C-29/10, *Koelzsch*, EU:C:2011:151.

98 S. Klosse and W. Rauws, 'Arbeidsrechtelijke aspecten van grensoverschrijdend werken', in H. Verschueren (ed.), *Werken over de grens België Nederland* (Antwerp: Intersentia, 2011), 85–86.

99 Under the legislation of the Netherlands, the employer's obligation of continued payment of the salary for a maximum period of two years when the worker falls ill, cannot be derogated from by agreement within the meaning of Article 8(1) Regulation 593/2008.

100 Article 27(5) and (6) Regulation 987/2009.

101 Case C-45/90, *Paletta*, EU:C:1992:236.

102 This is now stipulated in Article 1(q)(iv) Regulation 883/2004.

the worker pays his income taxes and social security contributions and where he is insured for pension, invalidity and sickness schemes. In this case, the worker pays his social security contributions in the Netherlands and is insured in the Netherlands for old age, invalidity and sickness schemes. In addition, he probably pays his income tax in the Netherlands.[103] There may also be further circumstances pointing to a close connection between the employment contract and the Netherlands. In such cases, the EU rules determining the applicable legislation in the fields of labour law and social security converge again.

If, however, the worker is unable to produce facts and circumstances leading to the applicability of Dutch labour law, the fundamental question arises again whether Union law precludes the application of Dutch legislation according to which a claim for Dutch sickness benefit is refused in all cases where an employment contract exists, even when there is not a sufficiently strong link between the Netherlands and the employment contract. The same reasoning for challenging the refusal of a Dutch sickness benefit as indicated above under 4.1.1. can be followed here. True, a posted worker is not a worker within the meaning of Article 45 TFEU, but he is nevertheless a person performing an 'activity as an employed person' within the meaning of Article 48 TFEU. In addition, the Court has underlined on several occasions that the purpose of the coordination regulations is not only to promote freedom of movement of workers, but also freedom to provide services.[104]

5. CONCLUSIONS

In many cases a mobile worker is subject to the social security legislation and to labour law of the same Member State. After all, the *lex loci laboris* is an important criterion used by conflict of law rules both in Regulation 883/2004 and Regulation 593/2008. However, such synchronism is no guarantee, since the conflict of law rules in both fields vary in their detail. In addition, they are based upon different principles.

In the field of social security, conflict of law rules are mandatory. The worker and his employer do not have the freedom to choose for themselves the applicable legislation. In order to ensure equal treatment of migrant and national workers, the *lex loci laboris*, namely the law of the country where the work is performed, is the main principle of the conflict of law rules. However, the application of this simple rule is not always possible or appropriate. A reference to *lex loci laboris* is not possible in situations where a worker normally pursues

103 Article 15 of Treaty to avoid double taxation of 5 June 2001 between Belgium and the Netherlands.

104 Case C-202/97, *Fitzwilliam*, EU:C:2000:75; Case C-56/01, *Inizan*, EU:C:2003:578; Case C-145/03, *Keller*, EU:C:2005:211; and Case C-372/04, *Watts*, EU:C:2006:325.

activities in two or more Member States. In addition, Regulation 883/2004 promotes not only free movement of workers but also the freedom to provide services. The application of the *lex loci laboris* for determining the applicable social security legislation of posted workers is considered as inappropriate, since it would lead to cumbersome complications for service providers, posted workers and social security institutions. Therefore, several special rules have been created to deal with specific situations of cross-border employment, using criteria for the determination of the applicable legislation other than the place of work. Furthermore, Article 16 Regulation 883/2004 empowers Member States to provide, by common agreement, for exceptions to the conflict of law rules laid down in this Regulation. Such agreements should be 'in the interest of' the workers concerned. Since there is not yet at Union level any clarification of this notion in either legislation or case-law, it is uncertain which criteria are used by the institutions of the various Member States to assess whether the agreement requested under Article 16 Regulation 883/2004 is indeed in the interest of the worker. In some cases, by putting pressure on the worker for making a 'mutual request' for applying Article 16, the employer may, on an indirect way, influence the determination of the applicable social security legislation. This is an undesirable phenomenon in itself, contrary to the spirit of Articles 45–48 TFEU. But the possible consequences of this phenomenon have become even worse after the *Schlecker* judgment according to which the result of the rules determining the applicable social security legislation could have an impact on the application of the conflict of law rules in labour law.

According to the letter of Regulation 883/2004, a mobile worker is subject to the social security legislation of one single Member State. However, a worker may also be covered by the social security legislation of a Member State other than the one designated by the Regulation, if there is a 'close connection' between the non-competent Member State and the worker. If this condition is fulfilled, it follows from the case-law of the Court that the conflict of law rules laid down in the social security regulations cannot prohibit a Member State from granting a worker broader social protection than that arising from the application of the regulations.

In the field of labour law, the starting point is the freedom of the worker and his employer to choose the applicable law. However, the conflict of law rules have curtailed to some extent this freedom of choice to protect the worker, being considered as the weaker party from a socio-economic point of view. In fact, the conflict of law rules guarantee that the worker cannot be deprived of the protection which he would enjoy under the mandatory rules of the 'objectively applicable law', namely the law of the country with which the employment contract is most closely connected. The criteria for determining the relevant country do not automatically result, in all cases, in the application of the law most favourable to the worker.[105] In most cases the 'objectively applicable law' for workers who make use of their right to free movement is the law of the host State where the work is 'habitually carried out'. Such workers are entitled to equal treatment as national workers with respect to any conditions of employment. However, for posted workers the 'objectively applicable law' is usually the law of the sending State. Directive 96/71 aims to reconcile the exercise of companies' fundamental freedom to provide cross-border services with appropriate protection of posted workers and workers of the host State. To this end the Directive lays down a number of mandatory rules to be observed during the posting period in the host State, even when the employment contract is governed by the law of the sending State. The notion of 'posted worker' within the meaning of Directive 96/71 differs from that laid down in Regulation 883/2004.

Due to the co-existence of different systems of conflict of law rules a migrant worker can be subject to the social security legislation of one Member State and to labour law of another Member State. This is especially true for posted workers who are posted for a period longer than two years and for workers who normally pursue an activity in two or more Member States.

For mobile workers and their employers, the situation might become rather complicated when the EU rules in the fields of labour law and social security lead to the applicability of different national laws concerning the same subject, for instance the social protection of the worker in case of sickness. In fact, the obligation of the employer to continue to pay wages during sickness of the worker – an obligation imposed by legislation – falls under the scope of Regulation 883/2004. Such a continued payment of the salary is a 'sickness benefit' within the meaning of this Regulation. On the other hand, it follows from the case-law of the Court that the social security regulations do not contain any conflict of law rule concerning the legislation applicable to the employment relationship between worker and employer. Some examples have illustrated the kind of difficulties a mobile worker has to face in practice, when he is subject to the social security legislation of one Member State and to labour law of another State. I have argued that it would go beyond the coordination of social security if the application of the EU rules determining the applicable social security legislation would result in intervening in the rights between employer and worker even in cases where there is no strong link between the employment contract and the competent Member State. In such situations the social security legislation of the competent State cannot unilaterally shift the responsibility for social protection of a person covered by its system either to the social security institutions of another Member State or to an employer bound by labour law of another Member State.

---

105 Case C-64/12, *Schlecker*, EU:C:2013:551, para. 34.

CHAPTER 13
CONFLICTING RULES OF CONFLICT: SOCIAL SECURITY AND LABOUR LAW
A Response

Maximilian Fuchs

1. THE SCOPE OF CONFLICT-OF-LAW RULES

Prof. Cornelissen has presented a thorough analysis of the case-law of the CJEU in which it evolves the reach of what is laid down in Articles 11–16 of Regulation 883/2004.[1] And he has shown the not easy relations between conflict-of-law rules in social security and those contained in Regulation Rome I.[2] He has not left any significant lacuna which I could fill.

Therefore I shall concentrate my discussion paper on the recent and very contested case-law of the CJEU concerning the doctrinal dimension of Article 11 *et seq.* of Regulation 883/2004. I understand my short statement as a legal narrative of that small piece of legal history which the CJEU has written beginning with *Bosmann*[3] and momentarily ending with *Franzen.*[4] My reading and analysis of these judgments is somewhat different from what most authors have thought and written. I see the messages the Court wanted to send out less critically. And I believe that examples can be offered which show that the main idea behind *Bosmann*, strictly interpreted, is reasonable and need not endanger the application of provisions on conflict-of-laws. But I join the critics where in my opinion the Court had crossed the Rubicon which forms the boundaries needed for an unambiguous determination of the applicable law.

1 Regulation (EC) 883/2004 of the European Parliament and of the Council of 29 April 2004 on the coordination of social security systems, OJ 2004, L 200/1 (hereinafter referred to as 'Regulation 883/2004').

2 Regulation (EC) No. 593/ 2008 17 June 2008 on the law applicable to contractual obligations (Rome I), OJ 2008, L 177/6 (hereinafter referred to as 'Rome I').

3 Case C-352/06, *Bosmann*, EU:C:2008:290.

4 Case C-382/13, *Franzen and Others*, EU:C:2015:261.

As Prof. Cornelissen has clearly documented, the CJEU in the beginning of its case-law on the provisions on conflicts of law followed a clear-cut approach insisting on the strict and mandatory character of the rules in question. The leading cases which established the scope and the reach of these provisions were *Ten Holder*[5] and *Luijten*.[6] The central message is that conflict-of-law rules 'constitute a complete system of conflict rules the effect of which is to divest the legislature of each Member State of the power to determine the ambit and the conditions for the application of its national legislation so far as the persons who are subject thereto and the territory within which the provisions of national law take effect are concerned'. This is what we call the mandatory character of the rules contained in Article 11 *et seq.* which also encompasses the exclusivity rule according to which every person is subject to the legislation of a single Member State only. The interpretation inherent to the case-law of the CJEU guaranteed – as Prof. Cornelissen rightly stated – 'the predictability of the conflict-of-law rules as well as legal certainty.'

2. THE *BOSMANN* CASE

Did the *Bosmann* judgment change this situation? This judgment, indeed, caused consternation as to how it should be read and understood. For example, an author wrote that there are two possibilities for interpretation.[7] Firstly, if no family benefits are to be paid under the law of the competent state, the chances of migrant workers and their families getting family benefits from the non-competent state are good if this is foreseen by its legislation. Secondly, the Court could mean that Article 68 in conjunction with Articles 2 and 11(3)(e) of Regulation 883/2004 should be applied and, as a consequence, the state of residence of the children must always check if there are benefits payable according to its law.

The CJEU clearly stated that its verdict in the *Bosmann* case was no derogation from *Ten Holder* and *Luijten*.[8] And this can be confirmed when we have a look at the Court's argumentation. It leaves no doubt that the legislation applicable is the Dutch one and from that 'follows that Community law does not require the competent German authorities to grant Mrs. Bosmann the family benefit in question'.[9] With this statement the second possibility for interpretation mentioned above is excluded. This is clear evidence that the Court does not make changes as to the conflict-of-law rules. The really new element which the Court adds is the statement that in the light of Article 42 EC (now Article 45 TFEU) 'the Member State of residence cannot be deprived of the right to grant child benefits

5 Case 302/84, *Ten Holder*, EU:C:1986:242.

6 Case 60/86, *Luijten*, EU:C:1986:307.

7 Cfr. S. Devetzi, 'The coordination of family benefits by Regulation 883/2004' (2009) 11 *European Journal of Social Security*, 213.

8 See Case C-352/06, *Bosmann*, EU:C:2008:290, para. 32.

9 Case C-352/06, *Bosmann*, EU:C:2009:290, para. 27.

to those resident within its territory while under Article 13(2)(a) of Regulation No. 1408/71 (=Article 11(3)(a) of Regulation 883/2004) a person employed in the territory of one Member State is to be subject to the legislation of that state even if he resides in the territory of another Member State, the fact remains that the purpose of that Regulation is not to prevent the Member State of residence from granting, pursuant to its legislation, child benefits to that person'.[10]

From this argumentation we can derive two consequences: (a) the competent Member State remains the competent Member State; (b) nevertheless the non-competent Member State may apply its legislation. I think that this line of thought is not in contrast with the mandatory character of conflict-of-law rules as they are laid down in Article 11 *et seq.* of Regulation 883/2004. It does not matter whether we explain this by referring to the *Petroni* principle. The most important aspect is that the judgment does not establish a duty or an obligation for the non-competent Member State to grant the benefit. The Court could have avoided irritation. If we construe the judgment in this way it may also be in line with what national legislation wants to achieve. Let me explain.

In Germany there is a consistent case-law of the Constitutional Court (Bundesverfassungsgericht) and the Federal Social Court (Bundessozialgericht) which was begun long before *Bosmann* and maintained to this day without any reference to *Bosmann*. The conflict-of-law rules contained in Article 11 *et seq.* of Regulation 883/2004 define the competent Member State according to clear-cut criteria. And the exclusivity rule makes a person subject to the legislation of a single Member State only. Nevertheless the Bundesverfassungsgericht and in its wake the Bundessozialgericht applied national law independently of conflict-of-law rules in the Co-ordination Regulation.[11] I will give you an example which is taken from the case-law of the Bundessozialgericht, a case decided in 2009.[12]

The plaintiff had been working and living in Aachen until 31 August 2003. From 1 September 2003 to 24 January 2004 he received a child-raising benefit. From July 2004 on he lived in the Netherlands. On 6 January 2006 he registered as unemployed with the Federal Labour Agency (the competent German institution for unemployment benefits) and made a request for an unemployment benefit.

It was a moot point of the trial as to whether Article 71 of Regulation 1408/71, the provision on frontier workers, was applicable and therefore Dutch law the competent legislation. And the lower court denied the claim due to the fact that the plaintiff had at the time of the request no residence in Germany. The Bundessozialgericht, however, argued that it does not matter whether the plaintiff was a frontier worker and consequently the state of residence, the Netherlands, had to decide on the claim. The Bundessozialgericht considered

---

10 Case C-352/06, *Bosmann*, EU:C:2008:290, para. 31.

11 Bundesverfassungsgericht 30.12.1999 – 1 BvR 809/95; Bundessozialgericht 03.07.2003 – B 7 AL 42/02 R.

12 Bundessozialgericht 07.10.2009 – B 11 AL 25/08.

the question about the qualification of the plaintiff as a frontier worker immaterial and applied German social security law. The plaintiff satisfied all the requirements for entitlement to the unemployment benefit, but he did not meet with the requirement under German conflict-of-law rules which for the benefit in question render residence of the applicant obligatory. But the Bundessozialgericht could invoke the consistent case-law of the Bundesverfassungsgericht which prohibits the denial of a claim to unemployment benefits on the sole ground that residence in Germany is not available. The rationale of this case-law of the Bundesverfassungsgericht which started in the 1990s of the last century lies in the constitutionally protected principle of equality of treatment. If an unemployed person – the Bundesverfassungsgericht holds – has made sufficient contributions within the qualifying period as provided for in unemployment insurance law, it would be a violation of equality of treatment if he was disadvantaged compared to other comparable claimants. The existence of a residence is no acceptable justification for unequal treatment.

The judgment of the Bundessozialgericht was delivered in October 2009, that is more than one year after the *Bosmann* case. The *Bosmann* judgment was not mentioned in the verdict. From this we may gather that German courts grant social benefits on condition that German legislation requires them to do so. And if all the requirements for entitlement to a social benefit are met, the fact that Germany is not the competent state does not rule out that a claim be awarded along the terms of its legislation. If we construe the ruling in the *Bosmann* case as containing the dictum that it is not the purpose of conflict-of-law rules to erect a bar which denies Member States achieving aims which are inherent to their legislation, then the case-law of both German courts fits within what was held in the *Bosmann* judgement. I think seen in this perspective conflict-of-law rules in the Regulation 883/2004 and the legal requirements of national legislation for granting benefits can peacefully co-exist. There is no change or shift of competence from the competent to the non-competent Member State. Abiding with its duties under national law a national court does not violate the rules of games contained in Article 11 *et seq.* of Regulation 883/2004. I do not know to what extent other courts in other Member States follow similar routes. At least in the *Franzen* case we meet an example of it.

3. THE *HUDZINSKI/WAWRZYNIAK* CASES

3.1. THE LINES OF ARGUMENTATION

What lesson do we have to draw from the *Hudzinski/Wawrzyniak* judgment?[13] Is it a mere continuation of *Bosmann* or does it add something different? To give

[13] Joined Cases C-611/10 and C-612/10, *Hudzinski and Wawrzyniak*, EU:C:2012:339.

an answer I think we have to discern two parts of the judgment. The first part is dedicated to the area and the application of conflict-of-law rules. The second part deals with the problem of the conformity of a domestic provision with Article 48 TFEU.

The first part of the judgment[14] contains answers responding to the first two questions submitted by the German highest court in tax matters, the Bundesfinanzhof (BFH). And these two questions should be read carefully. From them we can gather that the BFH has read and interpreted the *Bosmann* judgment as not imposing a duty on the non-competent Member State to award benefits. As a consequence, in both questions the BFH uses the formula 'the power to grant benefits'. And in respect of this power the BFH wants to know whether this power exists also in cases essentially different from the facts available in the *Bosmann* case. The plaintiffs Hudzinski and Wawrzyniak did not lose their rights to family benefits under Polish legislation. Should the *Bosmann* argumentation be restricted to cases in which persons concerned suffered from a disadvantage resulting from the exercise of the right to freedom of movement of workers?

My interpretation and my thesis is that as far as these questions are concerned and, as a consequence, as far as conflict-of-law rules contained in Article 13 *et seq.* of Regulation 1408/71 (now Article 11 *et seq.* of Regulation 883/2004) are concerned, the Court does not go beyond what it has already held in *the Bosmann* case. Let me explain.

Paragraphs 37–49 of the judgment contain a mere reference and a repetition of what has been outlined in the *Bosmann* judgment. Beginning with paragraph 50 the Court develops its answer to the specific questions by the BFH and therefore turns to the peculiar situation which is without any doubt different from *Bosmann*. In view of the purpose and the function of the provisions on the applicable legislation as it is laid down in the Preamble and in the light of Article 48 TFEU the CJEU clearly states and extends the validity of the – I call it from now on – *Bosmann* principle to cases in which persons affected are not disadvantaged. When – as the Court points out – the provisions of Regulation 1408/71 must be interpreted in the light of the purpose of Article 48 TFEU, which is to contribute to the establishment of the greatest possible freedom of movement for migrant workers and referring to the first Recital in the Preamble to Regulation 1408/71 the latter seeks to contribute to the improvement of the standard of living and conditions of employment for migrant workers, it is within this frame of reference when the Court holds that a migrant worker must not be deprived of benefits granted solely by virtue of the legislation of a single Member State. And with reference to the *Bosmann* case where the connecting factor was residence, since family benefits in Germany are based on residence, in

14 Joined Cases C-611/10 and C-612/10, *Hudzinski and Wawrzyniak*, EU:C:2012:339, paras. 37–68.

the *Hudzinski/Wawrzyniak* case the connecting factor was unlimited income tax liability. And so ends the argumentation by the Court with the identical result which we know from the *Bosmann* case. Even when the worker concerned has not suffered any legal disadvantage by reason of the fact that he has exercised his freedom of movement, Articles 14(1)(a) and 14a(1)(a) of Regulation 1408/71 must be interpreted as not precluding a Member State, which is not designated under those provisions as being the competent state, from granting child benefits in accordance with its national law to a migrant worker.[15]

The outcome is clear: The *Bosmann* principle is confirmed without reservations. Whether the plaintiff would lose a right or not is no relevant element of the principle. What, however, is important to see is that the CJEU does not change the contents of the provisions on the applicable legislation. The competent Member State is and remains the competent Member State, and the non-competent Member State is and remains the non-competent Member State. This is due to the fact that the Court never speaks of a duty or obligation to award a benefit, neither in the *Bosmann*, nor in the *Hudzinski/Wawrzyniak* case. In paragraph 70 of the judgment it emphasises this interpretation by stating that the state has the power, but not the obligation, to grant child benefits.

The study of the second part of the judgment[16] leads us to a different legal territory, away from the arena of conflict-of-law rules to that of primary law and in particular to freedom-of-movement provisions. The distinction of two different territories is indebted to the questions referred by the BFH. Whereas the first two questions concern the scope of the provisions on the applicable legislation, the last two questions aim at answers to the compatibility of the German tax provision which precludes entitlement to family benefits where a comparable benefit is paid in another country, with provisions of EU law. Linked to this problem is question number 4 with which the BFH wants to get an answer to the way with which rules on overlapping benefits should be applied.

Quite rightly the CJEU considers it appropriate to examine the third and the fourth question together. And the Court makes it clear from the beginning that we are now no longer in the domain of the provisions on the applicable legislation, and neither in the domain of coordination law at all. The yardstick against which the German law has to be measured is now substantive primary law. In other words, the well-known arena is opened in which the Court examines whether a specific provision is in tune with provisions on fundamental freedoms or is not.

Consequently, the Court refuses to examine the German law by relying on overlapping rules[17] on which the appellants in the proceedings had laid emphasis

---

15 Joined Cases C-611/10 and C-612/10, *Hudzinski and Wawrzyniak*, EU:C:2012:339, para. 68.

16 Joined Cases C-611/10 and C-612/10, *Hudzinski and Wawrzyniak*, EU:C:2012:339, paras. 69–85.

17 Article 76 of Council Regulation (EC) 1408/71 of 14 June 1971 on the application of social security schemes to employed persons, to self-employed persons and to members of their families moving within the Community, OJ 1971, L 149 (hereinafter referred to as 'Regulation

invoking the *Schwemmer* case.[18] Against this transfer of arguments, the Court holds that the situation at issue in the *Hudzinski/Wawrzyniak* proceedings is not covered by rules against overlapping since it does not concern a hypothetical overlapping of entitlements laid down by the legislation of the Member State of residence of the child concerned and of those resulting from the legislation of the Member State of employment designated as the competent state under that Regulation. A reason against this transfer is that the Republic of Poland is both the Member State of residence of the child concerned and the Member State of employment of the posted worker. From this follows that the rules against overlapping cannot preclude exclusion from entitlement to child benefit pursuant to the German tax provision.

The swerve in the examination begins with what is held in paragraph 76. The Court states that the rule of national law against overlapping which does not provide for a reduction in the amount of the benefits by the amount of that of a comparable benefit received in another state, but for exclusion from that benefit, is such as to constitute a substantial disadvantage affecting in reality a greater number of migrant workers than settled workers who have worked exclusively in the Member State concerned, this being a matter for the referring court to ascertain. With this statement the Court opens the door for the discrimination test on the basis of Articles 45 and 48 TFEU. The Court leaves no doubt that the disadvantage cannot be justified. Firstly, the fact that the benefit at issue is financed by tax revenue and that the appellants were entitled to that benefit by reason of the fact that they were subject to unlimited income tax liability is used by the Court as an element which makes the disadvantage 'even less justifiable.[19] In this connection the Court recalls former rulings, among others *Da Silva Martins*,[20] according to which the aim of Articles 45 and 48 TFEU would not be achieved if, as a result of the exercise of their freedom of movement, migrant workers were to lose social security advantages guaranteed to them by the legislation of one Member State. And it goes on and says that from the case-law of the Court it is clear that both Articles and Regulation 1408/71 are intended in particular to prevent the situation in which a worker who has exercised his right of free movement is treated, without objective justification, less favourably than one who has completed his entire career in only one Member State.

None of these arguments hold water.

Were Hudzinski and Wawrzyniak treated less favourably than persons who have completed their entire career in only one Member State? The answer is a clear

---

1408/71'); Article 10 of Council Regulation (EEC) 574/72 of 21 March 1972 laying down the procedure for implementing Regulation (EEC) 1408/71 on the application of social security schemes to employed person, to self-employed persons and to their families moving within the Community, OJ 1972, L 74 (hereinafter referred to as 'Regulation 574/72').

18 Case C-16/09, *Schwemmer*, EU:C:2010:605.

19 Joined Cases C-611/10 and C-612/10, *Hudzinski and Wawrzyniak*, EU:C:2012:339, para. 78.

20 Case C-388/09, *Da Silva Martins*, EU:C:2011:439.

no. They receive child benefits according to Polish law. In that respect there is no disadvantage for the appellants Hudzinski and Wawrzyniak. The Court gives the impression that the facts of the *Da Silva Martins* and *Hudzinski/Wawrzyniak* cases are similar and therefore should be solved on the same principles. But this is not the case, the facts in both situations are dissimilar. Da Silva Martins lost his entitlement to the German insurance of reliance on care due to exercising his right of freedom of movement. Staying in Germany would have given him the same right as those who pursue all their activities in this country. This situation is in clear contrast with that in which Hudzinski and Wawrzyniak were. The comparable person could be only another Polish worker who has spent his whole working life in Poland,[21] and compared to such a person they would not have been disadvantaged.

The second objection to the argumentation by the Court is the lack of examination according to the schema the CJEU itself has developed for proving whether there is a restriction to a fundamental freedom and whether this restriction is objectively justified which requires the legitimate aim and the proportionality test.[22] According to this schema it would have been necessary to inquire into the shape and function of the benefit in question, the child-raising benefit under German law. This inquiry is missing in the judgment. The Court singles out only one element: the tax financing of the benefit, neglecting all the other elements which constitute the legitimate aim and the proportionality of the requirements for entitlement to the benefit.

The family benefit in question (*Kindergeld*) is a typical non-contributory benefit. The child benefit in question was formerly contained in a specific social law, the law on child benefits.[23] For administrative reasons it was later transferred into tax law. The child benefit was formerly and is now financed by taxes. But this does not mean that financing has such a weight as the Court gave it. Giving unjustified weight to the finance aspect the Court does not seek for the essential characteristics of the benefit and its reasons which is normally on the examination agenda of the Court in similar cases.

Family benefits in Germany in general and child benefits in particular depend among other things on residence or the habitual stay of the claimant. The idea behind this requirement is that child-raising is a main contribution to the financing of the German social security system which is financed according to the pay-as-you-go method and according to the *Generationenvertrag* which sees children as the main resource for financing the system. And it is mainly these beneficiaries of child benefits who typically and overwhelmingly finance the social security system through their contributions taken from their salaries and the financial burden for child-raising. So child benefits are to a certain extent the

---

21 See L. Driguez, 'Note', *Europe – Revue mensuelle*, Lexis Nexis, Jurisclasseur 8/9 2012, 30–31.

22 See for this schema R. Streinz, *Europarecht, 9th edition* (Heidelberg: C.F. Müller, 2012), para. 811 *et seq*.

23 Bundeskindergeldgesetz of 1975, Bundesgesetzblatt 1975, I 412.

expression of social responsibility which the state assumes *vis-à-vis* its citizens and residents who typically and overwhelmingly finance the social security system. Posted workers do not contribute to German social security. That they pay taxes after a certain number of working days in Germany[24] is not a relevant criterion to make them eligible for child benefits; it is a merely accidental aspect due to the lack of harmonisation of tax laws. And their children are in their home countries and these children will not be the human source for financing German social security. In that respect their situation is different from people and their children the residence of whom is abroad but who have an insured working relation in Germany. People resident abroad, but with an employment relationship in Germany are entitled to child-raising benefits even if their children are resident in another Member State.[25] Employment in a Member State creates integration into the social security system of a Member State. The rationale is that persons pay social security contributions. That they, after a certain amount of time, pay taxes too, is of a secondary nature. Posted workers are not integrated into national social security systems and therefore cannot claim the same status as other groups and persons who pursuant to conflict-of-law rules are incorporated into national social security systems. So it seems to be an objective justification when posted workers are excluded from entitlement to child benefits.

To summarise, the *Hudzinski/Wawrzyniak* judgment in its first part has continued the road embarked upon in the *Bosmann* judgment and has not explicitly changed conflict-of-law rules within the framework of social security coordination. But due to the ruling in the second part the outcome of the judgment is as if it had. Germany has become the competent Member State, not in terms of social security coordination, but in terms of the free movement of workers. In practice, contrary to what the Court holds according to which the non-competent Member State in terms of conflict-of-law rules has the power, not the duty to grant a benefit, it undermines this ruling by introducing through the back door a duty to grant. From a doctrinal point of view this is unacceptable. I quote a passage from a review article by a French author in which the whole dilemma of the *Hudzinski/Wawrzyniak* decision is eloquently summarised:[26]

> '*force est de souligner le paradoxe selon lequel si l'Etat non compétent en vertu des règles de conflit de lois n'est pas obligé de servir une prestation familiale, l'absence totale de versement, dès lors que le demandeur possède un rattachement suffisant avec*

24 Typically 183 days, this is the usual time limit in bilateral tax agreements.

25 Article 73 of Regulation 1408/71; Article 67 of Regulation 883/2004.

26 J.-P. Lhernould, 'Ouverture de droits à prestations familiales dans deux Etats membres de l'Union: Consolidation de nouveaux principes?' (2012) *Revue de jurisprudence sociale*, 583–584.

cet Etat, a toutes les chances d'être condamné en tant qu'entrave à la libre circulation des travailleurs. Sauf à être en mesure de justifier cette entrave, il reste à l'Etat à mettre en place des dispositifs se limitant à diminuer le montant des prestations concernées, selon des mécanismes inspirés de l'article 68 du règlement 883/2004. Ainsi se poursuit la montée en puissance, au nom du traité, d'un "principe de faveur" qui va bien au-delà de la logique "neuter" des règles de coordination et qui dérange le principe cardinal d'unicité de la législation applicable. Il est bien difficile de savoir jusqu'où ce principe mènera, mais aussi comment les Etats membres seront en mesure de disposer concrètement de la liberté que leur accorde la Cour de justice.'

3.2. THE DANGER TO LEGAL CERTAINTY IN THE APPLICATION OF CONFLICT-OF-LAW RULES

The CJEU has decided against all opinions expressed in the proceedings by the German government, the European Commission and the Advocate General. The German government has asked for strict application of the conflict-of-law rules which are designed to determine, in accordance with objective criteria, the legislation applicable. As a consequence, the rules which determine the applicable legislation must not be watered down with a rule requiring 'application of the most favourable legislation.'

The Commission in its submission endorses these arguments, in particular referring to the fact that the plaintiffs had not lost their entitlement to child benefits, nor has either of them suffered a disadvantage because of exercising his right to freedom of movement. The Commission sees the danger if the conflict-of-law rules were construed in a way that there is more than one competent state and that there may also be accumulation of benefits. And as a consequence cautions against such an approach, which would not reflect the current legal situation and might thus be misleading for EU citizens.

The Advocate General in his opinion has made a thorough analysis both of the conflict-of-law rules and the case-law of the CJEU hereto and on this basis has stated clearly his position (see para. 77 *et seq.*). First of all the Advocate General's examination of the specific rules of Articles 14(1)(a) and 14a(1)(a) of Regulation 1408/71[27] are not incompatible with EU law, in particular with freedom of movement or the principle of equality. They are in the interest of both of the posted workers and the posting employer and in the interest of the administrative bodies involved. With reference to the *Bosmann* case he argues that even if the *Bosmann* rationale is applicable (as he suggests) to the circumstances of the pending case, only the option of granting child benefit, not an obligation to do so, can be inferred from that judgment, so far as Germany, as a Member State other than the competent state, is concerned.

---

27 Article 12 Regulation 883/2004.

The CJEU is sensitive to this line of criticism. In the *Hudzinski/Wawrzyniak* judgment it points out[28] that it does not appear that, in the situations in the main proceedings, the grant of that benefit, which is not subject to conditions of employment or insurance, is liable to affect disproportionally the predictability and effectiveness of the application of the coordination rules of Regulation 1408/71, requirements relating to legal certainty it also protects the interests of migrant workers.

On the basis of what I have said above I would agree to this statement by the Court if it had stopped its ruling with part 1 of the *Hudzinski/Wawrzyniak* judgment. Leaving it up to the law of the non-competent Member State to decide whether the benefit has to be granted or not, would not compromise conflict-of-law rules and would not endanger legal certainty and predictability. But the Court did not stop there. The approach taken by the Court in the second part of the *Hudzinski/Wawrzyniak* case gives rise to the risk that the aim of legal certainty and predictability of the application of the rules will not be achieved. And at this point I join all the critics of this case-law of the CJEU, although my criticism comes from a different angle.

I will give an example for this danger for legal certainty, predictability and coherence. Let's take the *Jeltes* case.[29] Applying the conflict-of-law rule contained in Article 65 of Regulation 883/2004, Belgium, the state of residence of the plaintiff, was the competent Member State to grant the unemployment benefit to the plaintiff Jeltes. He would have preferred to receive the unemployment benefit from the institution in the Netherlands, since the level of the benefit there is much higher. The Netherlands refused payment due to the claimant's lack of residence in the Netherlands.

Should the Court not have decided this case along the lines endorsed in the second part of the *Hudzinski/Wawrzyniak* judgment? The Netherlands refused payment of the unemployment benefit in full, since the plaintiff had no residence in the Netherlands. But the plaintiff had a very strong connecting factor, an employment relationship and a contribution record in unemployment insurance in the Netherlands. Why not say that the Dutch law is not in tune with Articles 45 and 48 TFEU, since a mere residence clause is no objective justification for the full exclusion of the benefit?

The Advocate General made no reference to *Bosmann* and *Hudzinski/Wawrzyniak*, but undertook an examination of whether the Dutch law was an obstacle or a deterrent to the exercise of freedom of movement.[30] Answering this question he called upon the settled case-law that a worker may not claim that his move will be neutral as regards social security. That is an inevitable consequence of the fact that Article 48 TFEU confers on the European Union a power only to

28 Joined Cases C-611/10 and C-612/10, *Hudzinski and Wawrzyniak*, EU:C:2012:339, para. 67.
29 Case C-443/11, *Jeltes*, EU:C:2013:224.
30 Case C-443/11, *Jeltes*, EU:C:2013:6, para. 53 *et seq.*

coordinate, and not to harmonise the laws of the Member States in the field of social security.

The Court picks up this argument and recalls that since Article 48 TFEU provides for the coordination, not the harmonisation of the legislation of the Member States, substantive and procedural differences between the social security systems of individual Member States and, hence, in the rights of persons insured under those schemes, are unaffected by that provision. In those circumstances the Treaty rules on freedom of movement cannot guarantee to an insured person that a move to another Member State will be neutral as regards social security. The fact that a person such as Mr Jeltes receives his unemployment benefit from the competent institution of the Member State of residence, in the present case the Kingdom of Belgium, results from the application, in accordance with Regulation 883/2004, of the law of that state on unemployment benefits. A difference between the benefits provided for in the legislation of the Member State of last employment and that granted pursuant to the legislation of the Member State of residence cannot, in those circumstances, be considered as a restriction on the freedom of movement for workers, since it results from the lack of harmonisation.[31]

Wasn't it appropriate, even necessary, to use the same reasoning in the *Hudzinski/Wawrzyniak* case? There is no material difference between *Jeltes* and *Hudzinski/Wawrzyniak*, at least not one which would be in favour of the Polish plaintiffs. On the contrary, Jeltes had a stronger connecting factor to the Netherlands, due to his employment relationship and, as a consequence, was integrated into the Dutch social security system and certainly paid taxes in the Netherlands. So *vis-à-vis* the Polish claimants Jeltes had better and stronger arguments to prove that the denial of the claim to unemployment benefits by Dutch authorities, relying merely on the residence clause, is an obstacle to free movement of workers protected by Articles 45 and 48 TFEU.

This is not to say that I had wished the CJEU had decided in this way in the *Jeltes* case. Not at all. What I wanted to show is the inconsistency of argumentation and, as a consequence, the rise of uncertainty in the application of conflict of law rules. It is to be desired that the CJEU stops examining the legislation of the non-competent Member State. The CJEU should recognise that in the *Hudzinski/Wawrzyniak* case it has changed the power to grant a benefit into a duty to grant the benefit. The conflict-of-law rules in Article 11 *et seq.* of Regulation 883/2004 mark the boundaries of social responsibility to which Member States are subject and they do this in implementing the requirements of Article 48 TFEU. And Article 4 of Regulation 883/2004 makes sure that all citizens are treated equally within these boundaries. There is no need to create new duties outside of this well-established system. With its idea that conflict-of law rules do not prevent Member States from granting benefits based on their

[31] Case C-443/11, *Jeltes*, EU:C:2013:224, para. 45.

legislation the Court has made a step towards leaving room for decisions by national institutions on the basis of their domestic national law. Not everybody is delighted with this case-law as the number of critics show. But there might be good reasons and aims inherent to national law which are in favour of granting benefits. The CJEU should not interfere with this decision-making.

4. THE *FRANZEN AND OTHERS* CASES[32]

The structure of the problem which the three joined cases show was the same. All three plaintiffs were employed in Germany on the basis of the so-called 'minor employment' (geringfügige Beschäftigung) in terms of a provision in German social insurance law[33] pursuant to which the employed persons were not affiliated to health insurance and pension insurance, but only to the accidents at work scheme.[34] With strict application of the *lex loci laboris* principle in Article 13 (now Article 11 of Regulation 883/2004) the competent Member State to grant social benefits was Germany. As a consequence, the plaintiffs lost family benefits and suffered from disadvantages under Dutch pension law.

The Court held that Article 13 of Regulation 1408/71 had to be applied. Referring to former case-law the fact that the plaintiffs worked only for very short periods was not material. From this we can gather that the CJEU in this case opted for a strict application of conflict-of-law rules.

The consequence would have been that the plaintiffs could not have claimed benefits according to Dutch law. The employment relationship in Germany stood in the way. The referring court asked therefore whether provisions concerning freedom of movement for workers could offer a remedy. In this context the Court came back to and relied on its case-law initiated with the *Bosmann* judgment and confirmed by the *Hudzinski/Wawrzyniak* judgment. One can say that the argumentation built exclusively on the *Bosmann* principle which holds that, in this case, Article 13(1) of Regulation 1408/71 does not preclude the granting of benefits by the non-competent Member State. The Court does not – as occurred in the *Hudzinski/Wawrzyniak* judgment – examine the relevant provisions of Dutch law with a view to Articles 45 and 48 TFEU. An explanation for this could be that the referring court had signalled that if the exclusion of Dutch law had to be accepted due to the strict application of Article 13 of Regulation 1408/71, it would apply a hardship clause under Dutch law. Here again we meet an example like that in Germany[35] that national social security law offers protection independently of what is required in strict application of conflict-of-law rules.

---

32 Case C-382/13, *Franzen and Others*, EU:C:2015:261.

33 §8 of the Sozialgesetzbuch IV.

34 Beginning with 1 January 2013 obligatory affiliation to pension insurance is provided for.

35 See above.

On the basis of the case-law of the CJEU the outcome of this judgment is satisfying. Since the Court opted for the strict application of conflict-of-law rules, the plaintiffs would have been denied social protection. To avoid this, the Court sought refuge with the *Bosmann* principle as it was developed in the first judgment in 2008. It did not interfere with national Dutch law. This is a further example of why the *Bosmann* principle makes sense, because it enables the non-competent Member State to apply its law in order to meet its aims. The question, however, may be allowed: would the Court have come back to the *Hudzinski/ Wawrzyniak* if the Dutch law had not provided for a hardship clause?

I would have preferred a different approach, not dissimilar to what the Advocate General had proposed.[36] In my opinion the case could have been solved on the basis of a purposive interpretation of Article 13(2)(a) of Regulation 1408/71. The *lex loci laboris* principle builds upon employment (or self-employment). The choice of employment as the overarching connecting factor for the establishment of the applicable legislation was made, since in practically all Member States employment is the link with affiliation to pension schemes and health insurance. If an employment relationship is without protection of these fundamental social security branches,[37] the *lex loci laboris* principle lacks its *raison d'être*. We should remember at this point what the CJEU had held in the case *Kits van Heijningen*.[38] It said that the conflict-of-law rules of Regulation 1408/71, among others Article 13, represent a complete system intended not only to prevent the simultaneous application of a number of national legislative systems and the complications which might ensue, but also to ensure that the persons covered by Regulation 1408/71 are not left without social security cover because there is no legislation applicable to them. The latter was the case here. As a consequence through purposive interpretation we may come to the conclusion that Article 13(2)(a) of Regulation 1408/71 is not applicable;[39] instead, pursuant to Article 13(2)(f), the Dutch legislation is the applicable law.

5. CONCLUDING REMARK

To conclude, I am of the opinion that if the judgments *Bosmann*, *Hudzinski/ Wawrzyniak* and *Franzen* remain in their nucleus limited to the literal statement according to which the non-competent Member State 'has the right to grant a benefit', or 'has the power to grant a benefit, not a duty', there is no interference

[36] Opinion of Advocate General Szpunar in Case C-382/13, *Franzen and Others*, EU:C:2014:2190, para. 79 *et seq.*

[37] Exactly this is the term the Advocate General quite rightly uses, see Case C-382/13, *Franzen and Others*, EU:C:2014:2190, para. 89.

[38] Case C-2/89, *Kits van Heijningen*, EU:C:1990:183, para. 12.

[39] From a methodological point of view it is about teleological reduction of the wording of Article 13(2)(a) of Regulation 1408/71.

with the provisions contained in Article 11 *et seq.* of Regulation 883/2004, and it does not arise legal uncertainty about the competent Member State. The competent Member State determined on the basis of these provisions keeps this status. And the non-competent Member State is legitimised to achieve its social policy aims *vis-à-vis* its citizens and those who are integrated in its social security sphere. The *Franzen* case is a good example for why the power to grant the benefit by the non-competent Dutch Member State is convincing. I do not see why this approach should endanger interests of the competent Member State, in this case Germany.

Nevertheless the flip side of the case-law is its temptation for prospective claimants to seek entitlement with the non-competent Member State even in otherwise hopeless cases. That this risk exists shows the recent judgment in the case *B.*[40] The competent Member State was France, the only element to make a request for family benefits with Czech institutions was a peculiar Czech provision giving a right to a parental allowance to persons registered as permanently resident in the Czech Republic. Since Regulation 1408/71 (the same is true of Regulation 883/2004) does not allow for two residences of a person[41] and the real residence of the defendant B. was unquestionably in France, to make a request in the Czech Republic was a lost case. But *Bosmann* gave hope. Against this background it has to be appreciated that the CJEU discouraged further legal actions which are based rather on speculation than on the spirit and purpose of the *Bosmann* verdict. The Court clearly stated that as there were no specific and particularly close connecting factors[42] to the territory of the Czech Republic, this (non-competent) Member State was precluded from granting the benefit requested.

A quite different bundle of problems emerges when the CJEU enters the area of substantive law of the non-competent Member State as it did in the second part of the *Hudzinski/Wawrzyniak* judgement. This is what I would call the crossing of the Rubicon. The power, the right to grant becomes a duty to grant. With this the social responsibility of the competent Member State, fixed and laid down in the conflict-of-law rules, is extended to the non-competent Member State. This approach goes too far in a system which is built on co-ordination, not on harmonisation of social security.

---

40 Case C-394/13, *B.*, EU:C:2014:2199.

41 See Case C 589/10, *Wencel*, EU:C:2013:303, para. 51.

42 Case C-394/13, *B.*, EU:C:2014:2199, paras. 28–30.

CHAPTER 14

WHERE DOES THE UK BELONG?

Jo Shaw

1. INTRODUCTION: MULLING OVER CONNECTIONS

What's in a connection? In this book, scholars across Europe have mulled over one of the most important issues which arise in migration or mobility situations, namely the character and legal regulation of the connections between the mobile person (and their family) and the home and host polities. Meanwhile, in the United Kingdom we have been mulling over another connection, that between the United Kingdom and its 27 fellow Member States, within the legal framework of the European Union. A referendum on UK membership of the EU was promised in the Conservative Party manifesto for the May 2015 General Election and, after the surprise victory of Prime Minister David Cameron and colleagues, legislation in the form of the European Union Referendum Act 2015 has been put in place to permit such a referendum to take place on the question whether the UK should remain in the EU or leave the EU. On 20 February 2016, Cameron announced that the referendum would take place on 23 June 2016.

Migration has become a central element in the debate about UK membership of the EU in recent years, even though it did not merit a mention when Cameron first announced that he supported a referendum in November 2013.[1] It was at the heart of the letter that PM Cameron sent to European Council (EUCO) President Donald Tusk in November 2015, setting out his demands for a 'renegotiation'.[2] Free movement – and the notion that perhaps the UK public might like it to be a little less 'free' (for others, if not for themselves)[3] – has played a central role in

---

1 See Prime Minister's Speech at Bloomberg, November 2013, available at https://www.gov.uk/government/speeches/eu-speech-at-bloomberg (last accessed on 1 March 2016).

2 Letter from David Cameron to Donald Tusk, A New Settlement for the United Kingdom in a reformed European Union, 10 November 2015, available at https://www.gov.uk/government/uploads/system/uploads/attachment_data/file/475679/Donald_Tusk_letter.pdf (last accessed on 1 March 2016).

3 D. Cameron, 'Free movement needs to be less free', *Financial Times*, 26 November 2013, available at www.ft.com/cms/s/0/add36222–56be-11e3-ab12–00144feabdc0.html#axzz39-

the 'renegotiation' of the UK's relationship with the European Union led by the UK's Conservative Government since its election in mid 2015. It featured heavily in the draft Decision of the Heads of State and Government published by Tusk at the beginning of February 2016, which was intended to accommodate the UK's 'special position' and from then on was contained in each successive draft. In the final version of the EUCO conclusions,[4] Section D of Annex 1, in its general considerations about free movement, refers to the need for a '*real and effective degree of connection* between the [mobile EU citizen] and the labour market of the host Member State' (emphasis added).

Hostility to immigration is undoubtedly a factor driving the various 'leave' campaigns, which have reacted to the Cameron 'Deal' by dismissing it as irrelevant to the concerns of the British public. This hostility to EU free movement, connecting to a more deep-seated concern about immigration discussed in more detail later in this chapter as well as to the ongoing refugee crisis and debate about the future of Schengen playing out across Europe during the course of 2015 and 2016, may in the end affect the outcome of the referendum, regardless of whether the renegotiation deal turns out to be salient in the campaign and regardless of what effects it might have in the future. Certainly at the time of writing that result was far too close to call and could go either way.

This concluding chapter has two tasks. It briefly considers the content of and uncertainty around the renegotiation deal, as regards the issue of free movement.[5] It then places these aspects of the deal in the wider context of the UK's longer term approach to navigating the boundaries between free movement under EU law and 'ordinary' immigration (i.e. from third countries), regulated (at least in the case of the UK) almost exclusively under national law.

YJSsk5W (last accessed on 1 March 2016); Prime Minister's Speech at JCB Staffordshire, 28 November 2014, available at https://www.gov.uk/government/speeches/jcb-staffordshire-prime-ministers-speech (last accessed on 1 March 2016).

4 *A New Settlement for the United Kingdom Within the European Union. Extract of the conclusions of the European Council of 18–19 February 2016*, OJ 2016, C 69 I/1. For analysis, see European Parliament Research Service, *The UK's 'new settlement' in the EU. Renegotiation and referendum*, In Depth Analysis, February 2016, available at www.europarl.europa.eu/RegData/etudes/IDAN/2016/577983/EPRS_IDA%282016%29577983_EN.pdf (last accessed on 1 March 2016); Full Fact, *The EU Deal*, available at https://fullfact.org/europe/eu-renegotiation-deal/ (last accessed on 1 March 2016); S. Weiss and S. Blockmans, *The EU deal to avoid Brexit: Take it or leave*, Special Report No. 131 (Brussels: CEPS, 2016).

5 See S. Peers, 'The final UK renegotiation deal: immigration issues', *EU Law Analysis Blog*, 20 February 2016, available at http://eulawanalysis.blogspot.co.uk/2016/02/the-final-uk-renegotiation-deal.html (last accessed on 1 March 2016) and J. Portes, 'Analysing the UK's deal: immigration, free movement, and benefits', *NIESR Blog*, 21 February 2016, available at www.niesr.ac.uk/blog/analysing-uk's-deal-immigration-free-movement-and-benefits (last accessed on 1 March 2016).

2. POLITICAL ARRANGEMENTS TO AVERT 'BREXIT'

At the time of writing, the ink was barely dry on the renegotiation deal. Right up to the last minute, it seemed possible that no deal would be finalised at the 18–19 February 2016 EUCO meeting in Brussels.[6] Many of the sticking points related to those aspects of the deal that concerned freedom of movement.[7]

The governments of the post-2004 Member States of Central and Eastern Europe have been wary of a UK 'renegotiation' containing measures which appeared to single out their citizens for more restrictive treatment as mobile workers, whether in relation to child benefit or 'in-work' benefits (housing benefit, child tax credits, access to public housing). They have become ever more concerned about the prospect that more than one Member State might attempt to introduce such restrictions after such a renegotiation – whether the indexing of child benefit payable in respect of children not resident in the host state, or the pulling of an emergency brake to restrict certain benefits said, by the EUCO conclusions, to act as a pull factor in relation to mobility. There is a fear that quite a number of Member States may seek to pull the new emergency brake to restrict access to 'in-work benefits' where there is said to be pressure on the domestic welfare state and on the labour market and that the roll back of free movement – however partial – would not be limited to the UK. To put it another way, the fear is that UK exceptionalism could end up resulting in a general watering down of the framework for the free movement of persons. Those fears are not far fetched. Already it has been mooted by the Social Democratic Party leader of the region of Burgenland in Austria that free movement for post-2004 Member State workers should be restricted in his *Land* because unemployment is rising.[8] The media often report that politicians in this or that Member State are eyeing the UK's approach with interest to see whether they can follow where the UK is leading. It is clear, as EUCO President Tusk has acknowledged, that it is the group of states from central and eastern Europe which have been asked to pay the biggest price for coming up with a deal designed to persuade the UK electorate to vote to remain in the EU.

While earlier versions of the EUCO decision seemed to be limited in their wording to the UK's situation alone (by reference to the UK's choice not to impose transitional labour market restrictions in 2004), the final version was

---

6 A. Duff, 'What could possibly go wrong at the European Council?', *Blogactiv.eu*, 18 February 2016, available at http://andrewduff.blogactiv.eu/2016/02/18/what-could-possibly-go-wrong-at-the-european-council/ (last accessed on 1 March 2016).

7 For a flavour of the final negotiations leading to the deal, see the *Open Europe* running blog: http://openeurope.org.uk/today/blog/deal-d-day-european-council-summit/ (last accessed on 1 March 2016).

8 'Niessl für Ende der Arbeitnehmerfreizügigkeit', *ORF.at*, 13 February 2016, available at http://burgenland.orf.at/news/stories/2757510/ (last accessed on 1 March 2016).

not. It should be noted that each and every Member State has had a veto on these conclusions, and that the UK is not the only Member State to be a prisoner of its domestic political system; domestic politics may therefore explain the wording of the final communiqué.[9] Given the restrictions on EU citizens that are likely to flow in the event of a UK vote to remain in the EU, the question arises as to what sweeteners for those states which are likely to be most affected were bargained for in the many bilateral meetings that took place on 18 and 19 February 2016. No such sweeteners appear in the actual conclusions, but that does not mean they do not exist. For while it is clear that strategically and economically it would be very much in the interests of the Central and Eastern European states to do whatever they could do to create the conditions under which the UK was more likely to remain in the EU, this could not be at any price. These matters may become public in the weeks, months and even years after the summit as those deals are paid out an in order to sweeten domestic audiences.

At the time of writing in early March 2016, the greatest uncertainty obviously concerned the result of the referendum on 23 June 2016. For many months at the end of 2015 and the beginning of 2016, all of the polls have pointed in the direction of a very close vote with both outcomes entirely possible. Either outcome breeds great uncertainty.

2.1. VOTE 'REMAIN'

In the event of a vote to 'remain', what will be the impact upon the domain of the free movement of persons?

The texts of the EUCO decision and the various Commission declarations on free movement related matters (on the emergency brake, on child benefit and on the alleged abuse of free movement rights) will be translated into formal legislative proposals amending existing EU legislative measures. These will require a qualified majority vote on the part of the Member States in the Council (probably a given, given that EUCO agreed unanimously on these matters in February 2016, but it is never possible wholly to predict how circumstances may change even over a few short months) as well as a (by no means assured) majority in the European Parliament, under the ordinary legislative procedure. National parliaments will also have their say through a scrutiny process.

Even if the legislation is duly approved, problems may still continue. Take the example of the emergency brake to restrict in-work benefits over a period of four years for newly arrived workers, and for a period of no more than seven

---

9 N. Watt, 'A prisoner to his party: David Cameron and his battle with the Tory right', *The Guardian*, 17 February 2016, available at www.theguardian.com/politics/2016/feb/17/prisoner-party-david-cameron-battle-tory-right (last accessed on 1 March 2016).

years in total, where an amendment to Regulation 492/2011 is needed.[10] The circumstances under which the emergency brake may be pulled are set out in the EUCO decision. The legislation will presumably contain some legally refined variant of this (politically agreed) wording:

> 'A Member State wishing to avail itself of the [emergency brake] would notify the Commission and the Council that such an exceptional situation [i.e. inflow of workers from other Member States of an exceptional magnitude over an extended period of time, including as a result of past policies following previous EU enlargements] exists on a scale that affects essential aspects of its social security system, including the primary purpose of its in-work benefits system, or which leads to difficulties which are serious and liable to persist in its employment market or are putting an excessive pressure on the proper functioning of its public services.'

Even in advance of the EUCO agreement, the Commission stated that it considered that the circumstances that would justify the pulling of the emergency brake were already in place in the case of the UK (in particular in view of its decision not to apply transitional restrictions in 2004), suggesting that measures will be forthcoming straight after a referendum vote to remain. However, the leaders of the European Parliament have indicated that a smooth passage for legislation in the Parliament cannot be guaranteed. The Commission's assertion is flatly contradicted by the overwhelming majority of informed economic opinion regarding the impact of EU migration in the UK, which tends to suggest that the UK labour market is in better health than almost any other labour market in the EU and that the fiscal effects of EU migration are positive.[11] Indeed it has been suggested that it was improper of the Commission to indicate, 'without due examination, that it accepts the dubious UK case that migrant costs are putting an exceptional burden on its budget, and has promised to rubber-stamp its application for special measures.' Given the more cautious approach of the European Parliament, the Irish Times has highlighted 'the irony [...] that the UK is supposedly trying to enhance the accountability of the "undemocratic" EU.'[12]

---

10 Regulation (EU) No. 492/2011 of the European Parliament and of the Council of 5 April 2011 on freedom of movement for workers within the Union, OJ 2011, L 141/1.

11 See J. Portes, 'Always crashing in the same car? An "emergency brake" on EU migration', *NIESR Blog*, 23 January 2016, available at www.niesr.ac.uk/blog/always-crashing-same-car-emergency-brake-eu-migration#.VshCxhhdHTF (last accessed on 1 March 2016). See also S. Peers, 'The "emergency brake" on EU citizens' benefits: Must the Commission or Council control it?', *EU Law Analysis Blog*, 31 January 2016, available at http://eulawanalysis.blogspot.co.uk/2016/01/the-emergency-brake-on-eu-citizens.html (last accessed on 1 March 2016).

12 Editorial, 'A necessary compromise on David Cameron's EU reform demands', *Irish Times*, 18 February 2016, available at www.irishtimes.com/opinion/editorial/a-necessary-compromise-on-david-cameron-s-eu-reform-demands-1.2538380 (last accessed on 1 March 2016).

But if the Commission has already tied its own hands in relation to this matter, who else might hold the national politicians to account in such a context by requiring the presentation of proper robust evidence? Could there be some role for judges to test the evidence demanded as the case for pulling the emergency brake? Given the limitations and non-interventionist character of the Court of Justice's approach to subsidiarity questions in the cases that have come before it, this seems relatively unlikely.[13] What might be the role of the European Parliament in the procedure to activate the safeguard mechanism? As it stands, it has not been given a role, as it would be the Council that would give the authorisation; however, a role in the process of scrutinising the pulling of the brake may be something for which the Parliament bargains when the originating legislation is adopted.

Moreover, the usefulness of the emergency brake is undermined by empirical evidence collected about the motivations of workers (especially from Central and Eastern Europe) coming to the UK, whose overwhelming desire is to work.[14] This suggests that even pulling the emergency brake may have no impact on migration flows, which tends to negate the reasoning given in the EUCO decision which connects together the restrictions on benefits and so-called 'pull factors' said to encourage migration. Some have commented upon how ironic it is that the effect of the widespread discussion of access to in-work benefits (including extensive press coverage in Poland of the matter) has resulted in incoming workers destined for low paid jobs having a much better idea of what their benefit entitlements currently are than they did before.

In the UK, there has been some discussion in the last few years about whether or not it was possible to introduce into EU law a measure restricting access on the part of newly arrived workers to in-work non-contributory benefits for four years by means of legislation, without amending the treaties. In other words, would such a discriminatory measure require changes to primary or secondary law? Stephen Booth and Damian Chalmers (the latter of the LSE, but writing in this case for the think tank Open Europe which is seen as close to No. 10 Downing Street) have argued that it would be possible to achieve this by means of amendments to existing legislation.[15] Steve Peers has argued the opposite case.[16] One proposal which was mooted as a means of getting around the problem of discriminating

---

13 T. Horsley, 'Reflections on the Role of the Court of Justice as the Motor of European Integration: Legal Limits to Judicial Lawmaking' (2013) 50 *CML Rev*, 931–964.

14 O. Cichowlas, 'Benefit ban wouldn't keep Poles out of UK', *Politico*, 17 February 2016, available at www.politico.eu/article/benefit-ban-poland-david-cameron-uk-in-eu-salary/ (last accessed on 1 March 2016).

15 See D. Chalmers and S. Booth, *A European labour market with national welfare systems: a proposal for a new Citizenship and Integration Directive*, *Open Europe*, November 2014, and for a summary see http://openeuropeblog.blogspot.co.uk/2014/12/free-movement-why-reforming-rules-on-in.html (last accessed on 1 March 2016).

16 See S. Peers, 'Amending EU free movement law: What are the legal limits?', *EU Law Analysis Blog*, 24 November 2014, available at http://eulawanalysis.blogspot.co.uk/2014/11/amending-eu-free-movement-law-what-are.html (last accessed on 1 March 2016).

against non-UK workers was to require *all* workers entering the UK labour market to wait four years before claiming in-work benefits, thus including also UK citizen/resident 16–20 year olds within the framework of the measure.

In the event, the UK and its partners have opted for an emergency brake short term derogation approach, and it remains to be seen whether this will survive judicial scrutiny in relation to its impact on different social or national groups, perhaps on grounds of its limited temporal effects and its appeal to the protection of national interests such as welfare states, labour markets and the delivery of public services.

The national courts in any state that 'pulls the brake' (and presumably the Court of Justice assuming that at least one national court will refer the question of EU law raised in such a case for a preliminary ruling under Article 267 TFEU) will be faced with the argument that such measures are directly discriminatory against citizens of other Member States denied access to benefits associated with integration in the labour market given to domestic workers. The treaties expressly prohibit discrimination against EU citizens on grounds of nationality within the scope of application of the treaty (Article 18 TFEU). Article 45(2) TFEU specifies that free movement entails the abolition of discrimination between EU workers as regards 'employment, remuneration and other conditions of work and employment'. The Court has consistently held that this extends to benefits which are associated with access to the labour market, and this would include so-called non-contributory in-work benefits. What arguments can be mustered to enable the Court of Justice to avoid the politically inconvenient conclusion of needing to strike down the UK's emergency brake? In that context, some have referred to the unwillingness of the Court of Justice to disturb hard won political settlements in the area of Eurozone legislation. It has been suggested that the case of *Bressol* provides an outlet.[17] In *Bressol*, the Court reviewed national rules that made it much easier for those who were resident in Belgium to access third level paramedical or medical courses, thus indirectly discriminating against citizens of other Member States. The case turned on the justification for such a measure. Rejecting a finding of an excessive burden on Belgium, the Court did not preclude that such measures could be justified on public health grounds.

Such an approach to restrictions on free movement, which seems sympathetic to the imperative concerns of Member States, as well as some of the 'health tourism' case-law, may be what EUCO had in mind when it included in its conclusions this somewhat tendentious summary of the scope of free movement:

> 'Whereas the free movement of workers under Article 45 TFEU entails the abolition of any discrimination based on nationality as regards employment, remuneration and other conditions of work and employment, this right may be subject to limitations on grounds of public policy, public security or public health. In addition, if overriding

17 Case C-73/08, *Bressol*, EU:C:2010:181.

> reasons of public interest make it necessary, free movement of workers may be restricted by measures proportionate to the legitimate aim pursued. Encouraging recruitment, reducing unemployment, protecting vulnerable workers and averting the risk of seriously undermining the sustainability of social security systems are reasons of public interest recognised in the jurisprudence of the Court of Justice of the European Union for this purpose, based on a case by case analysis.'[18]

This text, according to the European Parliament Library's summary of the UK renegotiation 'clarifies' EU free movement law, but in line with CJ case-law.[19] It can be anticipated that it will be subjected to close scrutiny over the coming years. As several commentators on the legal effects of the renegotiation have noted, the EUCO decision will take effect in international law and as such may have certain legal effects for the Member States and indeed for the EU. But it cannot modify the treaties, although it can – as the Court noted in respect of a similar type of measure, which was at issue in the *Rottman* case – serve as an instrument for the interpretation and clarification of the treaties.[20] But it is hard to 'interpret away' a clear principle of non-discrimination, and this is doubtless why Steve Peers, who has subjected the emergency brake provisions to a closer degree of legal analysis than any other scholar thus far, has concluded that their vulnerability to judicial challenge is 'high'.[21]

It is also worth noting that the deal on benefits may have negative effects on other social groups, in particular women, but also men if they are single parents. If women are the group overwhelmingly affected by measures to restrict in-work benefits paid to certain categories of low paid workers, especially those with families, because they are more likely to head a single parent household with children, then such a measure could also be said to be indirectly discriminatory on grounds of sex and would thus require justification.[22] Challenges based on

---

18 *A New Settlement for the United Kingdom within the European Union. Extract of the conclusions of the European Council of 18–19 February 2016*, Annex I, Section D, point 1, OJ 2016, C 69 I/7.

19 See European Parliament Research Service, *The UK's 'new settlement' in the EU. Renegotiation and referendum*, In Depth Analysis, February 2016, 20, available at www.europarl.europa.eu/RegData/etudes/IDAN/2016/577983/EPRS_IDA%282016%29577983_EN.pdf (last accessed on 1 March 2016).

20 Case C-135/08, *Rottman*, EU:C:2010:104.

21 See S. Peers, 'The final UK renegotiation deal: immigration issues', *EU Law Analysis Blog*, 20 February 2016, available at http://eulawanalysis.blogspot.co.uk/2016/02/the-final-uk-renegotiation-deal.html (last accessed on 1 March 2016). It is interesting to note that Chalmers, who originally championed a legislative measure to restrict access to benefits, cannot support the emergency brake in its current form, believing it to be vulnerable to challenge as well as based on the wrong premise: D. Chalmers, 'The deeply misguided "emergency brake"', *The UK in a Changing EU Analysis*, 17 February 2016, available at http://ukandeu.ac.uk/the-deeply-misguided-emergency-break/ (last accessed on 1 March 2016).

22 See C. O'Brien, 'Why the EU emergency brake on migrant benefits is sexist', *The Independent Voices*, 5 February 2016, available at www.independent.co.uk/voices/why-the-eu-emergency-brake-on-migrant-benefits-is-sexist-a6854936.html (last accessed on 1 March 2016).

this analysis could also hinder the practical application of the deal for many years to come.

The implementation of the free movement provisions of the EUCO decision would also require a range of other measures of EU secondary law, including an amendment to Regulation 883/2004 on the coordination of social security systems (to introduce restrictions on child benefit where it is paid in respect of children not resident in the host state) and an amendment to Directive 2004/38, the free movement or Citizens' Rights Directive.[23] The latter measure would be designed to introduce a requirement in relation to third-country national family members of migrant EU citizens, enabling Member States to require that such family members must have enjoyed a prior lawful residence elsewhere in the EU before moving to the host state along with their EU citizen family member, reversing earlier CJ case-law.[24] Steve Peers takes the view that these measures are much less vulnerable to judicial review for non-compliance with the principles of primary EU law and with the treaties.

As with the case of in-work benefits, it is generally agreed that the attempt to reduce child benefits by indexation to home state costs of living is a solution in search of a problem, not least because benefits paid outside the UK represent a very small percentage of the overall benefits bill for children.[25] By way of contrast, the proposal to reverse the Court of Justice's judgment in *Metock* on prior lawful residence of third-country national family members (which was itself based on an interpretation of the current terms of Directive 2004/38),[26] along with the Commission's promise to provide new interpretative guidance on the conditions applicable to the deportation of EU citizens who have committed serious criminal offences, suggests a resurgence of interest on the part of Member States to apply as much 'ordinary' immigration law to the case of free movement as possible. This point is explored in more detail in the latter sections of this chapter.

2.2. VOTE 'LEAVE'

It is important to note that the vote in the UK is based on a binary choice – leave/remain – and while there are some uncertainties in relation to legal and political

23 Directive 2004/38/EC of the European Parliament and of the Council of 29 April 2004 on the right of citizens of the Union and their family members to move and reside freely within the territory of the Member States, OJ 2004, L 158/77 (hereinafter referred to as 'Directive 2004/38' or 'Citizens' Rights Directive').

24 See further European Parliament Research Service, *The UK's 'new settlement' in the EU. Renegotiation and referendum*, In Depth Analysis, February 2016, 20, available at www.europarl.europa.eu/RegData/etudes/IDAN/2016/577983/EPRS_IDA%282016%29577983_EN.pdf (last accessed on 1 March 2016).

25 For facts and figures see http://bruegel.org/2016/02/child-benefits-for-eu-migrants-in-the-uk/ (last accessed on 1 March 2016).

26 Case C-127/08, *Metock*, EU:C:2008:449.

issues if the vote is to remain, there is absolutely no clarity about what legal position the UK may find itself in, in the event of 'vote leave'.

There will certainly be profound impacts upon EU citizens with a connection to the UK, i.e. non-UK citizens resident in the UK and UK citizens resident in other Member States, and upon their families, including third-country nationals. How will their situations be regulated at the EU and (most importantly) the national levels in order to recognise their acquired rights and interests once the protective blanket of EU citizenship (or its recognition in the UK) is removed? What may be the prospects for future mobility? In part, this will obviously depend upon the legal position that the UK negotiates for itself as a non-member. The consensual nature of withdrawal under Article 50 TEU, which itself will require international treaties to be drawn up, agreed and ratified, may see terms imposed upon the UK withdrawal. Furthermore, the UK has to figure out what types of relations it wants with the EU and the other Member States after withdrawal, and various analogies have been drawn to the existing cases of 'connected' third countries, including Norway, Switzerland or indeed Canada.[27] Depending upon the choice or choices made, this will have significant repercussions with regard to potentially restoring relations between the UK and the other Member States to a case governed by 'ordinary immigration law'.

3. HOW CAN WE BEST UNDERSTAND THE UK RENEGOTIATION?

The remainder of this chapter is devoted to offering some context for better understanding the UK's renegotiation in relation to matters of the free movement of persons.

The UK's approach to 'renegotiating' EU free movement law should be understood as continuing the trends set through its previous approach to implementation and enforcement of this part of EU law. The renegotiation needs to be seen in the much wider context of the politicisation and contested application of EU free movement law in the UK over many years, certainly dating back to the 2004 enlargement of the EU, and perhaps much further. It fits neatly into a previously developed framework for analysis of the interactions between EU law and national law,[28] which helps to explain why there a history of frequent misapplication, misinterpretation and misimplementation of EU free movement law in the UK arena. This framework suggests that elite actors within Member

27 S. Dhingra and T. Sampson, *Life after BREXIT: What are the UK's options outside the European Union?*, Briefing (Brussels: CEPS, 2016), available at http://cep.lse.ac.uk/pubs/download/brexit01.pdf (last accessed on 1 March 2016).

28 J. Shaw and N. Miller, 'When Legal Worlds Collide: An Exploration of What Happens when EU Free Movement Law Meets UK Immigration Law' (2013) 38 *EL Rev*, 137.

States, notably governments, but also legislatures, officials, lawyers and judges, are not passive bystanders who receive the tablets of stone on which EU law is written and then just do their best (or worst) with them at the domestic level. On the contrary, as theories of Europeanisation have often sought to show, there needs to be a multiperspectival observation of how these interactions between the different legal and political elements of a policy area develop iteratively over time and space and across the 'levels' of the EU's multilevel constitutional framework. In particular, a historical and contextual approach is needed to understand how the UK has come to apply EU law.

3.1. THE UK AND FREE MOVEMENT LAW

Historically, UK immigration law is based on permissions – leave to enter, leave to remain, etc. – and this, combined with a strong border culture resulting from the UK's position as an island state with land borders only to Ireland, does not necessarily provide a propitious framework into which an EU law regime based on rights granted to individuals – to free movement, to non-discrimination, etc. – could be inserted. And yet, the UK has always been an active participant in the free movement system, both as a recipient and a sender of mobile Europeans, across many different categories of students, workers, self-employed, retired people, etc.

So long as free movement rights were not heavily politicised in the UK, nationals of other Member States encountered relatively few problems living and working in the UK. The principle behind the UK's approach to implementing EU free movement law through domestic measures (in practice, through statutory instruments or 'Regulations') was to ensure that nationals of other Member States were not treated as persons subject to general immigration control. This took a little while to sediment in UK law and immigration practice as some early CJ case-law showed.[29] In the 1990s, the boundaries between UK immigration law and free movement law were tested in a number of cases at the domestic level.[30] These cases provide examples of cases where the UK authorities were minded to think that a national of a Member State was not – in the terms of the UK implementing legislation – a qualifying Community citizen (e.g. because he or she was not self-sufficient through work or other means). Such a person would be likely to receive a letter from the Home Office informing him or her of this fact. However, enforcement proceedings were rarely, if ever taken at that time. Throughout this time, the issues were rarely salient outside relatively narrow circles of lawyers and officials, although the lawyers who dealt with EU law implementation on a regular basis were rarely wholly content with the

29 Case C-157/79, *R. v Pieck*, EU:C:1980:179. See generally C. Vincenzi, 'European Citizenship and Free Movement Rights in the United Kingdom' (1995) *Public Law*, 259.

30 *R. v City of Westminster, ex parte Castelli* (1996) 28 HLR 616 (CA).

UK authorities' approach.[31] Indeed, back in 1997, in a judgment of the House of Lords, UK 'immigration exceptionalism' was already at the forefront of the judicial mind:[32]

> '[The Immigration Act 1971] contemplates that persons who are not British citizens will be entitled to be present here only if they have been given leave to enter and that their right to reside in the United Kingdom will be a consequence of the terms of that leave. The whole scheme relies upon the exercise of control at the frontier and is part of the explanation for the insistence of the United Kingdom in retaining such controls [...] The immigration controls of most European countries with land frontiers operate in a different way. Under their systems, the primary question is whether the non-citizen has a legal right to be present in the country, reside there, be employed or follow an occupation. His right to enter is a consequence of his having the right to be there rather than the other way round.'

The years since the turn of the millennium have seen many changes, which contribute in different ways to an altered political and legal environment for asking the question 'where do I belong?' and for reinforcing the sense of 'immigration exceptionalism' for the UK.

On the side of EU law, the formalisation of a concept of EU citizenship in 1993 in the Treaty of Maastricht eventually started to produce some concrete outcomes in the 2000s, including a line of case-law under which certain non-discrimination rights seemed to attach to EU citizens simply on the basis that they were (lawfully) resident in another Member State.[33] This seemed capable of posing quite considerable demands on the welfare states of the Member States to show 'a certain degree of solidarity', but all in the service of the postulation that 'citizenship of the Union is destined to be the fundamental status of the nationals of the Member States.'[34] The legislature was also not idle. The Citizens' Rights Directive was adopted in 2004. The Citizens' Rights Directive is partly a consolidation of previous instruments, but it also instantiates some key changes to the status of EU citizens, such as the right of permanent residence for those resident in the host state for five years or more. Other legislative changes, e.g. in relation to social security rights, were also introduced in that period.

The EU changed dramatically with the accession of new Member States in 2004, 2007 and 2013, in particular a large number of states that underwent disruptive economic and political transformations after 1989, which had severe

---

31 When I presented the preliminary findings of earlier research on EU free movement law to a group of stakeholders in the summer of 2012, one long-term and experienced observer of the story of UK implementation of the EU free movement suggested that our arguments regarding the restrictive approach taken by the UK government in the 2010s found an echo in her practical experience dating back to the 1970s.

32 Lord Hoffmann delivering the minority judgment in *Remilien v Secretary of State for Social Security; Chief Adjudication Officer v Wolke* [1998] 1 All ER 129; [1997] 1 WLR 1640.

33 See Case C-85/96, *Martínez Sala*, EU:C:1998:217.

34 See Case C-184/99, *Grzelczyk*, EU:C:2001:458.

impacts upon their labour markets. This has led to migration flows from East to West (and sometimes back again), which appear not to have been fully anticipated by political elites in all states. The UK was one of the few states not to apply transitional restrictions on access to the labour market of citizens of the states of Central and Eastern Europe (the so-called A8 states), which acceded to the EU in 2004, but it would seem that it did so not so much as a result of a liberal impulse but rather as a result of a miscalculation as to the potential numbers of EU citizens who might move to the UK. However, just a few years later the economic differences that led to these flows increasingly demanded to be viewed in conjunction with the effects of the global financial crisis of 2008, which became – as a result of a range of decisions made by different political actors – a sovereign debt crisis in parts of the Eurozone which persists even today. This has led to the introduction of heavy and often contested austerity policies in many states, which in turn has generated a significant element of south to north intra-EU migration, alongside the East-West movements.[35]

The particular factors affecting the economy in the late 2000s and 2010s have, moreover, also coalesced with broader concerns amongst electorates in the Member States regarding immigration more generally, including fears about the apparent lack of integration on the part of certain migrant communities which become linked in the public imagination to security concerns. These fears seemed to have been fully realised with the migrant and refugee crisis that has arisen across Europe in 2015 and 2016, mainly as a result of conflict and instability in states such as Iraq and Syria, and the rise of Islamic State. It is in large measure these fears that have led to increasing votes for anti-immigration and indeed anti-immigrant political parties in many countries.

There is, furthermore, a perception that the EU's own liberalisation of service sectors has opened up possibilities for exploitation of pay and conditions differentials across the Member States by transnational corporations evading host state labour regulation requirements by 'posting' workers employed under home state conditions. In that context, globalisation is a dirty word, and the EU's own single market is seen as complicit in this process of undermining the social compacts within individual Member States to the detriment of organised labour and 'ordinary working people'. This form of Euroscepticism certainly is not exclusive to the UK. In fact, it is strong in many states where organised labour still retains a higher degree of traction within the political sphere than it does these days in the UK.

Altogether, this amounts to a perfect storm in which free movement rights have come to be seen as part of the problem (of a loss of sovereignty) rather than an element of the solution (through a pooling of sovereignty to combat challenges collectively rather than individually). Public opinion polls thus

---

35 R. Verwiebe, 'New Forms of Intra-European Migration, Labour Market Dynamics and Social Inequality in Europe' (2014) 11 *Migration Letters*, 125.

demonstrate that free movement is simultaneously one of the most prized and one of the most feared elements of the integration process.

3.2. CONTESTING FREE MOVEMENT IN THE UK

Although not alone, the UK government has been at the forefront of these processes of contestation, and this position has manifested itself in a increasingly politicised and ever more complex legal framework for the implementation of free movement rights, with increasing levels of friction and overlap between the framework of EU free movement law and UK immigration law.[36] These frictions can be seen in the form of a much more energetic 'sorting' of EU citizens resident in the UK into good migrants and bad migrants by public authorities, with the latter more vulnerable to removal from the territory, in particular if they can be said to be an unreasonable burden upon the state. In the UK, various measures have been taken to restrict access to benefits – with problematic outcomes for many vulnerable migrants, as Charlotte O'Brien's work has shown.[37] In many cases, this has taken the form of tidying up a previously unclear legal situation which led to variations in practice across the UK, and creating avenues that public officials – e.g. the police, in conjunction with benefits officers and immigration officials – can pursue in order to make it clear to individuals, such as those who have lost their jobs, that they are definitely no longer welcome in the UK.

In addition, the UK has made full use of the new openings offered by a hardening of CJ case-law on EU citizenship, in particular from *Dano* onwards,[38] through *Alimanovic*[39] and most recently *Garcia-Nieto.*[40] Faced with fear of the demon 'welfare tourist', the Court has permitted Member States to reject claims for social assistance from EU citizens who have not worked and have no intention of working, and indeed from those who had worked but who have lost their status as a 'worker'. The Court has reversed its historic approach to the equality of EU citizens established in *Martínez Sala* by making it clear that the EU citizens can *only* claim equality with nationals provided they comply with the conditions for lawful residence. There is no longer ever an assumption of lawful residence as appeared to prevail in *Martínez Sala*. And in *Garcia-Nieto*, the Court has confirmed that in the first three months of residence there is no need

36 J. Shaw *et al.*, *Getting to Grips with EU Citizenship: Understanding the Friction Between UK Immigration Law and EU Free Movement Law*, Research Report, 2013, available at www.frictionandoverlap.ed.ac.uk/files/1693_fullreportlowres.pdf (last accessed on 1 March 2016).

37 C. O'Brien, 'The Pillory, the Precipice and the Slippery Slope: The Profound Effects of the UK's Legal Reform Programme Targeting EU Migrants' (2015) 37 *Journal of Social Welfare and Family Law*, 111.

38 Case C-333/11, *Dano*, EU:C:2014:2358.

39 Case C-67/14, *Alimanovic*, EU:C:2015:597.

40 Case C-299/14, *Garcia-Nieto*, EU:C:2016:114.

for an individualised assessment of the situation of the applicant EU citizens. A blanket rejection of all claims can suffice. There have been plenty of comments also about the changing shape of European Union citizenship, and it is certainly true that this is driven not just by national resistance to burden sharing but also by the increasingly disciplinary approach of the Court of Justice.[41]

In an endeavour to offer a typology of national approaches, I have argued that states such as the UK pursue three main strategies when implementing a body of law such as EU free movement law where they find themselves trapped between political contingencies and legal requirements.[42] On the one hand, we can see that public opinion in the UK and beyond has become increasingly hostile to immigration and its consequences, and in that respect has elided the distinction between immigration and free movement. For governments, the management of both immigration and free movement has to be seen increasingly on a continuum of migration governance, balancing between the politically possible and economically important for growth.[43] On the other hand, Member States remain generally committed to implementing EU law reasonably effectively, not least in order to maintain the credibility of their commitments to the other Member States under the EU treaties. There is non-compliance at the national level, but it is often of a subtle kind, and in practice compliance rates are often higher than the grumpy rhetoric of politicians about the impositions of EU law suggests they might be.

Thus states seek to exploit any uncertainties and wiggle room that the framework of EU law itself offers, creating new approaches to implementation that may or may not be in strict compliance with EU law, where it is likely to take months or years for courts to afford some clarity upon a new Member State strategy. Such uncertainties are legion in the field of free movement law, even after more than forty years of legal development, and they have been very effectively exploited by the UK. And in relation to social assistance for EU citizens who are not financially self-sufficient, it is clear that the protestations of Member States – not just the UK – about welfare tourism have not fallen on deaf ears in the Court of Justice, as we noted above.

States also try to read across from contiguous fields of national law. In the case of free movement, this means national immigration law. The UK authorities increasingly read EU free movement law as if it were a species of immigration law allowing, for example, the adoption of a position of scepticism towards the objectives of those who seek to rely upon EU free movement law that has no place

41 N. Nic Shuibhne, 'Limits rising, duties ascending: The changing legal shape of Union citizenship' (2015) 52 *CML Rev*, 889.

42 J. Shaw, 'Between Law and Political Truth? Member State Preferences, EU Free Movement Rules and National Immigration Law' (2016) 17 *Cambridge Yearbook of European Legal Studies*, 247.

43 E. Carmel, 'With What Implications? An Assessment of EU Migration Governance Between Union Regulation and National Diversity' (2014) 11 *Migration Letters*, 137.

in the EU legal order. To some extent UK judges have been willing to follow the lead of the government in this area.

Finally states – in this case the UK – can bargain for changes to the resources of EU free movement law, via amendments to the law. This is precisely what the UK renegotiation of the terms of membership sought to achieve. As we noted above, there are of course some limitations on what states can achieve, because of the restrictions of primary law in the form of the EU treaties. But I would argue that a renegotiation strategy attacking one of the central shibboleths of EU law such as the principle of free movement is much more likely to be successful in a case where it is based upon the prior effective use of other two strategies in order to restrict the exercise of free movement rights. The UK has previously raised most if not all elements of the final renegotiation deal – in particular those relating to abuse – before the Council of Ministers. It was generally met by a response from the Commission that asked for robust evidence (e.g. of welfare tourism or of abuse), not a response that posits *a priori* that the UK has in place the conditions for special treatment in relation to in-work benefits. Having pushed open the door on that question, the UK has been met with a friendly reaction on the part of other Member States resistant to the *Metock* case-law and indeed to the restrictions which the Citizens' Rights Directive currently imposes on the deportation of foreign national EU prisoners who have lengthy periods of residence in the host state. Spaventa's chapter in this volume makes clear that these areas are fertile ground for rollback of the protections that EU law currently provides for long-term resident EU citizens. It is in this domain, as much as in the domain of welfare benefits, that the connections between EU citizens and the host state will come under close scrutiny in future years.

Many comments have been delivered about the irrelevance of the renegotiation deal to the referendum debate in the UK. This may be true, but its impact on the future EU is likely to be profound, not least because it is rooted in a set of strategies that Member States already pursue to limit their duties under EU law, whilst maintaining a veneer of compliance. It could be argued that the capacity of the UK government to deliver on its promise to provide a comprehensive 'renegotiation' of the terms of membership was based not only on the plausibility of the threat to leave if concessions were not made, but also on a history of engaging in restrictive practices and interpretations in relation to free movement law which lent credibility to the precise content of the UK's requests. An interesting question for future research concerns what the Member States will learn from the UK renegotiation. There are fears, of course, of copycat referendum threats. But the effects will not all be at the macro level of blatant state resistance to EU law and EU obligations. There will also be a great deal of much less clearly visible policy learning across national boundaries in the wake of a UK vote to remain, and the implementation of the renegotiation deal. It is this policy learning that needs to be the subject of thorough future research.

www.ingramcontent.com/pod-product-compliance
Ingram Content Group UK Ltd.
Pitfield, Milton Keynes, MK11 3LW, UK
UKHW051920100926
8556IPUK00021B/1285

9 781780 684079